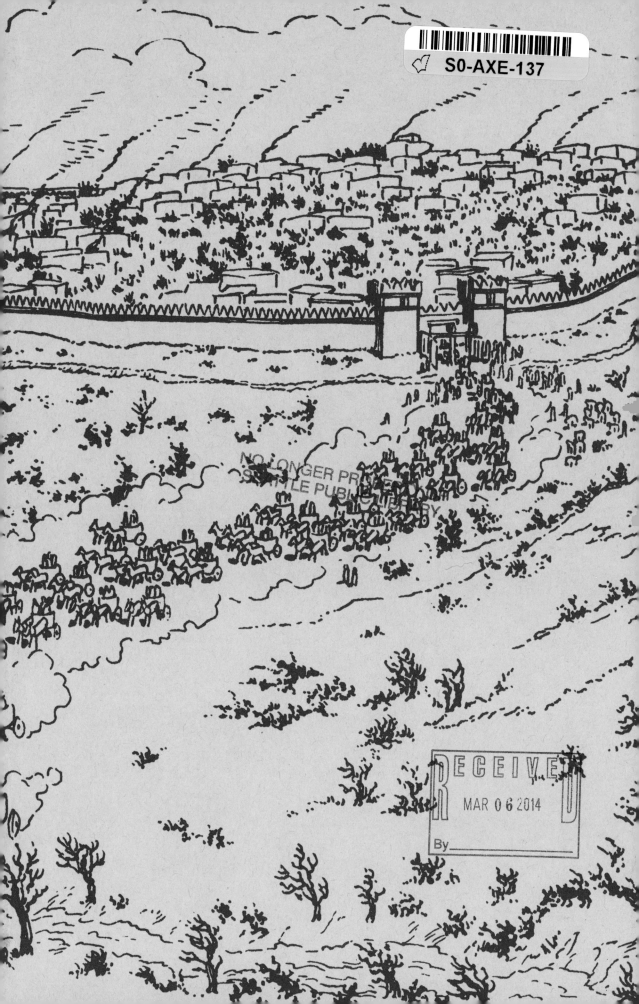

AGE OF BRONZE

Volume 3B

BETRAYAL

PART TWO

by Eric Shanower

image

Age of Bronze
Volume 3B
Betrayal Part Two
Copyright © 2013 by Eric Shanower. All rights reserved.

978-1-60706-758-0 (Trade Paperback)
978-1-60706-757-3 (Hardcover)

Published by Image Comics, Inc.
Office of Publication: 2001 Center Street, Sixth Floor
Berkeley, CA 94704
Image and its logos are ® and © 2013 by Image Comics, Inc.
All rights reserved.

Robert Kirkman *Chief Operating Officer*
Erik Larsen *Chief Financial Officer*
Todd McFarlane *President*
Marc Silvestri *Chief Executive Officer*
Jim Valentino *Vice President*
Eric Stephenson *Publisher*
Ron Richards *Director of Business Development*
Jennifer deGuzman *PR & Marketing Director*
Branwyn Bigglestone *Accounts Manager*
Emily Miller *Accounting Assistant*
Jamie Parreno *Marketing Assistant*
Susie Giroux *Administrative Assistant*
David Brothers *Content Manager*
Kevin Yuen *Digital Rights Coordinator*
Jonathan Chan *Production Manager*
Drew Gill *Art Director*
Jana Cook *Print Manager*
Vincent Kukua, Monica Garcia, Jenna Savage *Production Artists*

The story of *Betrayal Part Two*
was originally serialized in the comic book series
Age of Bronze, Issue 27 through 33.

First Printing November 2013

Visit the *Age of Bronze* website at:
www.age-of-bronze.com
Age of Bronze "Seen" is an app for iPad
available in the iTunes store.

Age of Bronze is a trademark of Eric Shanower.

Printed in the U.S.A.

Contents

Map
7

Our Story So Far
10

Betrayal
Part Two
19

Glossary of Names
162

Genealogical Charts
166

Bibliography
170

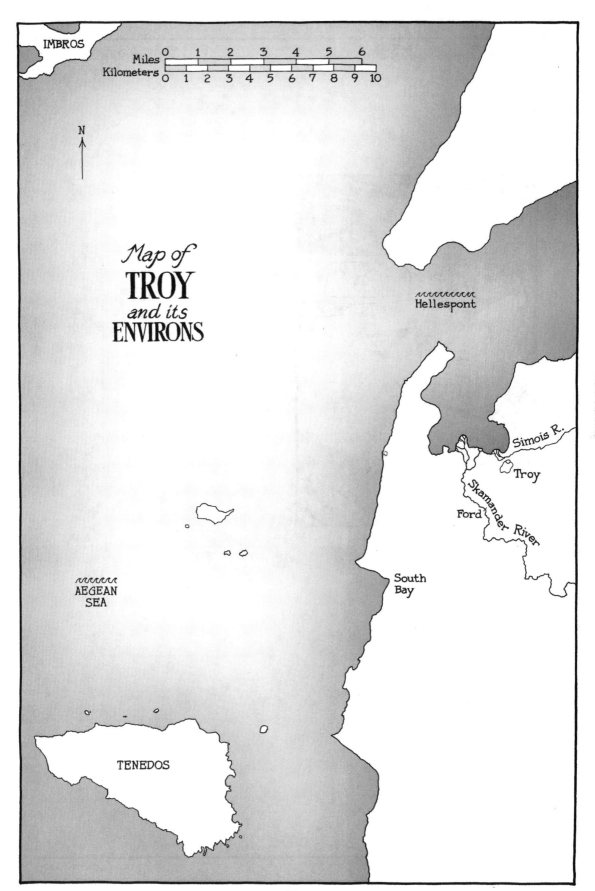

IMBROS

Miles
Kilometers

0 1 2 3 4 5 6
0 1 2 3 4 5 6 7 8 9 10

N

Map of
TROY
and its
ENVIRONS

Hellespont

Simois R.

Troy

Ford

Skamander River

South
Bay

AEGEAN
SEA

TENEDOS

TROILUS: O virtuous fight,
When right with right wars who shall be most right!
True swains in love shall in the world to come
Approve their truths by Troilus. When their rhymes,
Full of protest, of oath, and big compare,
Wants similes, truth tir'd with iteration,
As true as steel, as plantage to the moon,
As sun to day, as turtle to her mate,
As iron to adamant, as earth to th' center,
Yet, after all comparisons of truth,
As truth's authentic author to be cited,
'As true as Troilus' shall crown up the verse,
And sanctify the numbers.

CRESSIDA: Prophet may you be!
If I be false, or swerve a hair from truth,
When time is old and hath forgot itself,
When water drops have worn the stones of Troy
And blind oblivion swallow'd cities up,
And mighty states characterless are grated
To dusty nothing, yet let memory,
From false to false among false maids in love,
Upbraid my falsehood! When they've said, "As false
As air, as water, as wind, or sandy earth,
As fox to lamb, as wolf to heifer's calf,
Pard to the hind, or stepdame to her son,"
Yea, let them say, to stick the heart of falsehood,
"As false as Cressid."

PANDARUS: Go to, a bargain made! Seal it, seal it; I'll be the witness.
Here I hold your hand, here my cousin's. If ever you prove
false one to another, since I have taken such pains to bring
you together, let all pitiful goers-between be call'd to the
world's end after my name; call them all Pandars. Let all
constant men be Troiluses, all false women Cressids, and all
brokers-between Pandars! Say, "Amen."

Troilus and Cressida
Act III, Scene 2
William Shakespeare, circa 1602

TROY.

Our Story So Far

Paris

During the Late Bronze Age—about the 13th century BCE—the powerful city of Troy flourishes under the Great King Priam's rule. Years before, Priam's sister Hesione was captured by Achaean raiders during an assault on Troy. Now Priam commands Paris, a prince of Troy recently reunited with his father and his mother Hekuba, to bring Hesione back. Priam's daughter Kassandra and her twin brother Helenus predict calamity, but no one takes their warnings seriously.

MY GRANDSON.
HE MUST REMAIN IN TROY WHEN YOU LEAVE.

Priam

WE'RE HERE-- IT'S TRUE! TROY.
I WANT TO FEEL ITS WARM STONES BENEATH MY OWN HANDS...

Helen

Accompanied by his cousin Aeneas, Paris sails to the Achaean city of Sparta where Menelaus is king. Paris forgets his pregnant lover, the mountain nymph Oenone, and ignoring his brother Hektor's warning to follow their father Priam's instructions, he seduces Menelaus's wife Helen away from Sparta with her serving women and infant son Pleisthenes. They sail to Cyprus, then to Sidon.

Hektor

HOW LONG CAN WE EXPECT TO BEACH THERE BEFORE WE START FOR TROY AGAIN?

MENELAUS

Helen's brothers, Kastor and Polydeukes, pursue, but are lost in a storm at sea.

Menelaus is eager to recover his wife, while his brother Agamemnon, king of Mycenae and High King of the Achaeans, is eager to gain Troy's control of rich trade routes through the Hellespont. So they summon the many Achaean kings who once swore an oath to help Helen's husband for her sake. At the bay at Aulis a massive army with hundreds of ships and thousands of men assembles. The army pledges to follow High King Agamemnon as commander in an attack on Troy.

AGAMEMNON

The Achaean priestess Thetis foresees the death of her son, Achilles, at Troy. To circumvent this, she takes the boy from his teacher, the kentaur Cheiron, and hides him, disguised as a girl called Pyrrha, among the daughters of Lykomedes on the island of Skyros. There, Achilles rapes Lykomedes's eldest daughter Deidamia, who bears a son. Deidamia calls the child Pyrrhus; Achilles calls him Neoptolemus.

A prophecy foretells that if Odysseus, king of Ithaka, goes to Troy with the army, he'll return home to his wife Penelope and son Telemachus after twenty years, alone and unrecognized. To avoid this fate, Odysseus pretends to be mad. But Palamedes, prince of Nauplia, exposes Odysseus's ploy, thus earning his enmity.

Kalchas, Trojan priest of the sun god, has visions that show him Troy's fall. He joins the Achaeans, leaving his recently widowed daughter Cressida at Troy in the care of her uncle Pandarus. The Trojan prince Troilus falls in love with Cressida, but Pandarus discourages Troilus from pursuing her prematurely.

All signs point to eventual success for the Achaean army. The Delphic oracle predicts Achaean victory over Troy, contingent, however, upon conflict among Achaeans. And Kalchas foretells Achaean triumph in the tenth year, provided that Achilles joins the army.

OH--PANDARUS. HELLO--UH, YES ...THEY DO...
AH!

PANDARUS AND TROILUS

HE JUST SHOT A DEER--WHY IS HE IN A BAD MOOD?
YOU NEVER KNOW WHEN TO STOP, DO YOU, PALAMEDES?

PALAMEDES AND MENELAUS

Odysseus tricks Achilles into shedding his disguise and brings him to Aulis. Achilles assumes leadership of his father Peleus's Myrmidons from Phthia, choosing a short life fighting gloriously at Troy rather than a long life in obscurity.

After Palamedes remedies a food shortage by bringing supplies from Delos, the army at last sets sail for war with Troy.

Meanwhile, Paris and Helen finally reach Troy. Priam confronts them outside the city. Paris presents Helen as a substitute for Hesione. Priam resists. But when Paris reveals that Helen is pregnant with his child, Priam has no other choice but to welcome Helen to Troy.

FIRE!

KASSANDRA

Kassandra grows so frantic at Helen's presence in Troy that Priam has her shut away.

Aeneas claims the hand of Kreusa, daughter of Priam, in marriage. Priam refuses to grant this, so Aeneas and Kreusa secretly leave Troy.

OH! TROILUS... LITTLE TROILUS...
CRESSIDA, I--

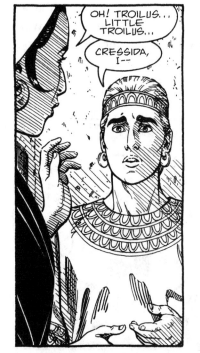

CRESSIDA AND TROILUS

Troilus tells Cressida that he loves her, but she laughs at him.

The Achaean fleet, having sailed from Aulis, mistakes the coast of Mysia for Troy. Achilles attacks the inhabitants, assuming they're Trojans. In response, Telephus, king of Mysia, assembles an army and marches against the Achaeans. Soon the Achaeans discover their mistake and make peace, but not before Achilles has wounded Telephus.

TELEPHUS

Upon departing Mysia, a massive storm scatters the Achaean fleet. The leaders and their armies return to their various homes. Odysseus accompanies Agamemnon to Mycenae where they nurse grudges against Palamedes and plot strategy for reattempting the attack on Troy. When Diomedes at last brings news that the Trojans are renewing their defences and gathering their own allies in preparation for war, Agamemnon re-summons the Achaeans to Aulis.

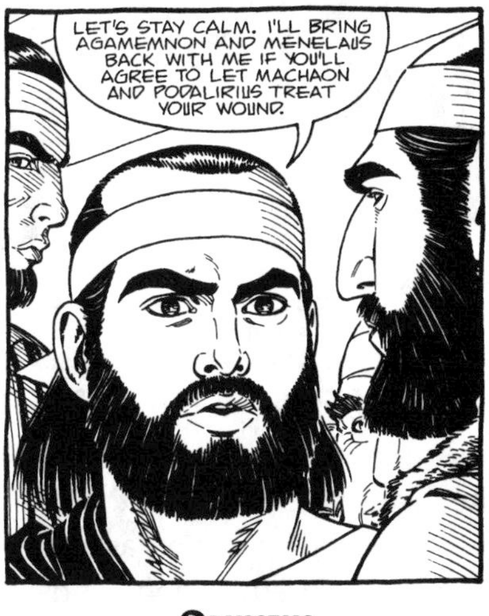
LET'S STAY CALM. I'LL BRING AGAMEMNON AND MENELAUS BACK WITH ME IF YOU'LL AGREE TO LET MACHAON AND PODALIRIUS TREAT YOUR WOUND.

Odysseus

Kalchas asks Agamemnon to save Cressida from the war, but the High King refuses, insulted by Kalchas's manipulative use of Agamemnon's daughters.

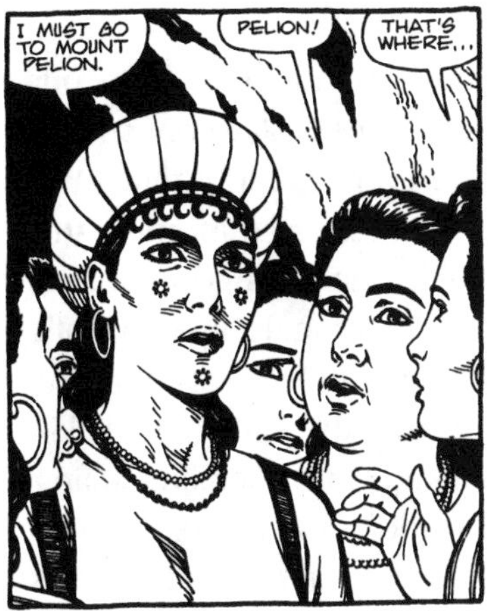
I MUST GO TO MOUNT PELION.
PELION!
THAT'S WHERE...

Thetis

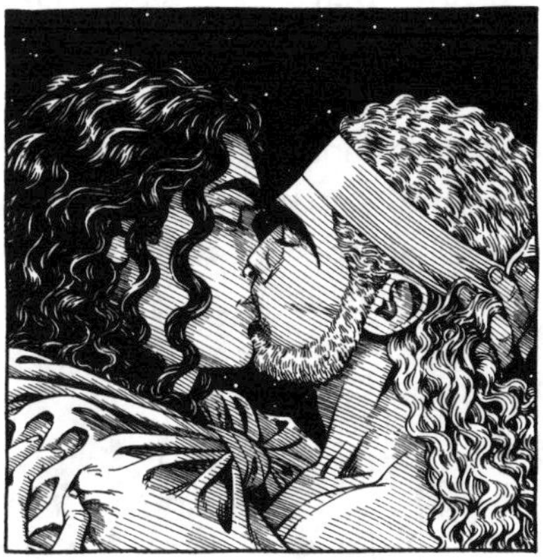

Achilles and Patroklus

On Skyros Achilles spurns Deidamia and declares his love for his companion, Patroklus. The two young men go to Phthia where Achilles receives summons to rejoin the Achaean army. Achilles's mother Thetis fails to prevent him from going, so she decides to go along, too.

Telephus appears unexpectedly in Mycenae, crazed with suffering from the now-infected wound Achilles inflicted. At Aulis, Achilles, with the help of the Achaean healers Machaon and Podalirius, heals Telephus's wound.

The army is finally at full strength again when a contrary wind springs up, preventing the fleet from sailing. Kalchas reveals to Agamemnon that the goddess Artemis requires the sacrifice of Agamemnon's first-born daughter, Iphigenia, in order to reverse the wind and release the fleet.

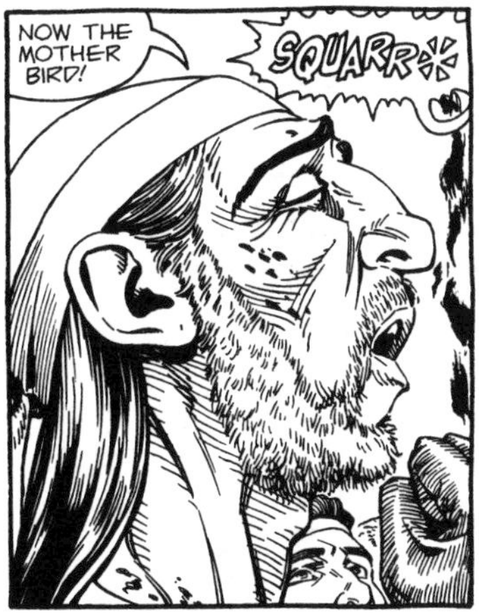
NOW THE MOTHER BIRD!
SQUARR

Kalchas

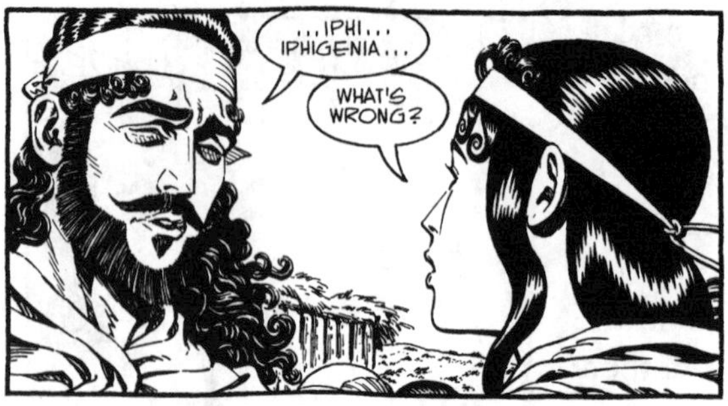
...IPHI...
IPHIGENIA...
WHAT'S WRONG?

Agamemnon and Iphigenia

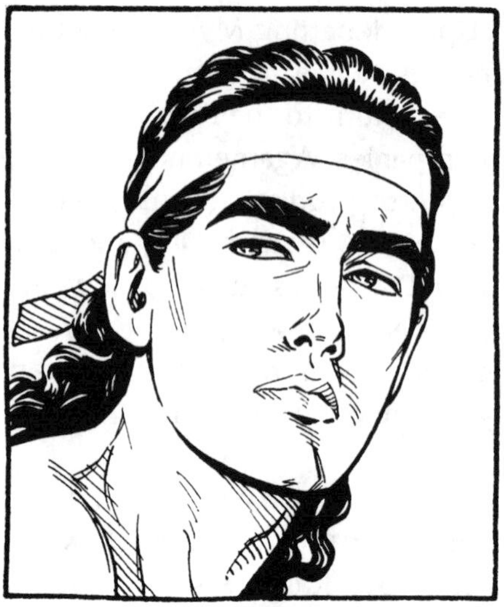

Achilles

Agamemnon is torn. Odysseus and Menelaus persuade him that he must submit to the goddess's demands. Prompted by Odysseus, Agamemnon sends a letter summoning Iphigenia to Aulis. The letter falsely explains that she will marry Achilles. Agamemnon secretly sends a second letter that countermands the first, but Menelaus intercepts it. Iphigenia arrives at Aulis with her mother, Klytemnestra.

Achilles and Klytemnestra uncover the truth. They hope to rescue Iphigenia, but the army, impatient to set sail, is against them. Iphigenia realizes that she can't escape, so she decides to accept death with grace. Achilles and his companions arm themselves in case Iphigenia calls on them to save her at the last moment.

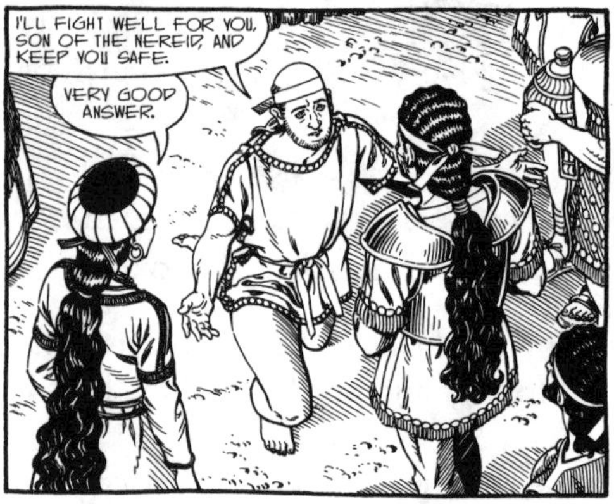
I'LL FIGHT WELL FOR YOU, SON OF THE NEREID, AND KEEP YOU SAFE.
VERY GOOD ANSWER.

Thetis, Mnemon, and Achilles

Thetis knows that the sun god will kill Achilles in retaliation for Achilles killing one of the sun god's sons. She charges Mnemon to accompany Achilles and steer him clear of all sons of the god.

At the altar Iphigenia accepts the knife without flinching. The wind turns favorable. Devastated, Klytemnestra departs Aulis.

The Achaean army sails for Troy. The Achaeans storm and capture the island

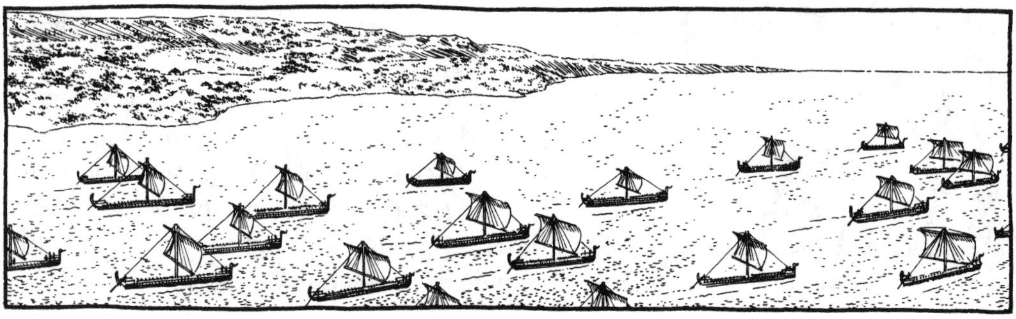

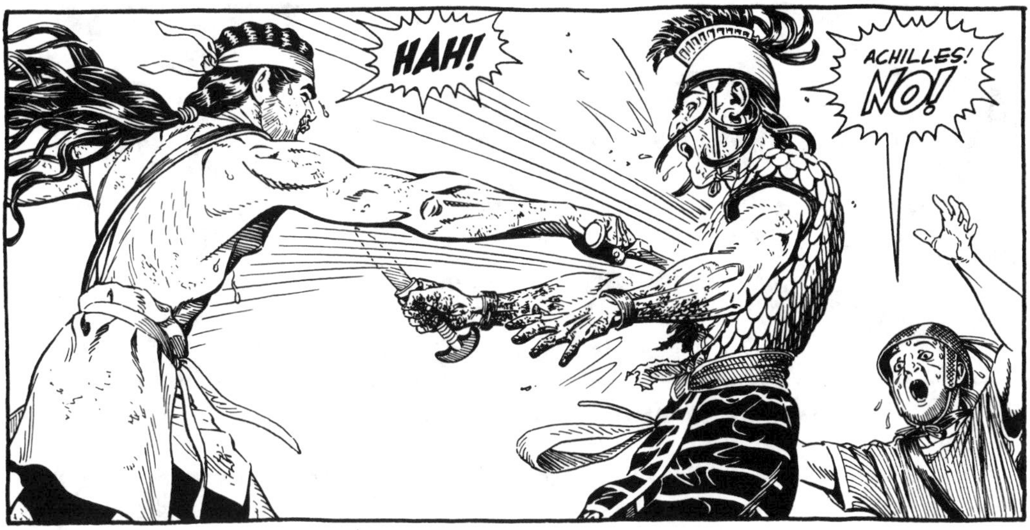
HAH!
ACHILLES! NO!

ACHILLES, TENNES, AND MNEMON

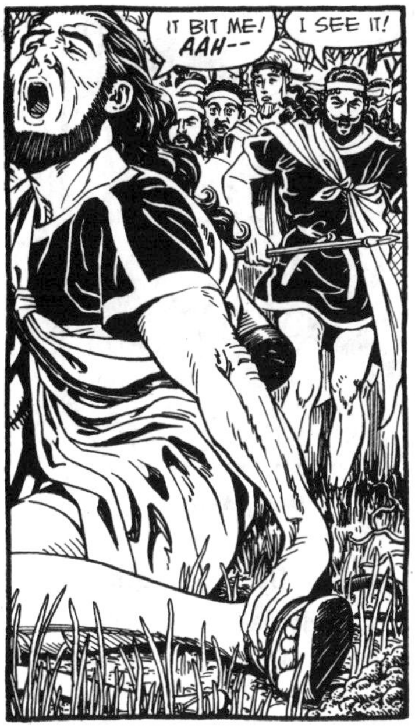
IT BIT ME! AAH--
I SEE IT!

PHILOKTETES

of Tenedos near Troy. Achilles kills King Tennes of Tenedos before Mnemon can warn Achilles that Tennes is reputed to be a son of the sun god. Achilles, in a rage, kills Mnemon.

While the Achaeans sacrifice to the gods for their victory, a snake from the altar bites Philoktetes's foot. Philoktetes screams loud curses at the pain. Fearing Philoktetes will offend the gods, the Achaeans strand him on the deserted island of Nea Chryse.

Trojan spies bring news that Kalchas has defected to the Achaeans. Cressida's uncle Pandarus fears that this betrayal will blacken the whole family. He fans the flames of Troilus's love for Cressida, hoping to gain royal protection. Pandarus persuades Cressida to give her veil to Troilus as a token of her friendship.

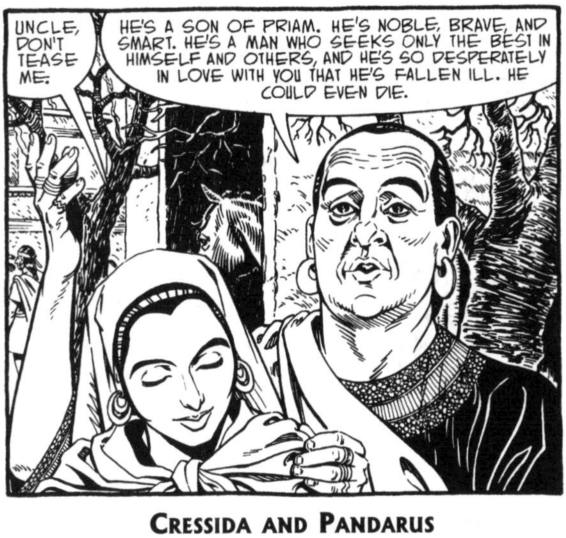
UNCLE, DON'T TEASE ME.
HE'S A SON OF PRIAM. HE'S NOBLE, BRAVE, AND SMART. HE'S A MAN WHO SEEKS ONLY THE BEST IN HIMSELF AND OTHERS, AND HE'S SO DESPERATELY IN LOVE WITH YOU THAT HE'S FALLEN ILL. HE COULD EVEN DIE.

CRESSIDA AND PANDARUS

> I PRESENT THE SON OF ATREUS, MENELAUS, KING OF LAKEDAEMON...

> ...THE SON OF NAUPLIUS, PALAMEDES, PRINCE OF NAUPLIA...

> ...THE SON OF LAERTES, ODYSSEUS, KING OF THE ISLAND OF ITHAKA...

> ...AND THE SON OF THESEUS, AKAMAS, PRINCE OF ATHENS.

MENELAUS, PALAMEDES, ODYSSEUS, AND AKAMAS

In a last gesture before attacking Troy, the Achaeans send a peace embassy to Priam to ask for Helen's return. It's an empty show, although Palamedes doesn't recognize this and Hektor attempts to negotiate in good faith. Menelaus sees Helen and their son Pleisthenes for the first time since they left Sparta. Helen, pregnant again by Paris, learns that her mother is dead by her own hand and that her brothers Kastor and Polydeukes are missing. Priam

LAODIKE AND AKAMAS

refuses to surrender Helen, even if the Achaeans were to offer Hesione in exchange. Menelaus vows to kill Helen and all the Trojans.

Laodike, a daughter of Priam, is smitten by the sight of Akamas of Athens, a member of the peace embassy. Philobia, wife of a Trojan ally, arranges for Laodike and Akamas to meet privately. Akamas mistakenly assumes Laodike is Philobia's servant and they make love.

Priam's counselor Antimachus and his sons plot to kill the members of the peace embassy. But the counselor Antenor and his sons escort the embassy safely out of Troy.

The peace embassy returns to Tenedos where the Achaean leaders assemble. They decide to attack Troy the next morning. Kalchas foretells that the first Achaean to set foot on the Trojan shore will die. Nevertheless, both Achilles and Iolaus vow to be first to reach the beach.

ANTENOR

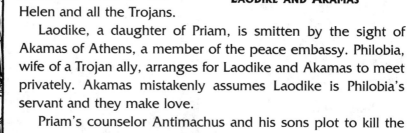

BETRAYAL
PART TWO

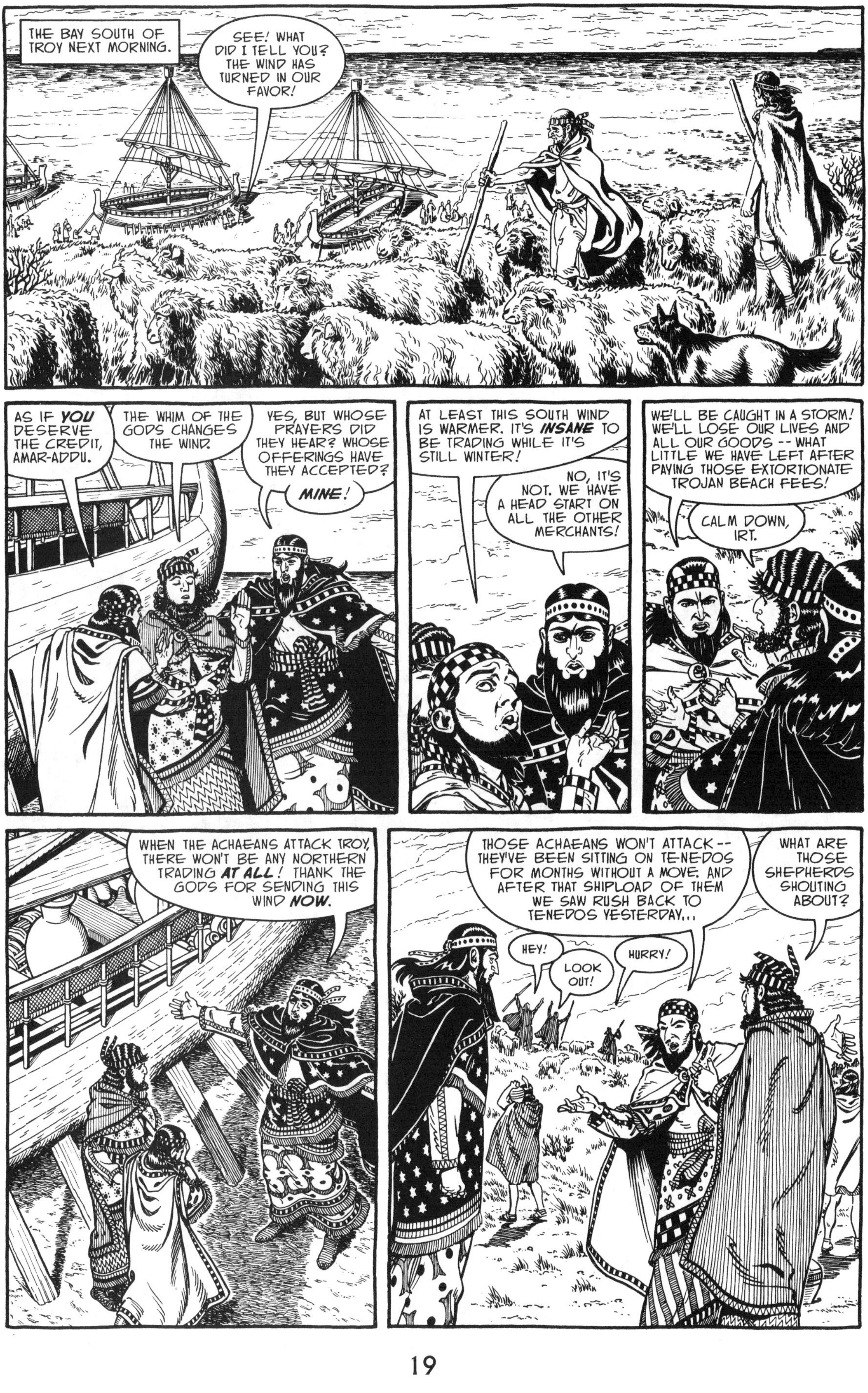
THE BAY SOUTH OF TROY NEXT MORNING.
SEE! WHAT DID I TELL YOU? THE WIND HAS TURNED IN OUR FAVOR!
AS IF **YOU** DESERVE THE CREDIT, AMAR-ADDU.
THE WHIM OF THE GODS CHANGES THE WIND.
YES, BUT WHOSE PRAYERS DID THEY HEAR? WHOSE OFFERINGS HAVE THEY ACCEPTED?
MINE!
AT LEAST THIS SOUTH WIND IS WARMER. IT'S **INSANE** TO BE TRADING WHILE IT'S STILL WINTER!
NO, IT'S NOT. WE HAVE A HEAD START ON ALL THE OTHER MERCHANTS!
WE'LL BE CAUGHT IN A STORM! WE'LL LOSE OUR LIVES AND ALL OUR GOODS -- WHAT LITTLE WE HAVE LEFT AFTER PAYING THOSE EXTORTIONATE TROJAN BEACH FEES!
CALM DOWN, IRT.
WHEN THE ACHAEANS ATTACK TROY, THERE WON'T BE ANY NORTHERN TRADING **AT ALL**! THANK THE GODS FOR SENDING THIS WIND **NOW**.
THOSE ACHAEANS WON'T ATTACK -- THEY'VE BEEN SITTING ON TENEDOS FOR MONTHS WITHOUT A MOVE. AND AFTER THAT SHIPLOAD OF THEM WE SAW RUSH BACK TO TENEDOS YESTERDAY...
HEY!
LOOK OUT!
HURRY!
WHAT ARE THOSE SHEPHERDS SHOUTING ABOUT?

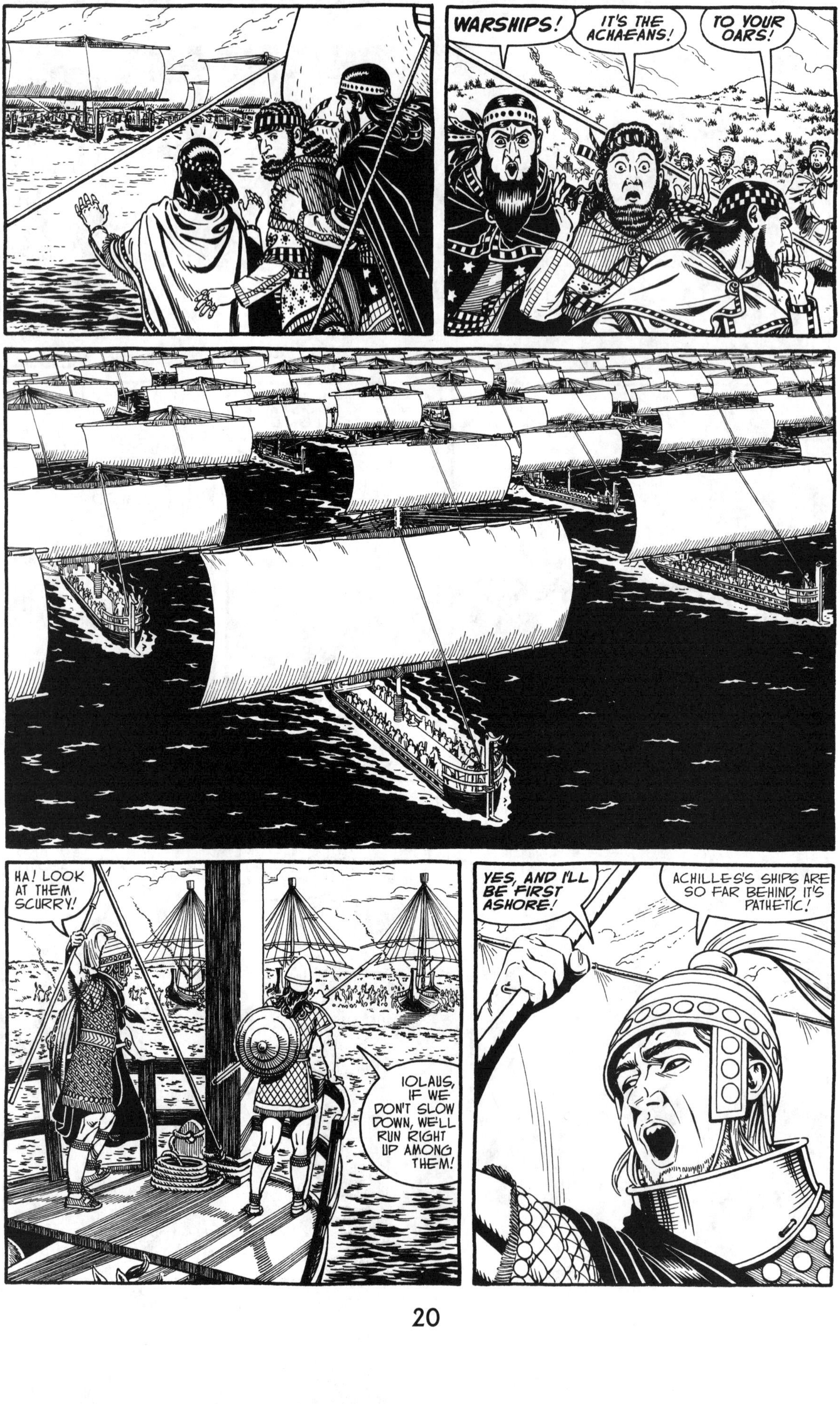
WARSHIPS!
IT'S THE ACHAEANS!
TO YOUR OARS!
HA! LOOK AT THEM SCURRY!
IOLAUS, IF WE DON'T SLOW DOWN, WE'LL RUN RIGHT UP AMONG THEM!
YES, AND I'LL BE FIRST ASHORE!
ACHILLES'S SHIPS ARE SO FAR BEHIND IT'S PATHETIC!

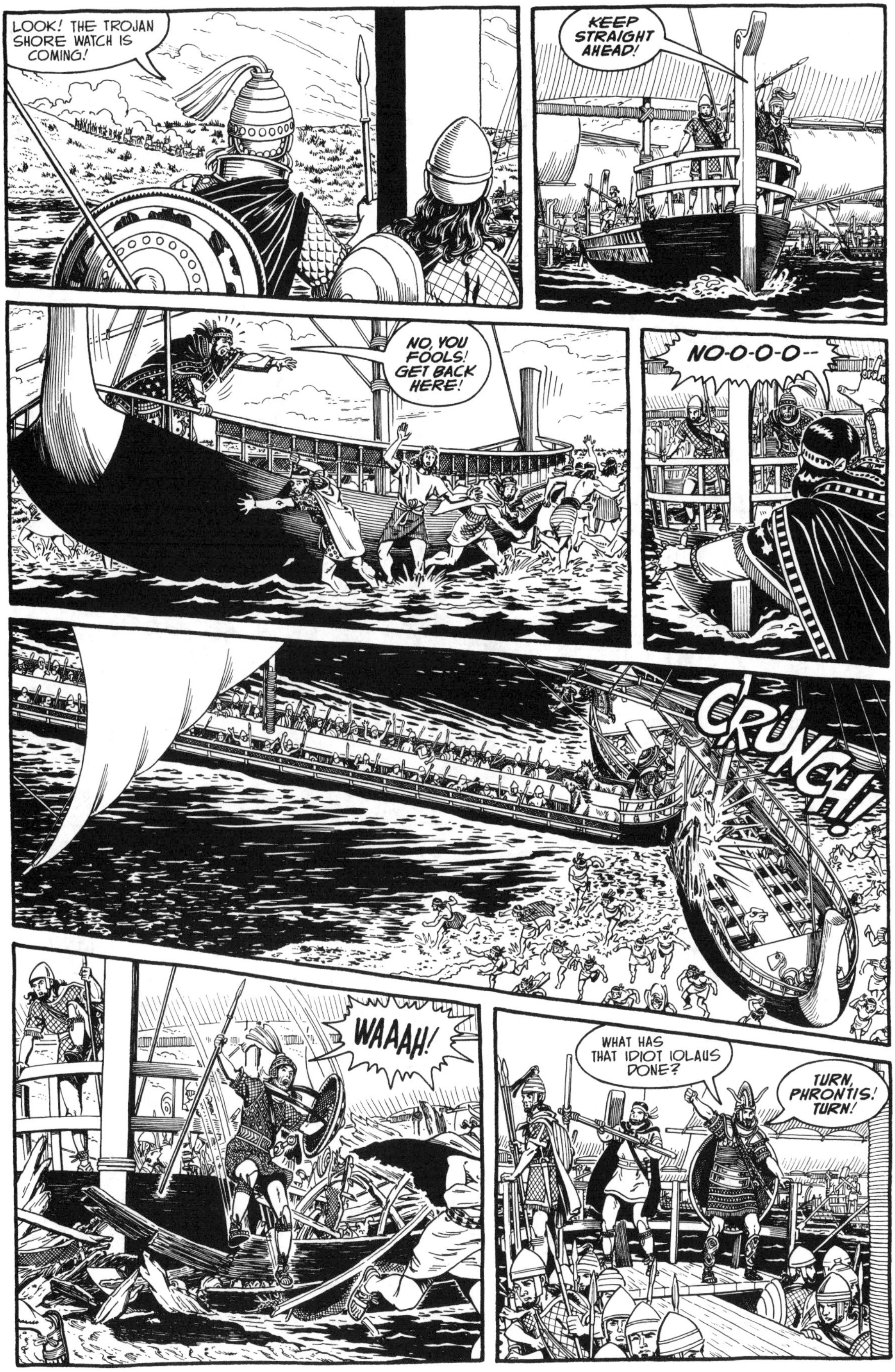
LOOK! THE TROJAN SHORE WATCH IS COMING!
KEEP STRAIGHT AHEAD!
NO, YOU FOOLS! GET BACK HERE!
NO-O-O-O--
CRUNCH!
WAAAH!
WHAT HAS THAT IDIOT IOLAUS DONE?
TURN, PHRONTIS! TURN!

IF WE TURN, WE'LL RUN INTO OUR OWN SHIPS!

THEN LOWER THAT SAIL! NOW!

CHOK

LOOK OUT!

CRUNCH

CRUNCH CACK CACK CACK

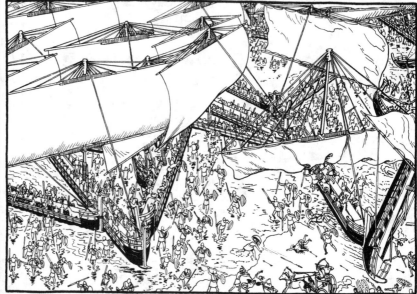

UNH!

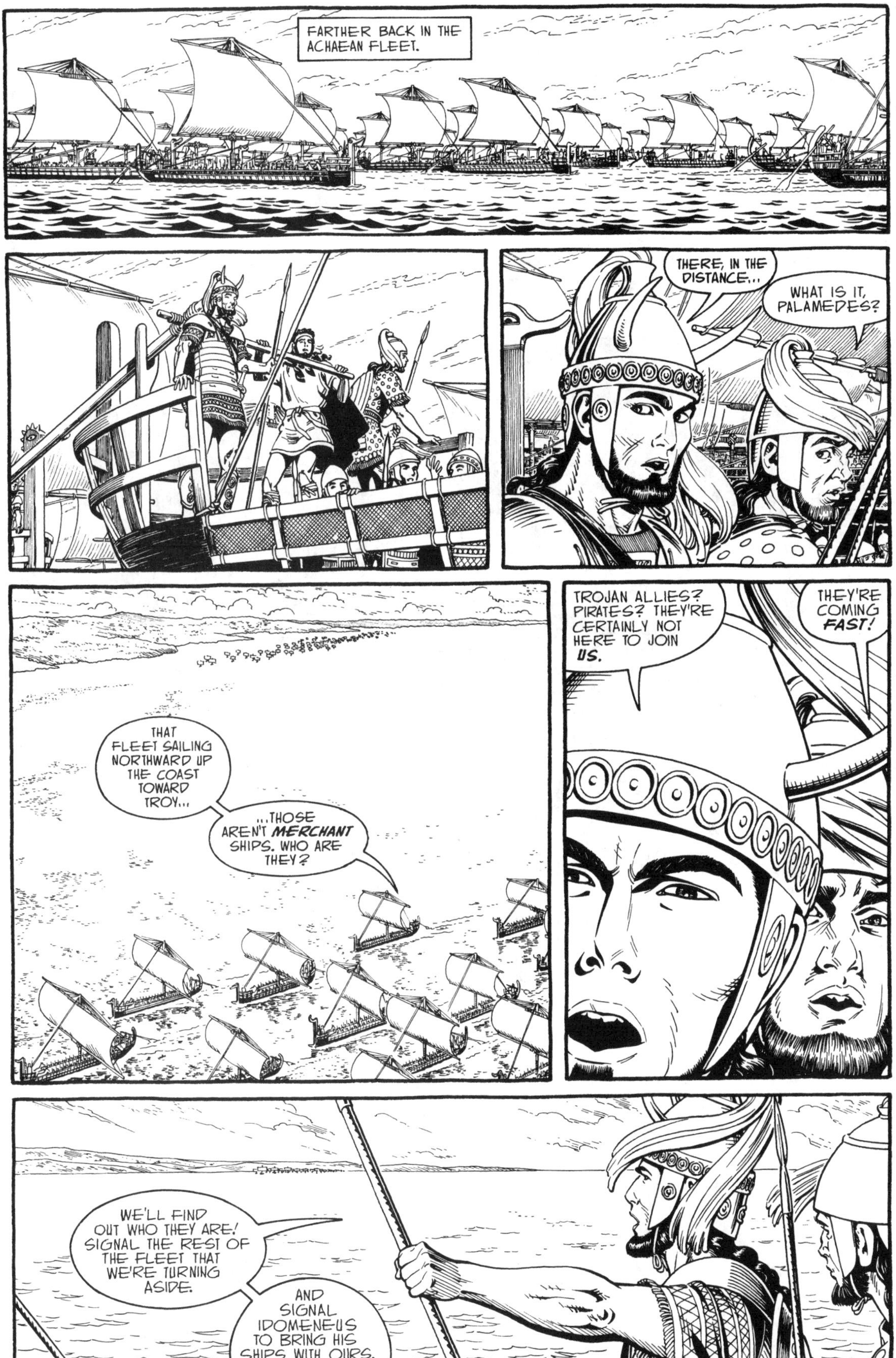
FARTHER BACK IN THE ACHAEAN FLEET.
THERE, IN THE DISTANCE...
WHAT IS IT, PALAMEDES?
THAT FLEET SAILING NORTHWARD UP THE COAST TOWARD TROY...
...THOSE AREN'T MERCHANT SHIPS. WHO ARE THEY?
TROJAN ALLIES? PIRATES? THEY'RE CERTAINLY NOT HERE TO JOIN US.
THEY'RE COMING FAST!
WE'LL FIND OUT WHO THEY ARE! SIGNAL THE REST OF THE FLEET THAT WE'RE TURNING ASIDE.
AND SIGNAL IDOMENEUS TO BRING HIS SHIPS WITH OURS.

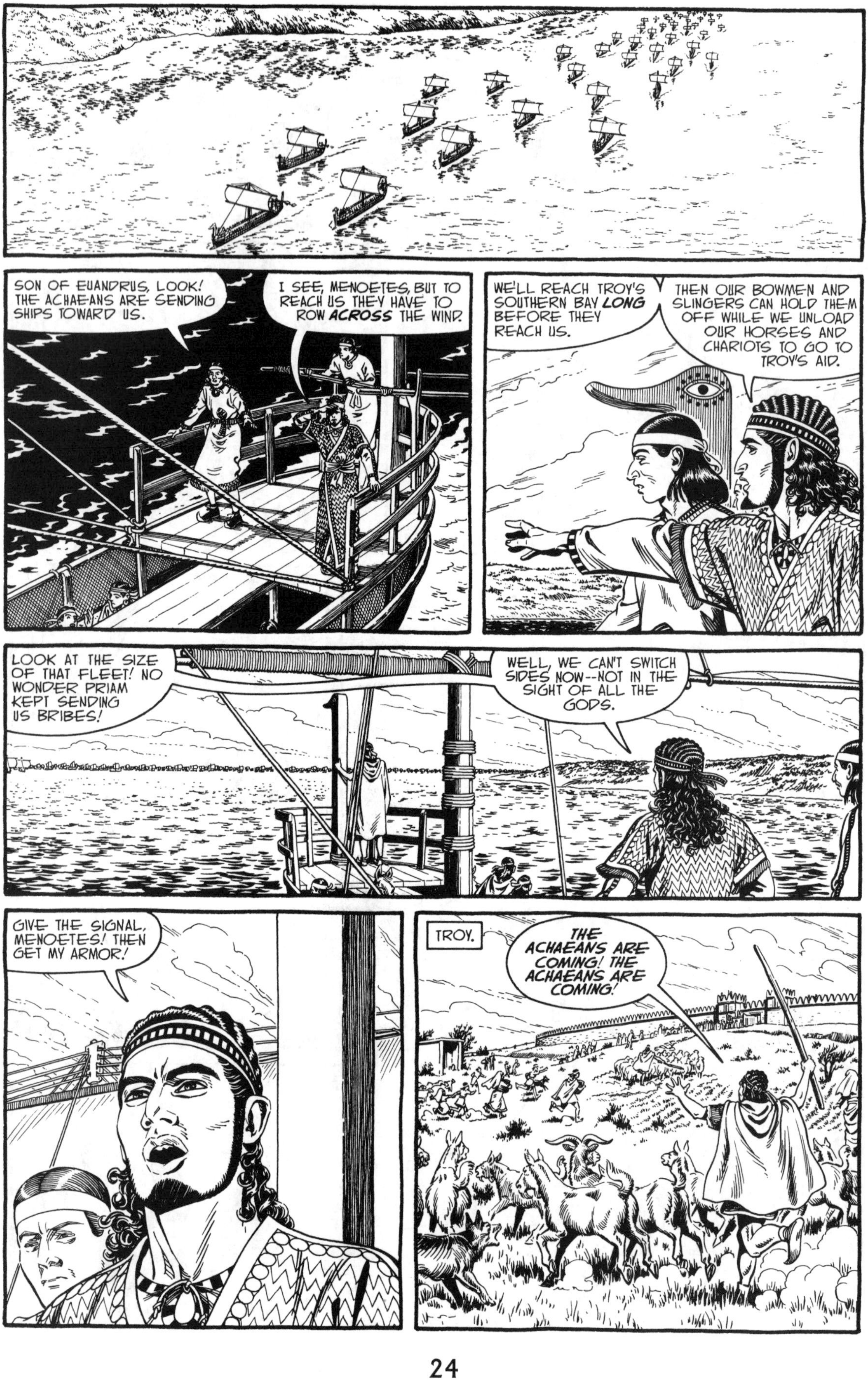
SON OF EUANDRUS, LOOK! THE ACHAEANS ARE SENDING SHIPS TOWARD US.
I SEE, MENOETES, BUT TO REACH US THEY HAVE TO ROW **ACROSS** THE WIND.
WE'LL REACH TROY'S SOUTHERN BAY **LONG** BEFORE THEY REACH US.
THEN OUR BOWMEN AND SLINGERS CAN HOLD THEM OFF WHILE WE UNLOAD OUR HORSES AND CHARIOTS TO GO TO TROY'S AID.
LOOK AT THE SIZE OF THAT FLEET! NO WONDER PRIAM KEPT SENDING US BRIBES!
WELL, WE CAN'T SWITCH SIDES NOW--NOT IN THE SIGHT OF ALL THE GODS.
GIVE THE SIGNAL, MENOETES! THEN GET MY ARMOR!
TROY.
THE ACHAEANS ARE COMING! THE ACHAEANS ARE COMING!

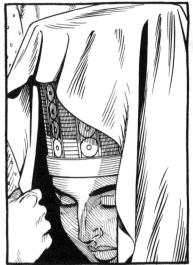

THE SEA-SHORE **SCREAMS!**

SCREAMS IN PAIN!

CRIES OUT FOR THE SNORTING OF HORSES!

THE RAGING WOLF PIERCES IT WITH SHARP FOOT!

FOUNTAINS GUSH FORTH!

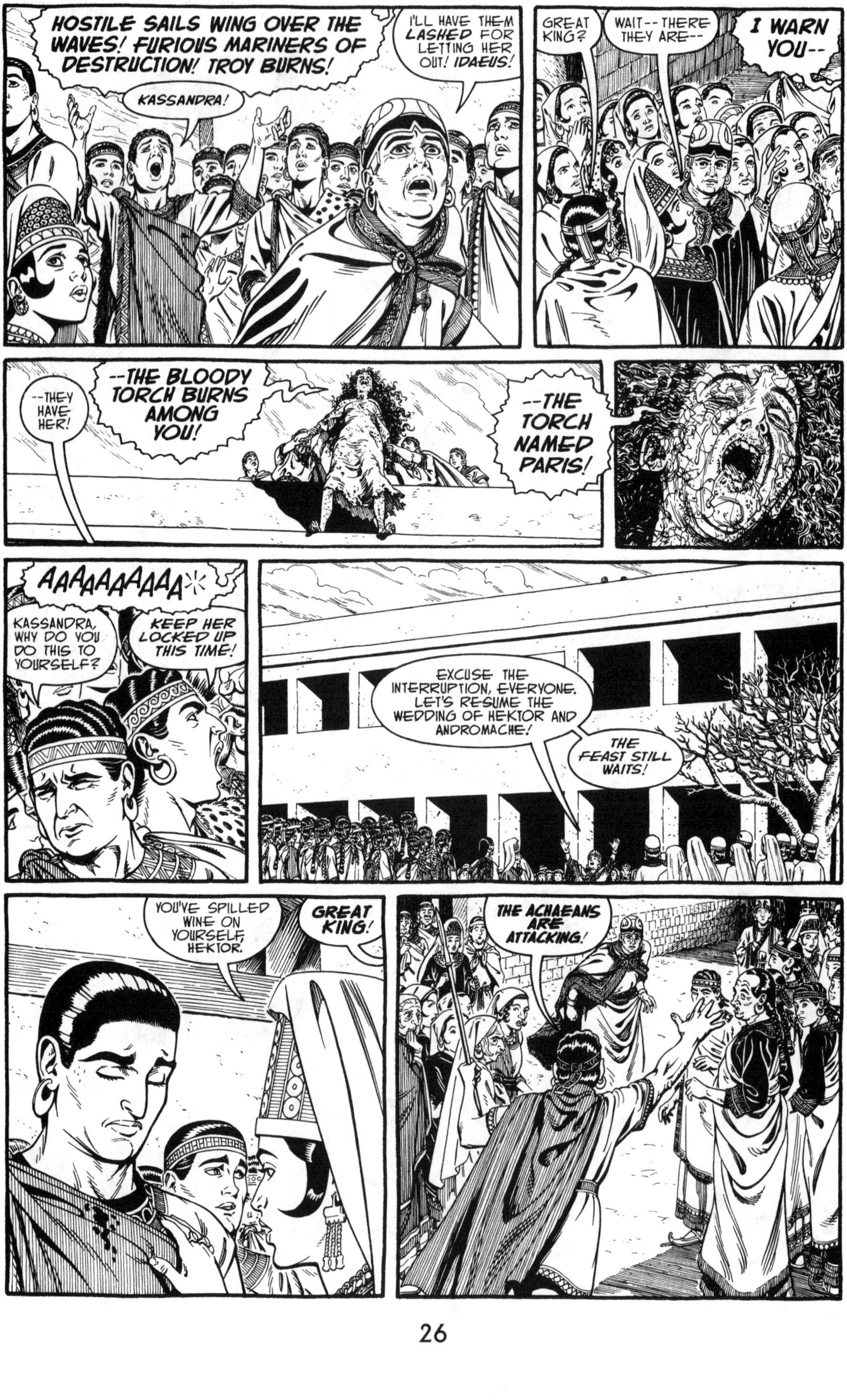
HOSTILE SAILS WING OVER THE WAVES! FURIOUS MARINERS OF DESTRUCTION! TROY BURNS!
KASSANDRA!
I'LL HAVE THEM LASHED FOR LETTING HER OUT! IDAEUS!
GREAT KING?
WAIT--THERE THEY ARE--
I WARN YOU--
--THEY HAVE HER!
--THE BLOODY TORCH BURNS AMONG YOU!
--THE TORCH NAMED PARIS!
AAAAAAAAAA
KASSANDRA, WHY DO YOU DO THIS TO YOURSELF?
KEEP HER LOCKED UP THIS TIME!
EXCUSE THE INTERRUPTION, EVERYONE. LET'S RESUME THE WEDDING OF HEKTOR AND ANDROMACHE!
THE FEAST STILL WAITS!
YOU'VE SPILLED WINE ON YOURSELF, HEKTOR.
GREAT KING!
THE ACHAEANS ARE ATTACKING!

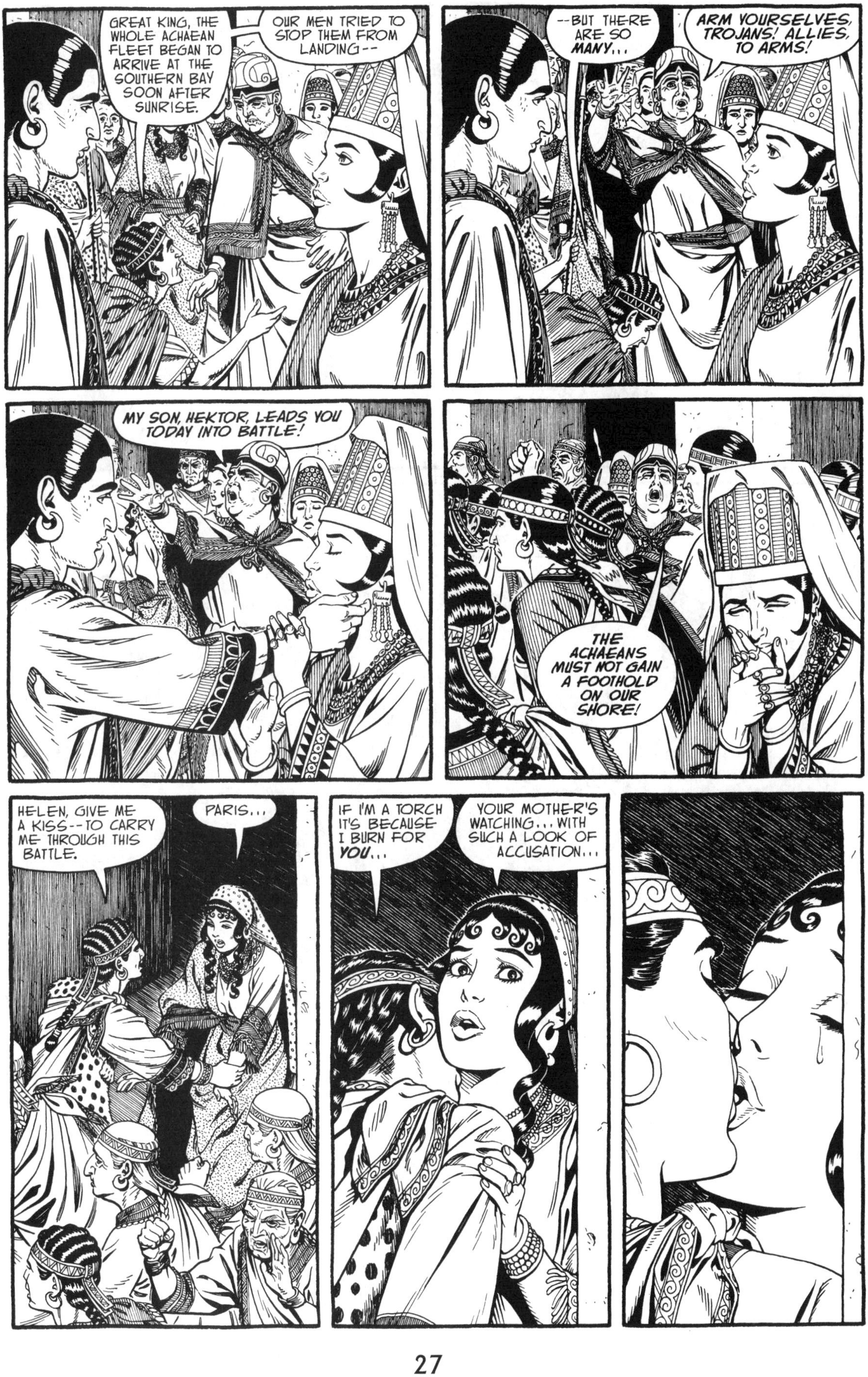
GREAT KING, THE WHOLE ACHAEAN FLEET BEGAN TO ARRIVE AT THE SOUTHERN BAY SOON AFTER SUNRISE.
OUR MEN TRIED TO STOP THEM FROM LANDING--
--BUT THERE ARE SO MANY...
ARM YOURSELVES, TROJANS! ALLIES, TO ARMS!
MY SON, HEKTOR, LEADS YOU TODAY INTO BATTLE!
THE ACHAEANS MUST NOT GAIN A FOOTHOLD ON OUR SHORE!
HELEN, GIVE ME A KISS--TO CARRY ME THROUGH THIS BATTLE.
PARIS...
IF I'M A TORCH IT'S BECAUSE I BURN FOR YOU...
YOUR MOTHER'S WATCHING... WITH SUCH A LOOK OF ACCUSATION...

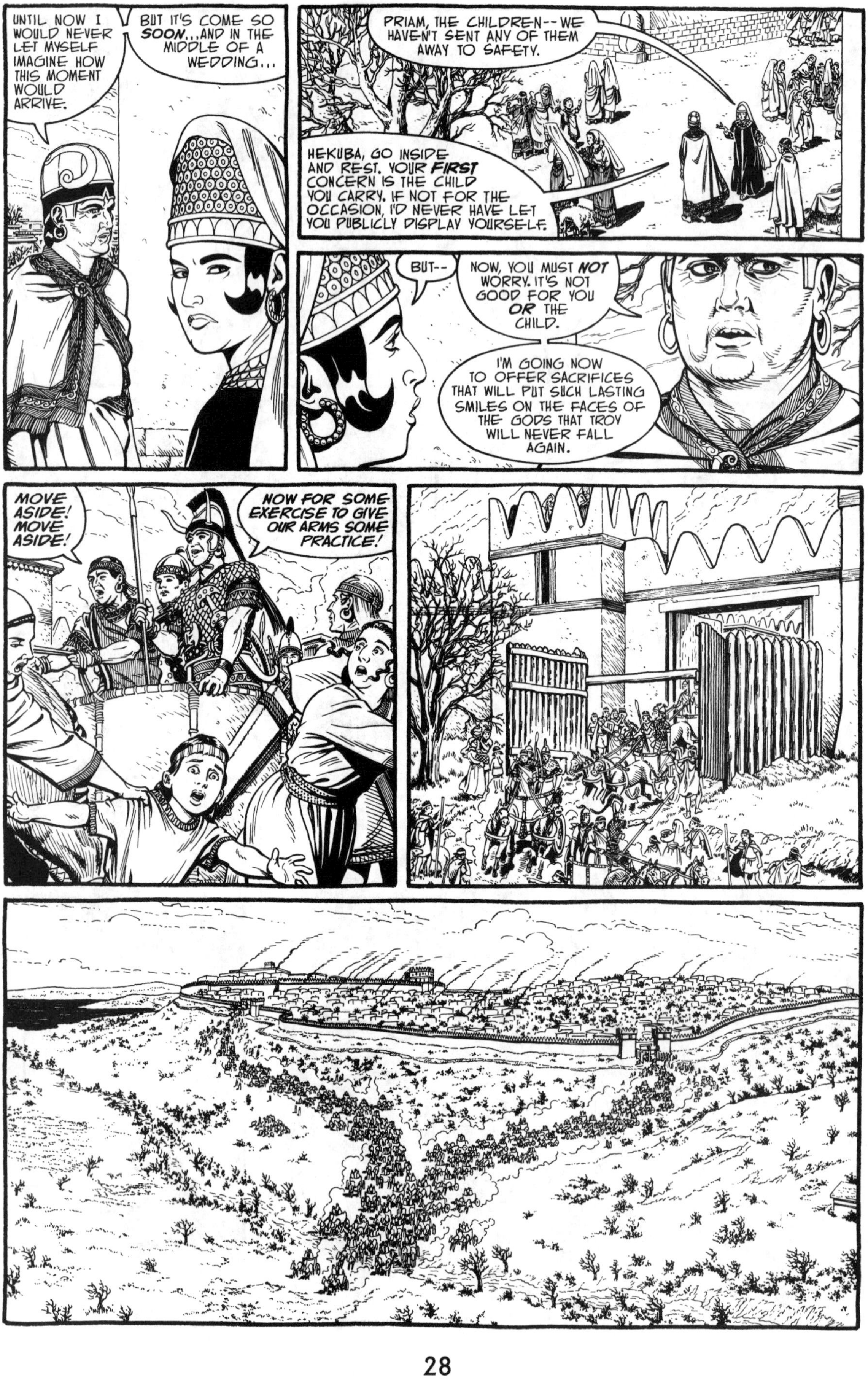
UNTIL NOW I WOULD NEVER LET MYSELF IMAGINE HOW THIS MOMENT WOULD ARRIVE.
BUT IT'S COME SO SOON...AND IN THE MIDDLE OF A WEDDING...
PRIAM, THE CHILDREN--WE HAVEN'T SENT ANY OF THEM AWAY TO SAFETY.
HEKUBA, GO INSIDE AND REST. YOUR FIRST CONCERN IS THE CHILD YOU CARRY. IF NOT FOR THE OCCASION, I'D NEVER HAVE LET YOU PUBLICLY DISPLAY YOURSELF.
BUT--
NOW, YOU MUST NOT WORRY. IT'S NOT GOOD FOR YOU OR THE CHILD.
I'M GOING NOW TO OFFER SACRIFICES THAT WILL PUT SUCH LASTING SMILES ON THE FACES OF THE GODS THAT TROY WILL NEVER FALL AGAIN.
MOVE ASIDE! MOVE ASIDE!
NOW FOR SOME EXERCISE TO GIVE OUR ARMS SOME PRACTICE!

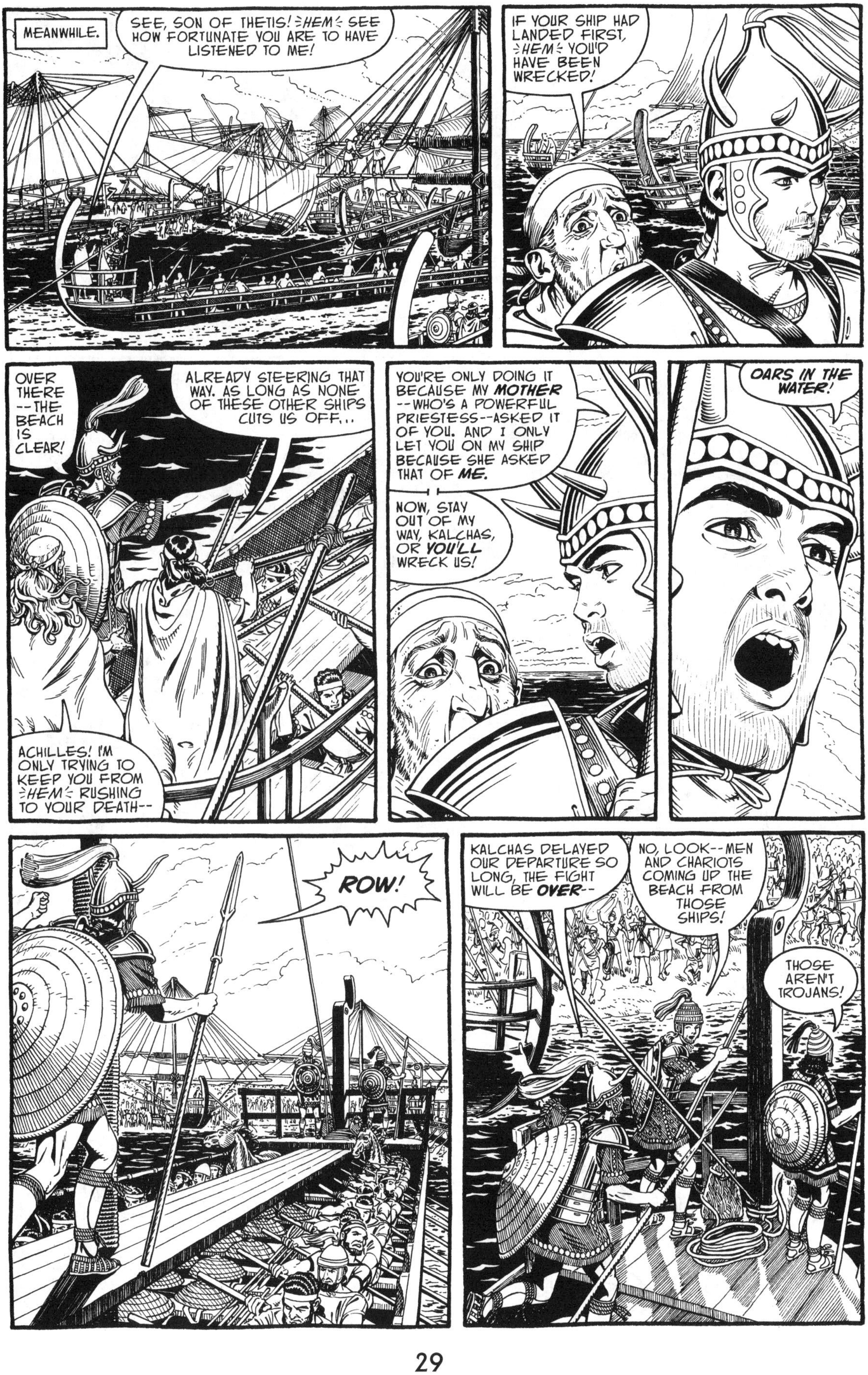
MEANWHILE.
SEE, SON OF THETIS! HEM SEE HOW FORTUNATE YOU ARE TO HAVE LISTENED TO ME!
IF YOUR SHIP HAD LANDED FIRST, HEM YOU'D HAVE BEEN WRECKED!
OVER THERE --THE BEACH IS CLEAR!
ALREADY STEERING THAT WAY. AS LONG AS NONE OF THESE OTHER SHIPS CUTS US OFF...
ACHILLES! I'M ONLY TRYING TO KEEP YOU FROM HEM RUSHING TO YOUR DEATH--
YOU'RE ONLY DOING IT BECAUSE MY MOTHER --WHO'S A POWERFUL PRIESTESS--ASKED IT OF YOU. AND I ONLY LET YOU ON MY SHIP BECAUSE SHE ASKED THAT OF ME.
NOW, STAY OUT OF MY WAY, KALCHAS, OR YOU'LL WRECK US!
OARS IN THE WATER!
ROW!
KALCHAS DELAYED OUR DEPARTURE SO LONG, THE FIGHT WILL BE OVER--
NO, LOOK--MEN AND CHARIOTS COMING UP THE BEACH FROM THOSE SHIPS!
THOSE AREN'T TROJANS!

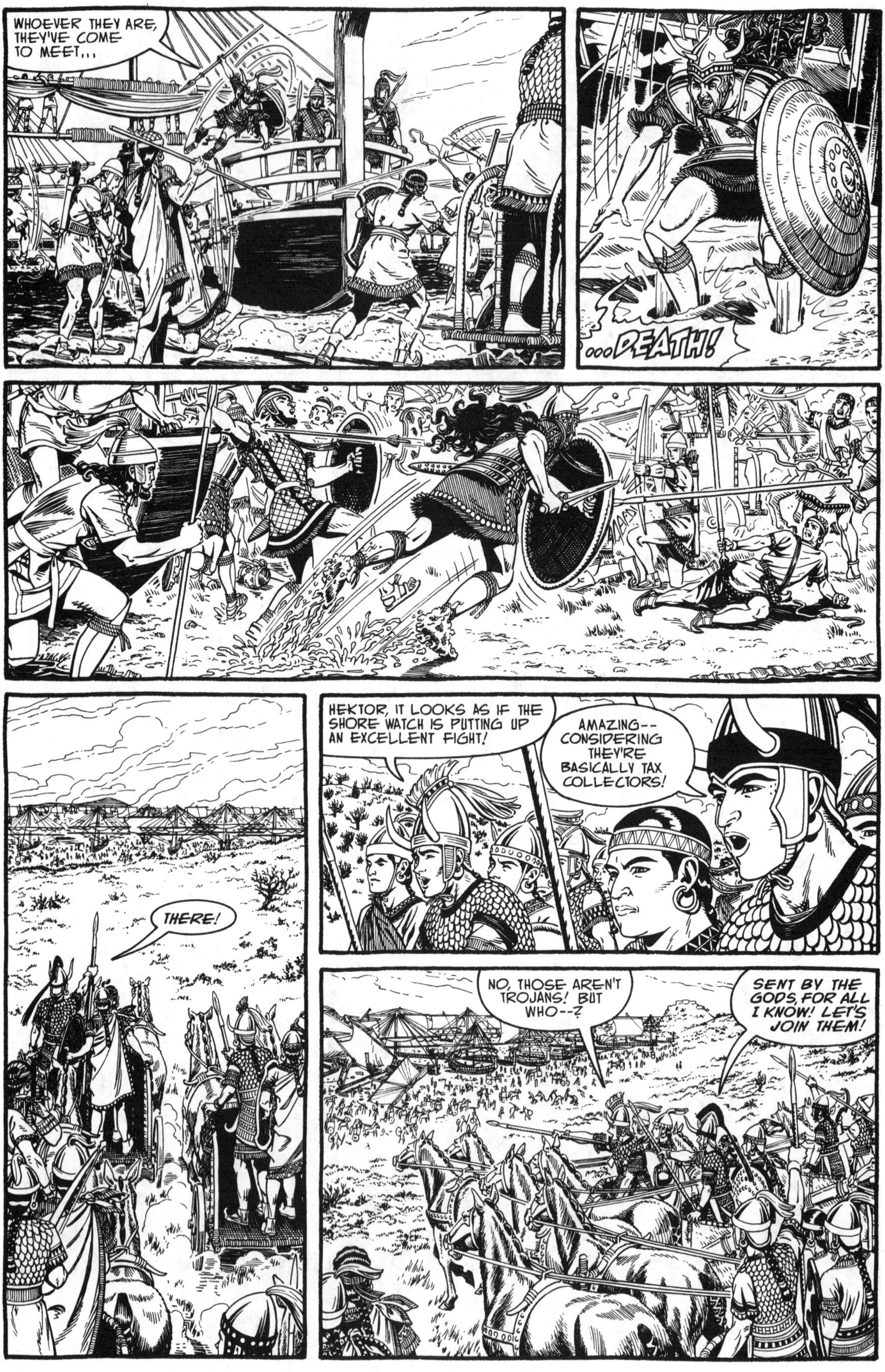
WHOEVER THEY ARE, THEY'VE COME TO MEET...
...DEATH!
THERE!
HEKTOR, IT LOOKS AS IF THE SHORE WATCH IS PUTTING UP AN EXCELLENT FIGHT!
AMAZING-- CONSIDERING THEY'RE BASICALLY TAX COLLECTORS!
NO, THOSE AREN'T TROJANS! BUT WHO--?
SENT BY THE GODS, FOR ALL I KNOW! LET'S JOIN THEM!

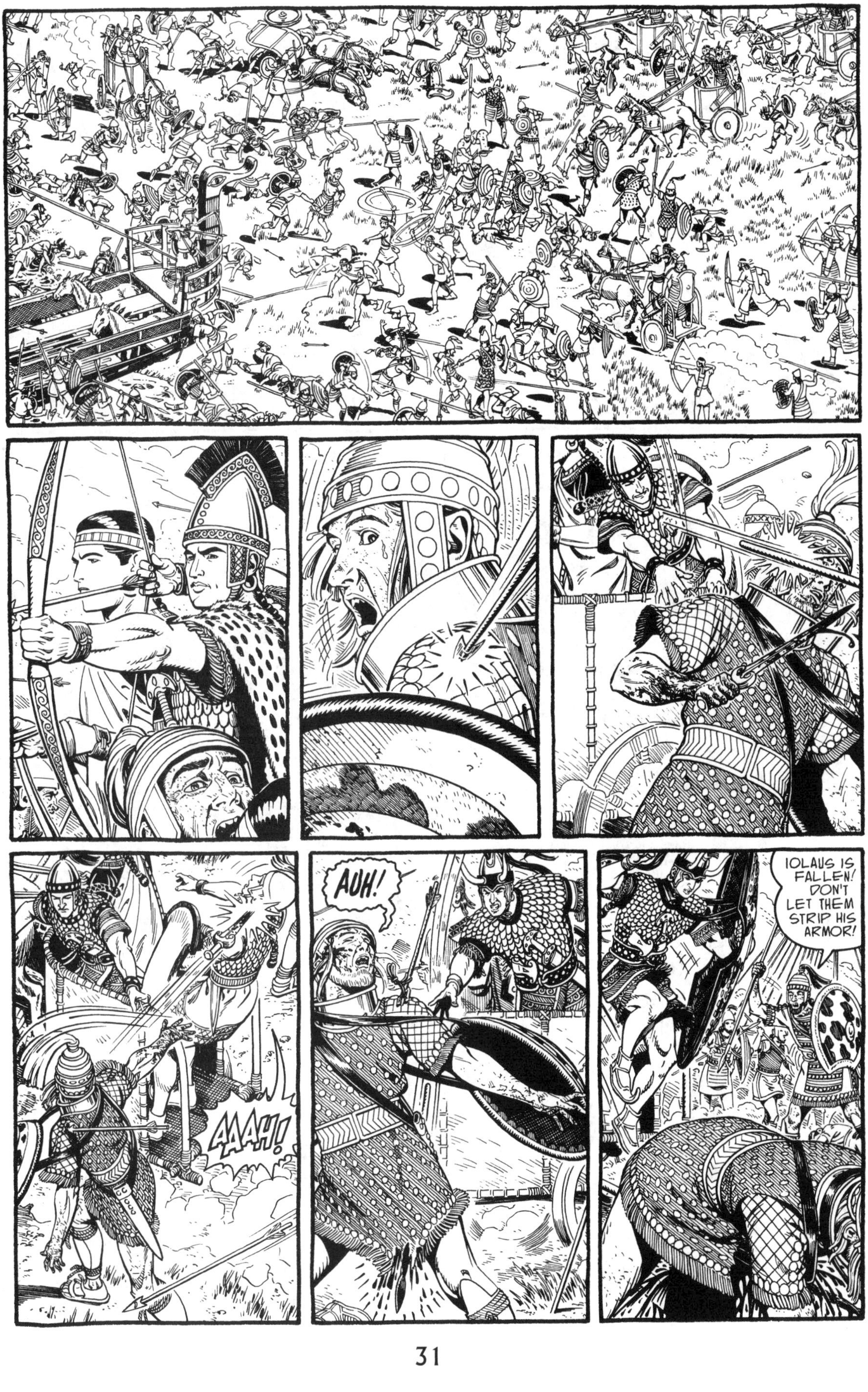
AAAH!
AUH!
IOLAUS IS FALLEN! DON'T LET THEM STRIP HIS ARMOR!

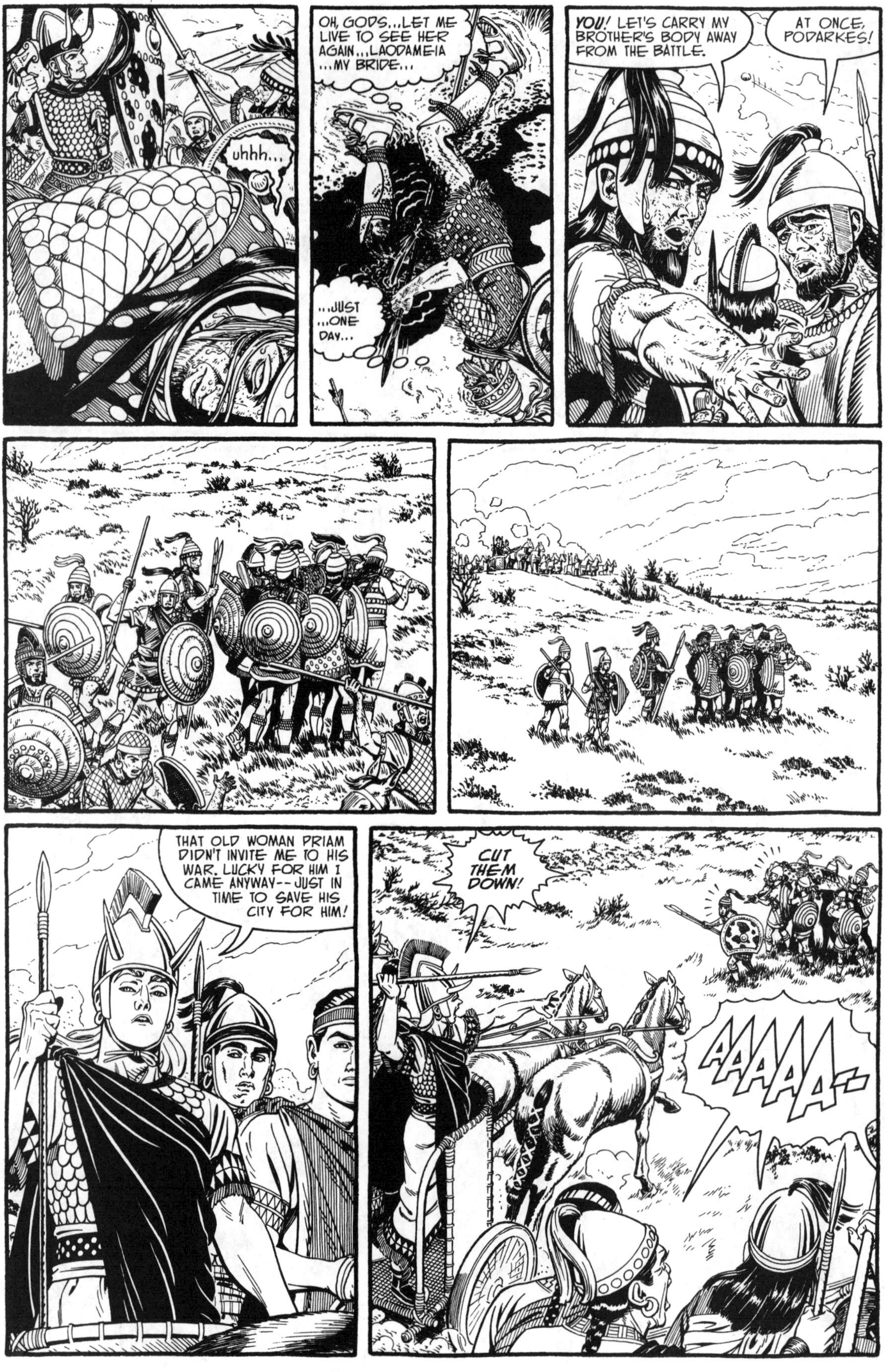
uhhh...
OH, GODS...LET ME LIVE TO SEE HER AGAIN...LAODAME-IA ...MY BRIDE...
...JUST ...ONE DAY...
YOU! LET'S CARRY MY BROTHER'S BODY AWAY FROM THE BATTLE.
AT ONCE, PODARKES!
THAT OLD WOMAN PRIAM DIDN'T INVITE ME TO HIS WAR. LUCKY FOR HIM I CAME ANYWAY-- JUST IN TIME TO SAVE HIS CITY FOR HIM!
CUT THEM DOWN!
AAAAA-

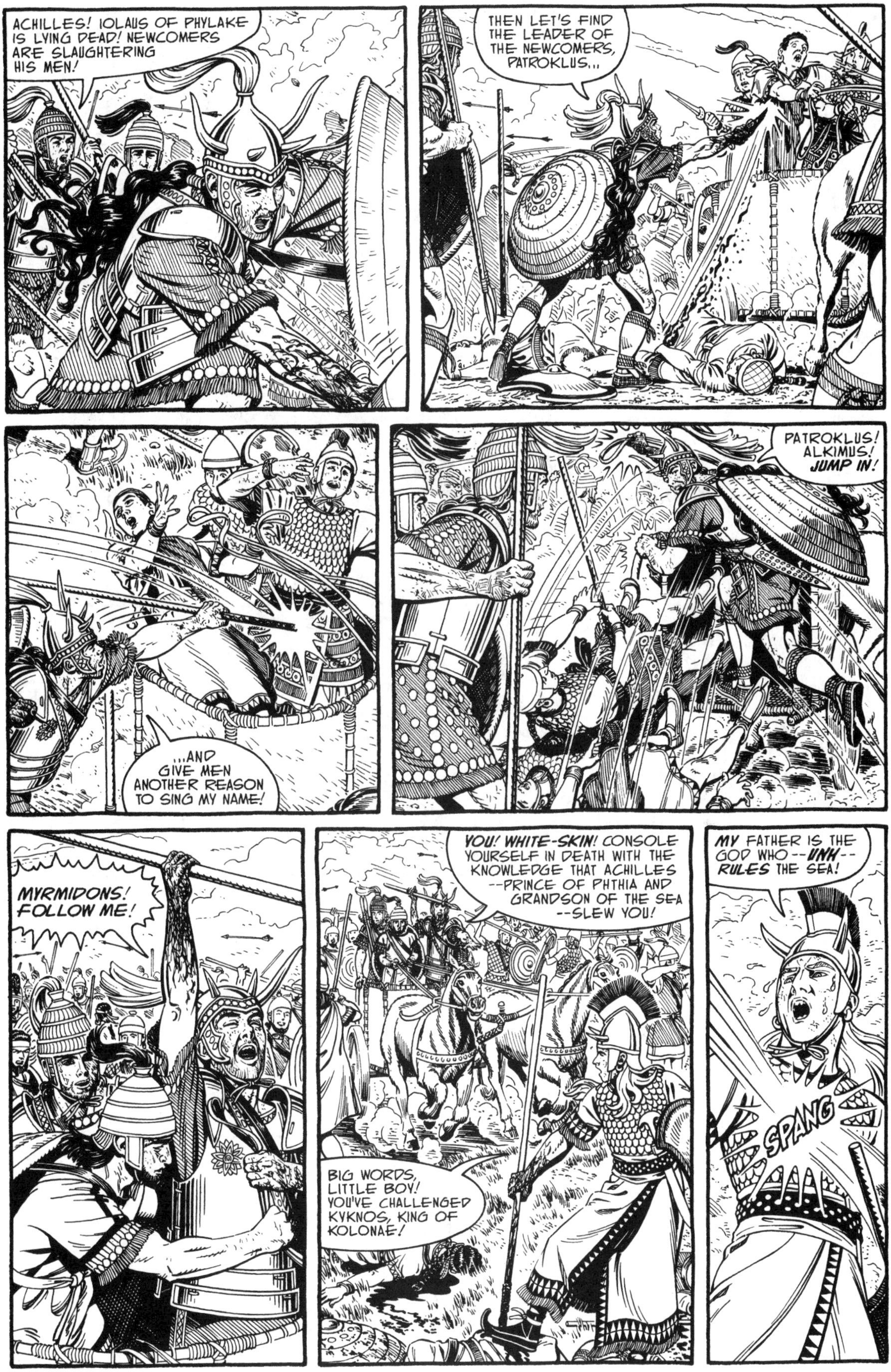
ACHILLES! IOLAUS OF PHYLAKE IS LYING DEAD! NEWCOMERS ARE SLAUGHTERING HIS MEN!
THEN LET'S FIND THE LEADER OF THE NEWCOMERS, PATROKLUS...
...AND GIVE MEN ANOTHER REASON TO SING MY NAME!
PATROKLUS! ALKIMUS! **JUMP IN!**
MYRMIDONS! FOLLOW ME!
YOU! WHITE-SKIN! CONSOLE YOURSELF IN DEATH WITH THE KNOWLEDGE THAT ACHILLES --PRINCE OF PHTHIA AND GRANDSON OF THE SEA --SLEW YOU!
BIG WORDS, LITTLE BOY! YOU'VE CHALLENGED KYKNOS, KING OF KOLONAE!
MY FATHER IS THE GOD WHO-- **UNH**-- **RULES** THE SEA!
SPANG

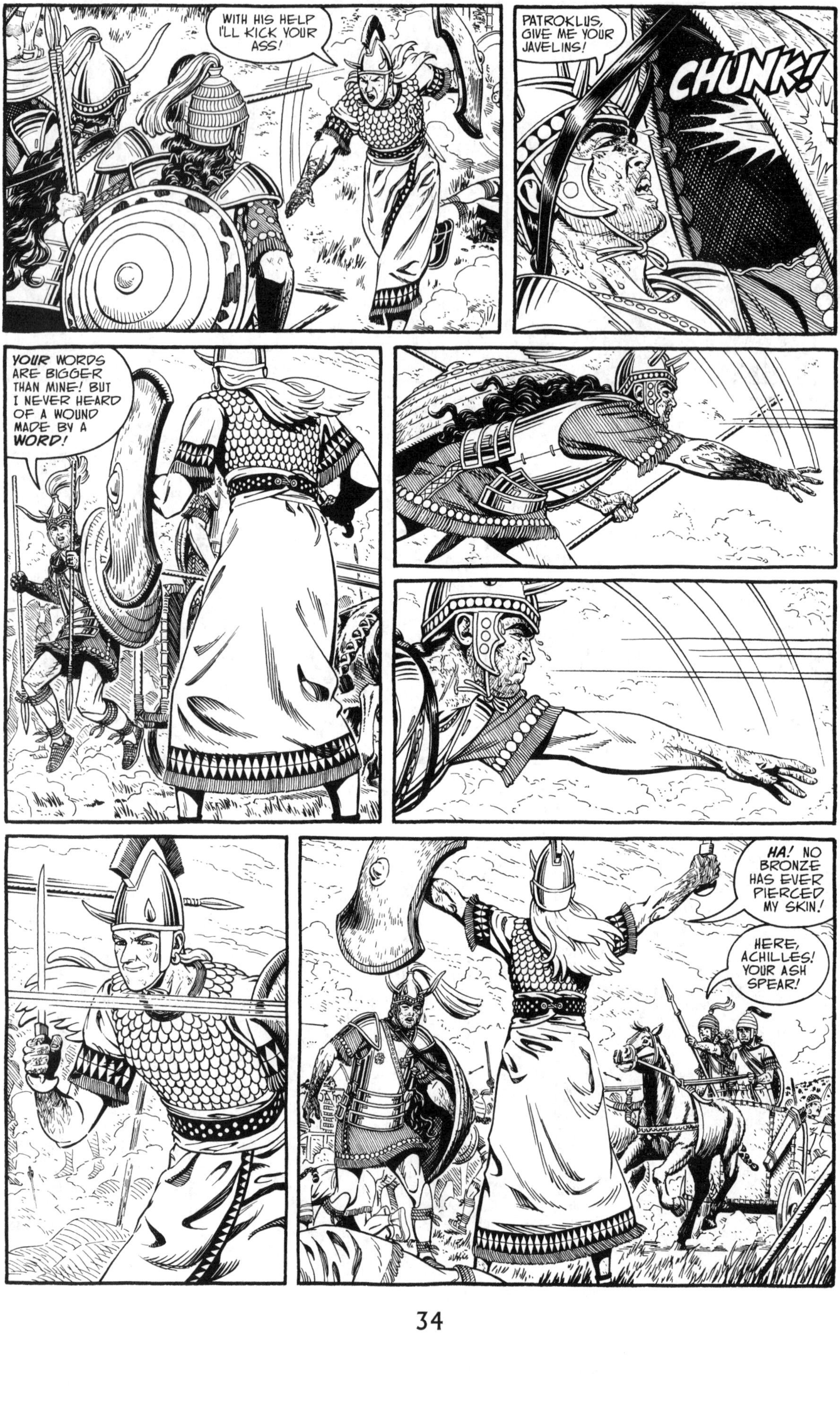
WITH HIS HELP I'LL KICK YOUR ASS!
PATROKLUS, GIVE ME YOUR JAVELINS!
CHUNK!
YOUR WORDS ARE BIGGER THAN MINE! BUT I NEVER HEARD OF A WOUND MADE BY A WORD!
HA! NO BRONZE HAS EVER PIERCED MY SKIN!
HERE, ACHILLES! YOUR ASH SPEAR!

IS SOMETHING WRONG WITH THE SPEAR? IT BOUNCED OFF HIM THE FIRST TIME.

THE TIP IS STILL ON AND SHARP! THEN IS IT MY THROWING ARM?

AUH!

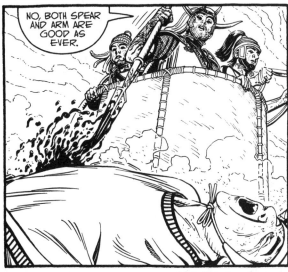

NO, BOTH SPEAR AND ARM ARE GOOD AS EVER.

I WON'T MISS HIM AGAIN!

CHANK!

AH! *THAT* DREW HIS BLOOD!

I THOUGHT YOU RAN AWAY.

NO, --THAT BLOOD'S FROM THE *OTHER* MAN I JUST KILLED!

35

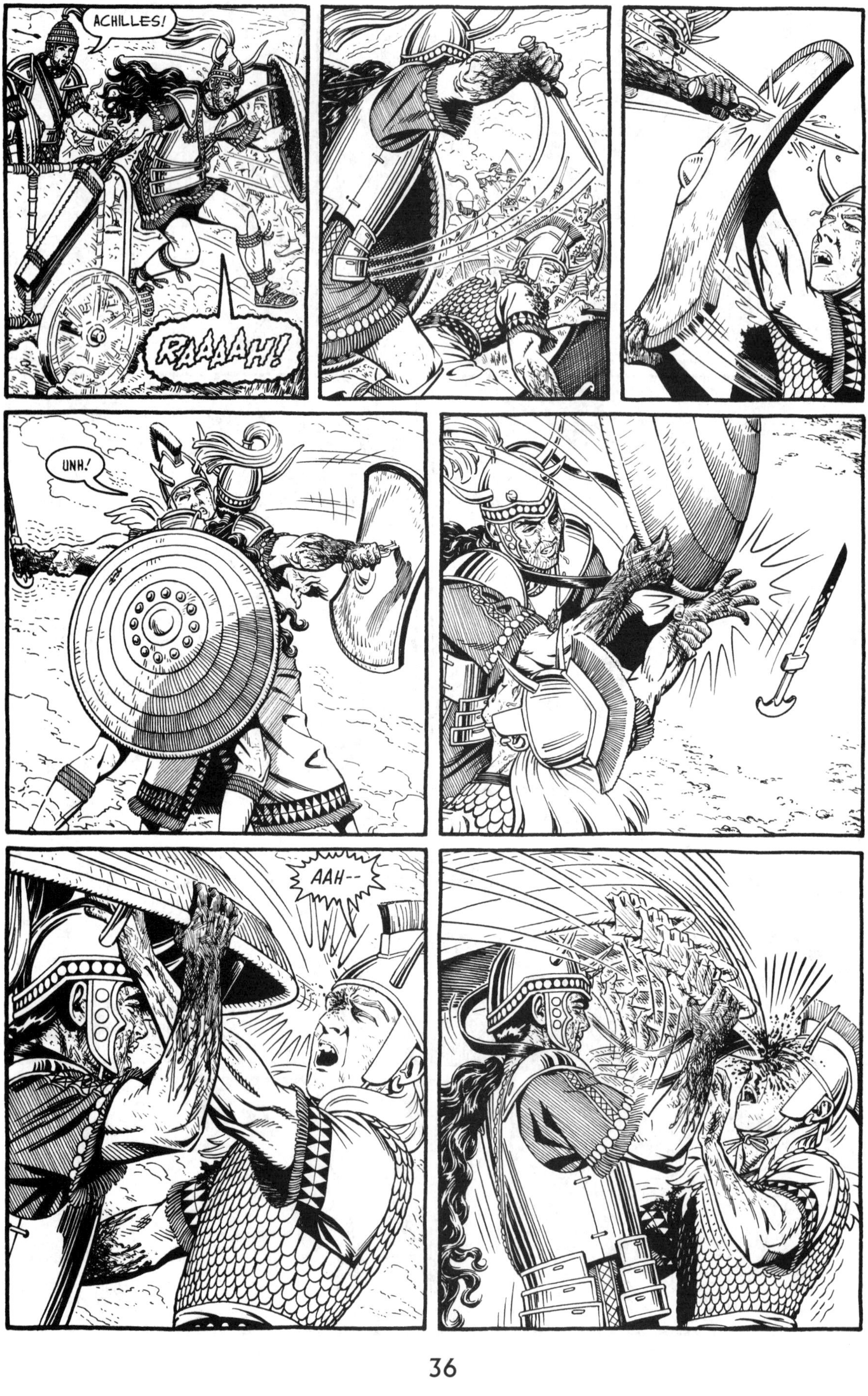
ACHILLES!
RAAAAH!
UNH!
AAH--

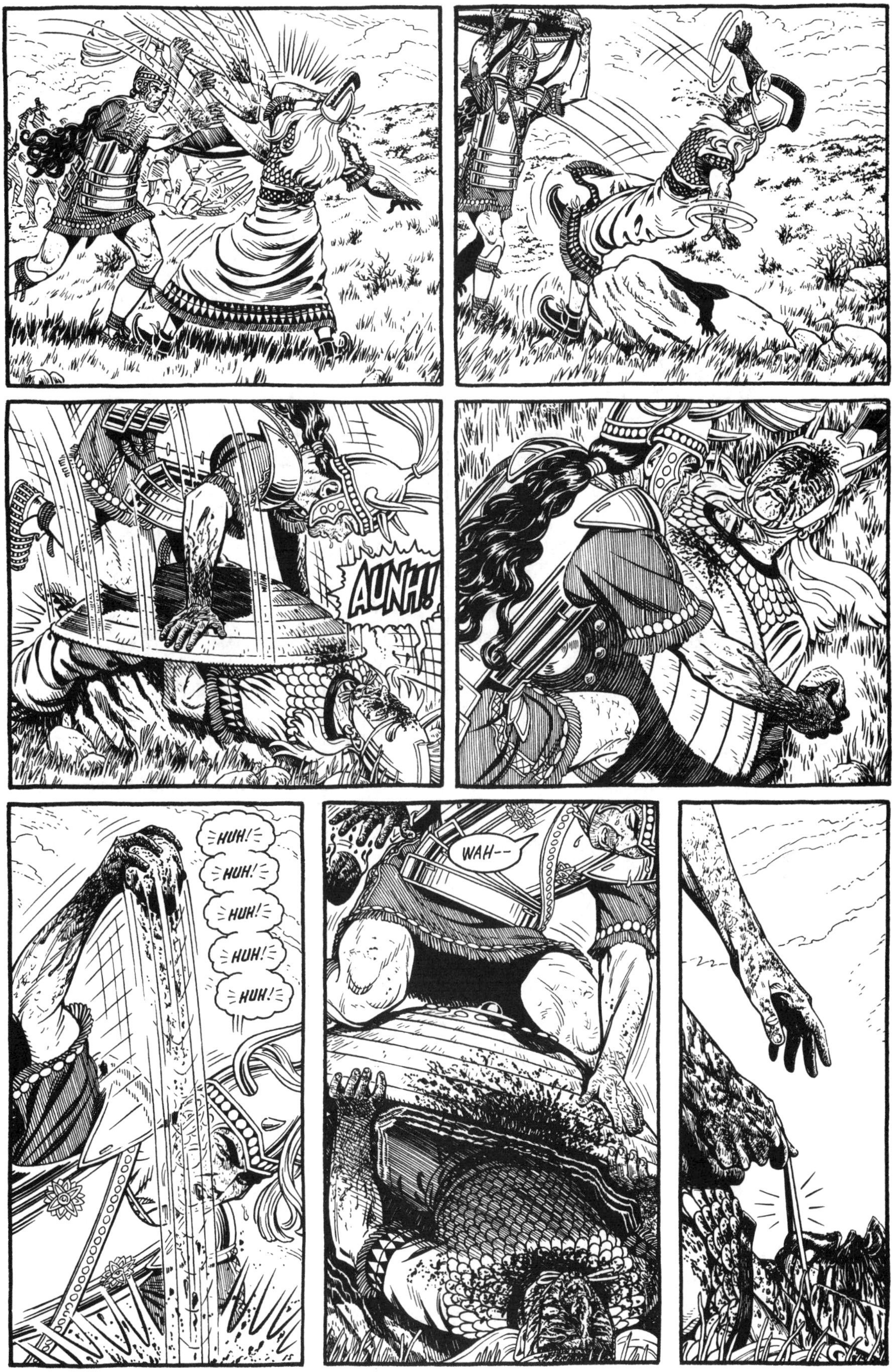
AUNH!
HUH!
HUH!
HUH!
HUH!
HUH!
WAH--

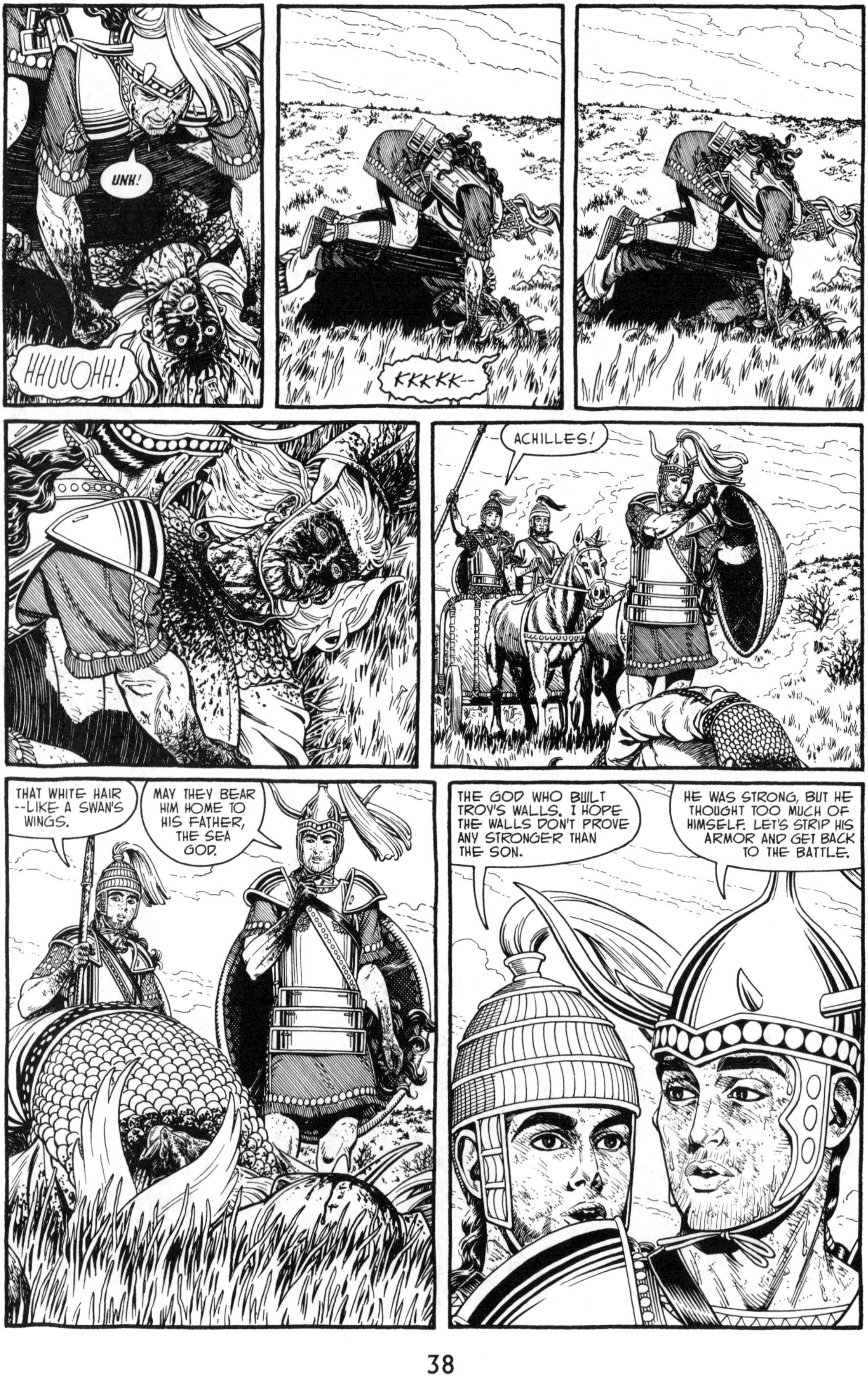

UNH!
HHUUOHH!
KKKKK--
ACHILLES!
THAT WHITE HAIR --LIKE A SWAN'S WINGS.
MAY THEY BEAR HIM HOME TO HIS FATHER, THE SEA GOD.
THE GOD WHO BUILT TROY'S WALLS. I HOPE THE WALLS DON'T PROVE ANY STRONGER THAN THE SON.
HE WAS STRONG, BUT HE THOUGHT TOO MUCH OF HIMSELF. LET'S STRIP HIS ARMOR AND GET BACK TO THE BATTLE.

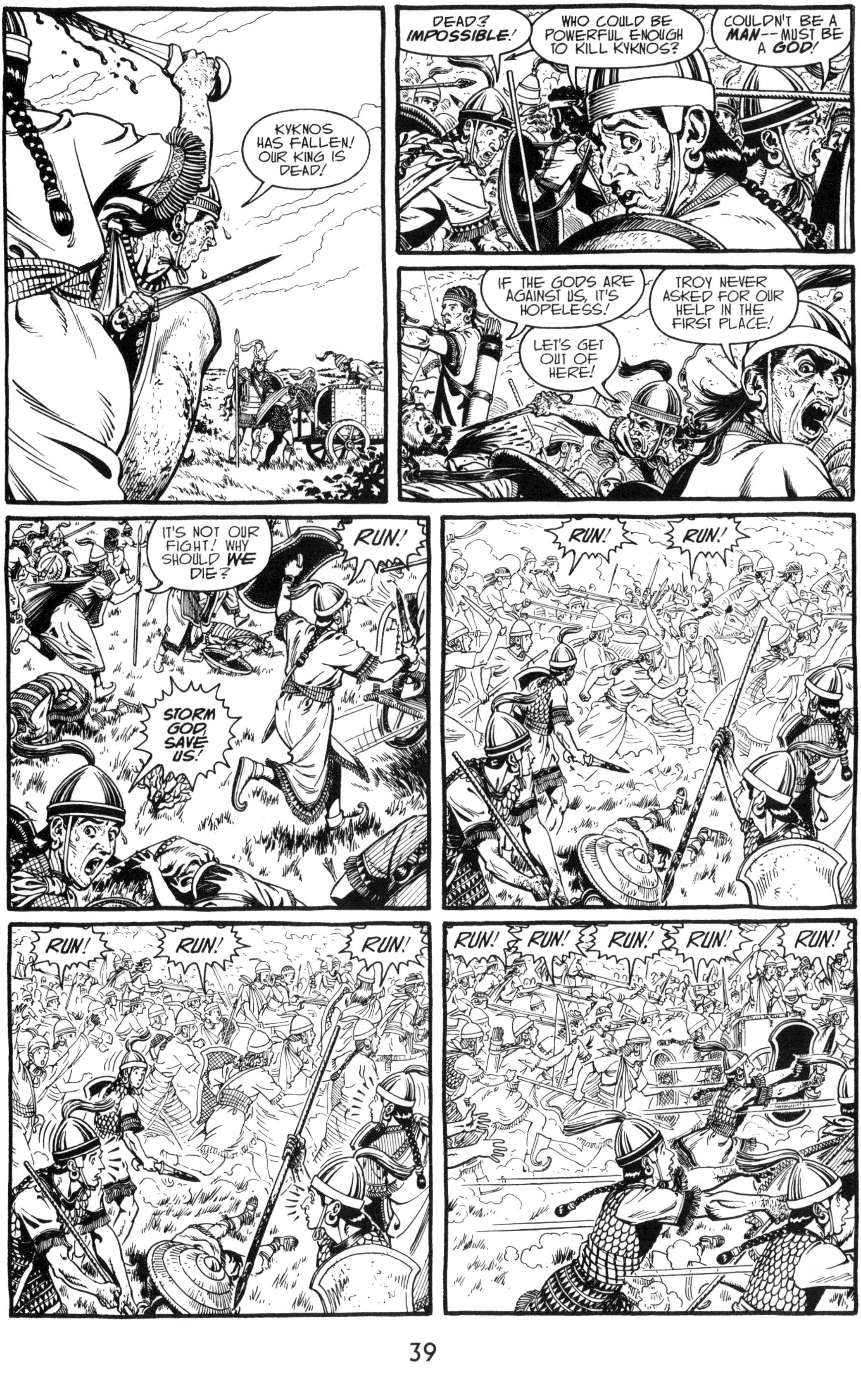
KYKNOS HAS FALLEN! OUR KING IS DEAD!
DEAD? **IMPOSSIBLE!**
WHO COULD BE POWERFUL ENOUGH TO KILL KYKNOS?
COULDN'T BE A **MAN**--MUST BE A **GOD!**
IF THE GODS ARE AGAINST US, IT'S HOPELESS!
LET'S GET OUT OF HERE!
TROY NEVER ASKED FOR OUR HELP IN THE FIRST PLACE!
IT'S NOT OUR FIGHT! WHY SHOULD **WE** DIE?
RUN!
STORM GOD, SAVE US!
RUN!
RUN!
RUN!
RUN!
RUN!
RUN!
RUN!
RUN!
RUN!
RUN!

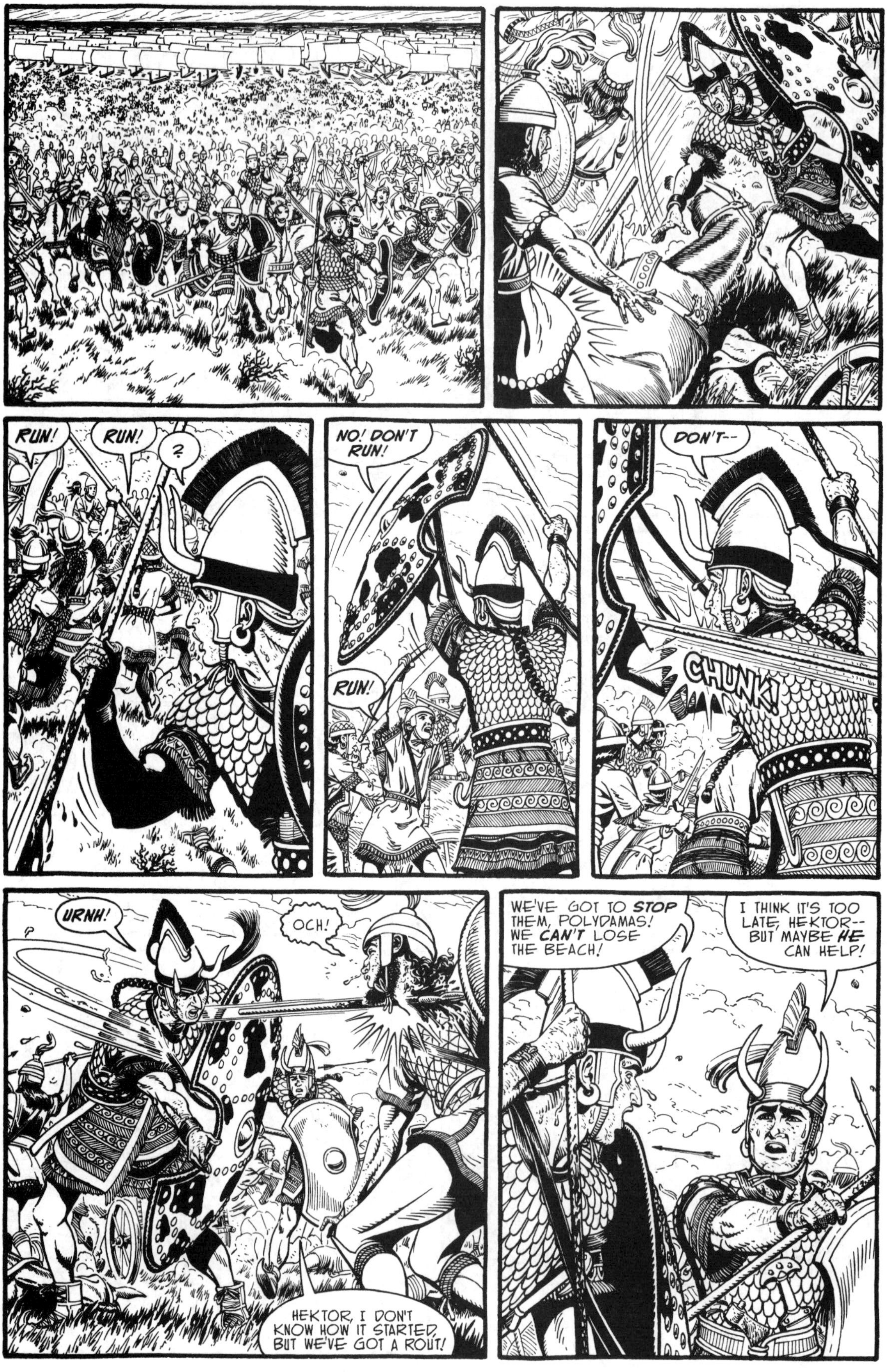
RUN!
RUN!
?
NO! DON'T RUN!
RUN!
DON'T--
CHUNK!
URNH!
OCH!
HEKTOR, I DON'T KNOW HOW IT STARTED, BUT WE'VE GOT A ROUT!
WE'VE GOT TO STOP THEM, POLYDAMAS! WE CAN'T LOSE THE BEACH!
I THINK IT'S TOO LATE, HEKTOR-- BUT MAYBE HE CAN HELP!

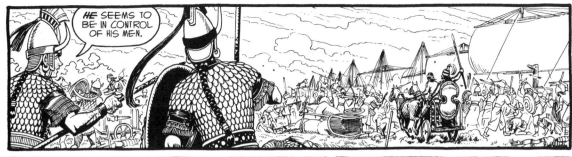

HE SEEMS TO BE IN CONTROL OF HIS MEN.

KEBRIONES, WHO'S THAT TROJAN ALLY OVER NEAR THE SHIPS--THE ONE IN THE PURPLE CHARIOT?

I DON'T KNOW, BUT I'LL TAKE YOU TO FIND OUT.

POLYDAMAS, FIND A CHARIOT AND RALLY AS MANY MEN AS YOU CAN!

STAND FIRM, LYKIANS!

I'M HEKTOR, SON OF PRIAM AND PRINCE OF TROY! WHO ARE YOU?

I AM SARPEDON OF LYKIA, SON OF EUANDRUS--

SARPEDON! AT LAST! THANK THE GODS!

CAN YOU HELP ME RALLY THE TROJANS AND THE REST OF OUR ALLIES?

GLAUKUS! TAKE OVER HERE!

DON'T LET THEM CUT US OFF FROM OUR SHIPS!

HEKTOR OF TROY AND I WILL TRY TO SALVAGE THIS BATTLE!

STAND AND FIGHT!

TO ME, TROJANS!

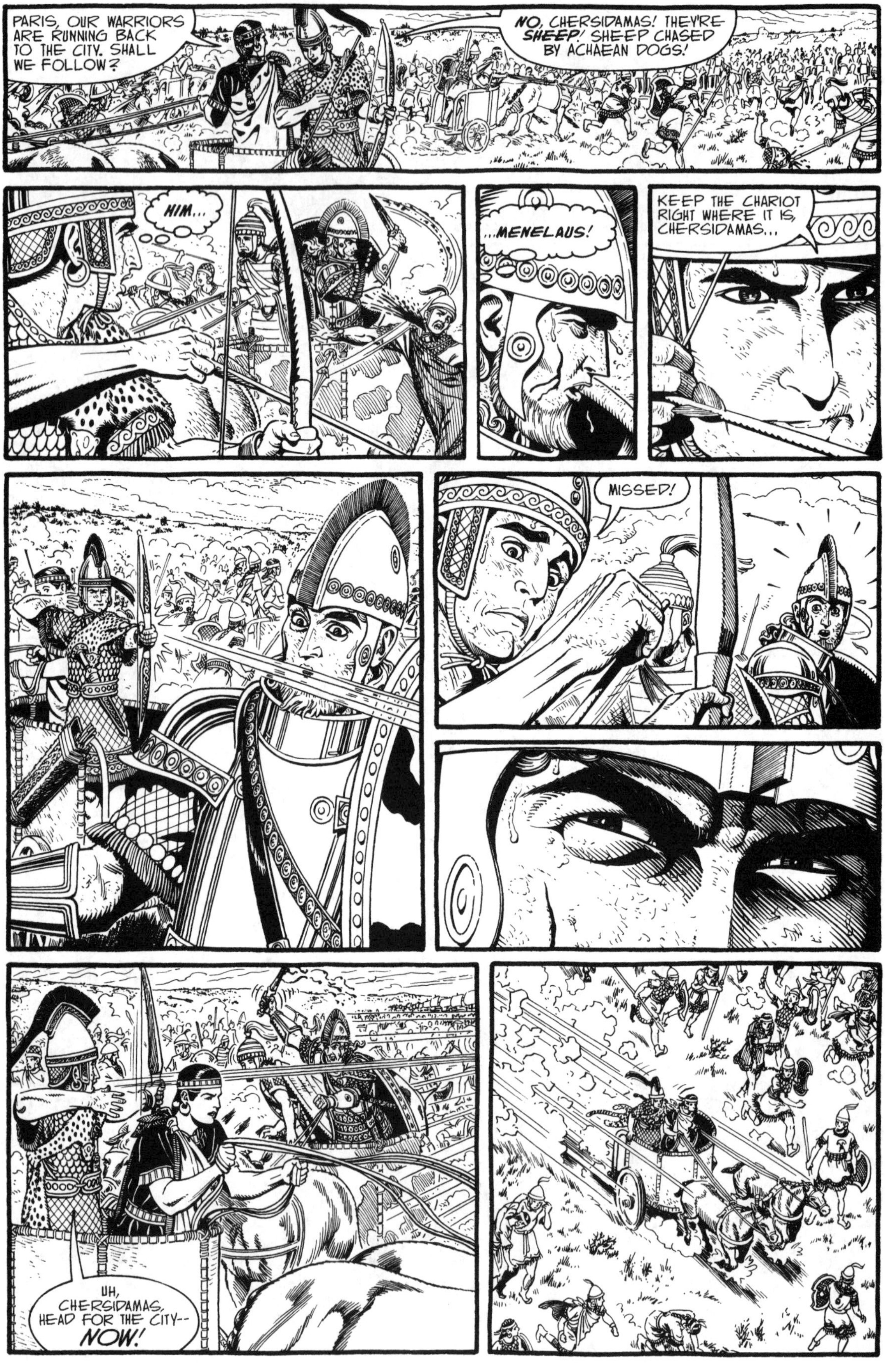
PARIS, OUR WARRIORS ARE RUNNING BACK TO THE CITY. SHALL WE FOLLOW?
NO, CHERSIDAMAS! THEY'RE SHEEP! SHEEP CHASED BY ACHAEAN DOGS!
HIM...
...MENELAUS!
KEEP THE CHARIOT RIGHT WHERE IT IS, CHERSIDAMAS...
MISSED!
UH, CHERSIDAMAS, HEAD FOR THE CITY-- NOW!

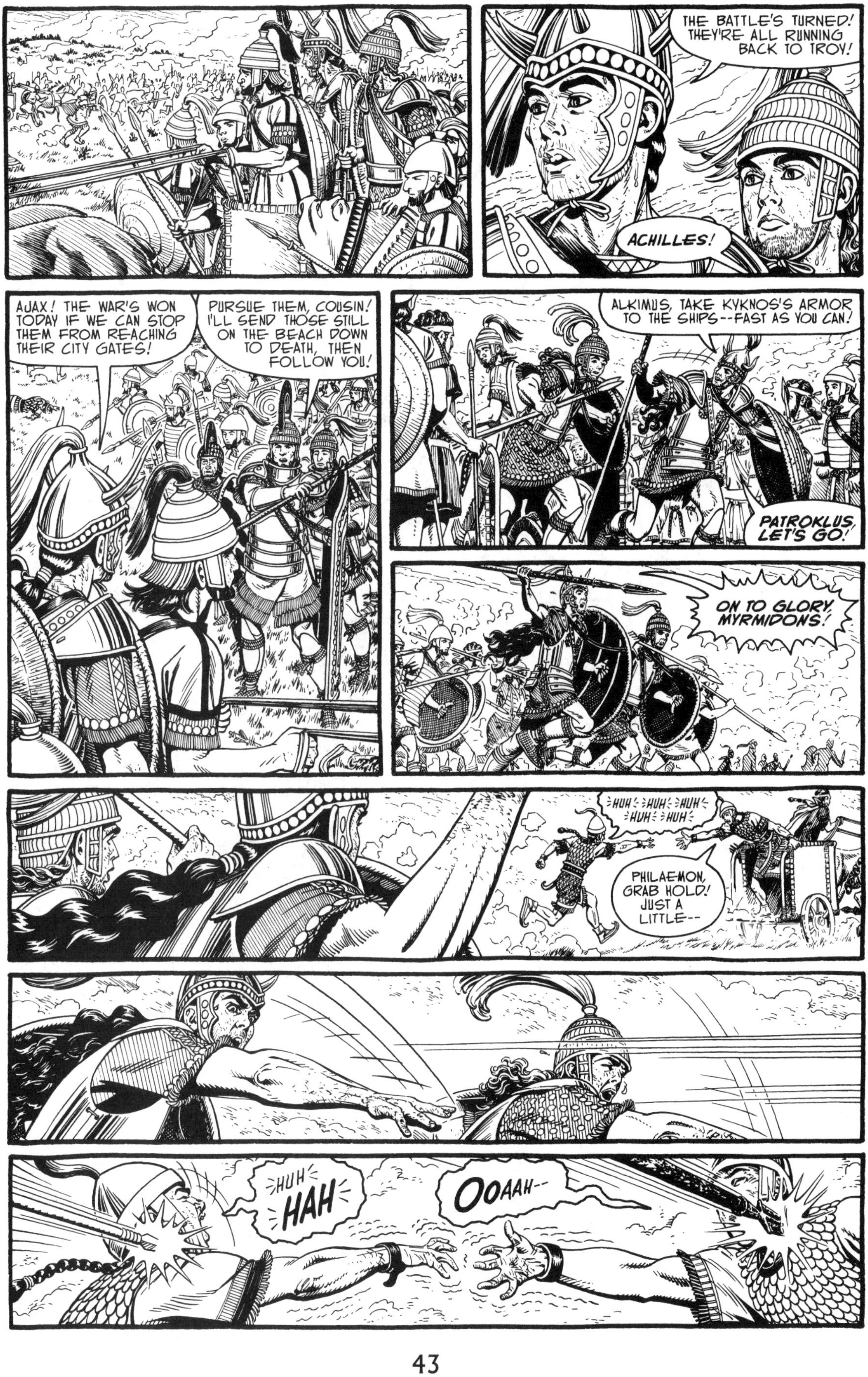
THE BATTLE'S TURNED! THEY'RE ALL RUNNING BACK TO TROY!
ACHILLES!
AJAX! THE WAR'S WON TODAY IF WE CAN STOP THEM FROM REACHING THEIR CITY GATES!
PURSUE THEM, COUSIN! I'LL SEND THOSE STILL ON THE BEACH DOWN TO DEATH, THEN FOLLOW YOU!
ALKIMUS, TAKE KYKNOS'S ARMOR TO THE SHIPS--FAST AS YOU CAN!
PATROKLUS, LET'S GO!
ON TO GLORY, MYRMIDONS!
HUH HUH HUH HUH HUH
PHILAEMON, GRAB HOLD! JUST A LITTLE--
HUH HAH
OOAAH--

STAND AND FIGHT!

ARE YOU WARRIORS --OR WOMEN?

KEBRIONES, LOOK OUT! YOU'LL FOUL--

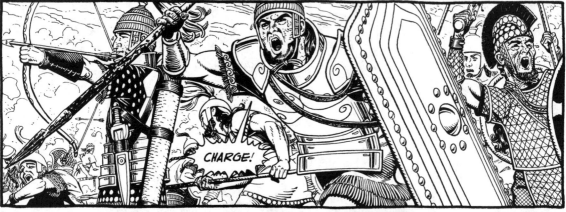

CHARGE!

YAAAAH!

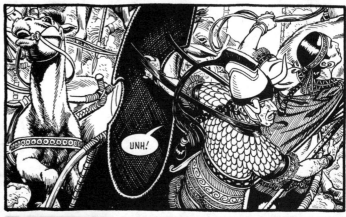

UNH!

44

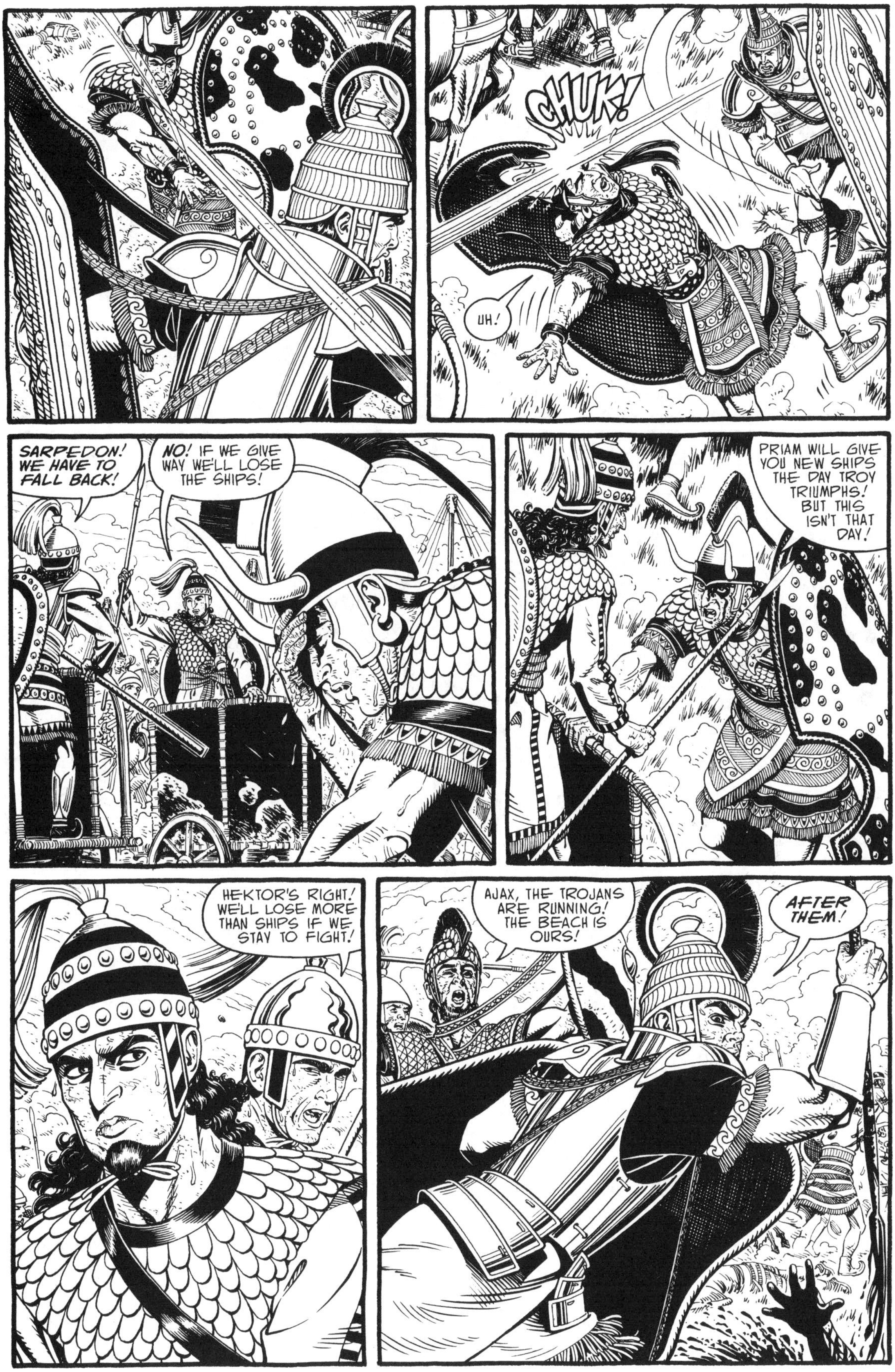
CHUK!
UH!
SARPEDON! WE HAVE TO FALL BACK!
NO! IF WE GIVE WAY WE'LL LOSE THE SHIPS!
PRIAM WILL GIVE YOU NEW SHIPS THE DAY TROY TRIUMPHS! BUT THIS ISN'T THAT DAY!
HEKTOR'S RIGHT! WE'LL LOSE MORE THAN SHIPS IF WE STAY TO FIGHT!
AJAX, THE TROJANS ARE RUNNING! THE BEACH IS OURS!
AFTER THEM!

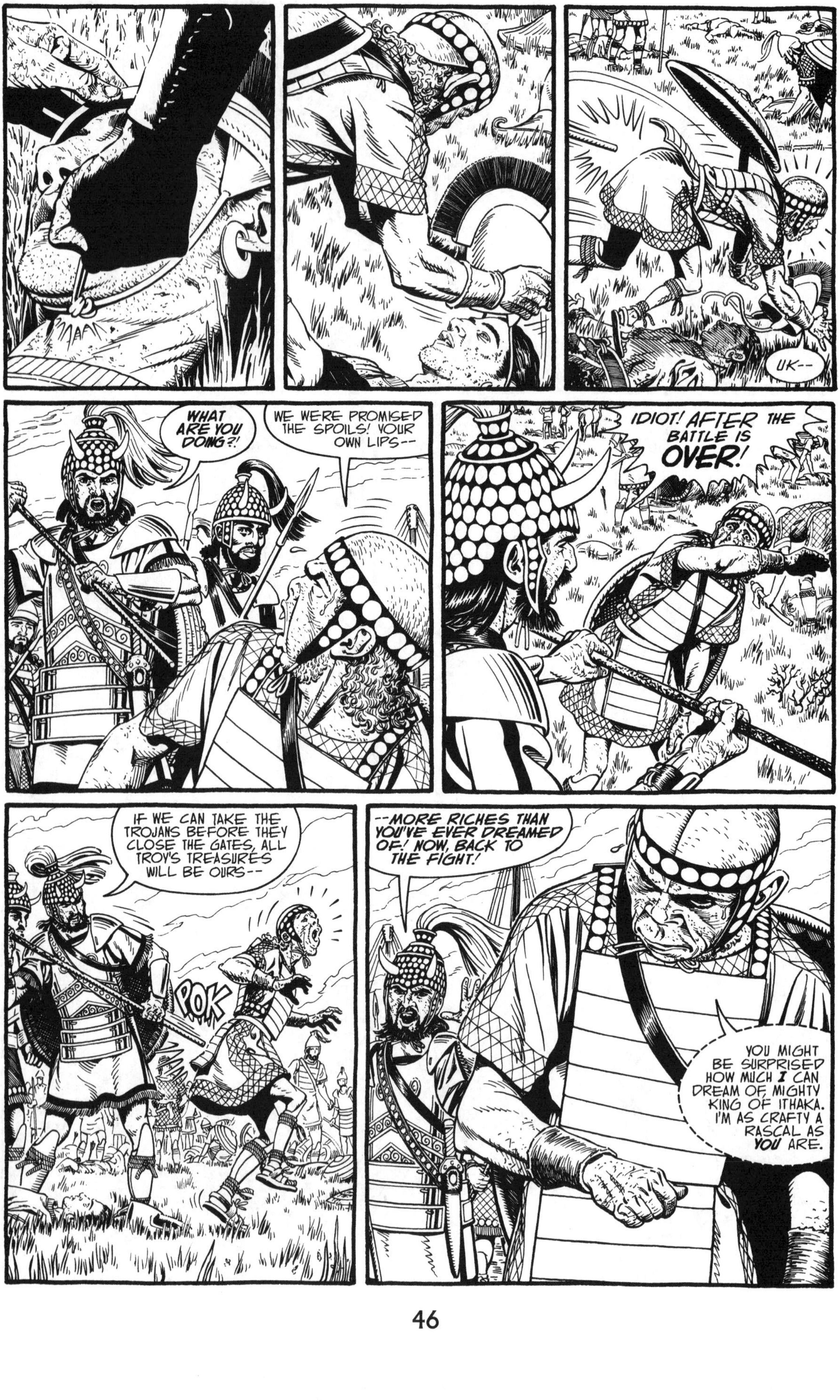
UK--
WHAT ARE YOU DOING?!
WE WERE PROMISED THE SPOILS! YOUR OWN LIPS--
IDIOT! AFTER THE BATTLE IS OVER!
IF WE CAN TAKE THE TROJANS BEFORE THEY CLOSE THE GATES, ALL TROY'S TREASURES WILL BE OURS--
POK
--MORE RICHES THAN YOU'VE EVER DREAMED OF! NOW, BACK TO THE FIGHT!
YOU MIGHT BE SURPRISED HOW MUCH I CAN DREAM OF, MIGHTY KING OF ITHAKA. I'M AS CRAFTY A RASCAL AS YOU ARE.

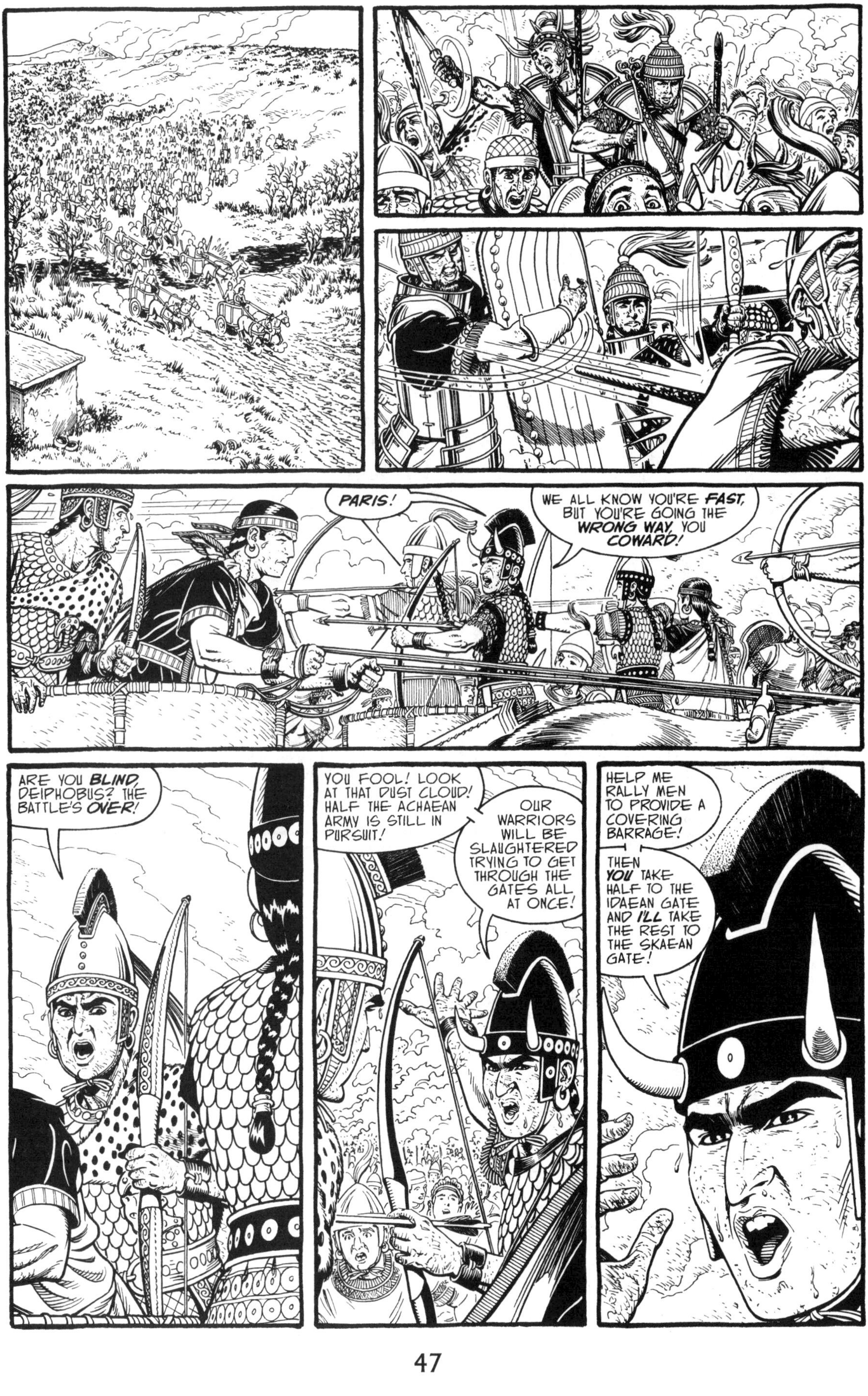
PARIS!
WE ALL KNOW YOU'RE **FAST,** BUT YOU'RE GOING THE **WRONG WAY,** YOU **COWARD!**
ARE YOU **BLIND,** DEIPHOBUS? THE BATTLE'S **OVER!**
YOU FOOL! LOOK AT THAT DUST CLOUD! HALF THE ACHAEAN ARMY IS STILL IN PURSUIT!
OUR WARRIORS WILL BE SLAUGHTERED TRYING TO GET THROUGH THE GATES ALL AT ONCE!
HELP ME RALLY MEN TO PROVIDE A COVERING BARRAGE!
THEN **YOU** TAKE HALF TO THE IDAEAN GATE AND **I'LL** TAKE THE REST TO THE SKAEAN GATE!

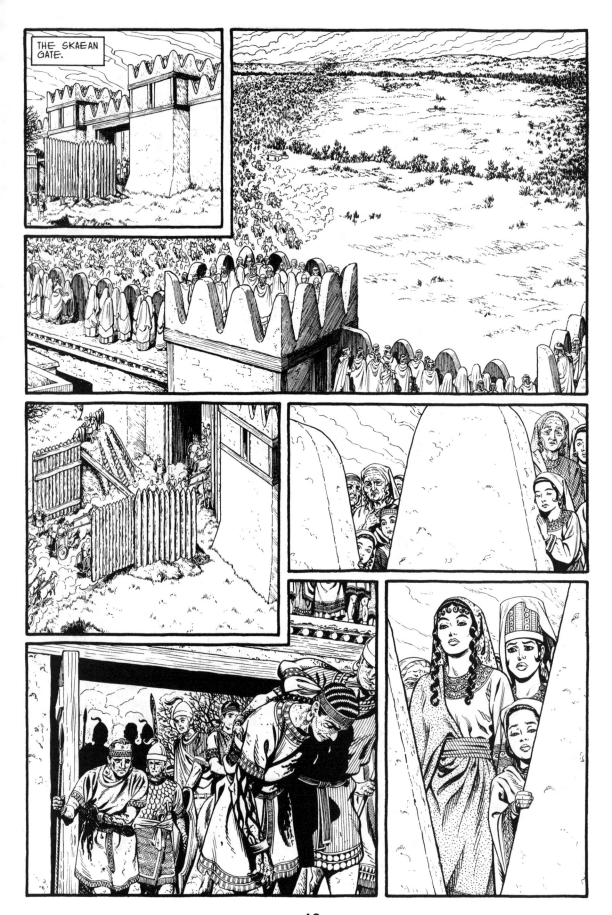

THE SKAEAN GATE.

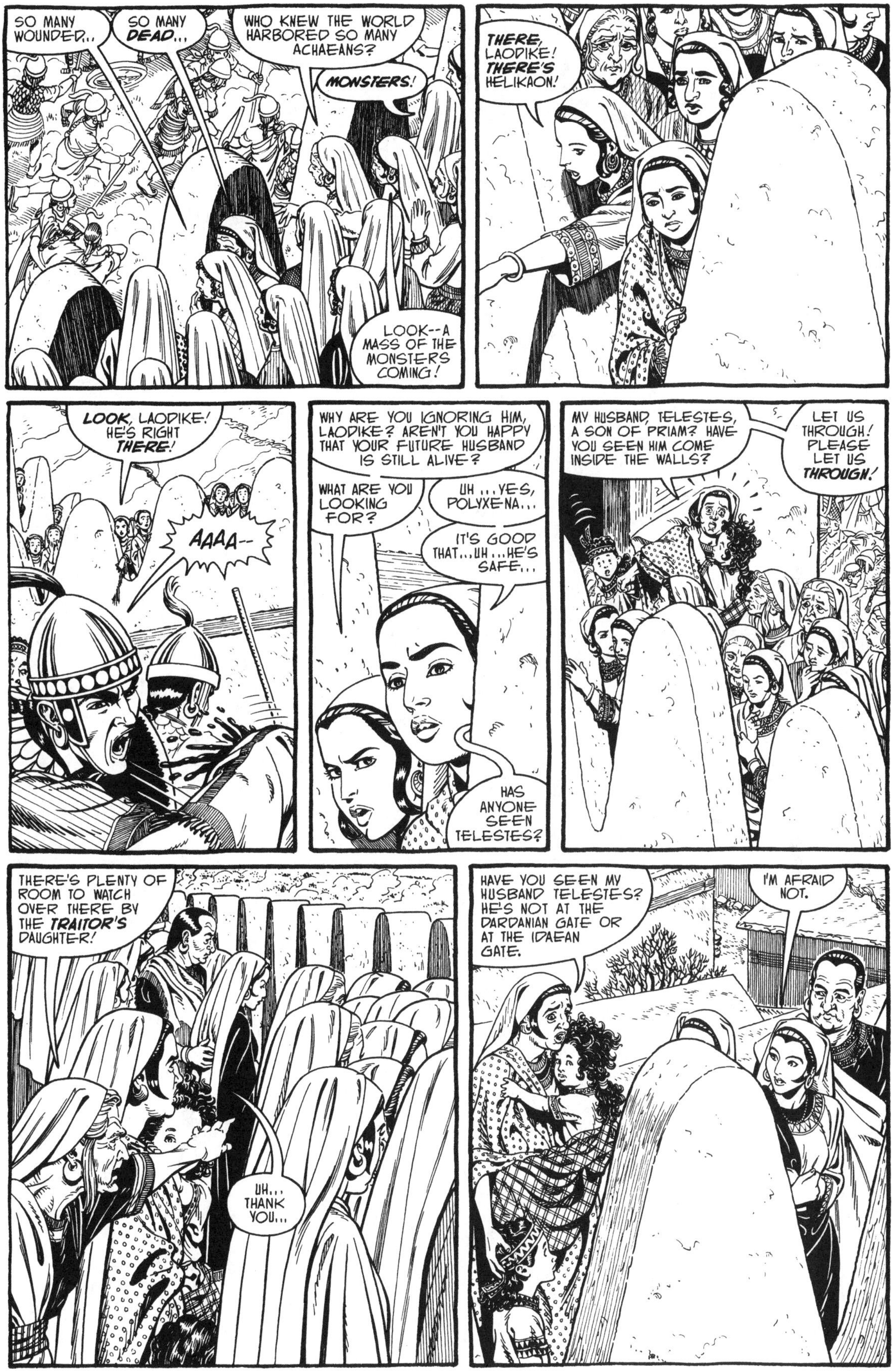
SO MANY WOUNDED...
SO MANY DEAD...
WHO KNEW THE WORLD HARBORED SO MANY ACHAEANS?
MONSTERS!
LOOK--A MASS OF THE MONSTERS COMING!
THERE, LAODIKE! THERE'S HELIKAON!
LOOK, LAODIKE! HE'S RIGHT THERE!
AAAA--
WHY ARE YOU IGNORING HIM, LAODIKE? AREN'T YOU HAPPY THAT YOUR FUTURE HUSBAND IS STILL ALIVE?
WHAT ARE YOU LOOKING FOR?
UH... YES, POLYXENA...
IT'S GOOD THAT...UH...HE'S SAFE...
HAS ANYONE SEEN TELESTES?
MY HUSBAND, TELESTES, A SON OF PRIAM? HAVE YOU SEEN HIM COME INSIDE THE WALLS?
LET US THROUGH! PLEASE LET US THROUGH!
THERE'S PLENTY OF ROOM TO WATCH OVER THERE BY THE TRAITOR'S DAUGHTER!
UH... THANK YOU...
HAVE YOU SEEN MY HUSBAND TELESTES? HE'S NOT AT THE DARDANIAN GATE OR AT THE IDAEAN GATE.
I'M AFRAID NOT.

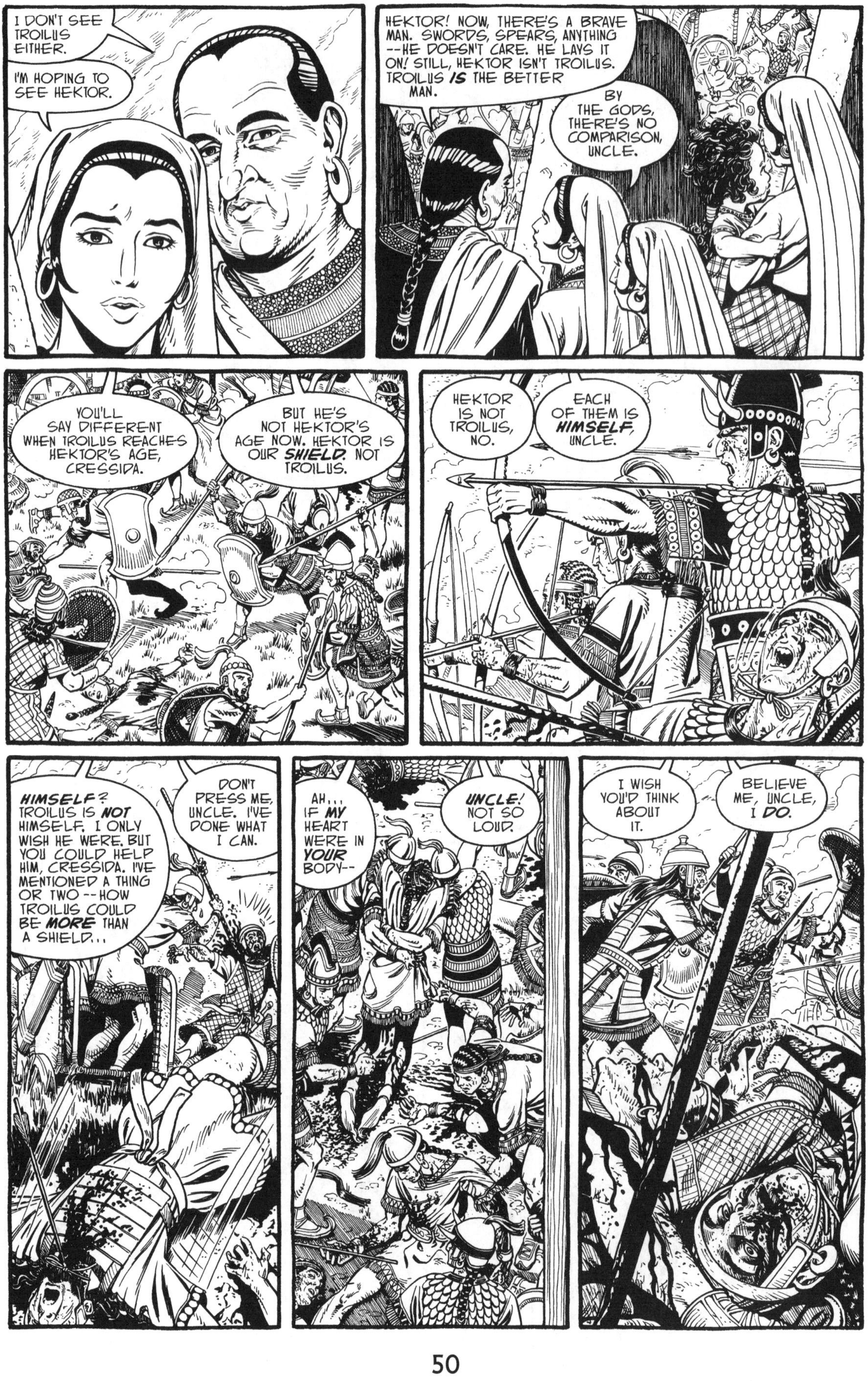
I DON'T SEE TROILUS EITHER.
I'M HOPING TO SEE HEKTOR.
HEKTOR! NOW, THERE'S A BRAVE MAN. SWORDS, SPEARS, ANYTHING --HE DOESN'T CARE. HE LAYS IT ON! STILL, HEKTOR ISN'T TROILUS. TROILUS *IS* THE BETTER MAN.
BY THE GODS, THERE'S NO COMPARISON, UNCLE.
YOU'LL SAY DIFFERENT WHEN TROILUS REACHES HEKTOR'S AGE, CRESSIDA.
BUT HE'S NOT HEKTOR'S AGE NOW. HEKTOR IS OUR *SHIELD.* NOT TROILUS.
HEKTOR IS NOT TROILUS, NO.
EACH OF THEM IS *HIMSELF,* UNCLE.
HIMSELF? TROILUS IS *NOT* HIMSELF. I ONLY WISH HE WERE. BUT YOU COULD HELP HIM, CRESSIDA. I'VE MENTIONED A THING OR TWO --HOW TROILUS COULD BE *MORE* THAN A SHIELD...
DON'T PRESS ME, UNCLE. I'VE DONE WHAT I CAN.
AH... IF *MY* HEART WERE IN *YOUR* BODY--
UNCLE! NOT SO LOUD.
I WISH YOU'D THINK ABOUT IT.
BELIEVE ME, UNCLE, I *DO.*

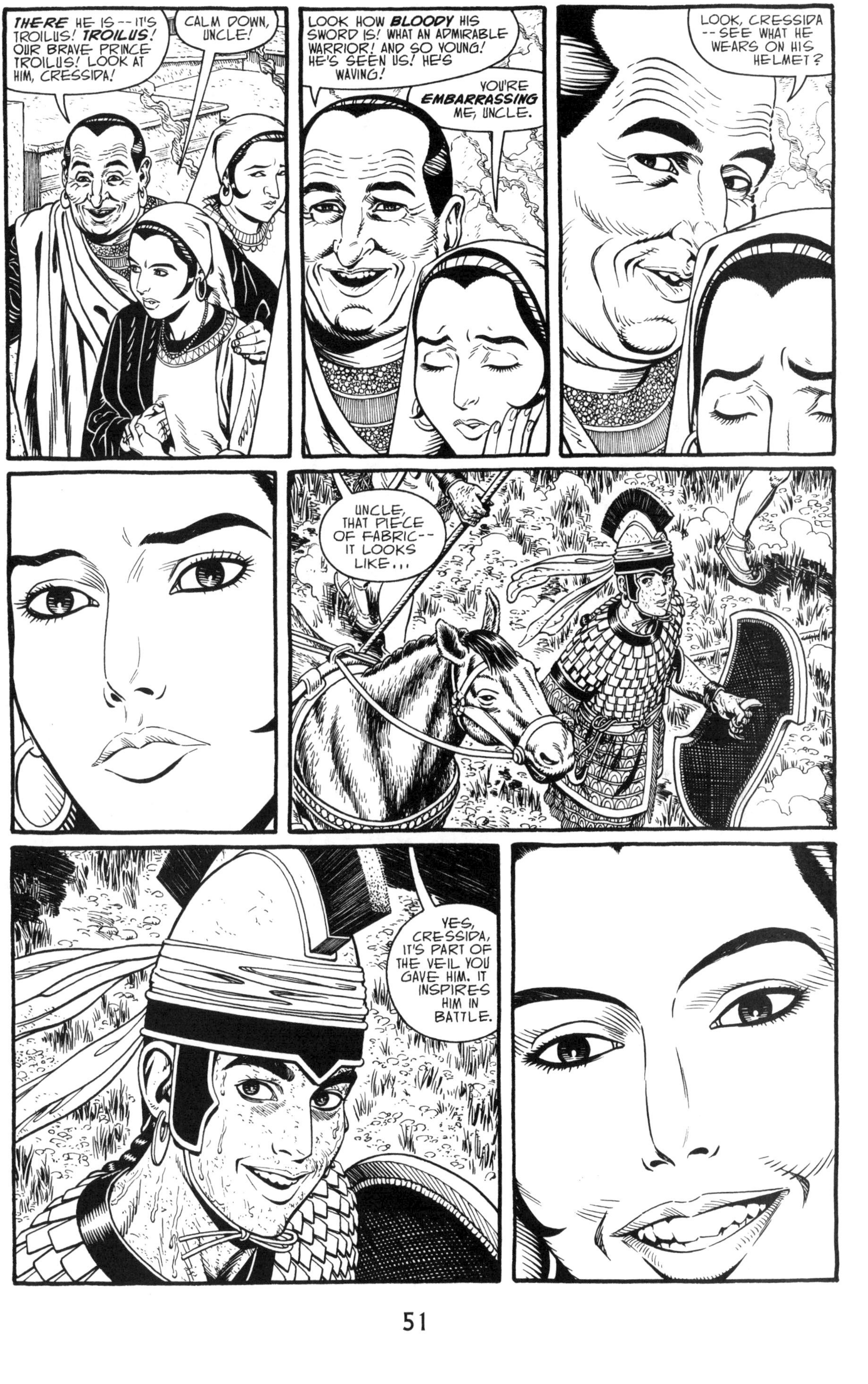
THERE HE IS -- IT'S TROILUS! TROILUS! OUR BRAVE PRINCE TROILUS! LOOK AT HIM, CRESSIDA!
CALM DOWN, UNCLE!
LOOK HOW BLOODY HIS SWORD IS! WHAT AN ADMIRABLE WARRIOR! AND SO YOUNG! HE'S SEEN US! HE'S WAVING!
YOU'RE EMBARRASSING ME, UNCLE.
LOOK, CRESSIDA -- SEE WHAT HE WEARS ON HIS HELMET?
UNCLE, THAT PIECE OF FABRIC-- IT LOOKS LIKE...
YES, CRESSIDA, IT'S PART OF THE VEIL YOU GAVE HIM. IT INSPIRES HIM IN BATTLE.

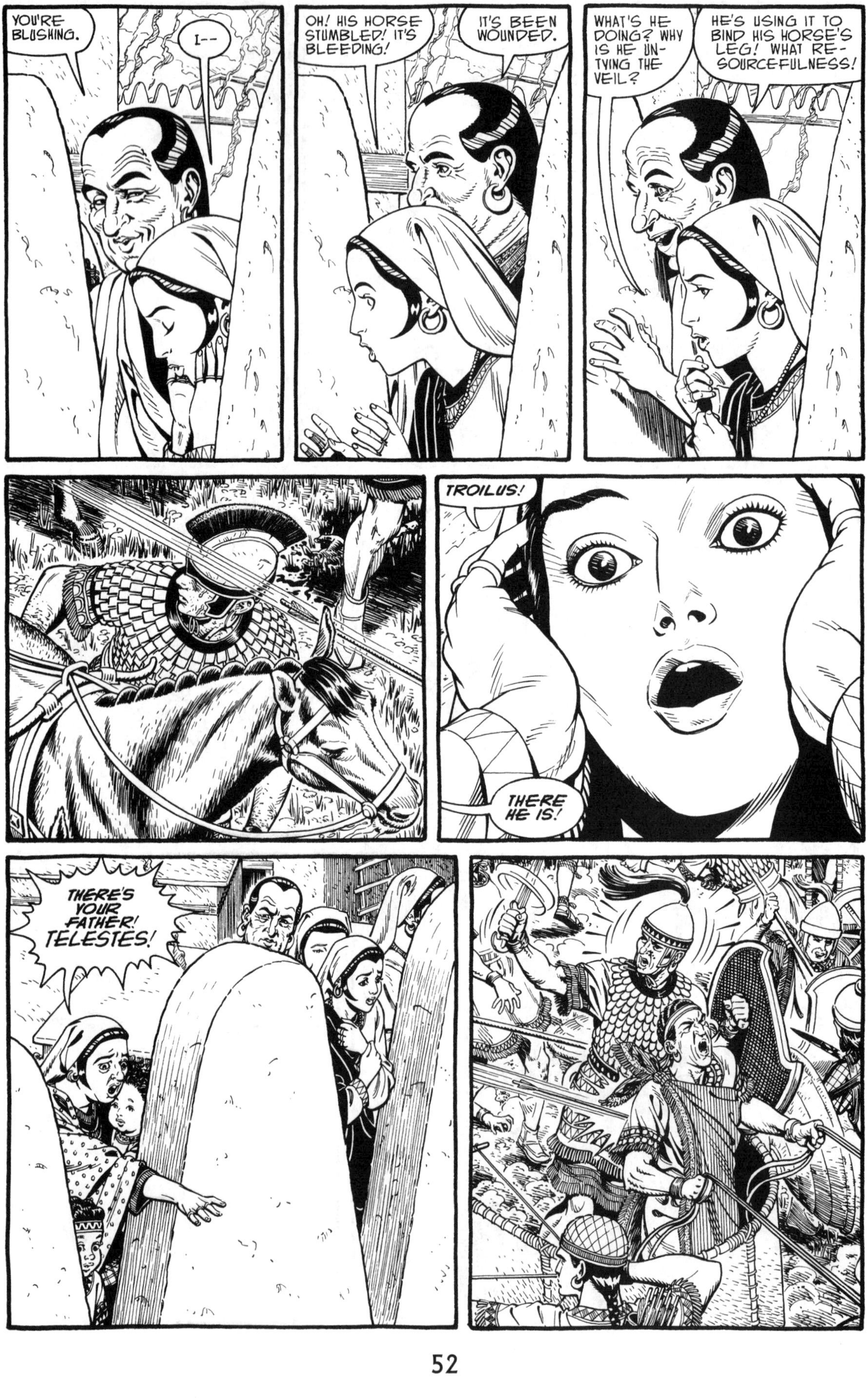
YOU'RE BLUSHING.
I--
OH! HIS HORSE STUMBLED! IT'S BLEEDING!
IT'S BEEN WOUNDED.
WHAT'S HE DOING? WHY IS HE UNTYING THE VEIL?
HE'S USING IT TO BIND HIS HORSE'S LEG! WHAT RESOURCEFULNESS!
TROILUS!
THERE HE IS!
THERE'S YOUR FATHER! TELESTES!

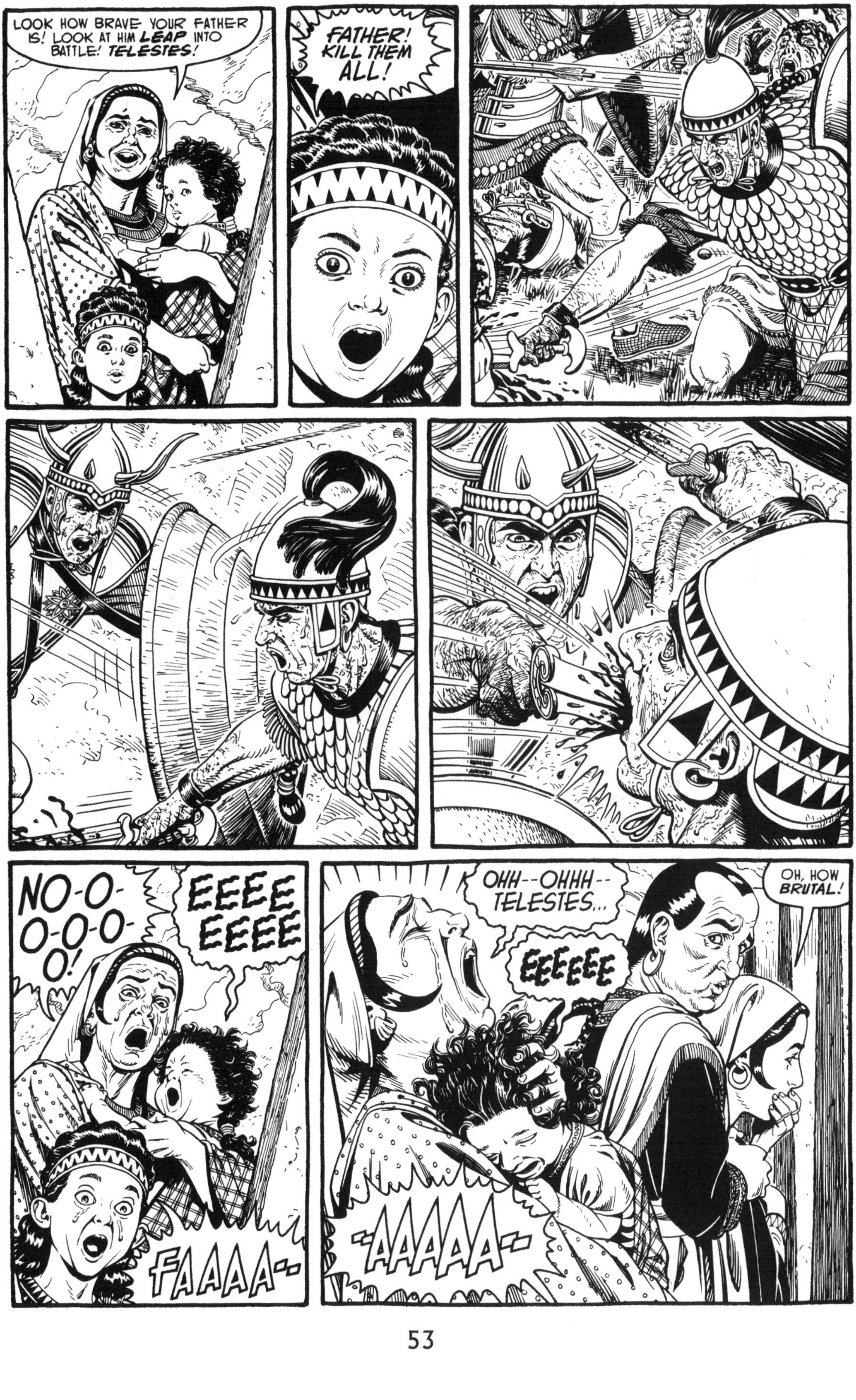
LOOK HOW BRAVE YOUR FATHER IS! LOOK AT HIM *LEAP* INTO BATTLE! *TELESTES!*
FATHER! KILL THEM ALL!
NO-O-O-O-O-O!
EEEE EEEE
FAAAA--
OHH--OHHH--TELESTES...
EEEEEE
OH, HOW *BRUTAL!*
-AAAAA--

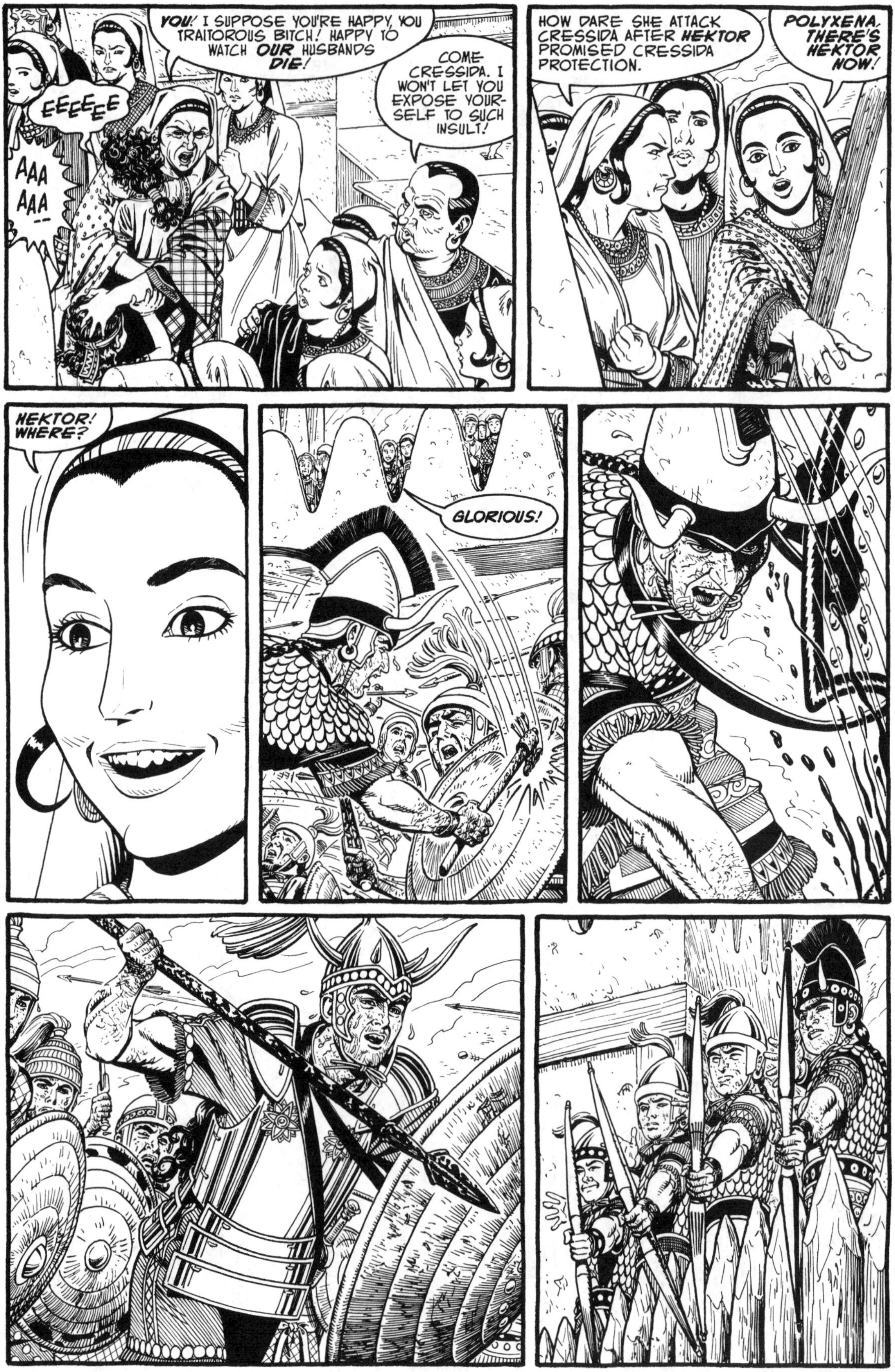
YOU! I SUPPOSE YOU'RE HAPPY, YOU TRAITOROUS BITCH! HAPPY TO WATCH OUR HUSBANDS DIE!
EEEEEE
AAA AAA --
COME CRESSIDA. I WON'T LET YOU EXPOSE YOURSELF TO SUCH INSULT!
HOW DARE SHE ATTACK CRESSIDA AFTER HEKTOR PROMISED CRESSIDA PROTECTION.
POLYXENA, THERE'S HEKTOR NOW!
HEKTOR! WHERE?
GLORIOUS!

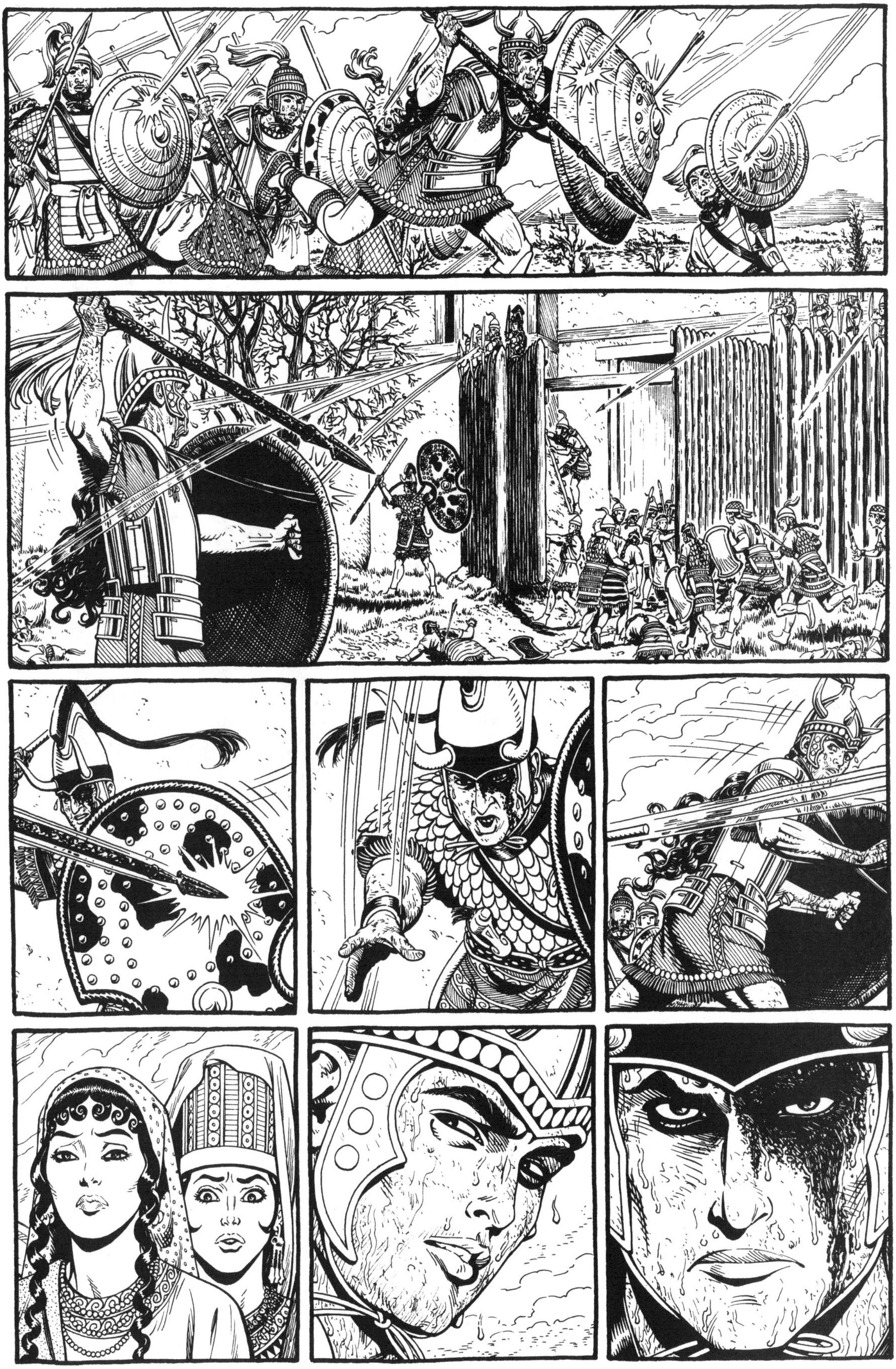

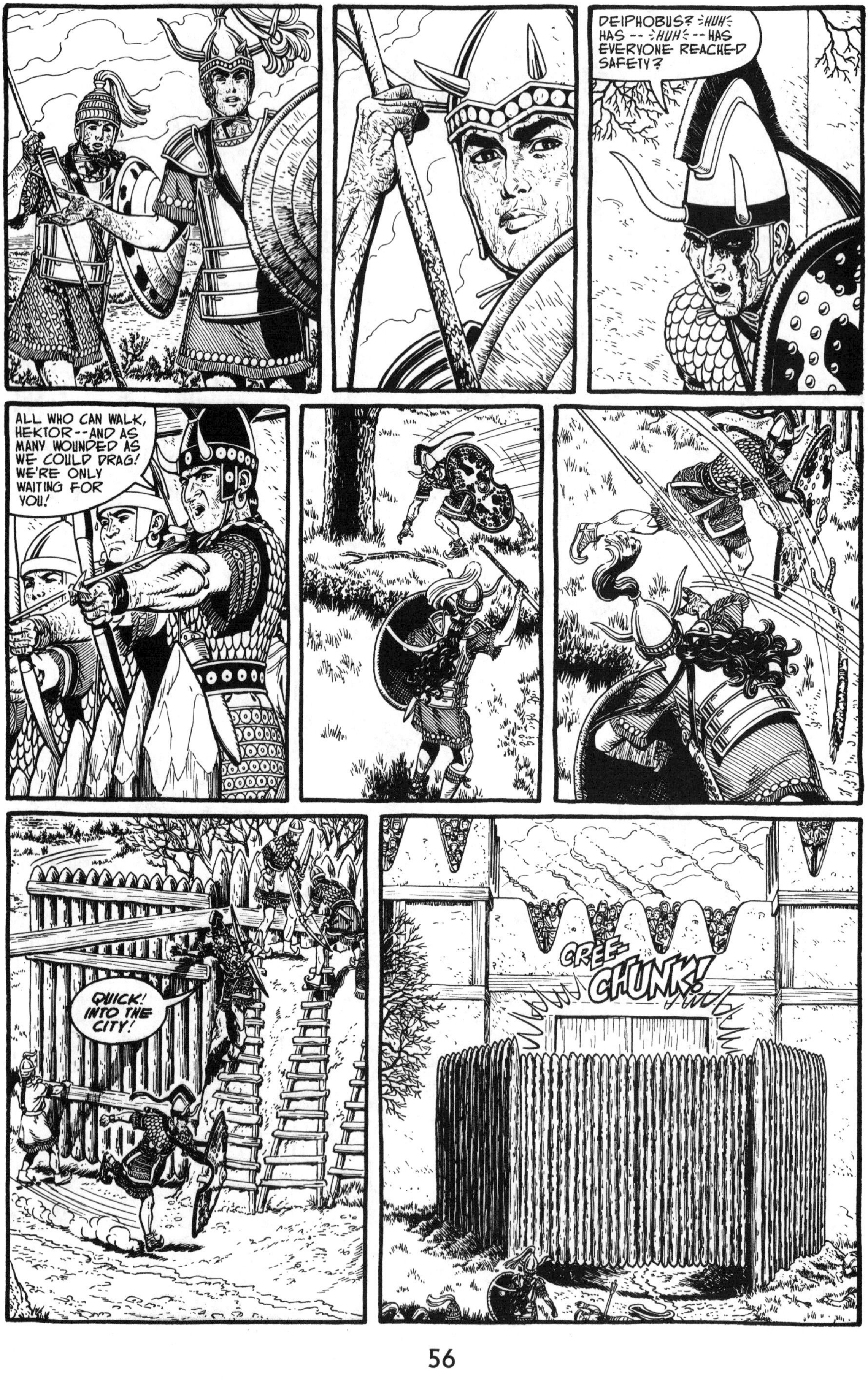
DEIPHOBUS? HUH HAS -- HUH -- HAS EVERYONE REACHED SAFETY?
ALL WHO CAN WALK, HEKTOR--AND AS MANY WOUNDED AS WE COULD DRAG! WE'RE ONLY WAITING FOR YOU!
QUICK! INTO THE CITY!
CREE-CHUNK!

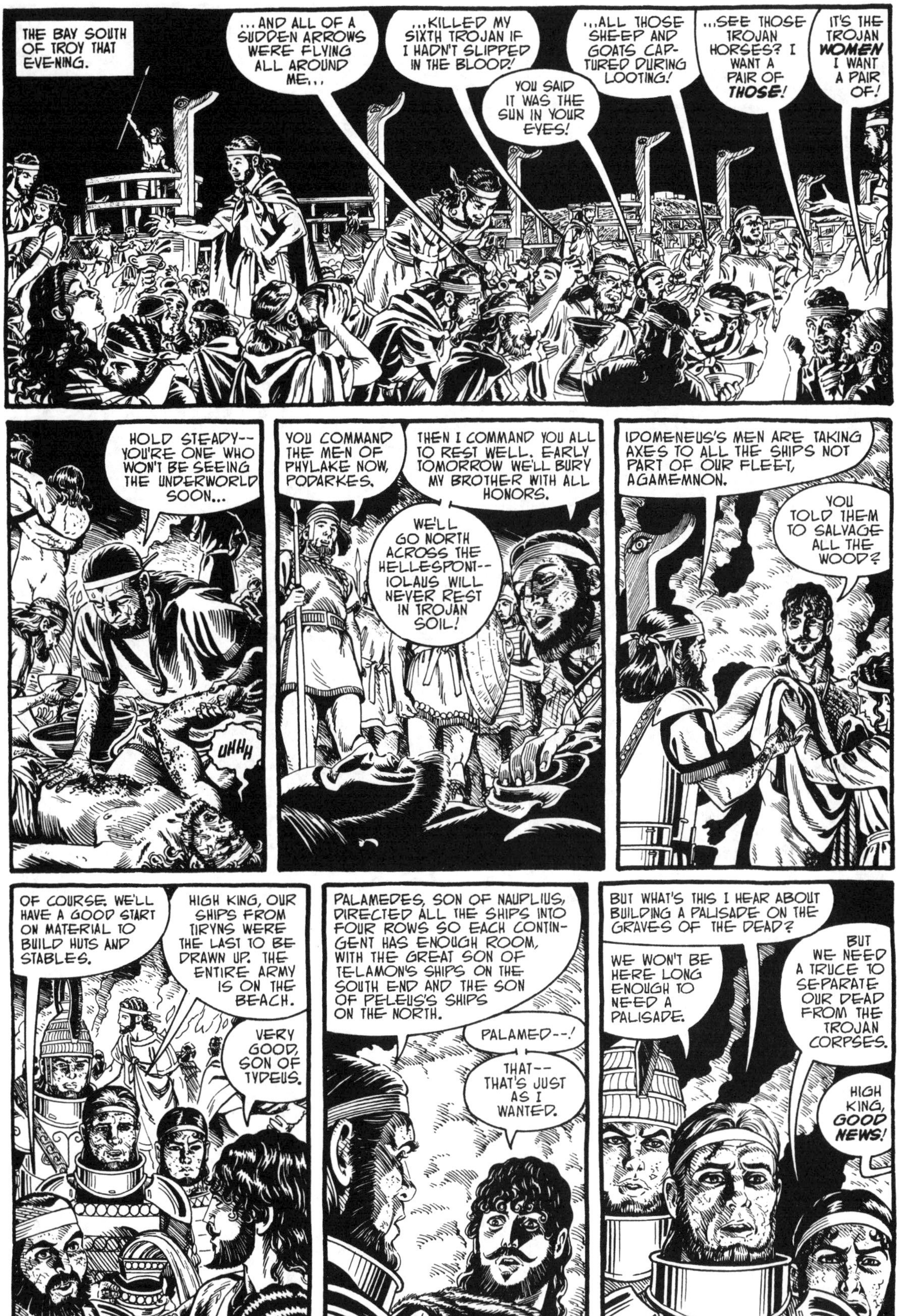
THE BAY SOUTH OF TROY THAT EVENING.
...AND ALL OF A SUDDEN ARROWS WERE FLYING ALL AROUND ME...
...KILLED MY SIXTH TROJAN IF I HADN'T SLIPPED IN THE BLOOD!
YOU SAID IT WAS THE SUN IN YOUR EYES!
...ALL THOSE SHEEP AND GOATS CAPTURED DURING LOOTING!
...SEE THOSE TROJAN HORSES? I WANT A PAIR OF **THOSE**!
IT'S THE TROJAN **WOMEN** I WANT A PAIR OF!
HOLD STEADY--YOU'RE ONE WHO WON'T BE SEEING THE UNDERWORLD SOON...
UHHH
YOU COMMAND THE MEN OF PHYLAKE NOW, PODARKES.
THEN I COMMAND YOU ALL TO REST WELL. EARLY TOMORROW WE'LL BURY MY BROTHER WITH ALL HONORS.
WE'LL GO NORTH ACROSS THE HELLESPONT--IOLAUS WILL NEVER REST IN TROJAN SOIL!
IDOMENEUS'S MEN ARE TAKING AXES TO ALL THE SHIPS NOT PART OF OUR FLEET, AGAMEMNON.
YOU TOLD THEM TO SALVAGE ALL THE WOOD?
OF COURSE. WE'LL HAVE A GOOD START ON MATERIAL TO BUILD HUTS AND STABLES.
HIGH KING, OUR SHIPS FROM TIRYNS WERE THE LAST TO BE DRAWN UP. THE ENTIRE ARMY IS ON THE BEACH.
VERY GOOD, SON OF TYDEUS.
PALAMEDES, SON OF NAUPLIUS, DIRECTED ALL THE SHIPS INTO FOUR ROWS SO EACH CONTINGENT HAS ENOUGH ROOM, WITH THE GREAT SON OF TELAMON'S SHIPS ON THE SOUTH END AND THE SON OF PELEUS'S SHIPS ON THE NORTH.
PALAMED--!
THAT--THAT'S JUST AS I WANTED.
BUT WHAT'S THIS I HEAR ABOUT BUILDING A PALISADE ON THE GRAVES OF THE DEAD?
WE WON'T BE HERE LONG ENOUGH TO NEED A PALISADE.
BUT WE NEED A TRUCE TO SEPARATE OUR DEAD FROM THE TROJAN CORPSES.
HIGH KING, **GOOD NEWS**!

HERE'S PALAMEDES NOW.

HIGH KING, I'M CONFIDENT THAT ALL OUR DAMAGED SHIPS CAN BE REPAIRED. ALSO, I'VE POSTED WATCHMEN TO THE HILLS ABOVE THE BEACH SINCE I KNEW YOU'D WANT THAT.

BEST OF ALL, IN THE POST-BATTLE LOOTING, MY MEN FOUND A WELL NEARBY. THE RETREATING TROJANS DUMPED IN STONES AND DIRT, EVIDENTLY IN AN ATTEMPT TO RENDER IT USELESS TO US, BUT WITH A LITTLE EFFORT, I BELIEVE--

ENOUGH!

WE'LL LEAVE ALL THESE QUESTIONS FOR *TOMORROW*--NOW WE'RE SUPPOSED TO BE CELEBRATING TODAY'S *VICTORY*.

CHECK YOUR ANGER FOR NOW, STHENELUS.

YOU ALL HEARD THE HIGH KING. NOW--WILL WE HAVE SONGS TONIGHT?

WHERE'S ACHILLES? *HE'S* THE ONE TO SING FOR US.

I THINK HE'S STILL PROPITIATING THE GODS FOR HIS SLAYING OF THAT PALE KING.

DID YOU SEE THAT HEIFER HE TOOK IN THE LOOTING? A *MAGNIFICENT SACRIFICE!*

WE CAN ALWAYS GET NESTOR TO TELL STORIES TILL ACHILLES IS READY.

BUT THEN CAN ANYONE GET NESTOR TO *STOP?*

GODS ON HIGH, IN YOUR WISDOM ACCEPT THIS SACRIFICE, BREATHE IN THE FRAGRANT SMOKE AS I CALL ON YOUR NAMES ONE BY ONE.

...EURYTUS GREW HOT WITH WINE OR LUST OR BOTH. HE SEIZED THE BRIDE TO TAKE HER THEN AND THERE. THE OTHER KENTAURS ALL SEIZED GIRLS, THE WEDDING FEAST BECAME A RAVAGED TOWN, WITH WOMEN SHRIEKING...

PATROKLUS, BRING MY HARP WHILE I WASH.

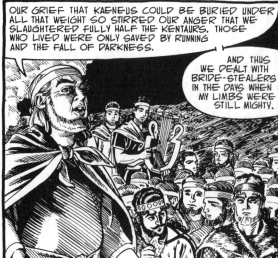

OUR GRIEF THAT KAENEUS COULD BE BURIED UNDER ALL THAT WEIGHT SO STIRRED OUR ANGER THAT WE SLAUGHTERED FULLY HALF THE KENTAURS. THOSE WHO LIVED WERE ONLY SAVED BY RUNNING AND THE FALL OF DARKNESS.

AND THUS WE DEALT WITH BRIDE-STEALERS IN THE DAYS WHEN MY LIMBS WERE STILL MIGHTY.

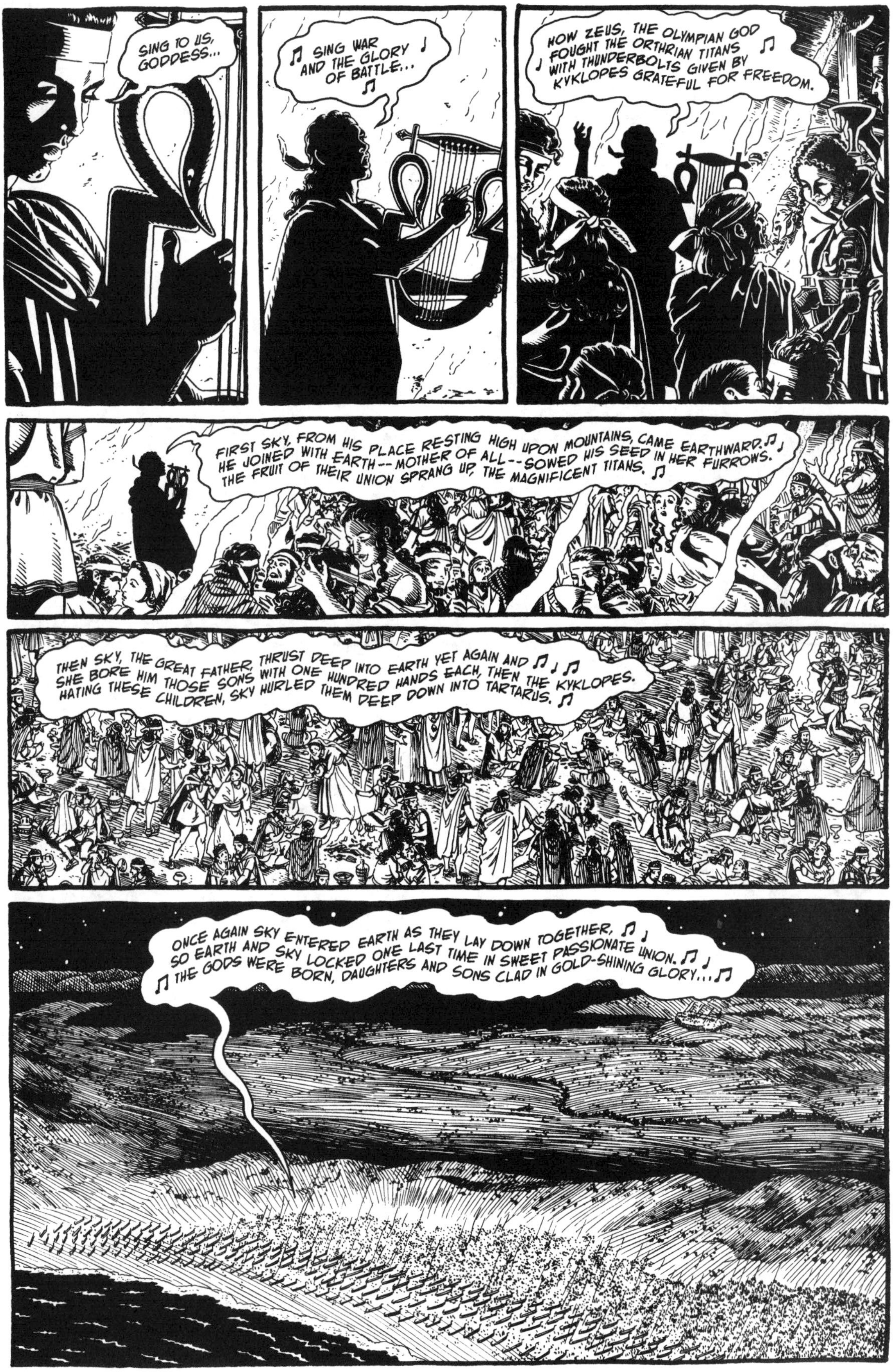
SING TO US, GODDESS...
♫ SING WAR ♩ AND THE GLORY OF BATTLE... ♫
HOW ZEUS, THE OLYMPIAN GOD ♩ FOUGHT THE ORTHRIAN TITANS ♫ WITH THUNDERBOLTS GIVEN BY KYKLOPES GRATEFUL FOR FREEDOM.
FIRST SKY, FROM HIS PLACE RESTING HIGH UPON MOUNTAINS, CAME EARTHWARD. ♫ ♩ HE JOINED WITH EARTH -- MOTHER OF ALL -- SOWED HIS SEED IN HER FURROWS. THE FRUIT OF THEIR UNION SPRANG UP, THE MAGNIFICENT TITANS. ♫
THEN SKY, THE GREAT FATHER, THRUST DEEP INTO EARTH YET AGAIN AND ♫ ♩ ♫ SHE BORE HIM THOSE SONS WITH ONE HUNDRED HANDS EACH, THEN THE KYKLOPES. HATING THESE CHILDREN, SKY HURLED THEM DEEP DOWN INTO TARTARUS. ♫
ONCE AGAIN SKY ENTERED EARTH AS THEY LAY DOWN TOGETHER, ♫ ♩ SO EARTH AND SKY LOCKED ONE LAST TIME IN SWEET PASSIONATE UNION. ♫ ♩ ♫ THE GODS WERE BORN, DAUGHTERS AND SONS CLAD IN GOLD-SHINING GLORY... ♫

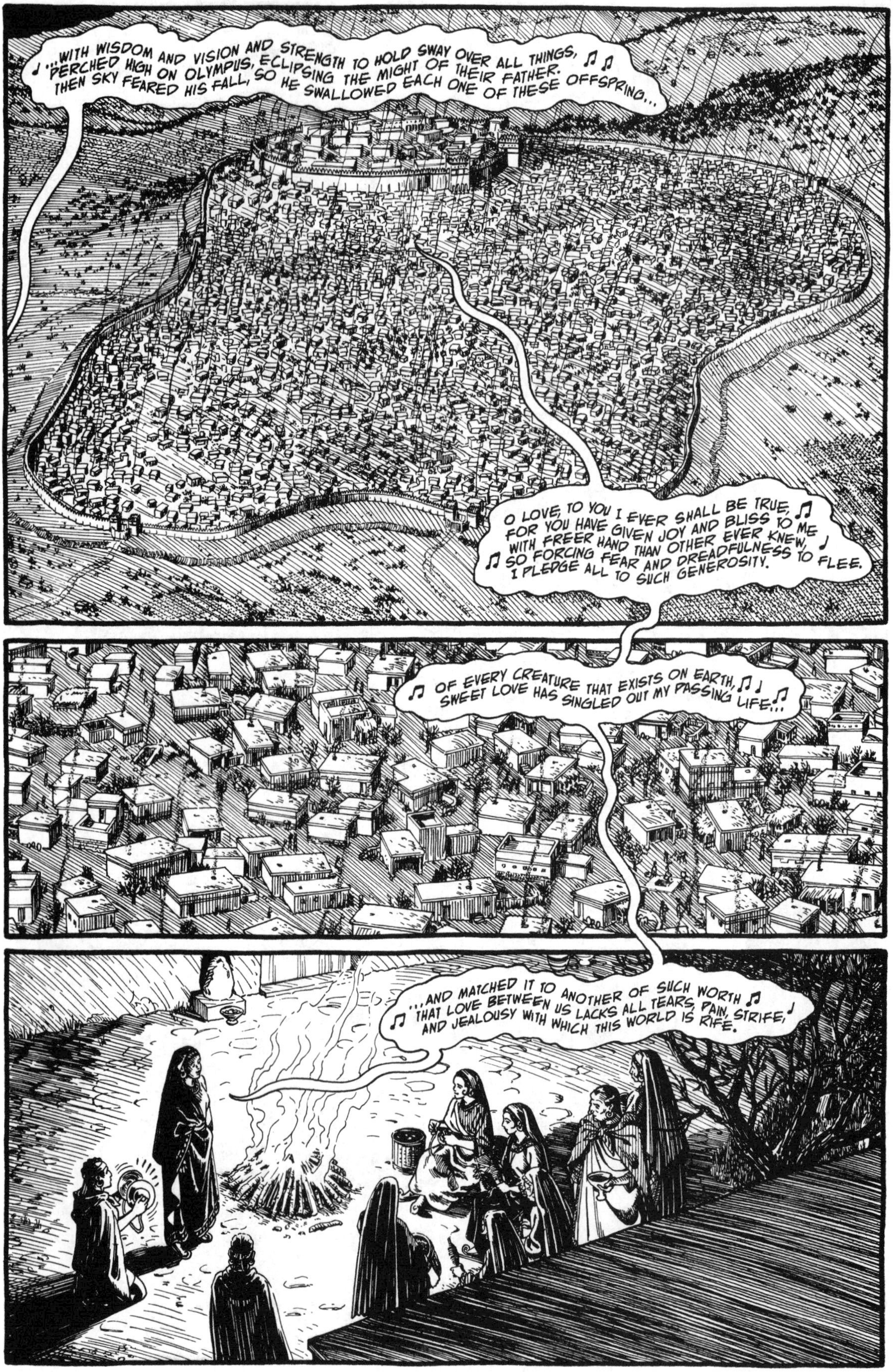
♩ ...WITH WISDOM AND VISION AND STRENGTH TO HOLD SWAY OVER ALL THINGS, PERCHED HIGH ON OLYMPUS, ECLIPSING THE MIGHT OF THEIR FATHER. ♫ ♫ THEN SKY FEARED HIS FALL, SO HE SWALLOWED EACH ONE OF THESE OFFSPRING...
O LOVE, TO YOU I EVER SHALL BE TRUE, ♫ FOR YOU HAVE GIVEN JOY AND BLISS TO ME WITH FREER HAND THAN OTHER EVER KNEW, ♫ SO FORCING FEAR AND DREADFULNESS TO FLEE. ♩ I PLEDGE ALL TO SUCH GENEROSITY.
♫ OF EVERY CREATURE THAT EXISTS ON EARTH, ♫ ♩ SWEET LOVE HAS SINGLED OUT MY PASSING LIFE... ♫
...AND MATCHED IT TO ANOTHER OF SUCH WORTH ♫ ♫ THAT LOVE BETWEEN US LACKS ALL TEARS, PAIN, STRIFE, ♩ AND JEALOUSY WITH WHICH THIS WORLD IS RIFE.

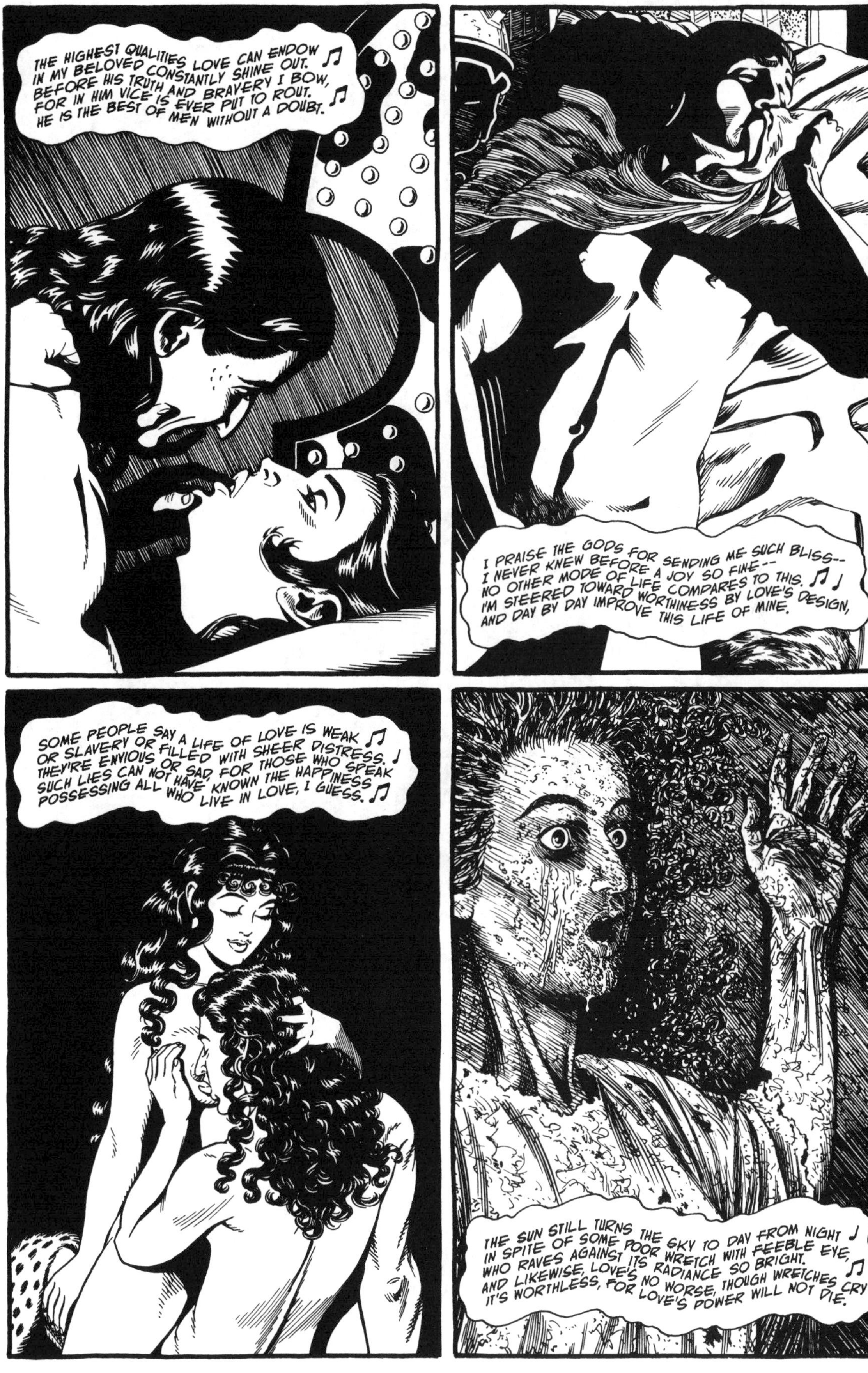
THE HIGHEST QUALITIES LOVE CAN ENDOW
IN MY BELOVED CONSTANTLY SHINE OUT. ♫
BEFORE HIS TRUTH AND BRAVERY I BOW,
FOR IN HIM VICE IS EVER PUT TO ROUT. ♫
HE IS THE BEST OF MEN WITHOUT A DOUBT.
I PRAISE THE GODS FOR SENDING ME SUCH BLISS--
I NEVER KNEW BEFORE A JOY SO FINE--
NO OTHER MODE OF LIFE COMPARES TO THIS. ♫♩
I'M STEERED TOWARD WORTHINESS BY LOVE'S DESIGN,
AND DAY BY DAY IMPROVE THIS LIFE OF MINE.
SOME PEOPLE SAY A LIFE OF LOVE IS WEAK ♫
OR SLAVERY OR FILLED WITH SHEER DISTRESS. ♩
THEY'RE ENVIOUS OR SAD, FOR THOSE WHO SPEAK
SUCH LIES CAN NOT HAVE KNOWN THE HAPPINESS
POSSESSING ALL WHO LIVE IN LOVE, I GUESS. ♫
THE SUN STILL TURNS THE SKY TO DAY FROM NIGHT ♩
IN SPITE OF SOME POOR WRETCH WITH FEEBLE EYE,
WHO RAVES AGAINST ITS RADIANCE SO BRIGHT.
AND LIKEWISE, LOVE'S NO WORSE, THOUGH WRETCHES CRY ♫
IT'S WORTHLESS, FOR LOVE'S POWER WILL NOT DIE.

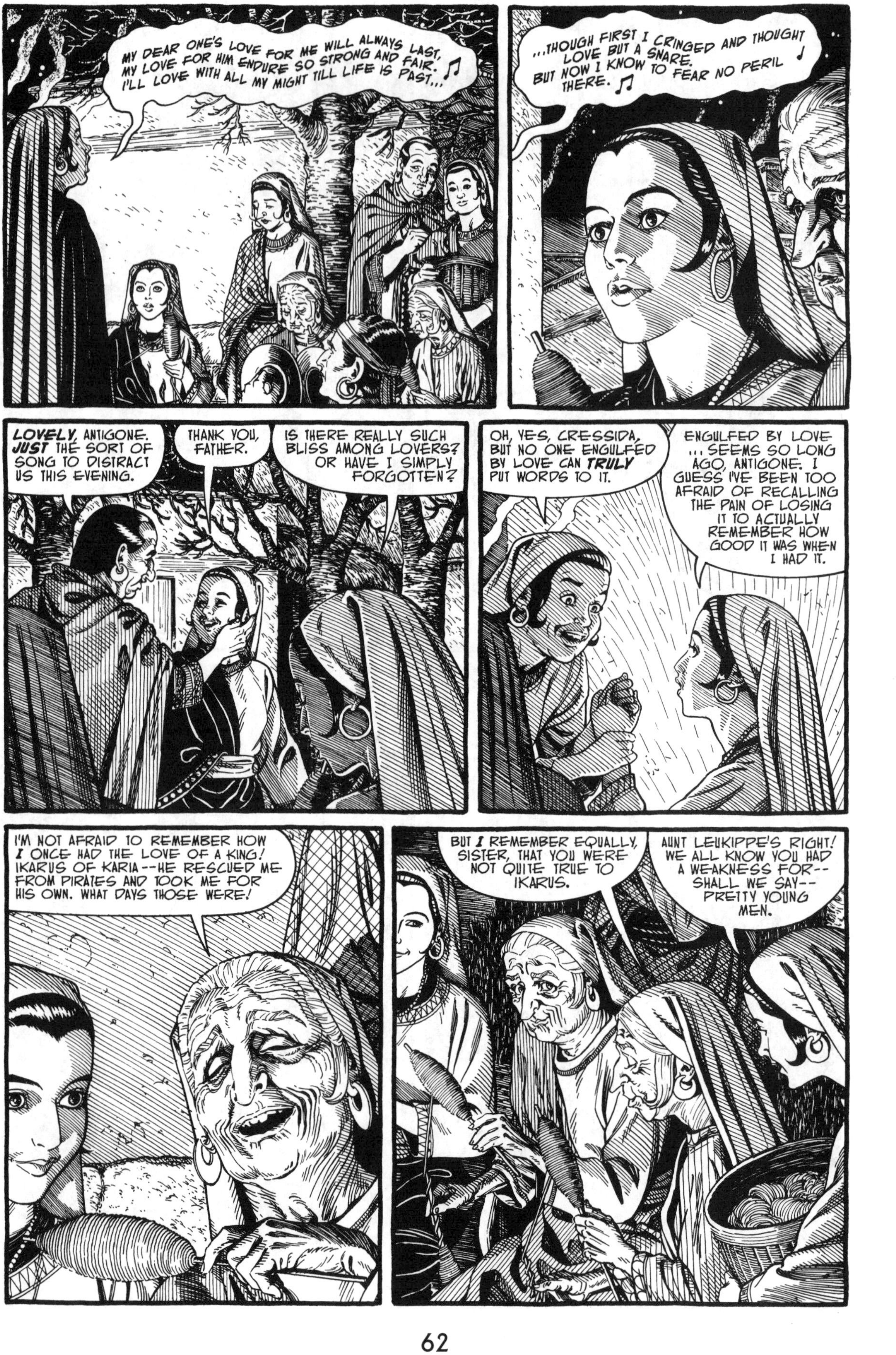
MY DEAR ONE'S LOVE FOR ME WILL ALWAYS LAST, MY LOVE FOR HIM ENDURE SO STRONG AND FAIR. I'LL LOVE WITH ALL MY MIGHT TILL LIFE IS PAST... ♫
...THOUGH FIRST I CRINGED AND THOUGHT LOVE BUT A SNARE. BUT NOW I KNOW TO FEAR NO PERIL THERE. ♫
LOVELY, ANTIGONE. ***JUST*** THE SORT OF SONG TO DISTRACT US THIS EVENING.
THANK YOU, FATHER.
IS THERE REALLY SUCH BLISS AMONG LOVERS? OR HAVE I SIMPLY FORGOTTEN?
OH, YES, CRESSIDA, BUT NO ONE ENGULFED BY LOVE CAN ***TRULY*** PUT WORDS TO IT.
ENGULFED BY LOVE ... SEEMS SO LONG AGO, ANTIGONE. I GUESS I'VE BEEN TOO AFRAID OF RECALLING THE PAIN OF LOSING IT TO ACTUALLY REMEMBER HOW GOOD IT WAS WHEN I HAD IT.
I'M NOT AFRAID TO REMEMBER HOW ***I*** ONCE HAD THE LOVE OF A KING! IKARUS OF KARIA--HE RESCUED ME FROM PIRATES AND TOOK ME FOR HIS OWN. WHAT DAYS THOSE WERE!
BUT ***I*** REMEMBER EQUALLY, SISTER, THAT YOU WERE NOT QUITE TRUE TO IKARUS.
AUNT LEUKIPPE'S RIGHT! WE ALL KNOW YOU HAD A WEAKNESS FOR-- SHALL WE SAY-- PRETTY YOUNG MEN.

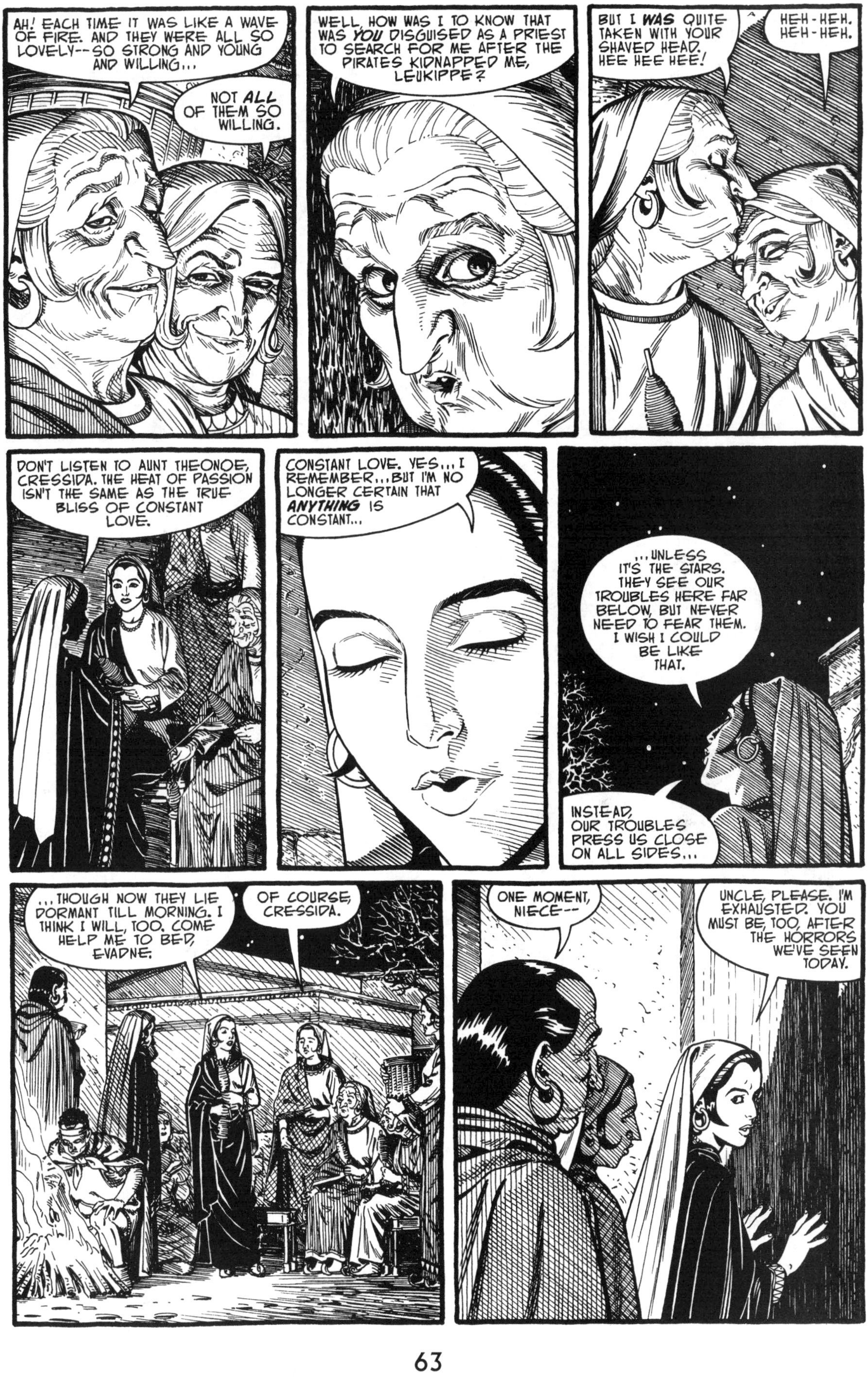
AH! EACH TIME IT WAS LIKE A WAVE OF FIRE. AND THEY WERE ALL SO LOVELY--SO STRONG AND YOUNG AND WILLING...
NOT ALL OF THEM SO WILLING.
WELL, HOW WAS I TO KNOW THAT WAS YOU DISGUISED AS A PRIEST TO SEARCH FOR ME AFTER THE PIRATES KIDNAPPED ME, LEUKIPPE?
BUT I WAS QUITE TAKEN WITH YOUR SHAVED HEAD. HEE HEE HEE!
HEH-HEH-HEH. HEH-HEH-HEH.
DON'T LISTEN TO AUNT THEONOE, CRESSIDA. THE HEAT OF PASSION ISN'T THE SAME AS THE TRUE BLISS OF CONSTANT LOVE.
CONSTANT LOVE. YES... I REMEMBER... BUT I'M NO LONGER CERTAIN THAT ANYTHING IS CONSTANT...
...UNLESS IT'S THE STARS. THEY SEE OUR TROUBLES HERE FAR BELOW, BUT NEVER NEED TO FEAR THEM. I WISH I COULD BE LIKE THAT.
INSTEAD, OUR TROUBLES PRESS US CLOSE ON ALL SIDES...
...THOUGH NOW THEY LIE DORMANT TILL MORNING. I THINK I WILL, TOO. COME HELP ME TO BED, EVADNE.
OF COURSE, CRESSIDA.
ONE MOMENT, NIECE--
UNCLE, PLEASE. I'M EXHAUSTED. YOU MUST BE, TOO, AFTER THE HORRORS WE'VE SEEN TODAY.

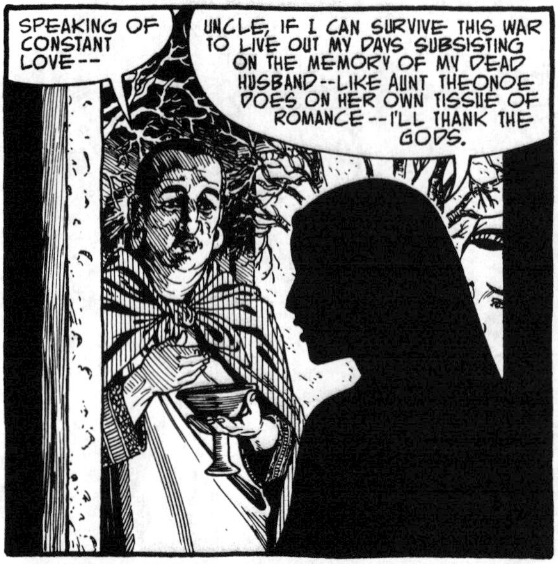
SPEAKING OF CONSTANT LOVE--
UNCLE, IF I CAN SURVIVE THIS WAR TO LIVE OUT MY DAYS SUBSISTING ON THE MEMORY OF MY DEAD HUSBAND--LIKE AUNT THEONOE DOES ON HER OWN TISSUE OF ROMANCE--I'LL THANK THE GODS.

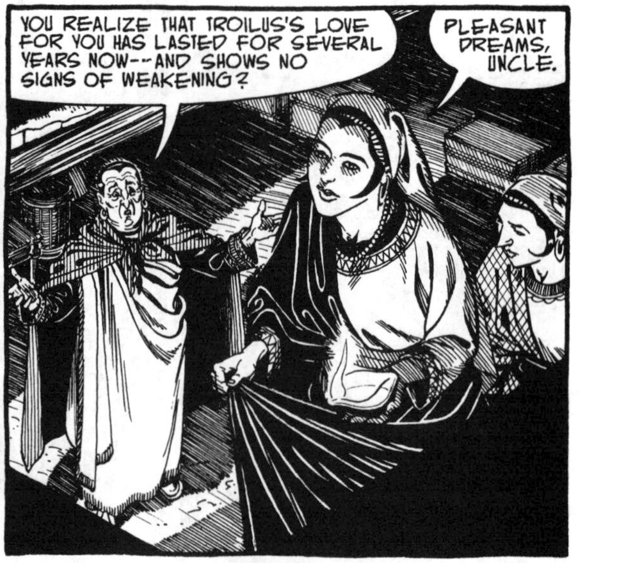
YOU REALIZE THAT TROILUS'S LOVE FOR YOU HAS LASTED FOR SEVERAL YEARS NOW--AND SHOWS NO SIGNS OF WEAKENING?
PLEASANT DREAMS, UNCLE.

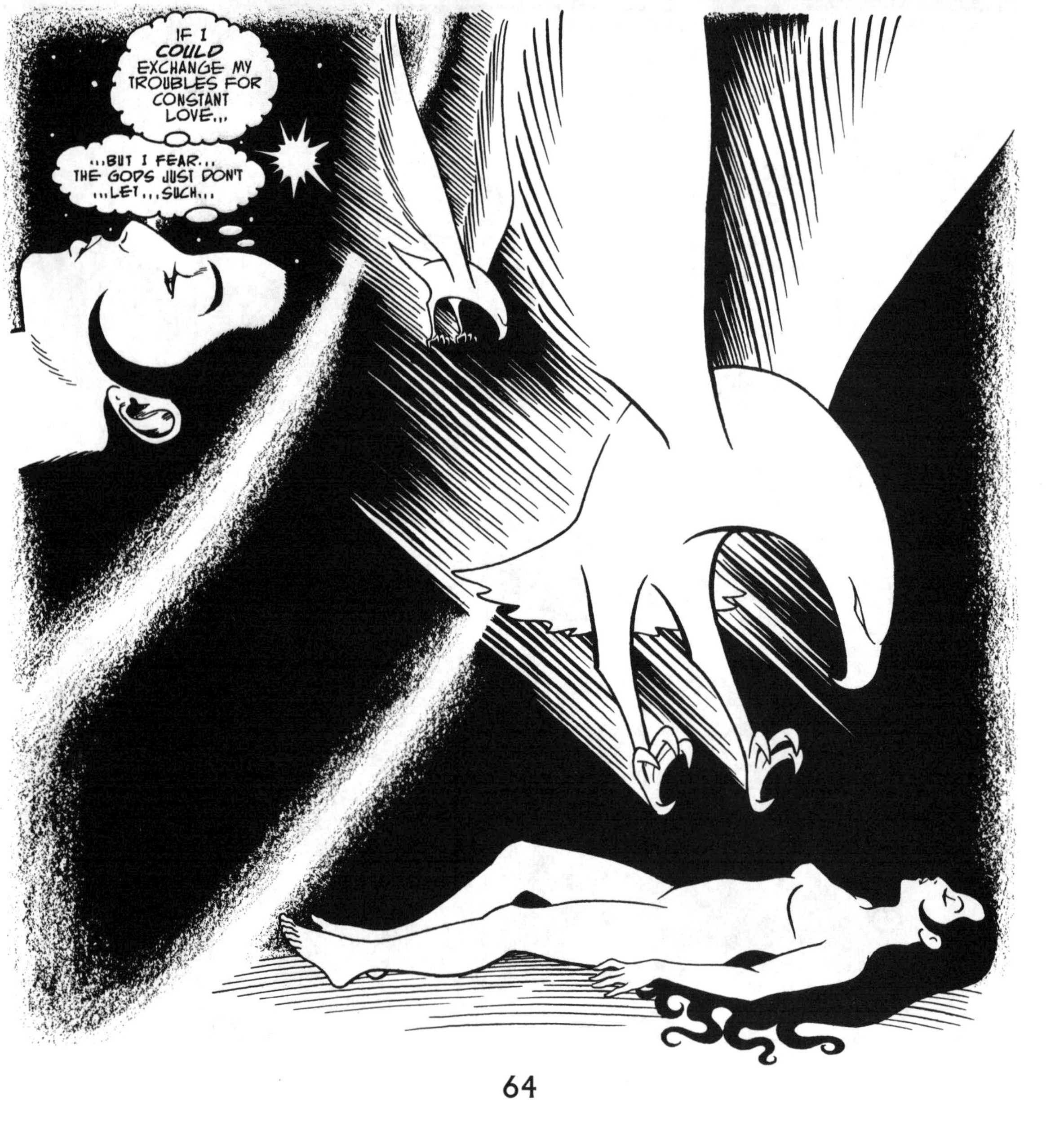
IF I *COULD* EXCHANGE MY TROUBLES FOR CONSTANT LOVE...
...BUT I FEAR... THE GODS JUST DON'T ...LET...SUCH...

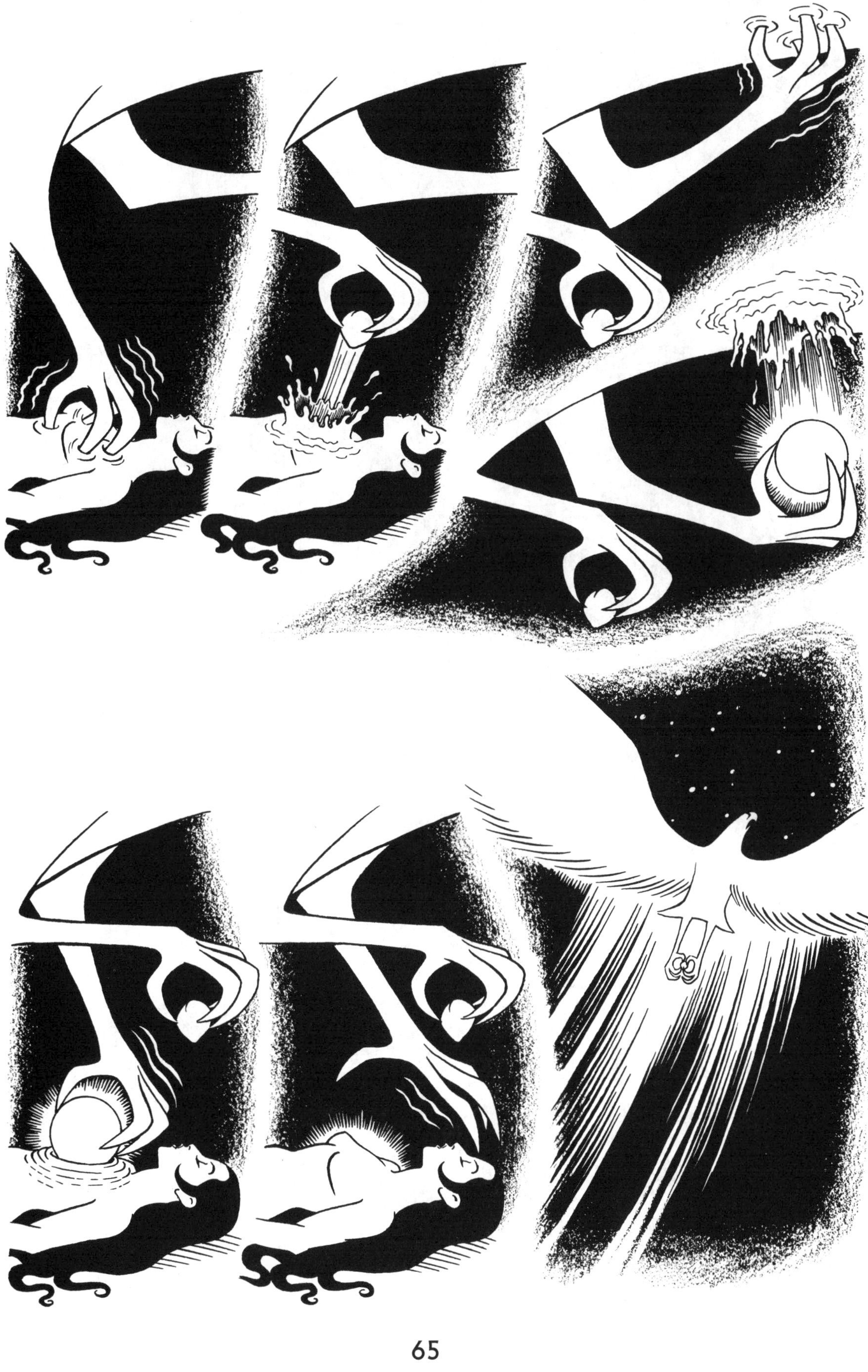

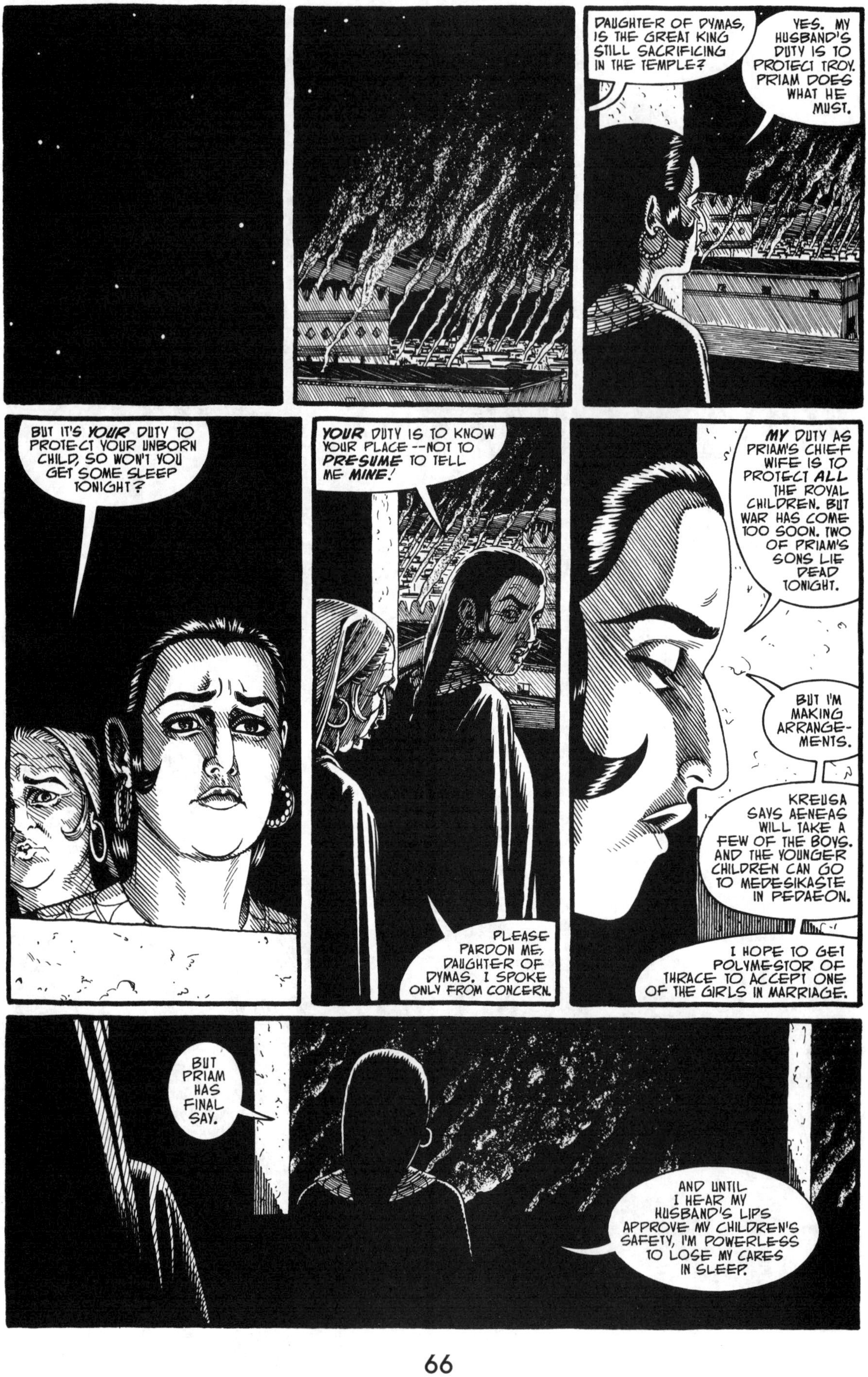
DAUGHTER OF DYMAS, IS THE GREAT KING STILL SACRIFICING IN THE TEMPLE?
YES. MY HUSBAND'S DUTY IS TO PROTECT TROY. PRIAM DOES WHAT HE MUST.
BUT IT'S **YOUR** DUTY TO PROTECT YOUR UNBORN CHILD, SO WON'T YOU GET SOME SLEEP TONIGHT?
YOUR DUTY IS TO KNOW YOUR PLACE --NOT TO **PRESUME** TO TELL ME **MINE**!
PLEASE PARDON ME, DAUGHTER OF DYMAS. I SPOKE ONLY FROM CONCERN.
MY DUTY AS PRIAM'S CHIEF WIFE IS TO PROTECT **ALL** THE ROYAL CHILDREN. BUT WAR HAS COME TOO SOON. TWO OF PRIAM'S SONS LIE DEAD TONIGHT.
BUT I'M MAKING ARRANGE-MENTS.
KREUSA SAYS AENEAS WILL TAKE A FEW OF THE BOYS. AND THE YOUNGER CHILDREN CAN GO TO MEDESIKASTE IN PEDAEON.
I HOPE TO GET POLYMESTOR OF THRACE TO ACCEPT ONE OF THE GIRLS IN MARRIAGE.
BUT PRIAM HAS FINAL SAY.
AND UNTIL I HEAR MY HUSBAND'S LIPS APPROVE MY CHILDREN'S SAFETY, I'M POWERLESS TO LOSE MY CARES IN SLEEP.

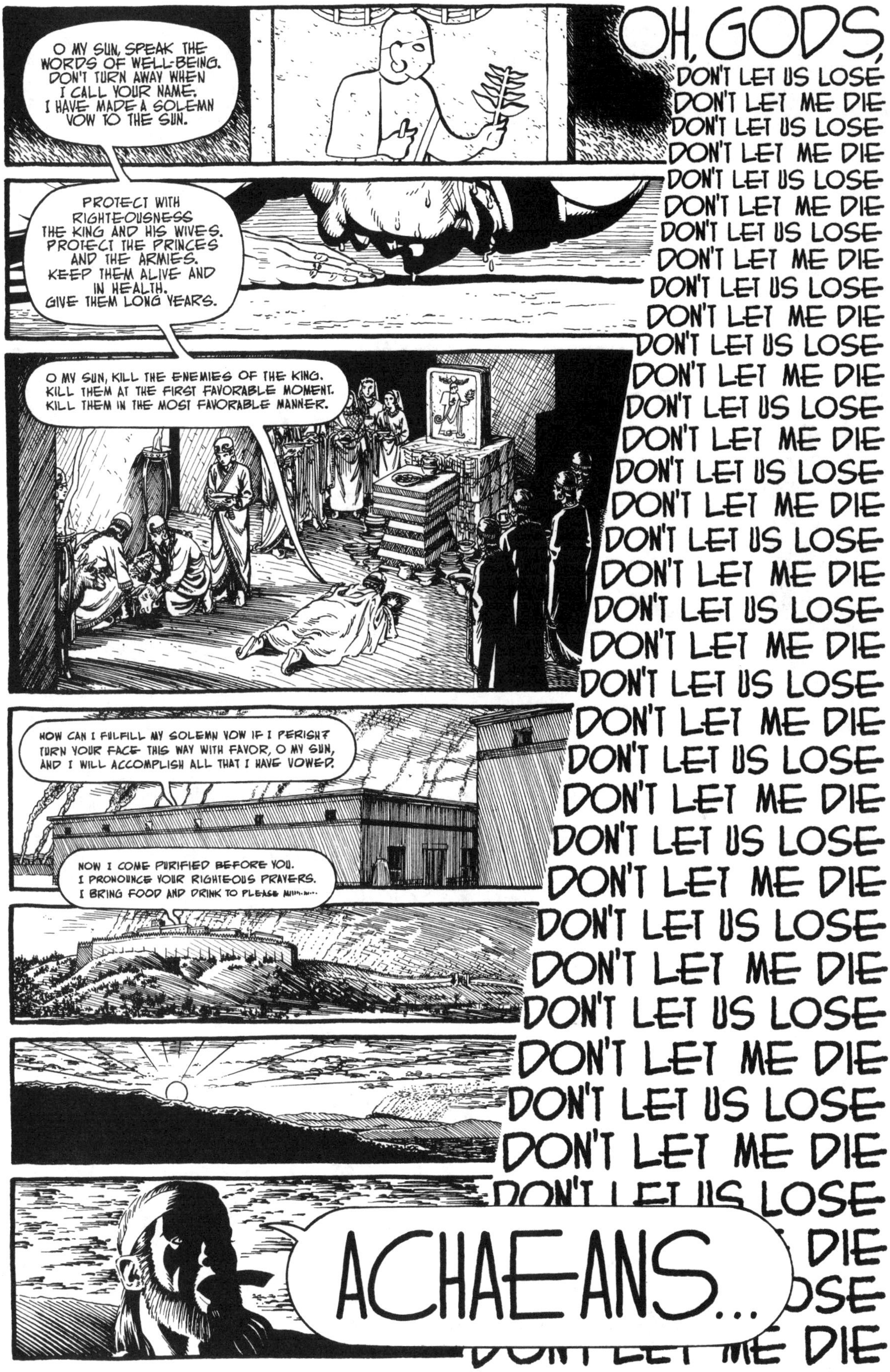
OH, GODS,
DON'T LET US LOSE
DON'T LET ME DIE
DON'T LET US LOSE
DON'T LET ME DIE
DON'T LET US LOSE
DON'T LET ME DIE
DON'T LET US LOSE
DON'T LET ME DIE
DON'T LET US LOSE
DON'T LET ME DIE
DON'T LET US LOSE
DON'T LET ME DIE
DON'T LET US LOSE
DON'T LET ME DIE
DON'T LET US LOSE
DON'T LET ME DIE
DON'T LET US LOSE
DON'T LET ME DIE
DON'T LET US LOSE
DON'T LET ME DIE
DON'T LET US LOSE
DON'T LET ME DIE
DON'T LET US LOSE
DON'T LET ME DIE
DON'T LET US LOSE
DON'T LET ME DIE
DON'T LET US LOSE
DON'T LET ME DIE
DON'T LET US LOSE
DON'T LET ME DIE
DON'T LET US LOSE
DON'T LET ME DIE
DON'T LET US LOSE
O MY SUN, SPEAK THE WORDS OF WELL-BEING. DON'T TURN AWAY WHEN I CALL YOUR NAME. I HAVE MADE A SOLEMN VOW TO THE SUN.
PROTECT WITH RIGHTEOUSNESS THE KING AND HIS WIVES. PROTECT THE PRINCES AND THE ARMIES. KEEP THEM ALIVE AND IN HEALTH. GIVE THEM LONG YEARS.
O MY SUN, KILL THE ENEMIES OF THE KING. KILL THEM AT THE FIRST FAVORABLE MOMENT. KILL THEM IN THE MOST FAVORABLE MANNER.
HOW CAN I FULFILL MY SOLEMN VOW IF I PERISH? TURN YOUR FACE THIS WAY WITH FAVOR, O MY SUN, AND I WILL ACCOMPLISH ALL THAT I HAVE VOWED.
NOW I COME PURIFIED BEFORE YOU. I PRONOUNCE YOUR RIGHTEOUS PRAYERS. I BRING FOOD AND DRINK TO PLEASE ...
ACHAEANS...

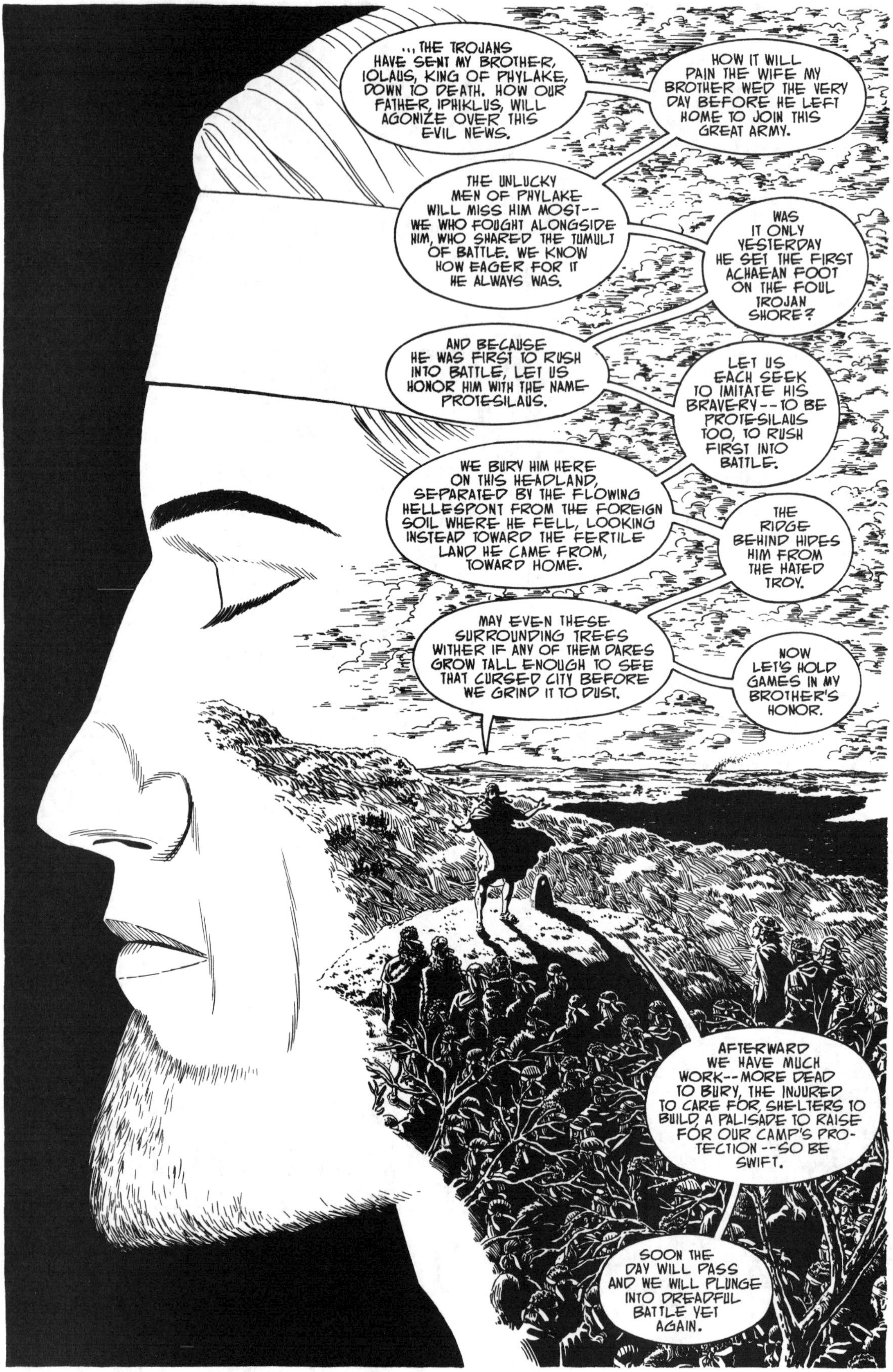
...THE TROJANS HAVE SENT MY BROTHER, IOLAUS, KING OF PHYLAKE, DOWN TO DEATH. HOW OUR FATHER, IPHIKLUS, WILL AGONIZE OVER THIS EVIL NEWS.
HOW IT WILL PAIN THE WIFE MY BROTHER WED THE VERY DAY BEFORE HE LEFT HOME TO JOIN THIS GREAT ARMY.
THE UNLUCKY MEN OF PHYLAKE WILL MISS HIM MOST-- WE WHO FOUGHT ALONGSIDE HIM, WHO SHARED THE TUMULT OF BATTLE. WE KNOW HOW EAGER FOR IT HE ALWAYS WAS.
WAS IT ONLY YESTERDAY HE SET THE FIRST ACHAEAN FOOT ON THE FOUL TROJAN SHORE?
AND BECAUSE HE WAS FIRST TO RUSH INTO BATTLE, LET US HONOR HIM WITH THE NAME PROTESILAUS.
LET US EACH SEEK TO IMITATE HIS BRAVERY--TO BE PROTESILAUS TOO, TO RUSH FIRST INTO BATTLE.
WE BURY HIM HERE ON THIS HEADLAND, SEPARATED BY THE FLOWING HELLESPONT FROM THE FOREIGN SOIL WHERE HE FELL, LOOKING INSTEAD TOWARD THE FERTILE LAND HE CAME FROM, TOWARD HOME.
THE RIDGE BEHIND HIDES HIM FROM THE HATED TROY.
MAY EVEN THESE SURROUNDING TREES WITHER IF ANY OF THEM DARES GROW TALL ENOUGH TO SEE THAT CURSED CITY BEFORE WE GRIND IT TO DUST.
NOW LET'S HOLD GAMES IN MY BROTHER'S HONOR.
AFTERWARD WE HAVE MUCH WORK--MORE DEAD TO BURY, THE INJURED TO CARE FOR, SHELTERS TO BUILD, A PALISADE TO RAISE FOR OUR CAMP'S PROTECTION--SO BE SWIFT.
SOON THE DAY WILL PASS AND WE WILL PLUNGE INTO DREADFUL BATTLE YET AGAIN.

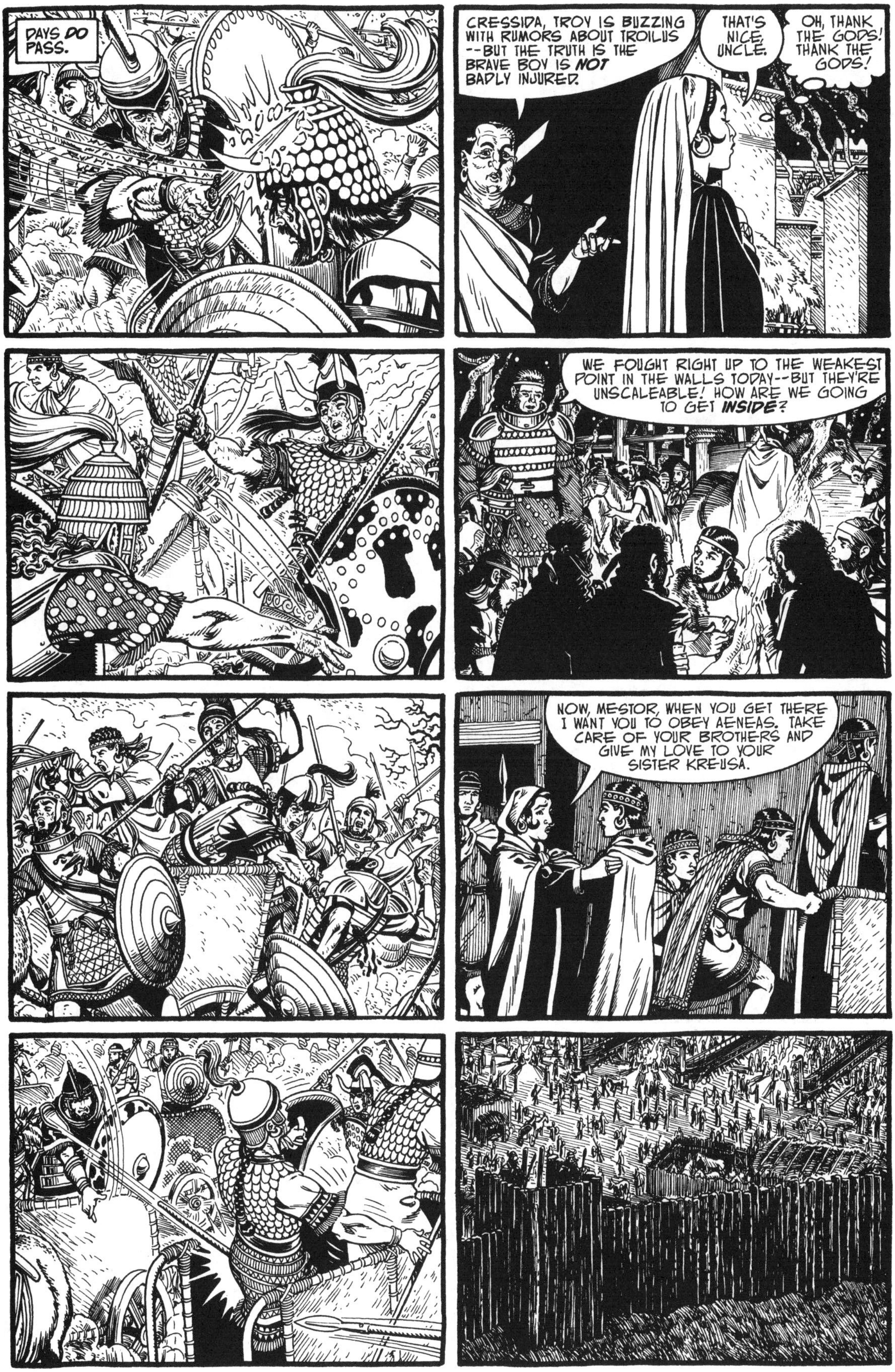
DAYS *DO* PASS.
CRESSIDA, TROY IS BUZZING WITH RUMORS ABOUT TROILUS --BUT THE TRUTH IS THE BRAVE BOY IS *NOT* BADLY INJURED.
THAT'S NICE, UNCLE.
OH, THANK THE GODS! THANK THE GODS!
WE FOUGHT RIGHT UP TO THE WEAKEST POINT IN THE WALLS TODAY--BUT THEY'RE UNSCALEABLE! HOW ARE WE GOING TO GET *INSIDE*?
NOW, MESTOR, WHEN YOU GET THERE I WANT YOU TO OBEY AENEAS. TAKE CARE OF YOUR BROTHERS AND GIVE MY LOVE TO YOUR SISTER KREUSA.

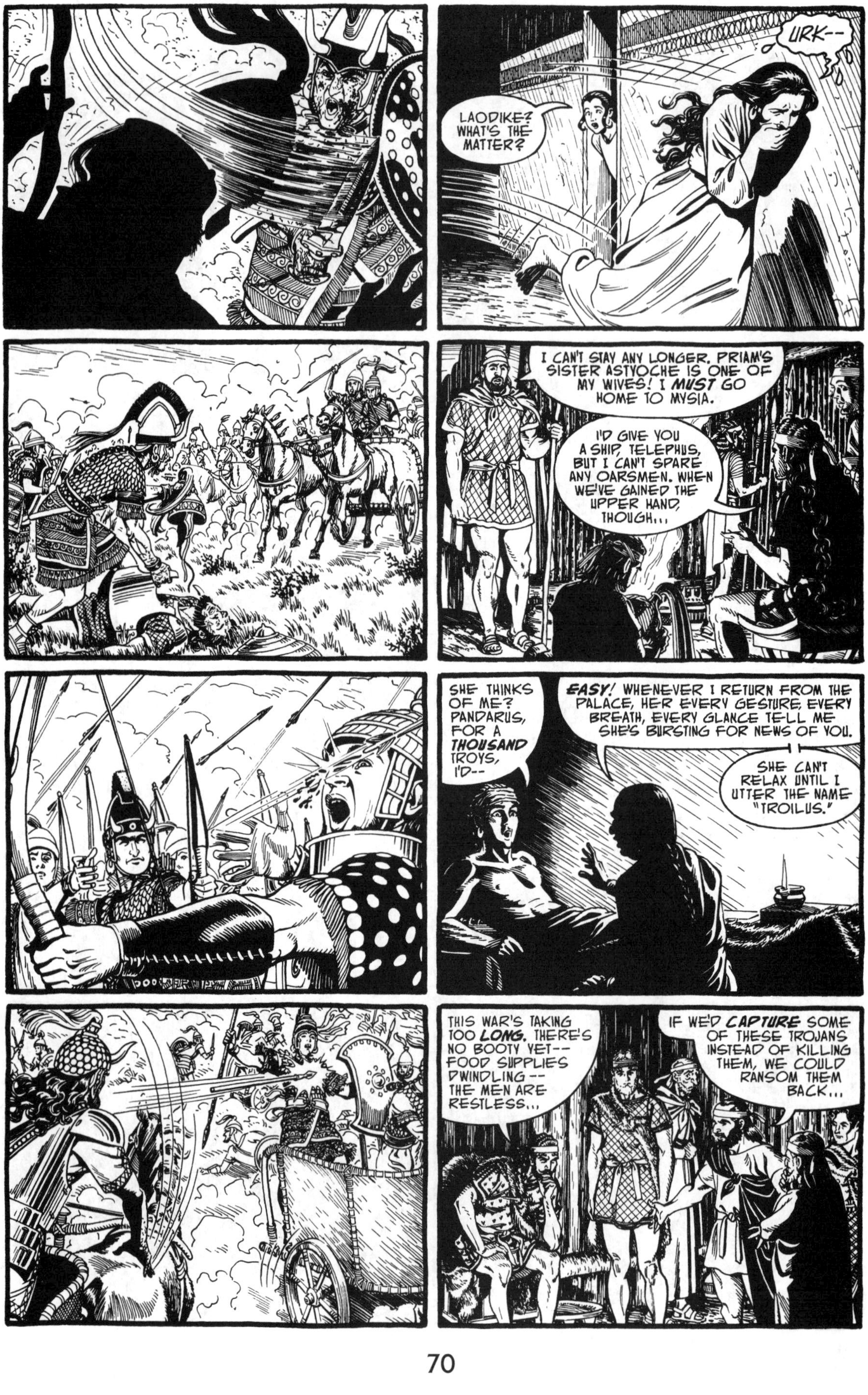
URK--
LAODIKE? WHAT'S THE MATTER?
I CAN'T STAY ANY LONGER. PRIAM'S SISTER ASTYOCHE IS ONE OF MY WIVES! I MUST GO HOME TO MYSIA.
I'D GIVE YOU A SHIP, TELEPHUS, BUT I CAN'T SPARE ANY OARSMEN. WHEN WE'VE GAINED THE UPPER HAND, THOUGH...
SHE THINKS OF ME? PANDARUS, FOR A THOUSAND TROYS, I'D--
EASY! WHENEVER I RETURN FROM THE PALACE, HER EVERY GESTURE, EVERY BREATH, EVERY GLANCE TELL ME SHE'S BURSTING FOR NEWS OF YOU.
SHE CAN'T RELAX UNTIL I UTTER THE NAME "TROILUS."
THIS WAR'S TAKING TOO LONG. THERE'S NO BOOTY YET-- FOOD SUPPLIES DWINDLING -- THE MEN ARE RESTLESS...
IF WE'D CAPTURE SOME OF THESE TROJANS INSTEAD OF KILLING THEM, WE COULD RANSOM THEM BACK...

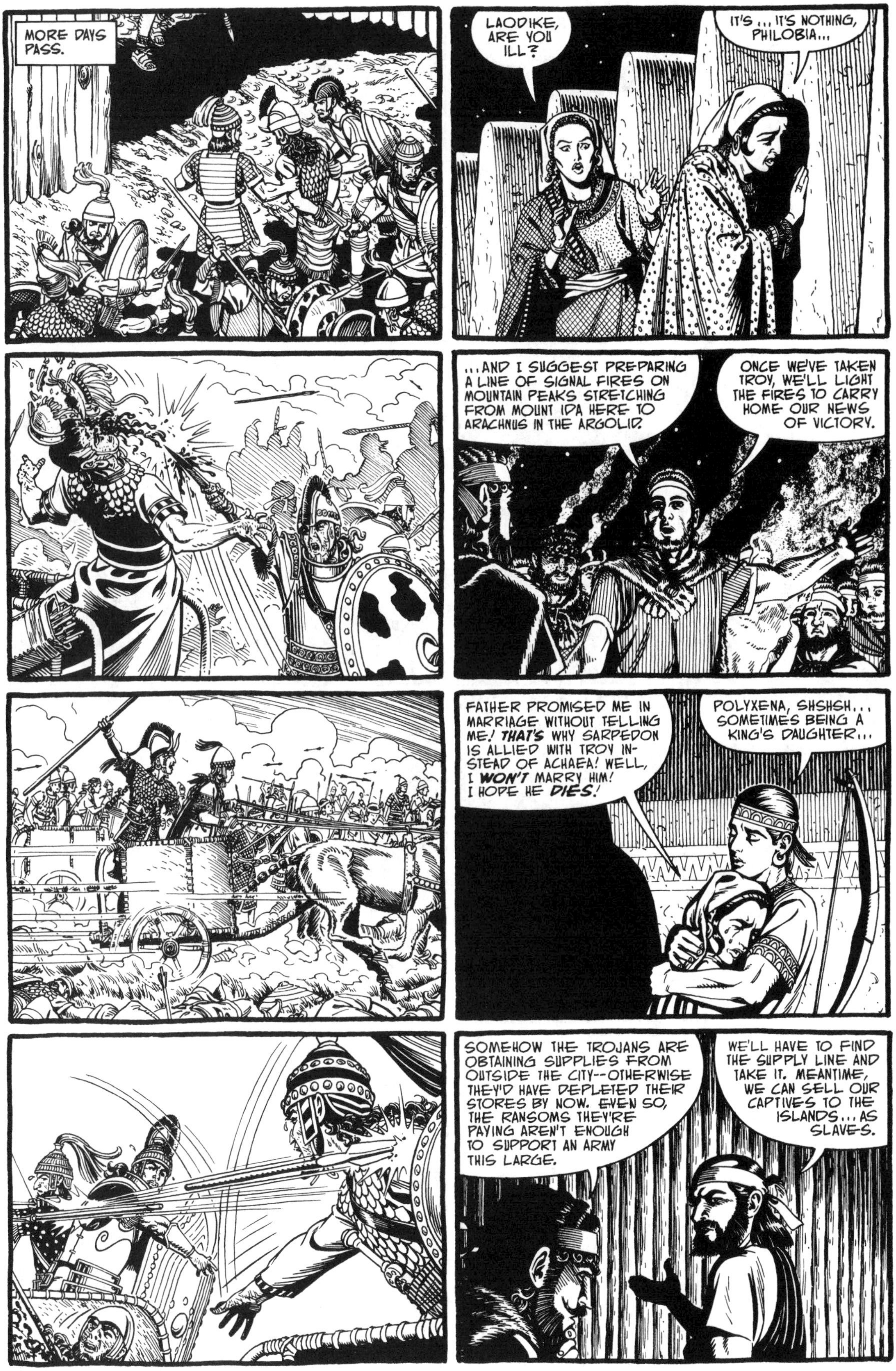
MORE DAYS PASS.
LAODIKE, ARE YOU ILL?
IT'S ... IT'S NOTHING, PHILOBIA...
...AND I SUGGEST PREPARING A LINE OF SIGNAL FIRES ON MOUNTAIN PEAKS STRETCHING FROM MOUNT IDA HERE TO ARACHNUS IN THE ARGOLID.
ONCE WE'VE TAKEN TROY, WE'LL LIGHT THE FIRES TO CARRY HOME OUR NEWS OF VICTORY.
FATHER PROMISED ME IN MARRIAGE WITHOUT TELLING ME! THAT'S WHY SARPEDON IS ALLIED WITH TROY INSTEAD OF ACHAEA! WELL, I WON'T MARRY HIM! I HOPE HE DIES!
POLYXENA, SHSHSH... SOMETIMES, BEING A KING'S DAUGHTER...
SOMEHOW THE TROJANS ARE OBTAINING SUPPLIES FROM OUTSIDE THE CITY--OTHERWISE THEY'D HAVE DEPLETED THEIR STORES BY NOW. EVEN SO, THE RANSOMS THEY'RE PAYING AREN'T ENOUGH TO SUPPORT AN ARMY THIS LARGE.
WE'LL HAVE TO FIND THE SUPPLY LINE AND TAKE IT. MEANTIME, WE CAN SELL OUR CAPTIVES TO THE ISLANDS... AS SLAVES.

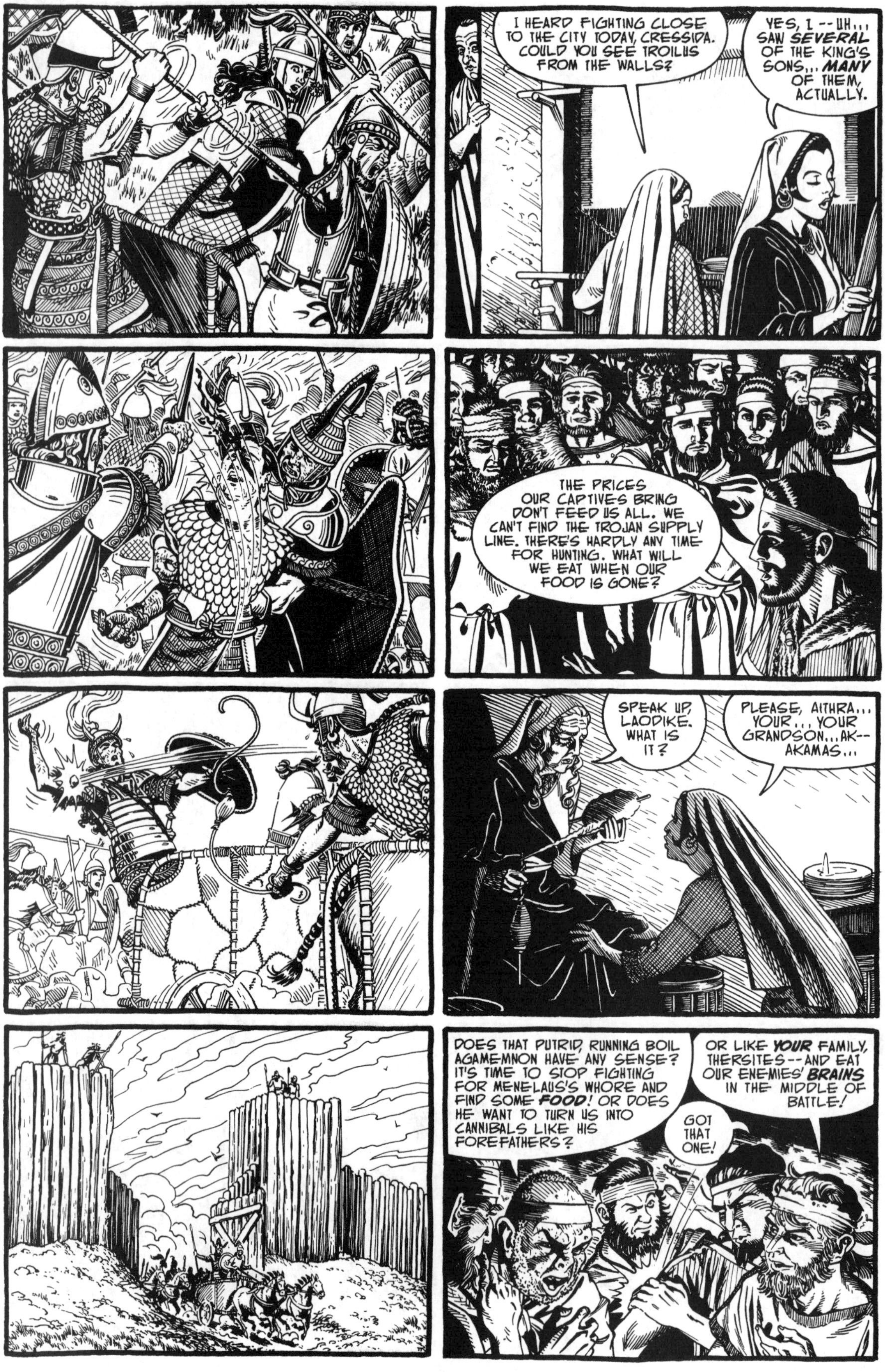

I HEARD FIGHTING CLOSE TO THE CITY TODAY, CRESSIDA. COULD YOU SEE TROILUS FROM THE WALLS?
YES, I --UH... SAW **SEVERAL** OF THE KING'S SONS... **MANY** OF THEM, ACTUALLY.
THE PRICES OUR CAPTIVES BRING DON'T FEED US ALL. WE CAN'T FIND THE TROJAN SUPPLY LINE. THERE'S HARDLY ANY TIME FOR HUNTING. WHAT WILL WE EAT WHEN OUR FOOD IS GONE?
SPEAK UP, LAODIKE. WHAT IS IT?
PLEASE, AITHRA... YOUR... YOUR GRANDSON... AK-- AKAMAS...
DOES THAT PUTRID, RUNNING BOIL AGAMEMNON HAVE ANY SENSE? IT'S TIME TO STOP FIGHTING FOR MENELAUS'S WHORE AND FIND SOME **FOOD**! OR DOES HE WANT TO TURN US INTO CANNIBALS LIKE HIS FOREFATHERS?
GOT THAT ONE!
OR LIKE **YOUR** FAMILY, THERSITES--AND EAT OUR ENEMIES' **BRAINS** IN THE MIDDLE OF BATTLE!

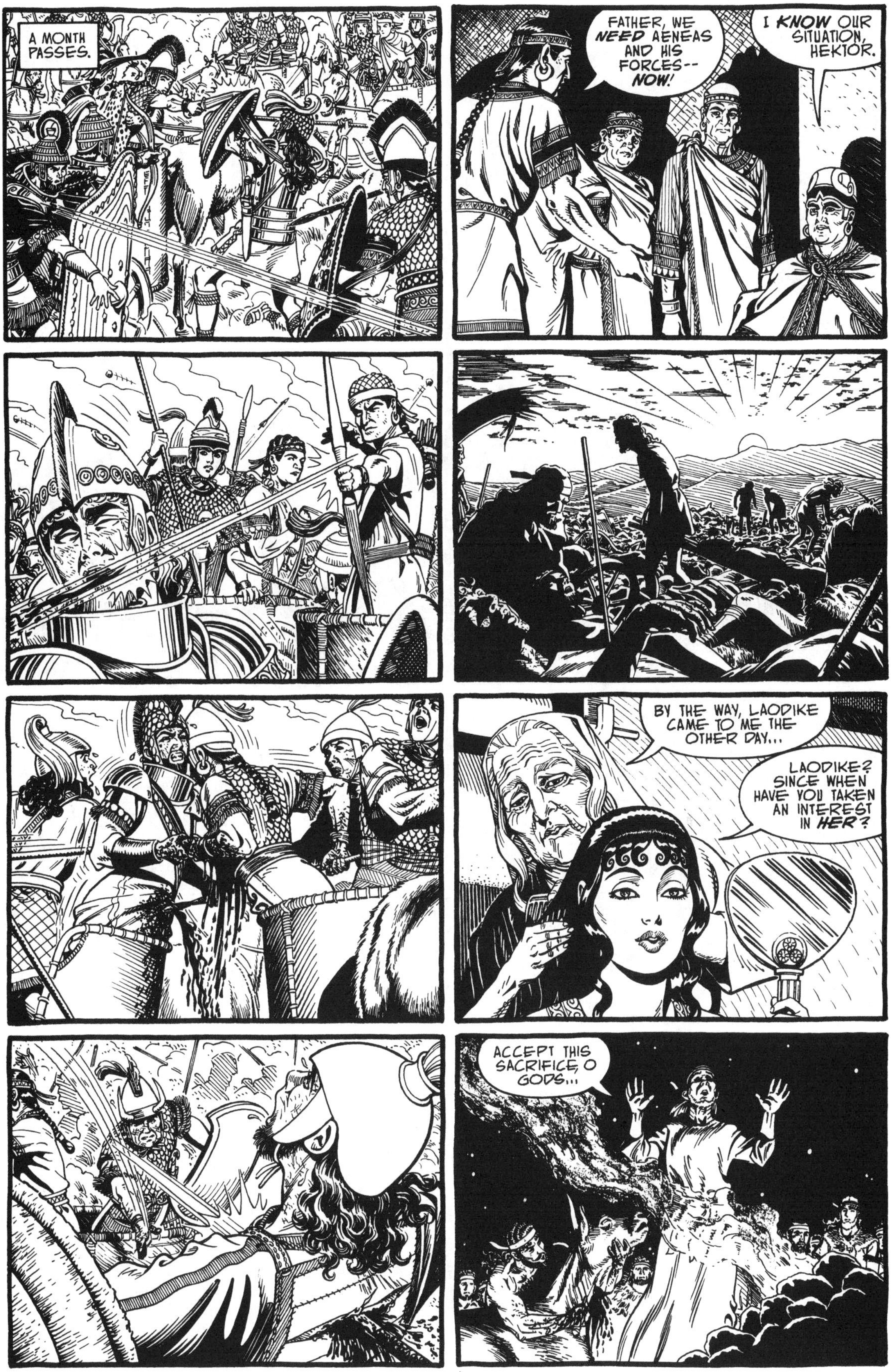
A MONTH PASSES.
FATHER, WE NEED AENEAS AND HIS FORCES-- NOW!
I KNOW OUR SITUATION, HEKTOR.
BY THE WAY, LAODIKE CAME TO ME THE OTHER DAY...
LAODIKE? SINCE WHEN HAVE YOU TAKEN AN INTEREST IN HER?
ACCEPT THIS SACRIFICE, O GODS...

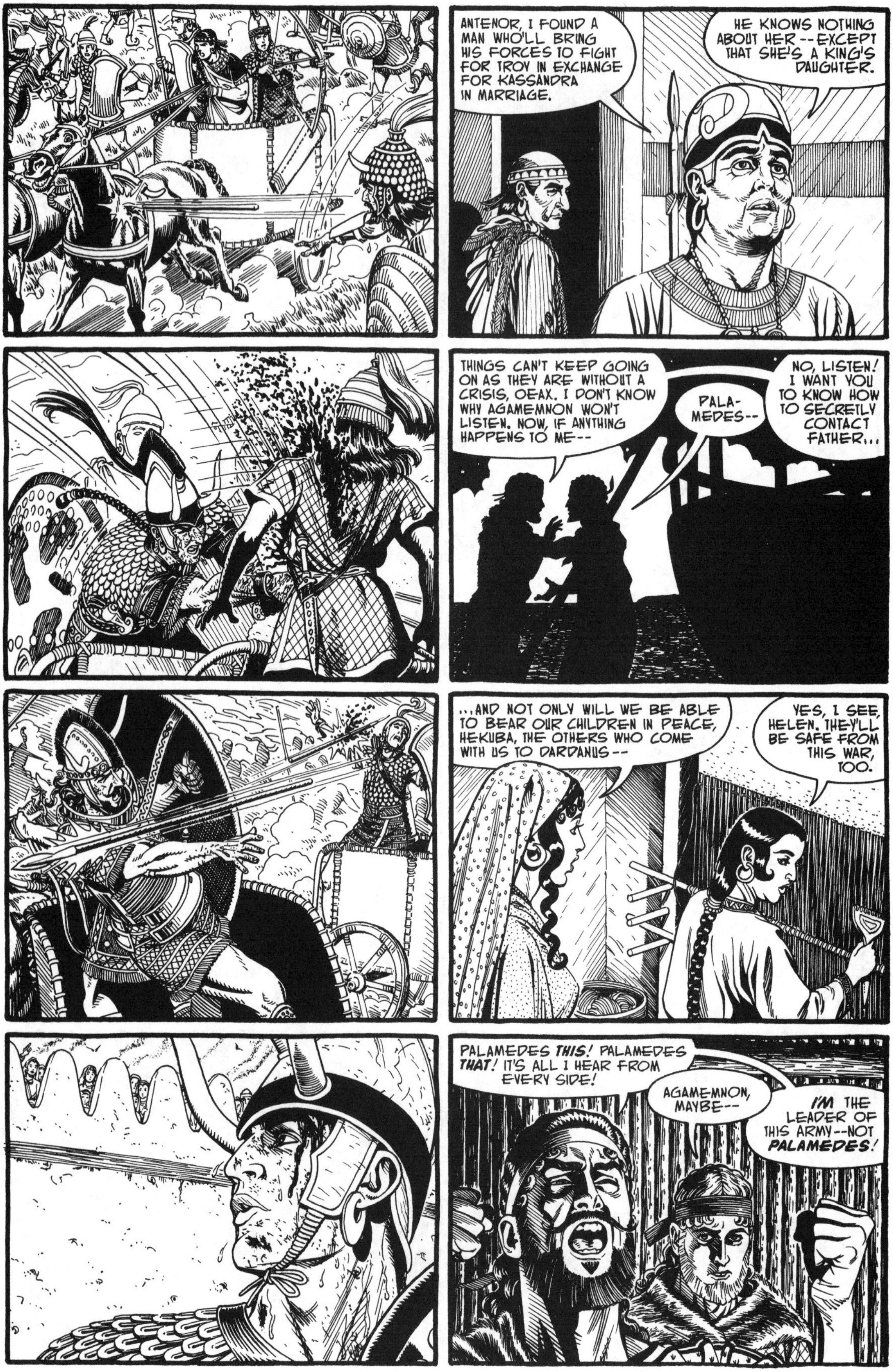
ANTENOR, I FOUND A MAN WHO'LL BRING HIS FORCES TO FIGHT FOR TROY IN EXCHANGE FOR KASSANDRA IN MARRIAGE.
HE KNOWS NOTHING ABOUT HER--EXCEPT THAT SHE'S A KING'S DAUGHTER.
THINGS CAN'T KEEP GOING ON AS THEY ARE WITHOUT A CRISIS, OEAX. I DON'T KNOW WHY AGAMEMNON WON'T LISTEN. NOW, IF ANYTHING HAPPENS TO ME--
PALA-MEDES--
NO, LISTEN! I WANT YOU TO KNOW HOW TO SECRETLY CONTACT FATHER...
...AND NOT ONLY WILL WE BE ABLE TO BEAR OUR CHILDREN IN PEACE, HEKUBA, THE OTHERS WHO COME WITH US TO DARDANUS--
YES, I SEE, HELEN. THEY'LL BE SAFE FROM THIS WAR, TOO.
PALAMEDES **THIS!** PALAMEDES **THAT!** IT'S ALL I HEAR FROM EVERY SIDE!
AGAMEMNON, MAYBE--
I'M THE LEADER OF THIS ARMY--NOT ***PALAMEDES!***

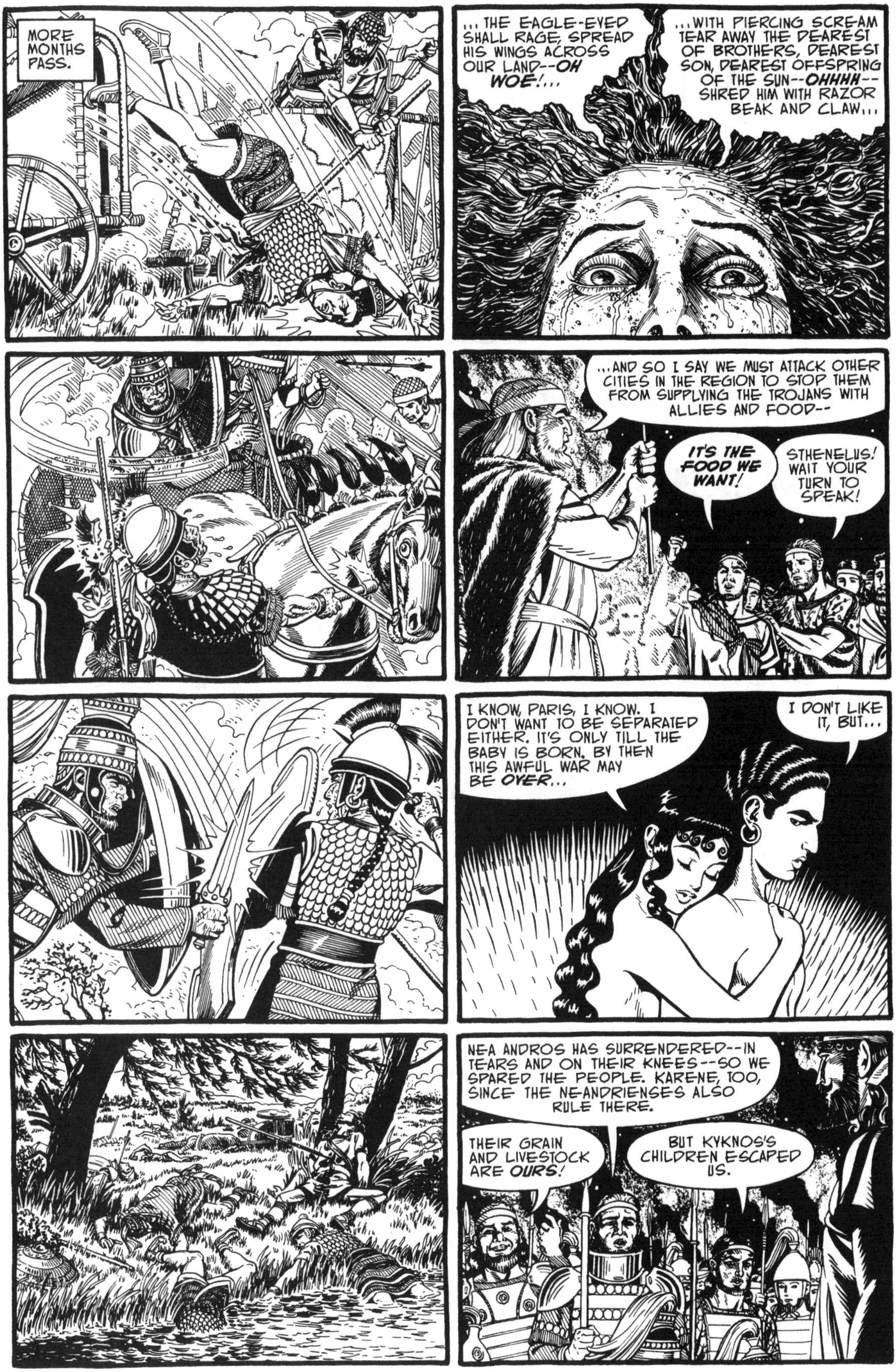
MORE MONTHS PASS.
...THE EAGLE-EYED SHALL RAGE, SPREAD HIS WINGS ACROSS OUR LAND--OH WOE!...
...WITH PIERCING SCREAM TEAR AWAY THE DEAREST OF BROTHERS, DEAREST SON, DEAREST OFFSPRING OF THE SUN--OHHHH--SHRED HIM WITH RAZOR BEAK AND CLAW...
...AND SO I SAY WE MUST ATTACK OTHER CITIES IN THE REGION TO STOP THEM FROM SUPPLYING THE TROJANS WITH ALLIES AND FOOD--
IT'S THE FOOD WE WANT!
STHENELUS! WAIT YOUR TURN TO SPEAK!
I KNOW, PARIS, I KNOW. I DON'T WANT TO BE SEPARATED EITHER. IT'S ONLY TILL THE BABY IS BORN. BY THEN THIS AWFUL WAR MAY BE OVER...
I DON'T LIKE IT, BUT...
NEA ANDROS HAS SURRENDERED--IN TEARS AND ON THEIR KNEES--SO WE SPARED THE PEOPLE. KARENE, TOO, SINCE THE NEANDRIENSES ALSO RULE THERE.
THEIR GRAIN AND LIVESTOCK ARE OURS!
BUT KYKNOS'S CHILDREN ESCAPED US.

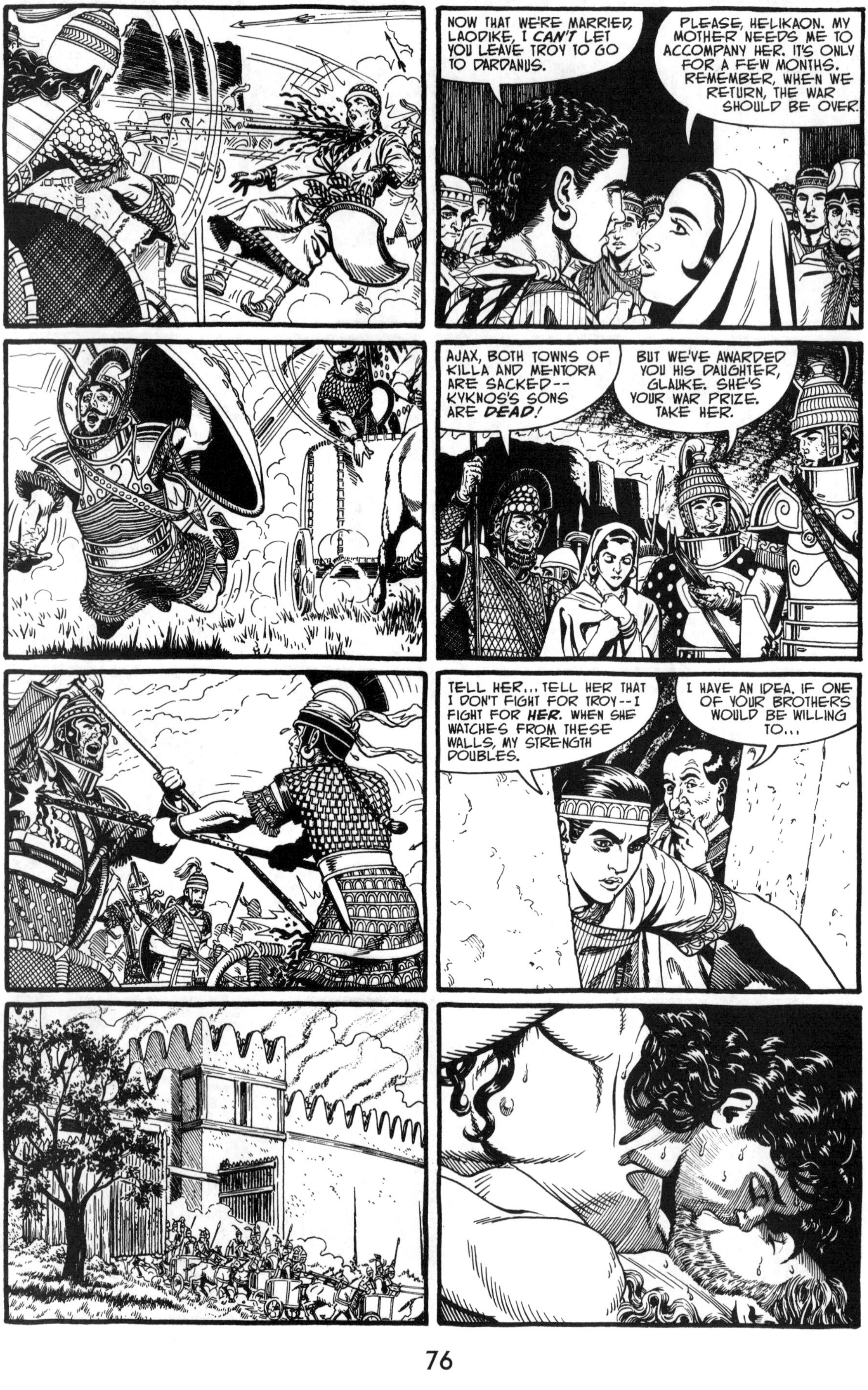
NOW THAT WE'RE MARRIED, LAODIKE, I CAN'T LET YOU LEAVE TROY TO GO TO DARDANUS.
PLEASE, HELIKAON. MY MOTHER NEEDS ME TO ACCOMPANY HER. IT'S ONLY FOR A FEW MONTHS. REMEMBER, WHEN WE RETURN, THE WAR SHOULD BE OVER.
AJAX, BOTH TOWNS OF KILLA AND MENTORA ARE SACKED-- KYKNOS'S SONS ARE DEAD!
BUT WE'VE AWARDED YOU HIS DAUGHTER, GLAUKE. SHE'S YOUR WAR PRIZE. TAKE HER.
TELL HER... TELL HER THAT I DON'T FIGHT FOR TROY--I FIGHT FOR HER. WHEN SHE WATCHES FROM THESE WALLS, MY STRENGTH DOUBLES.
I HAVE AN IDEA. IF ONE OF YOUR BROTHERS WOULD BE WILLING TO...

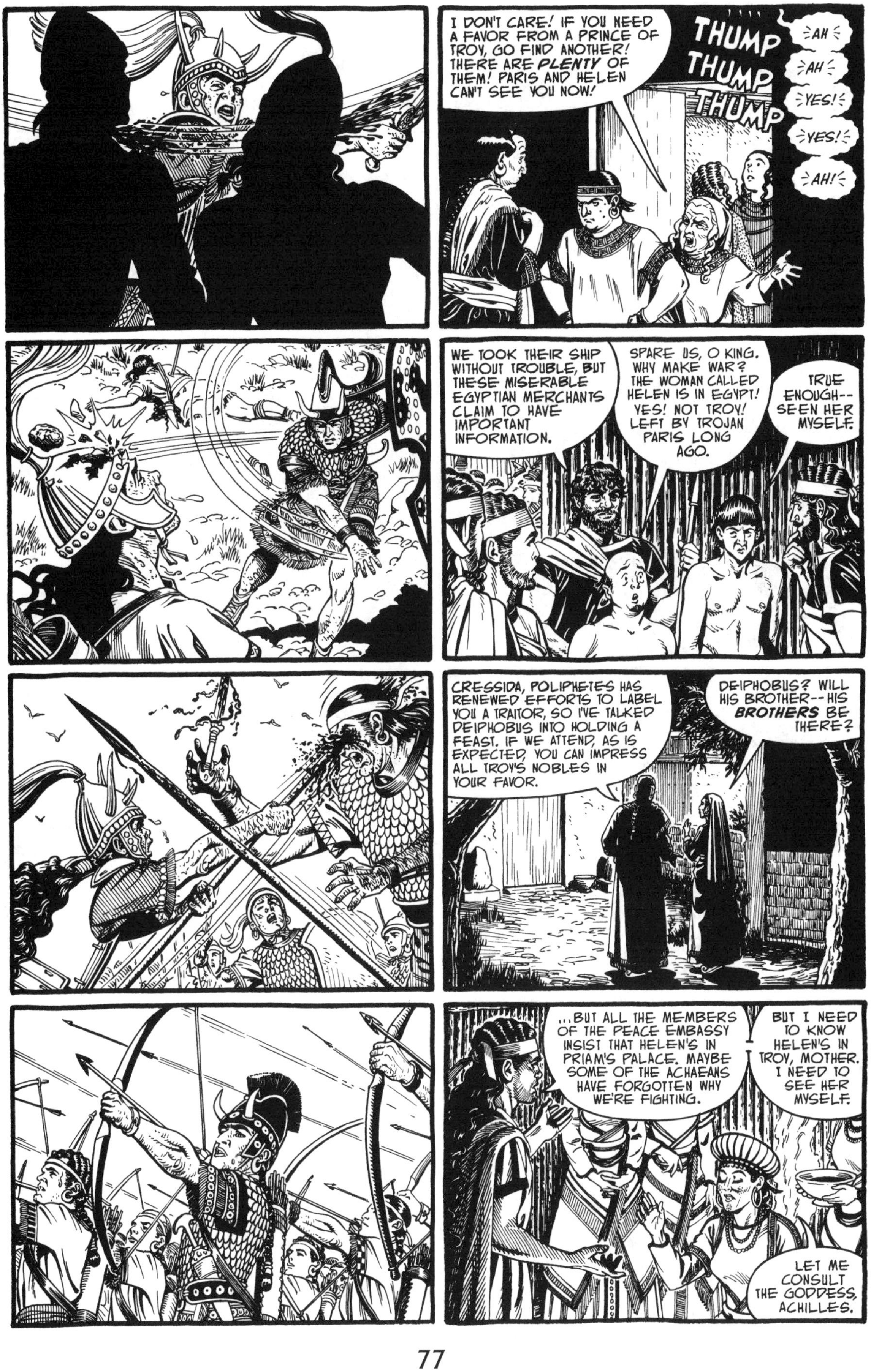
I DON'T CARE! IF YOU NEED A FAVOR FROM A PRINCE OF TROY, GO FIND ANOTHER! THERE ARE PLENTY OF THEM! PARIS AND HELEN CAN'T SEE YOU NOW!
THUMP
AH
THUMP
AH
THUMP
YES!
YES!
AH!
WE TOOK THEIR SHIP WITHOUT TROUBLE, BUT THESE MISERABLE EGYPTIAN MERCHANTS CLAIM TO HAVE IMPORTANT INFORMATION.
SPARE US, O KING. WHY MAKE WAR? THE WOMAN CALLED HELEN IS IN EGYPT! YES! NOT TROY! LEFT BY TROJAN PARIS LONG AGO.
TRUE ENOUGH-- SEEN HER MYSELF.
CRESSIDA, POLIPHETES HAS RENEWED EFFORTS TO LABEL YOU A TRAITOR, SO I'VE TALKED DEIPHOBUS INTO HOLDING A FEAST. IF WE ATTEND, AS IS EXPECTED, YOU CAN IMPRESS ALL TROY'S NOBLES IN YOUR FAVOR.
DEIPHOBUS? WILL HIS BROTHER--HIS BROTHERS BE THERE?
...BUT ALL THE MEMBERS OF THE PEACE EMBASSY INSIST THAT HELEN'S IN PRIAM'S PALACE. MAYBE SOME OF THE ACHAEANS HAVE FORGOTTEN WHY WE'RE FIGHTING.
BUT I NEED TO KNOW HELEN'S IN TROY, MOTHER. I NEED TO SEE HER MYSELF.
LET ME CONSULT THE GODDESS, ACHILLES.

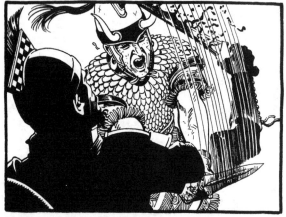

HOW DO MEN FIGHT A WAR WITHOUT FOOD, AGAMEMNON?

TURN ASIDE THE EVIL DAYS, O MY SUN. LET YOUR ANGER BE CALMED, O MY SUN. THE EVIL TONGUES OF THE MULTITUDES HAVE DISPLEASED YOU.

OFF TO MYSIA AT LAST!

AGAMEMNON WOULD NEVER BE SENDING US IF WE DIDN'T NEED YOUR GRAIN, TELEPHUS.

DON'T FORGET, ACHILLES, WE'VE GOT TO STOP AT MOUNT IDA ON THE WAY BACK TO PREPARE THE SIGNAL FIRE.

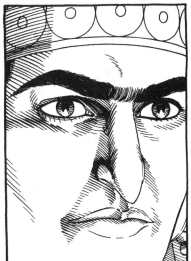

MY FRIENDS!

I'M GIVING THIS LITTLE FEAST TONIGHT SO THAT WE CAN BID FAREWELL TO SOMEONE WE'RE ALL FOND OF.

SHE'S LEAVING TROY TO BEAR HER CHILD IN SAFETY, FAR FROM THIS WAR WITH THE ACHAEANS.

SO FILL YOUR CUPS AND LET'S SALUTE THE MOST BEAUTIFUL WOMAN IN THE WORLD--

--MY SISTER, HELEN.

THANK YOU, DEIPHOBUS. AND MY THANKS TO ALL OF YOU, MY FRIENDS. EVERY MOMENT I'M AWAY, I'LL BE LONGING FOR TROY.

MY ADOPTED HOME IS ALL THE SWEETER BECAUSE I WASN'T BORN TO IT.

I BESEECH YOU TO DRIVE AWAY OUR ATTACKERS. AND IF THEY WON'T BE DRIVEN, THEN SEND THEM TO THEIR FINAL SLEEP.

I LOOK FORWARD TO MY SWIFT RETURN TO A VICTORIOUS TROY.

WHAT A WOMAN! HER WORDS ARE AS CHARMING AS HER FACE.

OBVIOUSLY SHE'S WASTED ON PARIS.

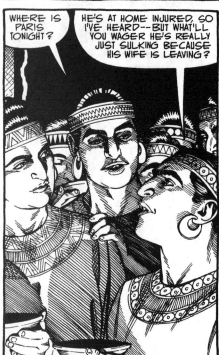

WHERE IS PARIS TONIGHT?

HE'S AT HOME INJURED. SO I'VE HEARD--BUT WHAT'LL YOU WAGER HE'S REALLY JUST SULKING BECAUSE HIS WIFE IS LEAVING?

AT LEAST SHE HAS REASON TO LEAVE. MY WIFE'S GOING WITH HELEN AND ALL THE OTHER PREGNANT WOMEN, BUT--

BUT LAODIKE'S NOT PREGNANT? IS THAT YOUR TROUBLE, HELIKAON?

NOT PREGNANT YET?

HELIKAON, I'M SHOCKED!

WHAT'S TAKING SO LONG?

GET BUSY!

HOW CAN I "GET BUSY" IF LAODIKE LEAVES? HEKUBA CHOSE HER AS AN ATTENDANT AND I HAVE NO SAY!

CALM DOWN. MY MOTHER'S BORNE CHILDREN OFTEN ENOUGH, THE GODS KNOW, BUT SHE'S NOT SO YOUNG ANYMORE. SHE NEEDS A LITTLE HELP.

DEIPHOBUS, IF I MAY? YOUR SECOND REASON FOR THIS FEAST-- THE OTHER YOUNG WOMAN...?

PANDARUS, WHAT--? OH, YES! YOUR NIECE. WELL, YOU KNOW THE SITUATION BEST. UNLEASH YOUR ORATORICAL SKILL.

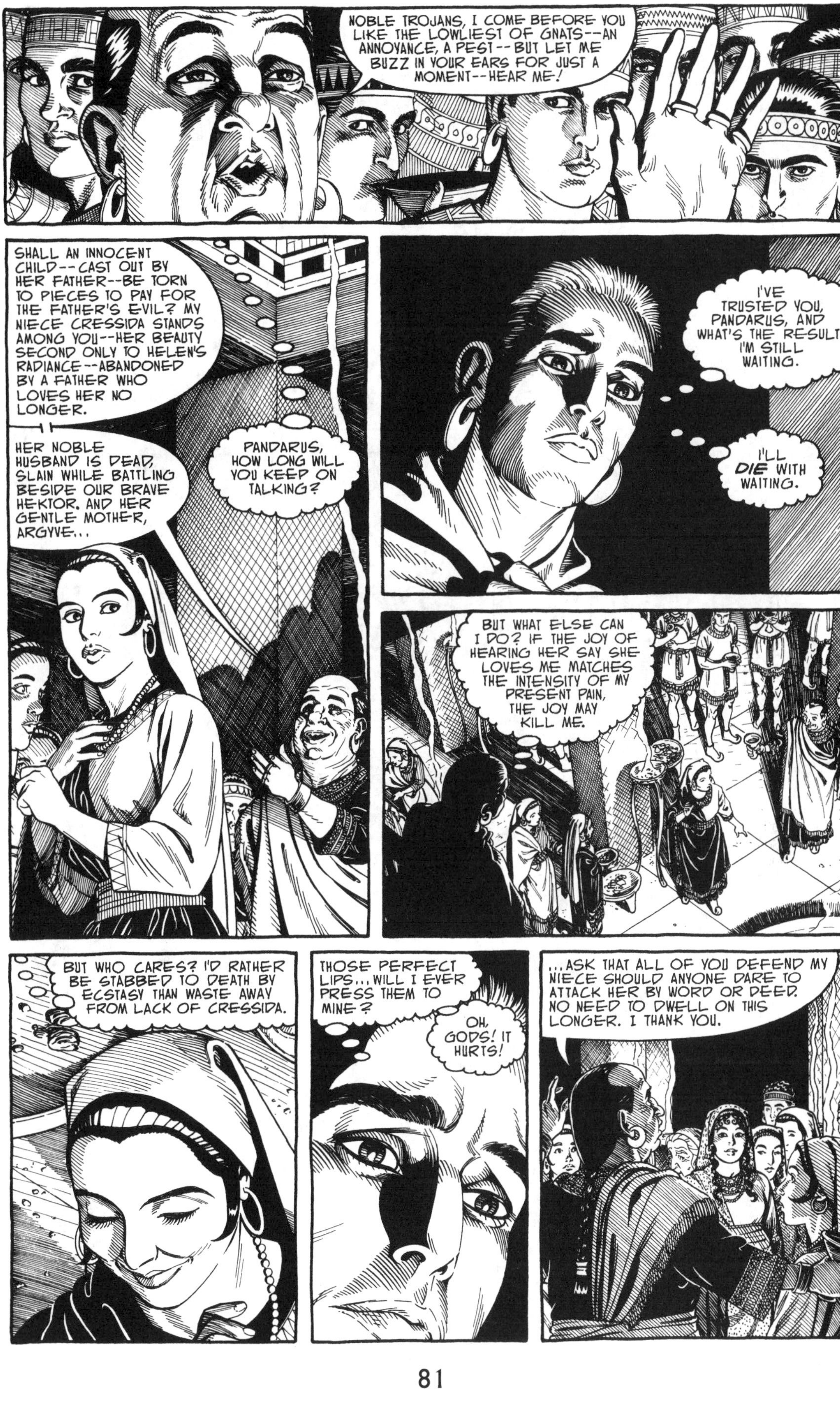
NOBLE TROJANS, I COME BEFORE YOU LIKE THE LOWLIEST OF GNATS--AN ANNOYANCE, A PEST--BUT LET ME BUZZ IN YOUR EARS FOR JUST A MOMENT--HEAR ME!
SHALL AN INNOCENT CHILD--CAST OUT BY HER FATHER--BE TORN TO PIECES TO PAY FOR THE FATHER'S EVIL? MY NIECE CRESSIDA STANDS AMONG YOU--HER BEAUTY SECOND ONLY TO HELEN'S RADIANCE--ABANDONED BY A FATHER WHO LOVES HER NO LONGER.
HER NOBLE HUSBAND IS DEAD, SLAIN WHILE BATTLING BESIDE OUR BRAVE HEKTOR. AND HER GENTLE MOTHER, ARGYVE...
PANDARUS, HOW LONG WILL YOU KEEP ON TALKING?
I'VE TRUSTED YOU, PANDARUS, AND WHAT'S THE RESULT? I'M STILL WAITING.
I'LL **DIE** WITH WAITING.
BUT WHAT ELSE CAN I DO? IF THE JOY OF HEARING HER SAY SHE LOVES ME MATCHES THE INTENSITY OF MY PRESENT PAIN, THE JOY MAY KILL ME.
BUT WHO CARES? I'D RATHER BE STABBED TO DEATH BY ECSTASY THAN WASTE AWAY FROM LACK OF CRESSIDA.
THOSE PERFECT LIPS... WILL I EVER PRESS THEM TO MINE?
OH, GODS! IT HURTS!
...ASK THAT ALL OF YOU DEFEND MY NIECE SHOULD ANYONE DARE TO ATTACK HER BY WORD OR DEED. NO NEED TO DWELL ON THIS LONGER. I THANK YOU.

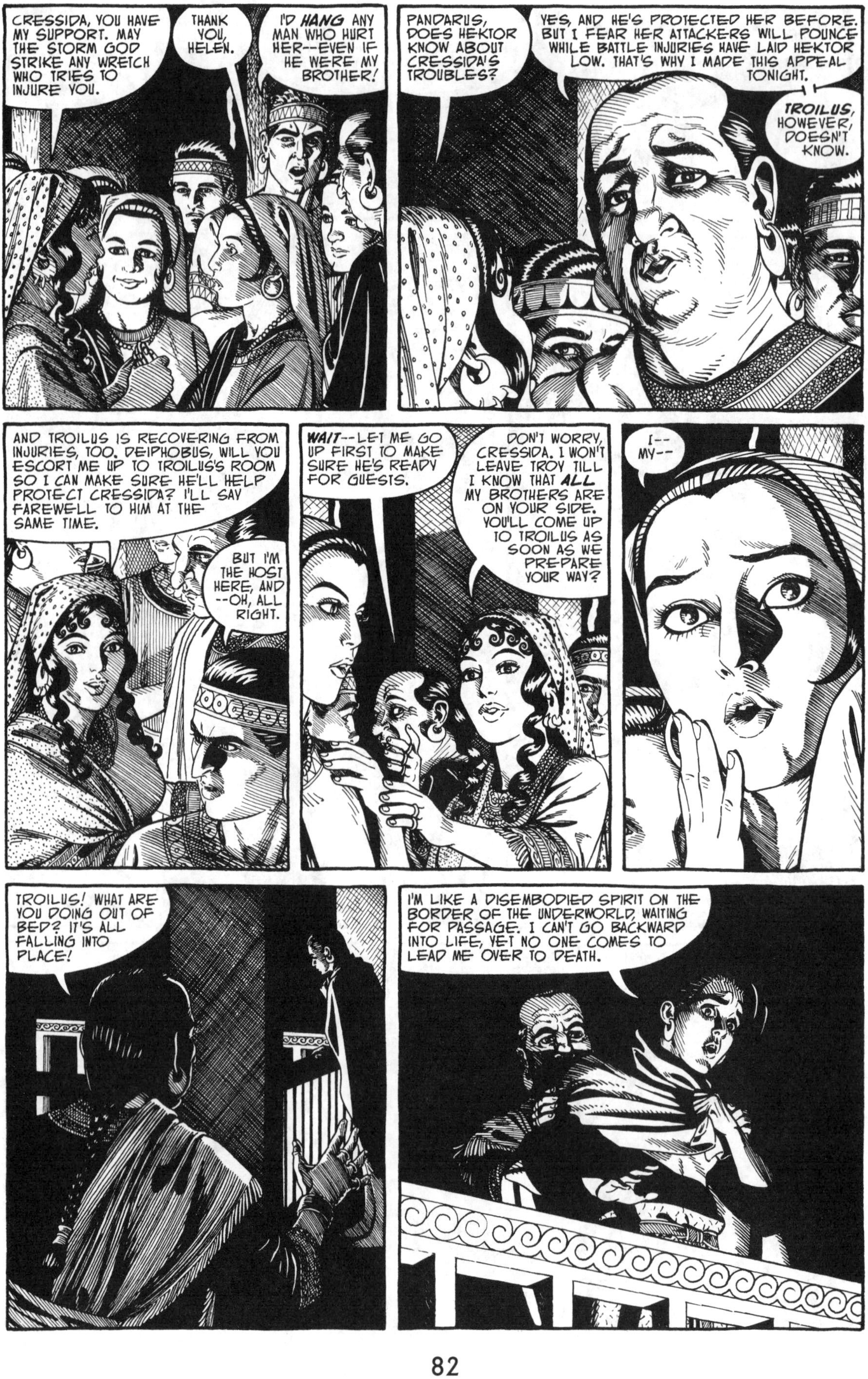
CRESSIDA, YOU HAVE MY SUPPORT. MAY THE STORM GOD STRIKE ANY WRETCH WHO TRIES TO INJURE YOU.
THANK YOU, HELEN.
I'D HANG ANY MAN WHO HURT HER--EVEN IF HE WERE MY BROTHER!
PANDARUS, DOES HEKTOR KNOW ABOUT CRESSIDA'S TROUBLES?
YES, AND HE'S PROTECTED HER BEFORE. BUT I FEAR HER ATTACKERS WILL POUNCE WHILE BATTLE INJURIES HAVE LAID HEKTOR LOW. THAT'S WHY I MADE THIS APPEAL TONIGHT.
TROILUS, HOWEVER, DOESN'T KNOW.
AND TROILUS IS RECOVERING FROM INJURIES, TOO. DEIPHOBUS, WILL YOU ESCORT ME UP TO TROILUS'S ROOM SO I CAN MAKE SURE HE'LL HELP PROTECT CRESSIDA? I'LL SAY FAREWELL TO HIM AT THE SAME TIME.
BUT I'M THE HOST HERE, AND --OH, ALL RIGHT.
WAIT--LET ME GO UP FIRST TO MAKE SURE HE'S READY FOR GUESTS.
DON'T WORRY, CRESSIDA. I WON'T LEAVE TROY TILL I KNOW THAT ALL MY BROTHERS ARE ON YOUR SIDE. YOU'LL COME UP TO TROILUS AS SOON AS WE PREPARE YOUR WAY?
I-- MY--
TROILUS! WHAT ARE YOU DOING OUT OF BED? IT'S ALL FALLING INTO PLACE!
I'M LIKE A DISEMBODIED SPIRIT ON THE BORDER OF THE UNDERWORLD, WAITING FOR PASSAGE. I CAN'T GO BACKWARD INTO LIFE, YET NO ONE COMES TO LEAD ME OVER TO DEATH.

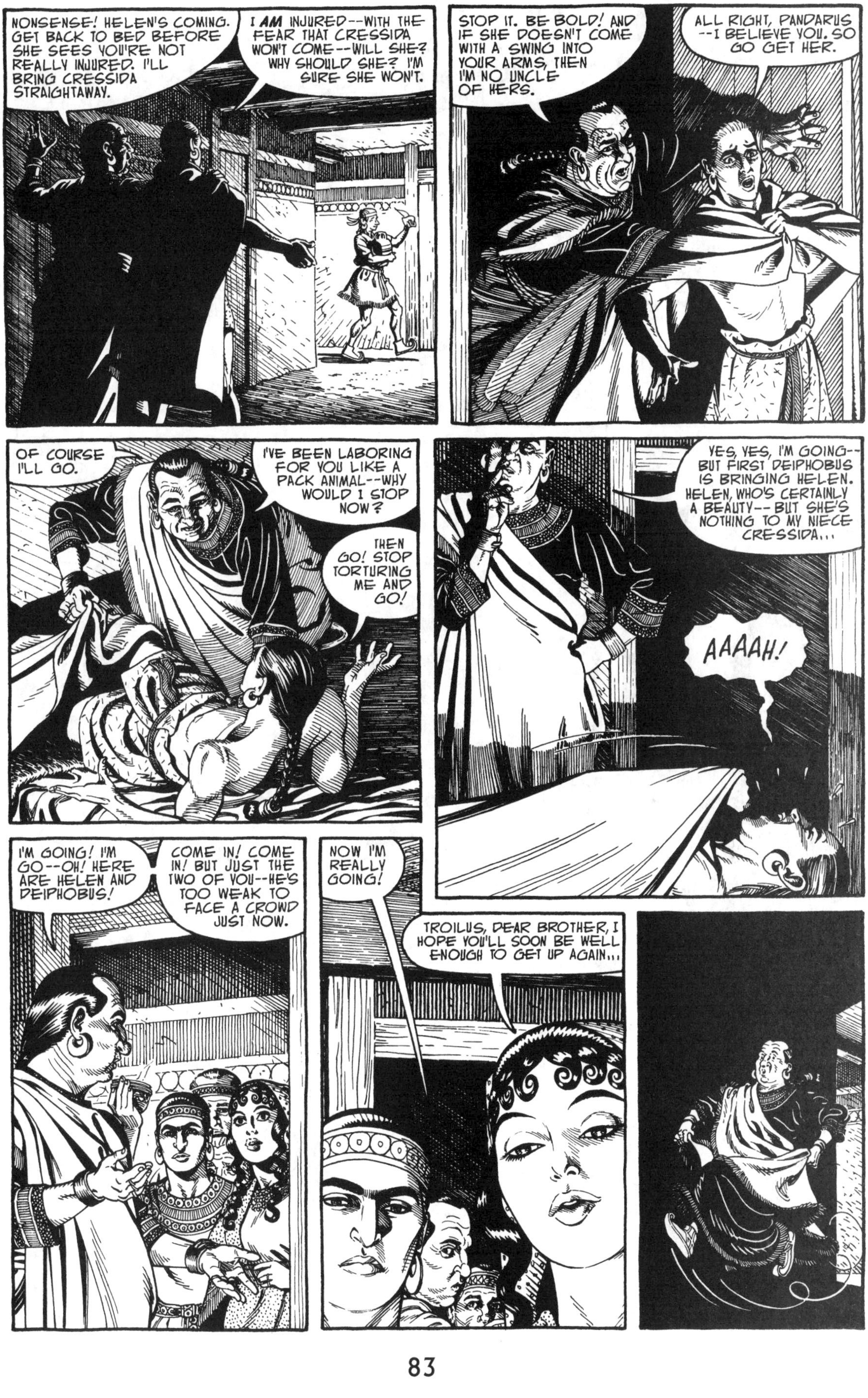
NONSENSE! HELEN'S COMING. GET BACK TO BED BEFORE SHE SEES YOU'RE NOT REALLY INJURED. I'LL BRING CRESSIDA STRAIGHTAWAY.
I AM INJURED--WITH THE FEAR THAT CRESSIDA WON'T COME--WILL SHE? WHY SHOULD SHE? I'M SURE SHE WON'T.
STOP IT. BE BOLD! AND IF SHE DOESN'T COME WITH A SWING INTO YOUR ARMS, THEN I'M NO UNCLE OF HERS.
ALL RIGHT, PANDARUS --I BELIEVE YOU. SO GO GET HER.
OF COURSE I'LL GO.
I'VE BEEN LABORING FOR YOU LIKE A PACK ANIMAL--WHY WOULD I STOP NOW?
THEN GO! STOP TORTURING ME AND GO!
YES, YES, I'M GOING-- BUT FIRST DEIPHOBUS IS BRINGING HELEN. HELEN, WHO'S CERTAINLY A BEAUTY-- BUT SHE'S NOTHING TO MY NIECE CRESSIDA...
AAAAH!
I'M GOING! I'M GO--OH! HERE ARE HELEN AND DEIPHOBUS!
COME IN! COME IN! BUT JUST THE TWO OF YOU--HE'S TOO WEAK TO FACE A CROWD JUST NOW.
NOW I'M REALLY GOING!
TROILUS, DEAR BROTHER, I HOPE YOU'LL SOON BE WELL ENOUGH TO GET UP AGAIN...

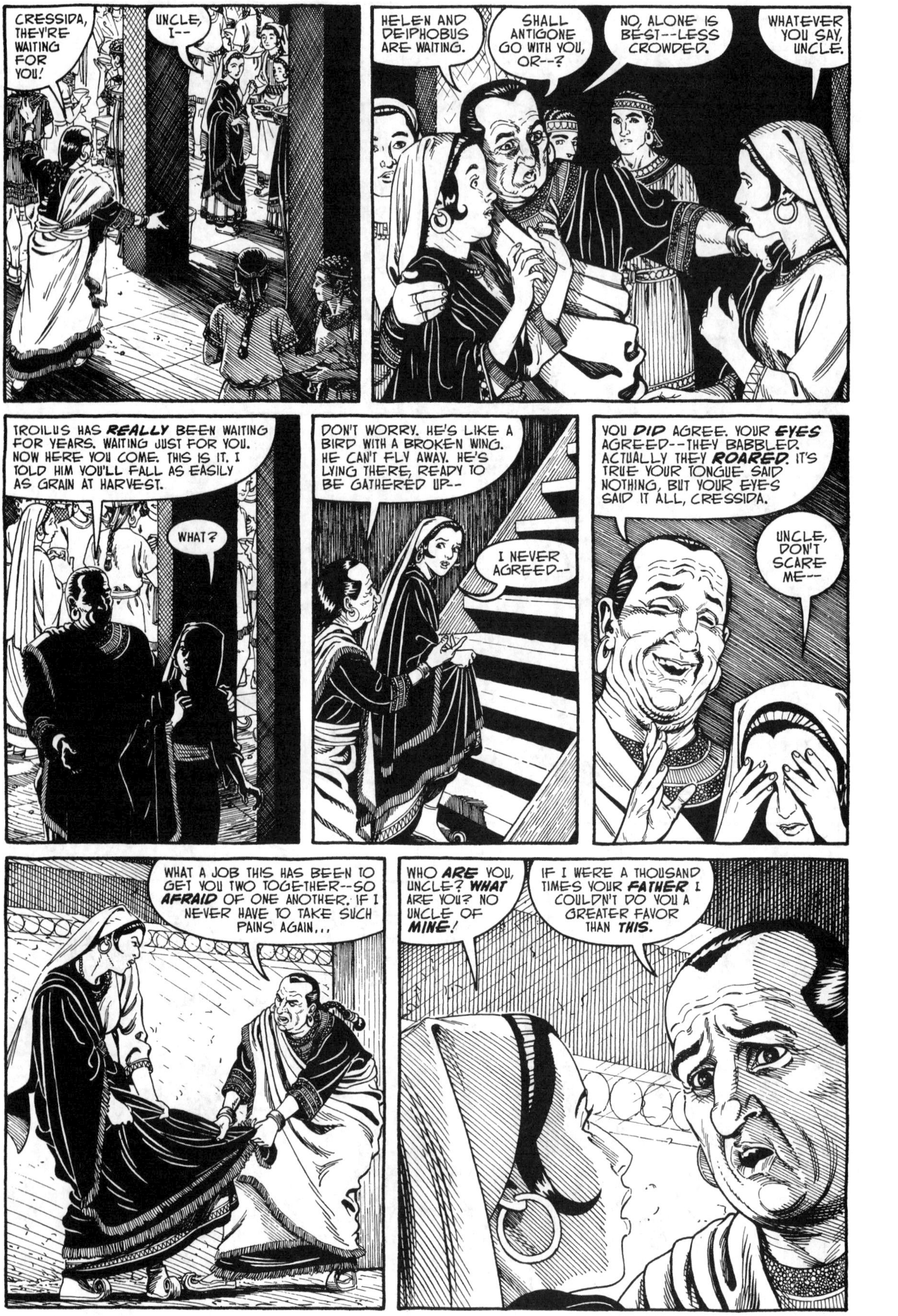
CRESSIDA, THEY'RE WAITING FOR YOU!
UNCLE, I--
HELEN AND DEIPHOBUS ARE WAITING.
SHALL ANTIGONE GO WITH YOU, OR--?
NO, ALONE IS BEST--LESS CROWDED.
WHATEVER YOU SAY, UNCLE.
TROILUS HAS **REALLY** BEEN WAITING FOR YEARS. WAITING JUST FOR YOU. NOW HERE YOU COME. THIS IS IT. I TOLD HIM YOU'LL FALL AS EASILY AS GRAIN AT HARVEST.
WHAT?
DON'T WORRY. HE'S LIKE A BIRD WITH A BROKEN WING. HE CAN'T FLY AWAY. HE'S LYING THERE, READY TO BE GATHERED UP--
I NEVER AGREED--
YOU **DID** AGREE. YOUR **EYES** AGREED--THEY BABBLED. ACTUALLY THEY **ROARED**. IT'S TRUE YOUR TONGUE SAID NOTHING, BUT YOUR EYES SAID IT ALL, CRESSIDA.
UNCLE, DON'T SCARE ME--
WHAT A JOB THIS HAS BEEN TO GET YOU TWO TOGETHER--SO **AFRAID** OF ONE ANOTHER. IF I NEVER HAVE TO TAKE SUCH PAINS AGAIN...
WHO **ARE** YOU, UNCLE? **WHAT** ARE YOU? NO UNCLE OF **MINE**!
IF I WERE A THOUSAND TIMES YOUR **FATHER** I COULDN'T DO YOU A GREATER FAVOR THAN **THIS**.

HERE WE ARE. GO AHEAD AND DENY HIM AT FIRST, NIECE. THAT'LL BE DECENT. BUT DON'T BE OBSTINATE FOR LONG. YOU'LL NEVER HAVE ANOTHER CHANCE LIKE THIS.

HELEN, ARE YOU GOING? PLEASE STAY.

I CAN'T. I STILL HAVE FAR TO GO TONIGHT--

--AND YOUR UNCLE IS HERE FOR CHAPERONE.

BUT YOU'LL HAVE NO WORRIES. IT'S CLEAR THAT OUR GALLANT YOUNG TROILUS WISHES YOU ONLY THE BEST. FAREWELL, CRESSIDA.

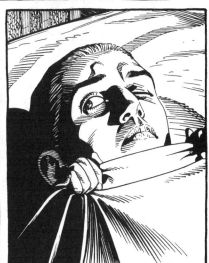

SWEET CRESSIDA, I--I SHOULD GET UP. THIS IS NO WAY TO GREET YOU.

OH, DON'T-- DON'T! YOU'RE INJURED...

85

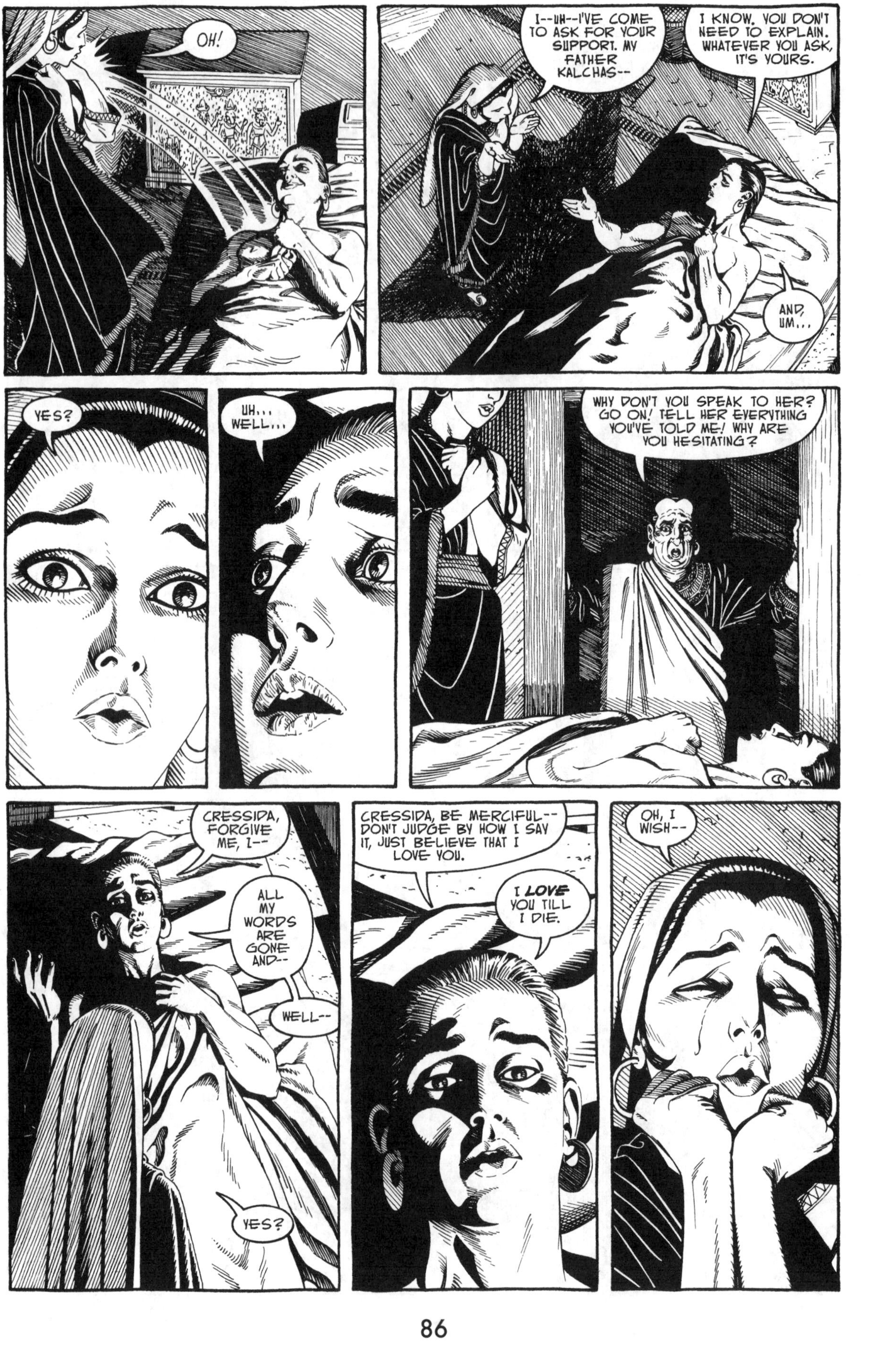

OH!
I--UH--I'VE COME TO ASK FOR YOUR SUPPORT. MY FATHER KALCHAS--
I KNOW. YOU DON'T NEED TO EXPLAIN. WHATEVER YOU ASK, IT'S YOURS.
AND, UM...
YES?
UH... WELL...
WHY DON'T YOU SPEAK TO HER? GO ON! TELL HER EVERYTHING YOU'VE TOLD ME! WHY ARE YOU HESITATING?
CRESSIDA, FORGIVE ME, I--
ALL MY WORDS ARE GONE AND--
WELL--
YES?
CRESSIDA, BE MERCIFUL--DON'T JUDGE BY HOW I SAY IT, JUST BELIEVE THAT I LOVE YOU.
I **LOVE** YOU TILL I DIE.
OH, I WISH--

WISH WHAT? OH, GODS, IF I'VE HURT HER LET ME DIE NOW!

NO, TROILUS, LISTEN--I--I'VE LOVED YOU NIGHT AND DAY FOR MANY MONTHS--SINCE I DREAMED OF A WHITE EAGLE THAT EXCHANGED ITS HEART FOR MINE.

MY FATHER USED TO TELL ME HOW TO READ BIRD FLIGHTS--SO I KNEW YOUR LOVE WAS TRUE.

OR MAYBE I LOVED YOU EARLIER --SINCE THE DAY YOU FIRST CARRIED MY VEIL IN BATTLE--OR MAYBE...

WHY AM I TELLING YOU EVEN NOW? SOME DAY I'LL REGRET THIS, I JUST KNOW IT.

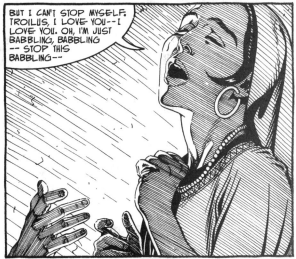

BUT I CAN'T STOP MYSELF, TROILUS, I LOVE YOU--I LOVE YOU. OH, I'M JUST BABBLING, BABBLING --STOP THIS BABBLING--

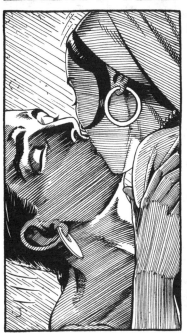

I--I WASN'T-- WASN'T BEGGING FOR A KISS. OH GODS, WHAT AM I DOING?

YOU'RE INJURED. I SHOULD GO. UNCLE, LET'S GO!

87

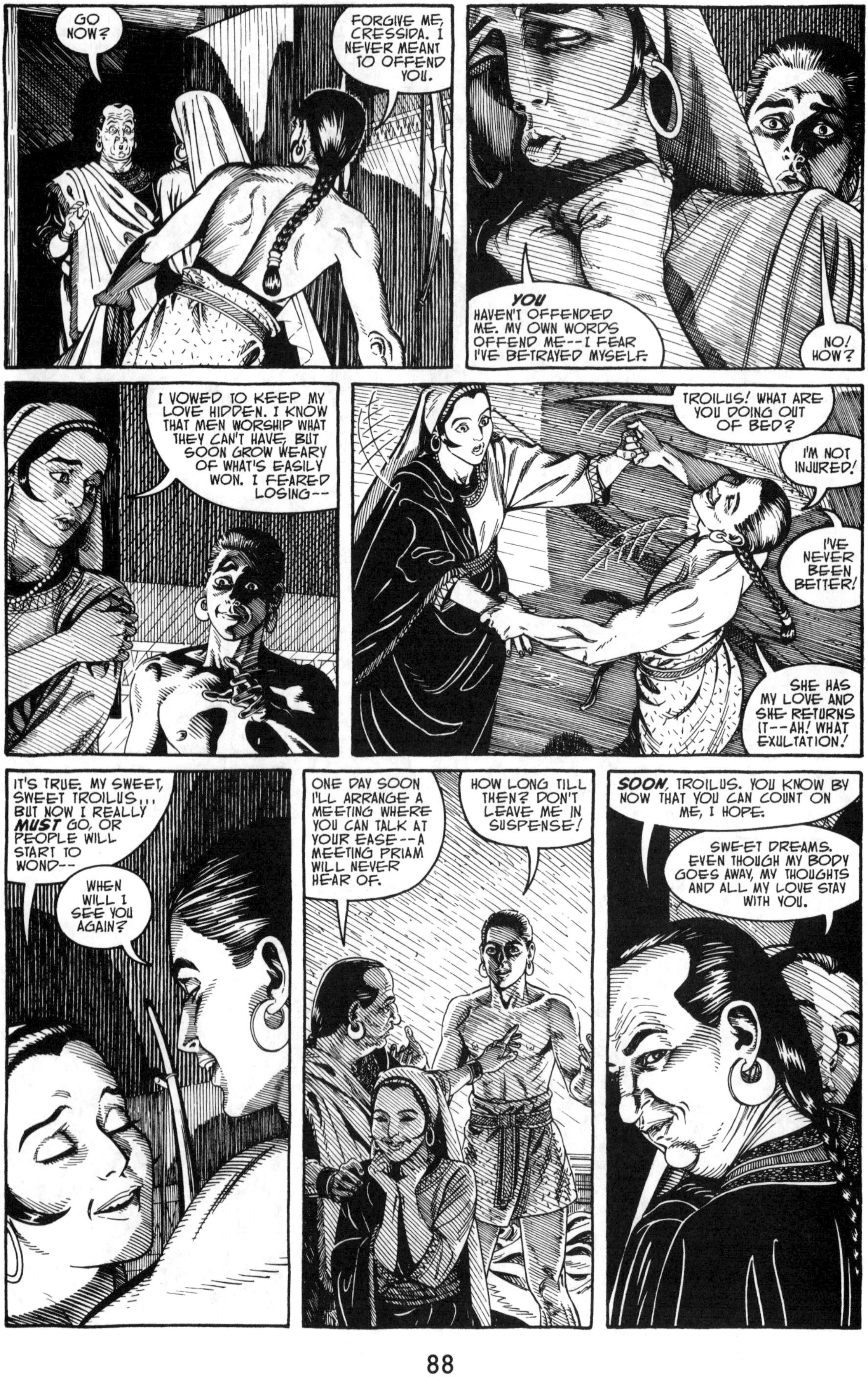
GO NOW?
FORGIVE ME, CRESSIDA. I NEVER MEANT TO OFFEND YOU.
YOU HAVEN'T OFFENDED ME. MY OWN WORDS OFFEND ME--I FEAR I'VE BETRAYED MYSELF.
NO! HOW?
I VOWED TO KEEP MY LOVE HIDDEN. I KNOW THAT MEN WORSHIP WHAT THEY CAN'T HAVE, BUT SOON GROW WEARY OF WHAT'S EASILY WON. I FEARED LOSING--
TROILUS! WHAT ARE YOU DOING OUT OF BED?
I'M NOT INJURED!
I'VE NEVER BEEN BETTER!
SHE HAS MY LOVE AND SHE RETURNS IT--AH! WHAT EXULTATION!
IT'S TRUE, MY SWEET, SWEET TROILUS... BUT NOW I REALLY MUST GO, OR PEOPLE WILL START TO WOND--
WHEN WILL I SEE YOU AGAIN?
ONE DAY SOON I'LL ARRANGE A MEETING WHERE YOU CAN TALK AT YOUR EASE--A MEETING PRIAM WILL NEVER HEAR OF.
HOW LONG TILL THEN? DON'T LEAVE ME IN SUSPENSE!
SOON, TROILUS. YOU KNOW BY NOW THAT YOU CAN COUNT ON ME, I HOPE.
SWEET DREAMS. EVEN THOUGH MY BODY GOES AWAY, MY THOUGHTS AND ALL MY LOVE STAY WITH YOU.

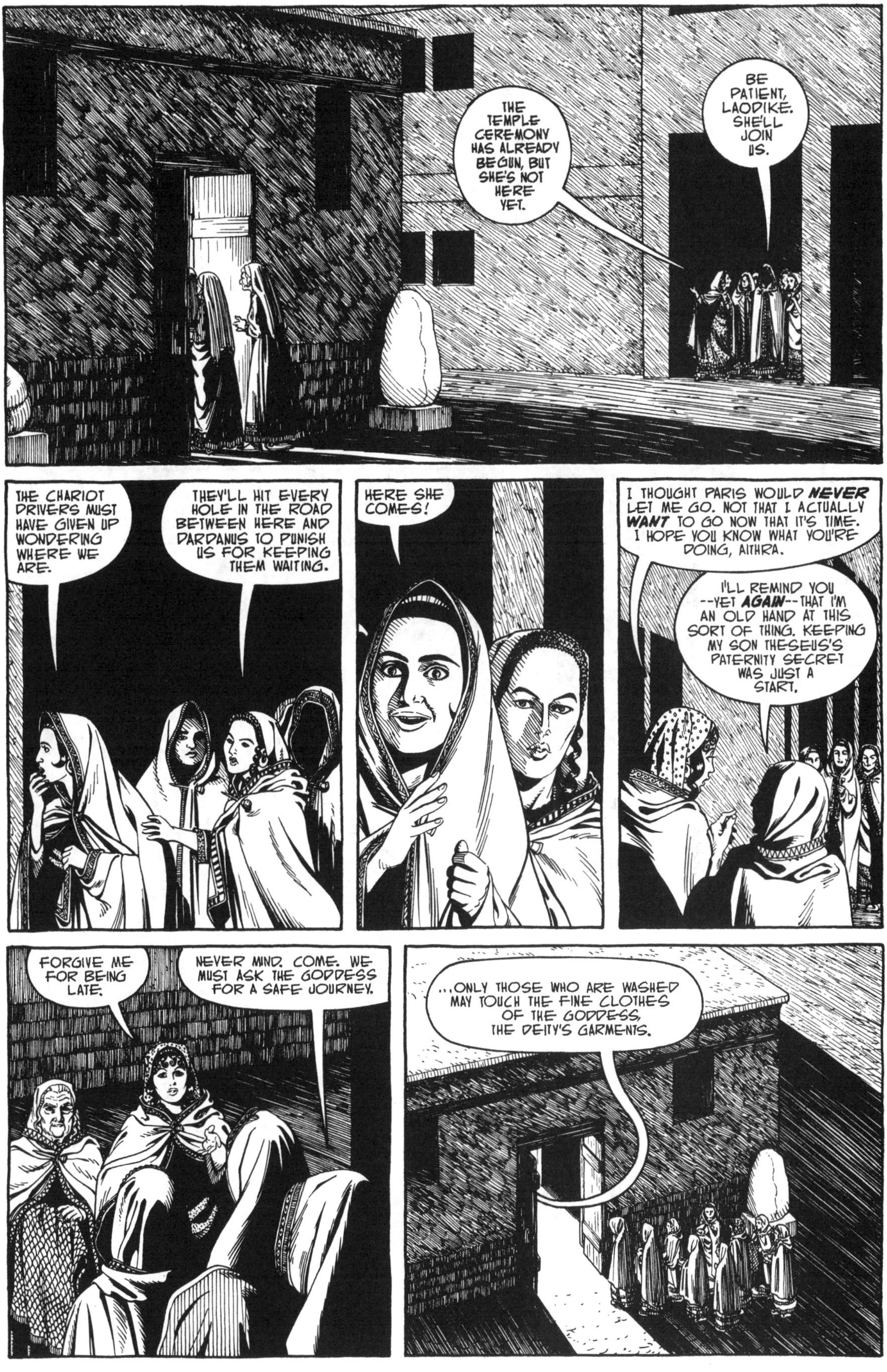
THE TEMPLE CEREMONY HAS ALREADY BEGUN, BUT SHE'S NOT HERE YET.
BE PATIENT, LAODIKE. SHE'LL JOIN US.
THE CHARIOT DRIVERS MUST HAVE GIVEN UP WONDERING WHERE WE ARE.
THEY'LL HIT EVERY HOLE IN THE ROAD BETWEEN HERE AND DARDANUS TO PUNISH US FOR KEEPING THEM WAITING.
HERE SHE COMES!
I THOUGHT PARIS WOULD NEVER LET ME GO. NOT THAT I ACTUALLY WANT TO GO NOW THAT IT'S TIME. I HOPE YOU KNOW WHAT YOU'RE DOING, AITHRA.
I'LL REMIND YOU --YET AGAIN-- THAT I'M AN OLD HAND AT THIS SORT OF THING. KEEPING MY SON THESEUS'S PATERNITY SECRET WAS JUST A START.
FORGIVE ME FOR BEING LATE.
NEVER MIND. COME. WE MUST ASK THE GODDESS FOR A SAFE JOURNEY.
...ONLY THOSE WHO ARE WASHED MAY TOUCH THE FINE CLOTHES OF THE GODDESS, THE DEITY'S GARMENTS.

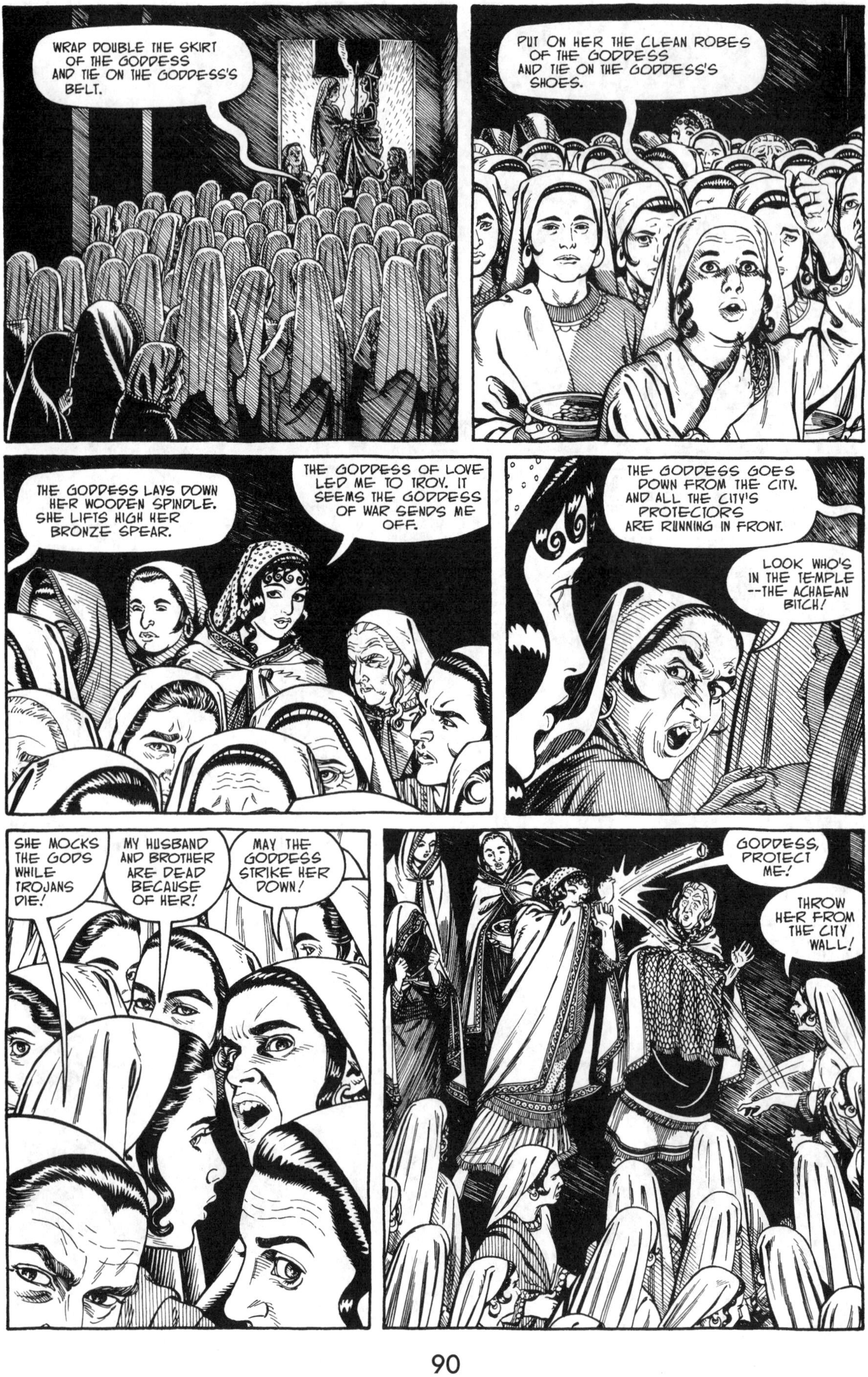
WRAP DOUBLE THE SKIRT OF THE GODDESS AND TIE ON THE GODDESS'S BELT.
PUT ON HER THE CLEAN ROBES OF THE GODDESS AND TIE ON THE GODDESS'S SHOES.
THE GODDESS LAYS DOWN HER WOODEN SPINDLE. SHE LIFTS HIGH HER BRONZE SPEAR.
THE GODDESS OF LOVE LED ME TO TROY. IT SEEMS THE GODDESS OF WAR SENDS ME OFF.
THE GODDESS GOES DOWN FROM THE CITY. AND ALL THE CITY'S PROTECTORS ARE RUNNING IN FRONT.
LOOK WHO'S IN THE TEMPLE --THE ACHAEAN BITCH!
SHE MOCKS THE GODS WHILE TROJANS DIE!
MY HUSBAND AND BROTHER ARE DEAD BECAUSE OF HER!
MAY THE GODDESS STRIKE HER DOWN!
GODDESS, PROTECT ME!
THROW HER FROM THE CITY WALL!

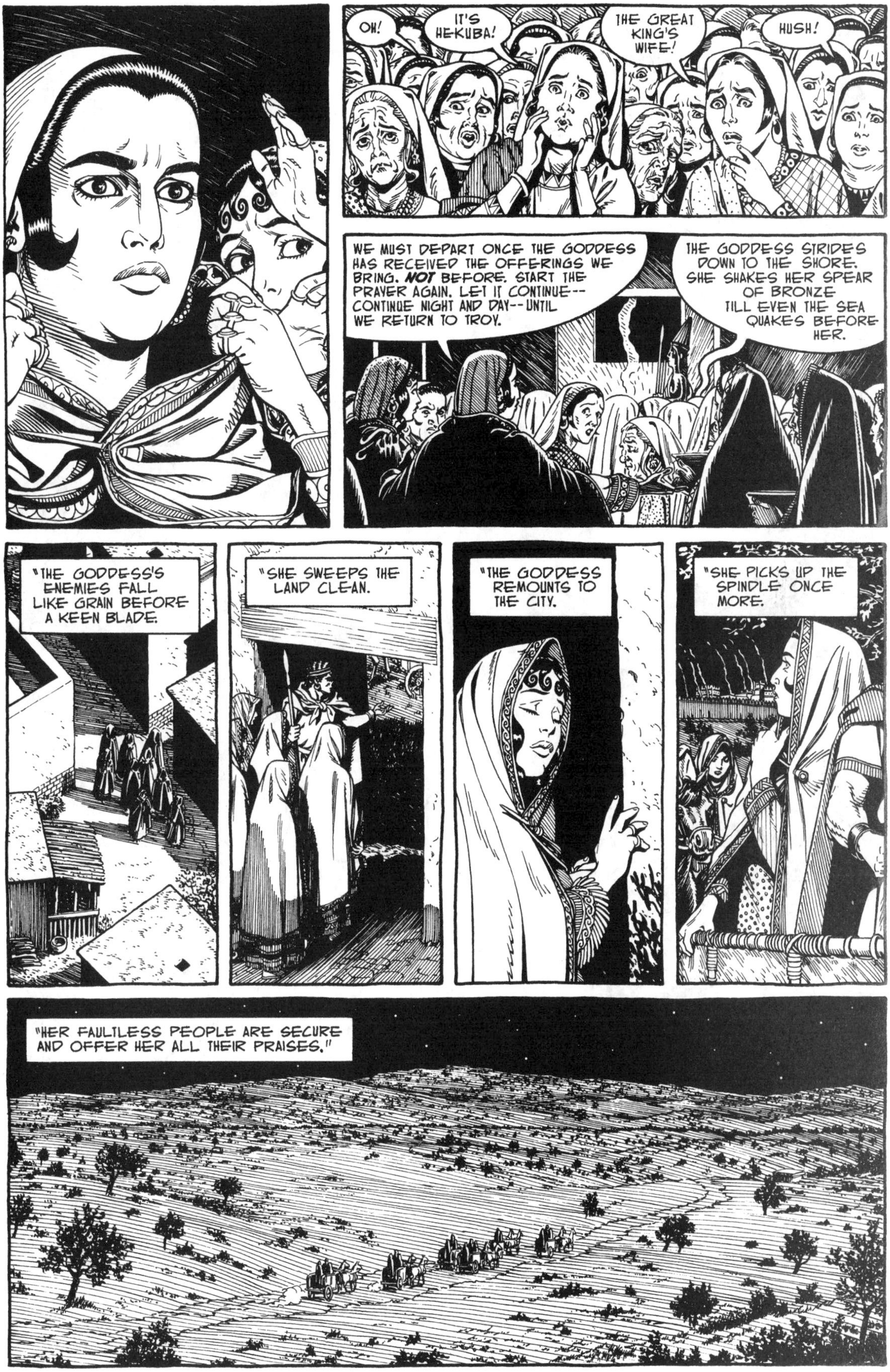
OH!
IT'S HE-KUBA!
THE GREAT KING'S WIFE!
HUSH!
WE MUST DEPART ONCE THE GODDESS HAS RECEIVED THE OFFERINGS WE BRING. **NOT** BEFORE. START THE PRAYER AGAIN. LET IT CONTINUE-- CONTINUE NIGHT AND DAY--UNTIL WE RETURN TO TROY.
THE GODDESS STRIDES DOWN TO THE SHORE. SHE SHAKES HER SPEAR OF BRONZE TILL EVEN THE SEA QUAKES BEFORE HER.
"THE GODDESS'S ENEMIES FALL LIKE GRAIN BEFORE A KEEN BLADE.
"SHE SWEEPS THE LAND CLEAN.
"THE GODDESS REMOUNTS TO THE CITY.
"SHE PICKS UP THE SPINDLE ONCE MORE.
"HER FAULTLESS PEOPLE ARE SECURE AND OFFER HER ALL THEIR PRAISES."

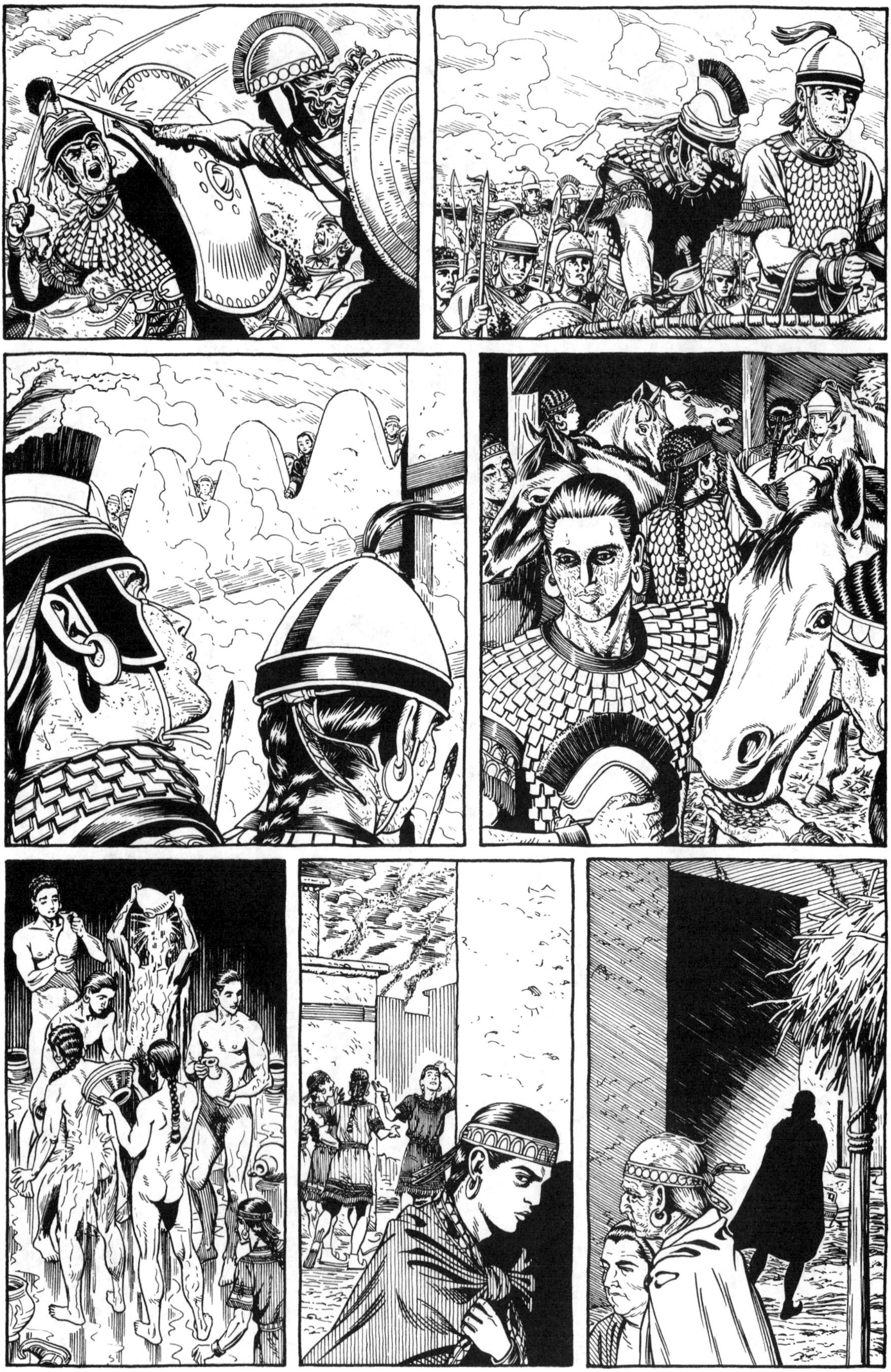

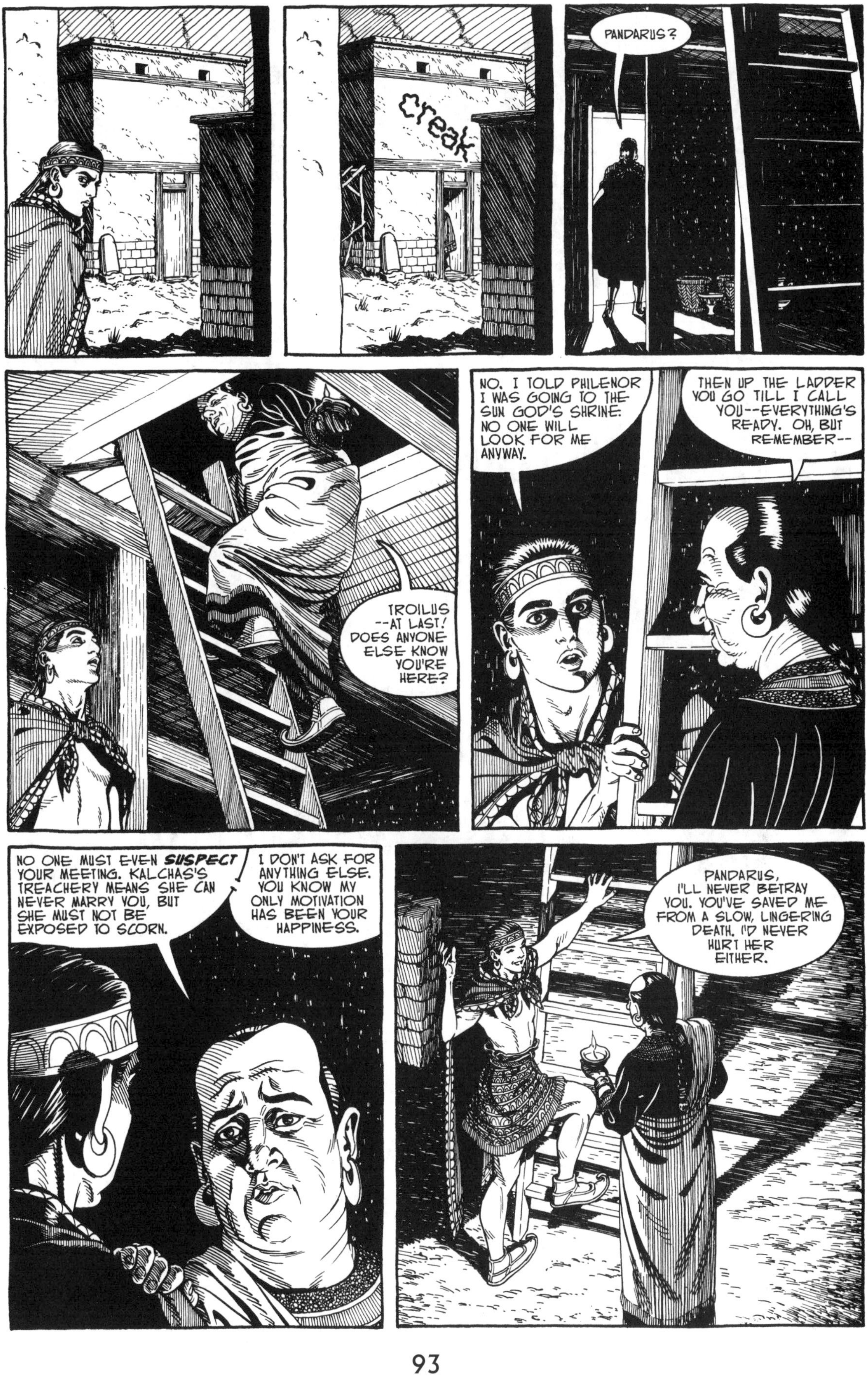
creak
PANDARUS?
TROILUS --AT LAST! DOES ANYONE ELSE KNOW YOU'RE HERE?
NO. I TOLD PHILENOR I WAS GOING TO THE SUN GOD'S SHRINE. NO ONE WILL LOOK FOR ME ANYWAY.
THEN UP THE LADDER YOU GO TILL I CALL YOU--EVERYTHING'S READY. OH, BUT REMEMBER--
NO ONE MUST EVEN **SUSPECT** YOUR MEETING. KALCHAS'S TREACHERY MEANS SHE CAN NEVER MARRY YOU, BUT SHE MUST NOT BE EXPOSED TO SCORN.
I DON'T ASK FOR ANYTHING ELSE. YOU KNOW MY ONLY MOTIVATION HAS BEEN YOUR HAPPINESS.
PANDARUS, I'LL NEVER BETRAY YOU. YOU'VE SAVED ME FROM A SLOW, LINGERING DEATH. I'D NEVER HURT HER EITHER.

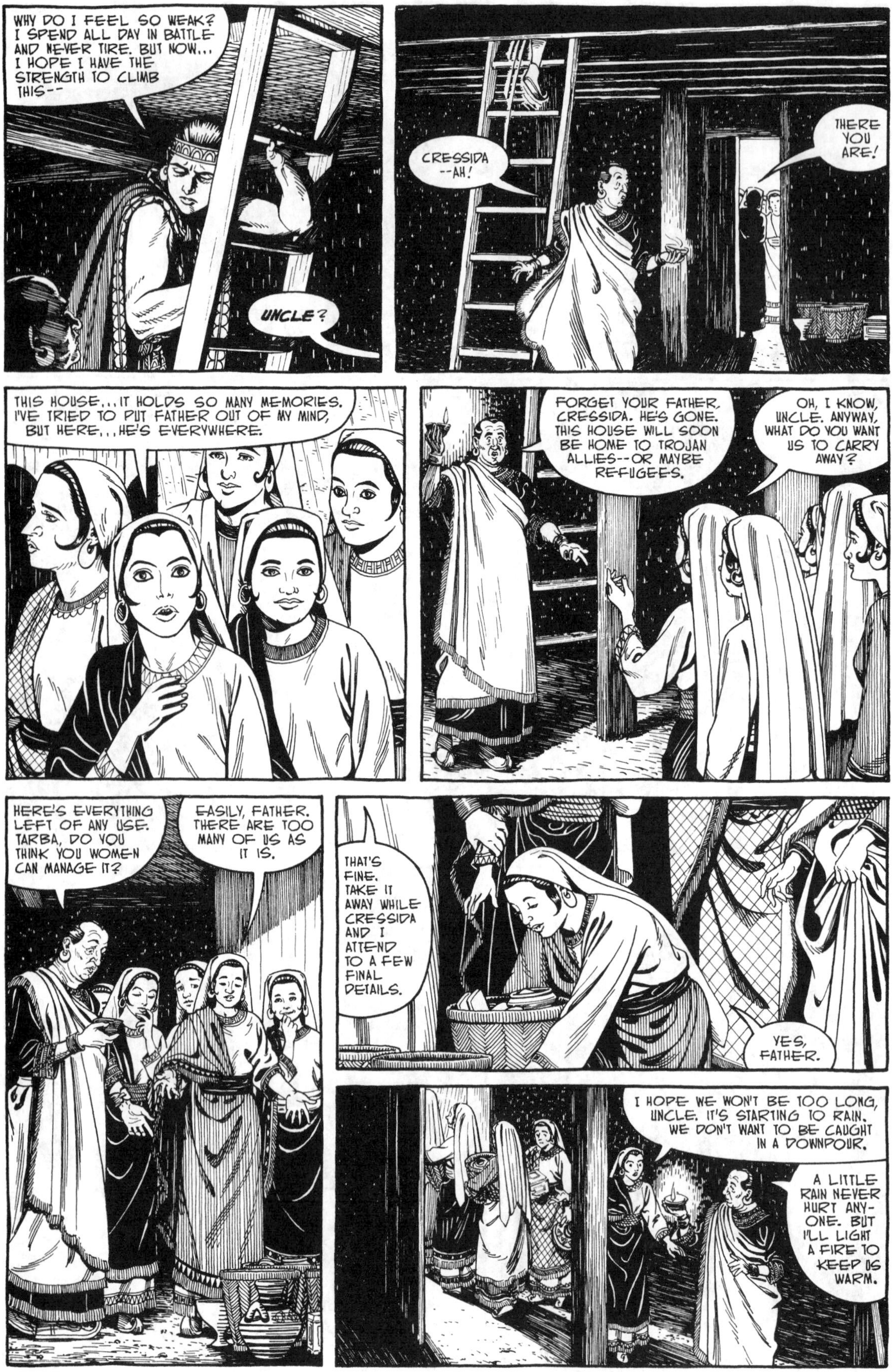
WHY DO I FEEL SO WEAK? I SPEND ALL DAY IN BATTLE AND NEVER TIRE. BUT NOW... I HOPE I HAVE THE STRENGTH TO CLIMB THIS--
UNCLE?
CRESSIDA --AH!
THERE YOU ARE!
THIS HOUSE... IT HOLDS SO MANY MEMORIES. I'VE TRIED TO PUT FATHER OUT OF MY MIND, BUT HERE... HE'S EVERYWHERE.
FORGET YOUR FATHER, CRESSIDA. HE'S GONE. THIS HOUSE WILL SOON BE HOME TO TROJAN ALLIES--OR MAYBE REFUGEES.
OH, I KNOW, UNCLE. ANYWAY, WHAT DO YOU WANT US TO CARRY AWAY?
HERE'S EVERYTHING LEFT OF ANY USE. TARBA, DO YOU THINK YOU WOMEN CAN MANAGE IT?
EASILY, FATHER. THERE ARE TOO MANY OF US AS IT IS.
THAT'S FINE. TAKE IT AWAY WHILE CRESSIDA AND I ATTEND TO A FEW FINAL DETAILS.
YES, FATHER.
I HOPE WE WON'T BE TOO LONG, UNCLE. IT'S STARTING TO RAIN. WE DON'T WANT TO BE CAUGHT IN A DOWNPOUR.
A LITTLE RAIN NEVER HURT ANYONE. BUT I'LL LIGHT A FIRE TO KEEP US WARM.

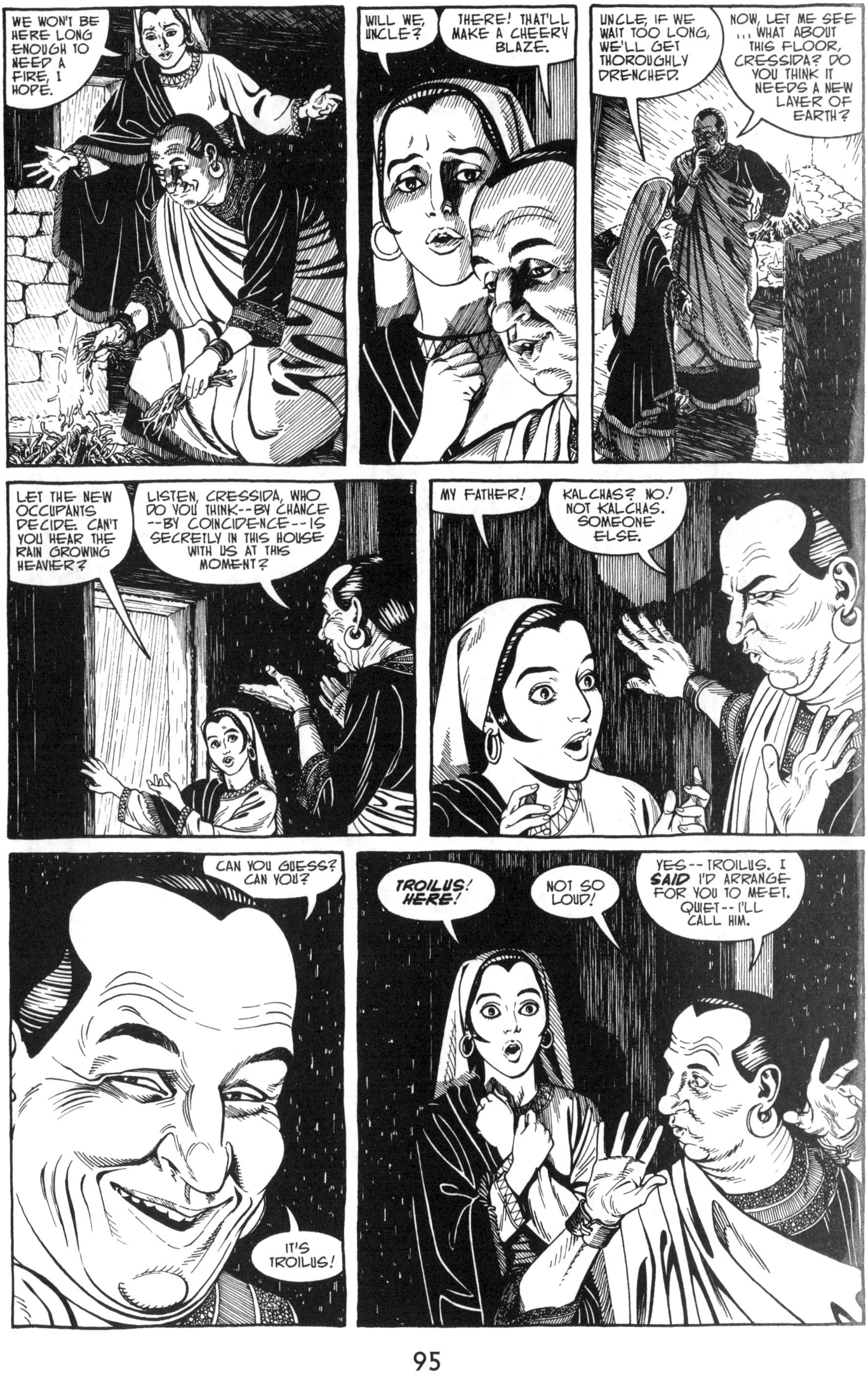
WE WON'T BE HERE LONG ENOUGH TO NEED A FIRE, I HOPE.
WILL WE, UNCLE?
THERE! THAT'LL MAKE A CHEERY BLAZE.
UNCLE, IF WE WAIT TOO LONG, WE'LL GET THOROUGHLY DRENCHED.
NOW, LET ME SEE ... WHAT ABOUT THIS FLOOR, CRESSIDA? DO YOU THINK IT NEEDS A NEW LAYER OF EARTH?
LET THE NEW OCCUPANTS DECIDE. CAN'T YOU HEAR THE RAIN GROWING HEAVIER?
LISTEN, CRESSIDA, WHO DO YOU THINK--BY CHANCE --BY COINCIDENCE--IS SECRETLY IN THIS HOUSE WITH US AT THIS MOMENT?
MY FATHER!
KALCHAS? NO! NOT KALCHAS. SOMEONE ELSE.
CAN YOU GUESS? CAN YOU?
IT'S TROILUS!
TROILUS! HERE!
NOT SO LOUD!
YES--TROILUS. I SAID I'D ARRANGE FOR YOU TO MEET. QUIET--I'LL CALL HIM.

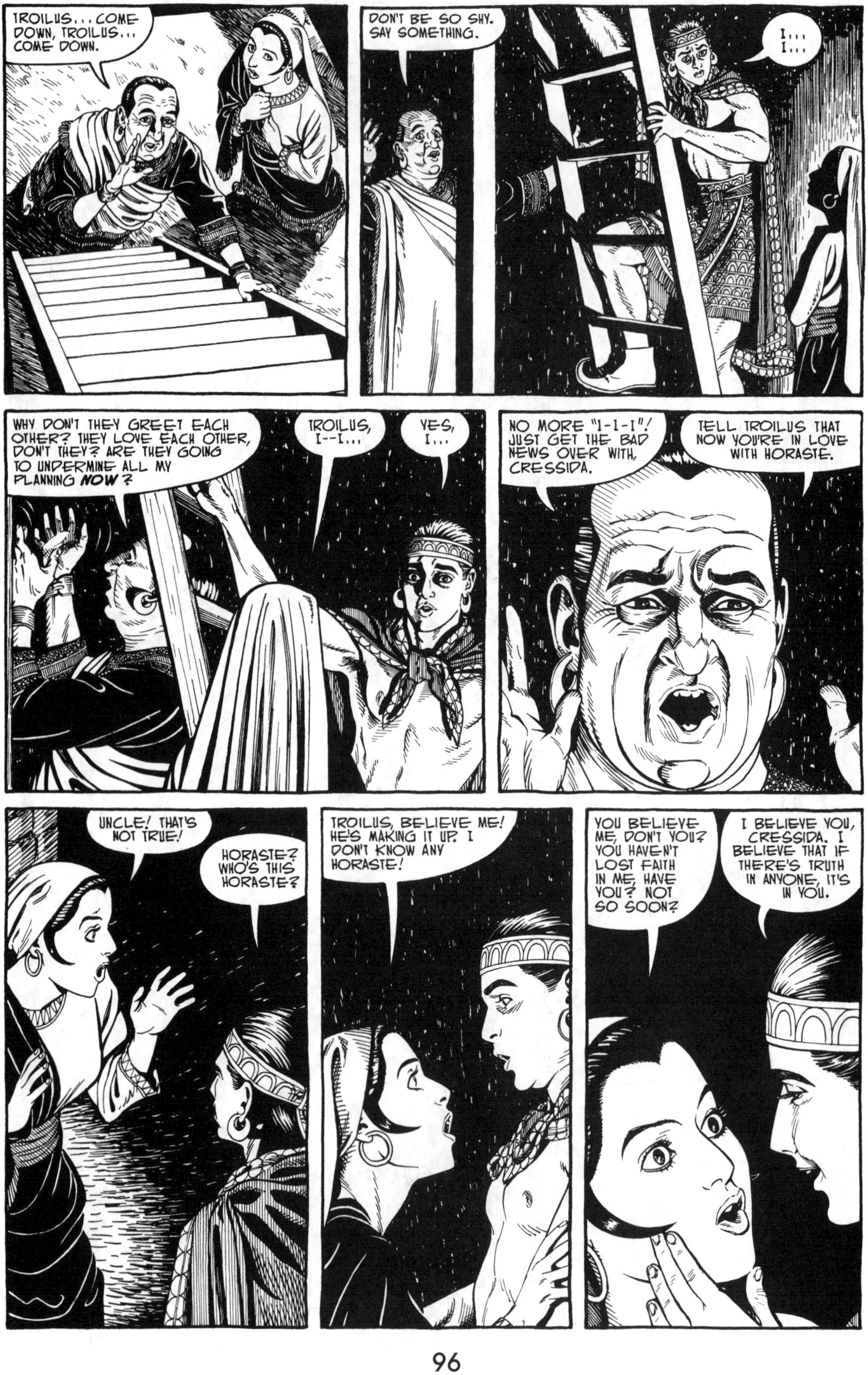
TROILUS... COME DOWN, TROILUS... COME DOWN.
DON'T BE SO SHY. SAY SOMETHING.
I... I...
WHY DON'T THEY GREET EACH OTHER? THEY LOVE EACH OTHER, DON'T THEY? ARE THEY GOING TO UNDERMINE ALL MY PLANNING NOW?
TROILUS, I--I...
YES, I...
NO MORE "I-I-I"! JUST GET THE BAD NEWS OVER WITH, CRESSIDA.
TELL TROILUS THAT NOW YOU'RE IN LOVE WITH HORASTE.
UNCLE! THAT'S NOT TRUE!
HORASTE? WHO'S THIS HORASTE?
TROILUS, BELIEVE ME! HE'S MAKING IT UP. I DON'T KNOW ANY HORASTE!
YOU BELIEVE ME, DON'T YOU? YOU HAVEN'T LOST FAITH IN ME, HAVE YOU? NOT SO SOON?
I BELIEVE YOU, CRESSIDA. I BELIEVE THAT IF THERE'S TRUTH IN ANYONE, IT'S IN YOU.

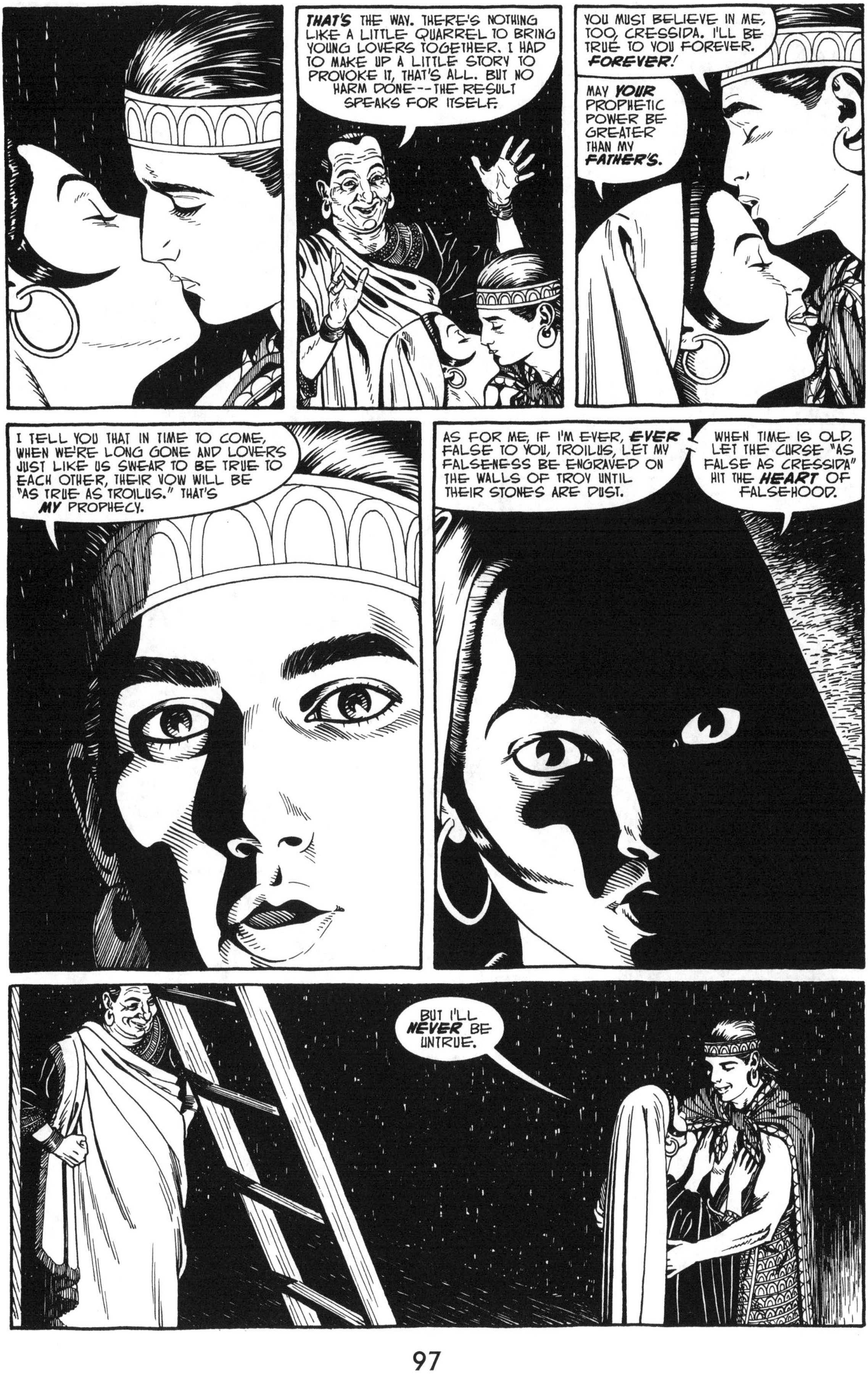
THAT'S THE WAY. THERE'S NOTHING LIKE A LITTLE QUARREL TO BRING YOUNG LOVERS TOGETHER. I HAD TO MAKE UP A LITTLE STORY TO PROVOKE IT, THAT'S ALL. BUT NO HARM DONE--THE RESULT SPEAKS FOR ITSELF.
YOU MUST BELIEVE IN ME, TOO, CRESSIDA. I'LL BE TRUE TO YOU FOREVER. FOREVER!
MAY YOUR PROPHETIC POWER BE GREATER THAN MY FATHER'S.
I TELL YOU THAT IN TIME TO COME, WHEN WE'RE LONG GONE AND LOVERS JUST LIKE US SWEAR TO BE TRUE TO EACH OTHER, THEIR VOW WILL BE "AS TRUE AS TROILUS." THAT'S MY PROPHECY.
AS FOR ME, IF I'M EVER, EVER FALSE TO YOU, TROILUS, LET MY FALSENESS BE ENGRAVED ON THE WALLS OF TROY UNTIL THEIR STONES ARE DUST.
WHEN TIME IS OLD, LET THE CURSE "AS FALSE AS CRESSIDA" HIT THE HEART OF FALSEHOOD.
BUT I'LL NEVER BE UNTRUE.

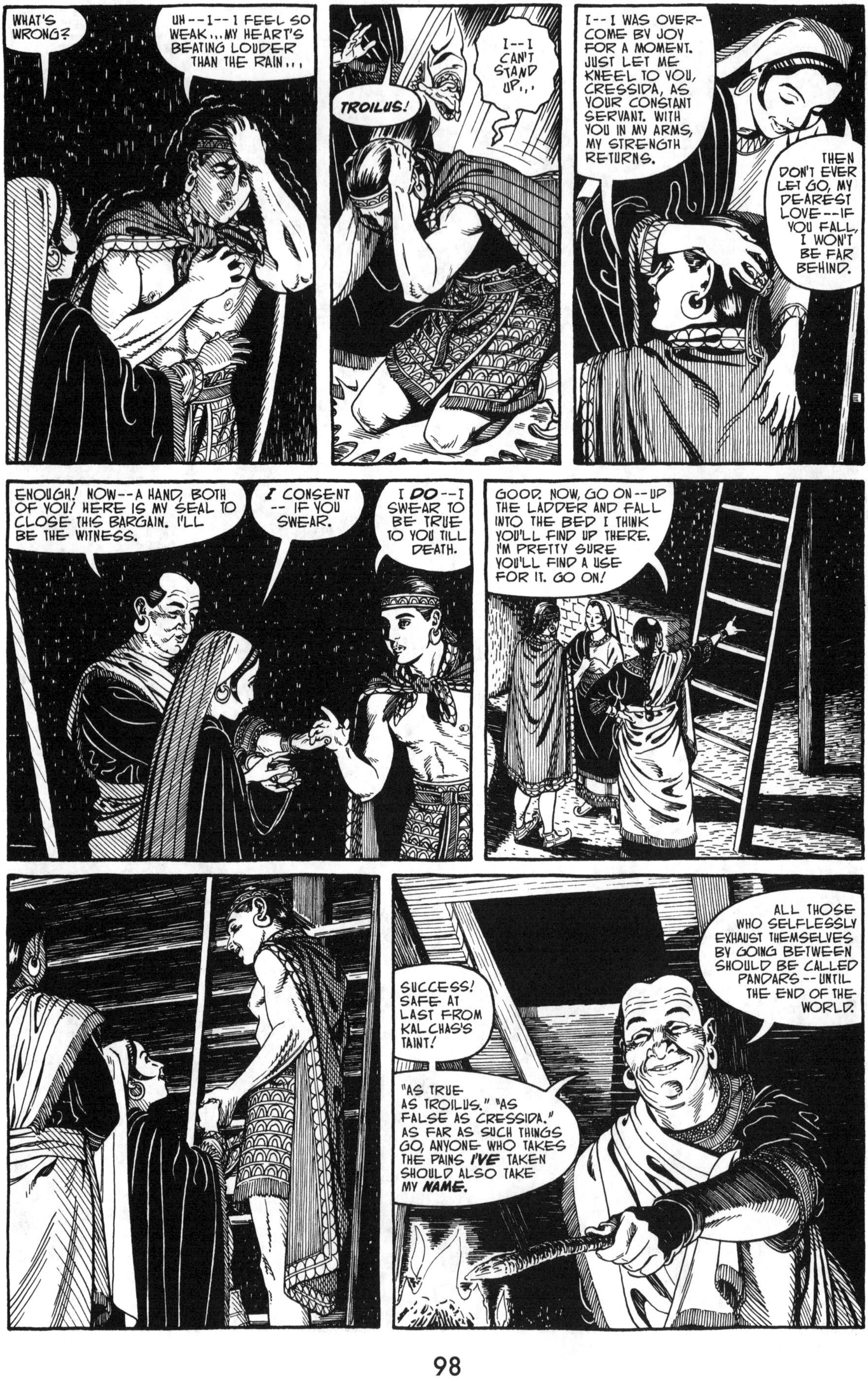
WHAT'S WRONG?
UH--I--I FEEL SO WEAK...MY HEART'S BEATING LOUDER THAN THE RAIN...
TROILUS!
I--I CAN'T STAND UP...
I--I WAS OVERCOME BY JOY FOR A MOMENT. JUST LET ME KNEEL TO YOU, CRESSIDA, AS YOUR CONSTANT SERVANT. WITH YOU IN MY ARMS, MY STRENGTH RETURNS.
THEN DON'T EVER LET GO, MY DEAREST LOVE--IF YOU FALL, I WON'T BE FAR BEHIND.
ENOUGH! NOW--A HAND, BOTH OF YOU! HERE IS MY SEAL TO CLOSE THIS BARGAIN. I'LL BE THE WITNESS.
I CONSENT -- IF YOU SWEAR.
I DO--I SWEAR TO BE TRUE TO YOU TILL DEATH.
GOOD. NOW, GO ON--UP THE LADDER AND FALL INTO THE BED I THINK YOU'LL FIND UP THERE. I'M PRETTY SURE YOU'LL FIND A USE FOR IT. GO ON!
SUCCESS! SAFE AT LAST FROM KALCHAS'S TAINT!
"AS TRUE AS TROILUS." "AS FALSE AS CRESSIDA." AS FAR AS SUCH THINGS GO, ANYONE WHO TAKES THE PAINS I'VE TAKEN SHOULD ALSO TAKE MY NAME.
ALL THOSE WHO SELFLESSLY EXHAUST THEMSELVES BY GOING BETWEEN SHOULD BE CALLED PANDARS--UNTIL THE END OF THE WORLD.

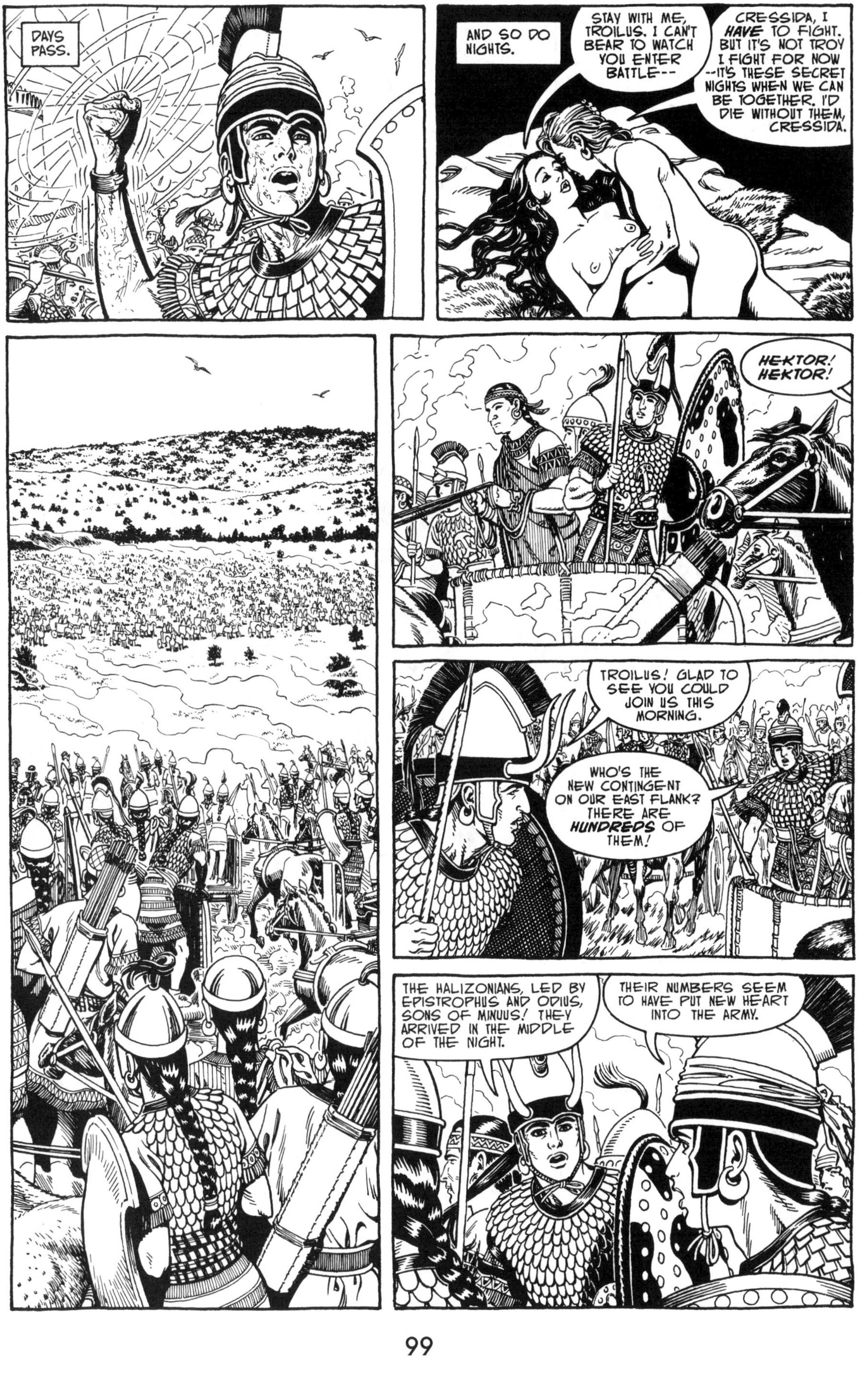
DAYS PASS.
AND SO DO NIGHTS.
STAY WITH ME, TROILUS. I CAN'T BEAR TO WATCH YOU ENTER BATTLE--
CRESSIDA, I **HAVE** TO FIGHT. BUT IT'S NOT TROY I FIGHT FOR NOW --IT'S THESE SECRET NIGHTS WHEN WE CAN BE TOGETHER. I'D DIE WITHOUT THEM, CRESSIDA.
HEKTOR! HEKTOR!
TROILUS! GLAD TO SEE YOU COULD JOIN US THIS MORNING.
WHO'S THE NEW CONTINGENT ON OUR EAST FLANK? THERE ARE **HUNDREDS** OF THEM!
THE HALIZONIANS, LED BY EPISTROPHUS AND ODIUS, SONS OF MINUUS! THEY ARRIVED IN THE MIDDLE OF THE NIGHT.
THEIR NUMBERS SEEM TO HAVE PUT NEW HEART INTO THE ARMY.

YES, THANK THE GODS! AFTER THE LAST FEW DAYS, WE NEEDED *SOMETHING* TO GIVE US HOPE. EPISTROPHUS HAS BROUGHT A REALLY UNUSUAL WARRIOR. THEY SAY HE'S A MIGHTY ARCHER AND HE RIDES--

SHIELDS UP!

TOK THOK
TOK
TUNK

AAAAAAAAAAAAAA!

TOK
THUK
TUNK

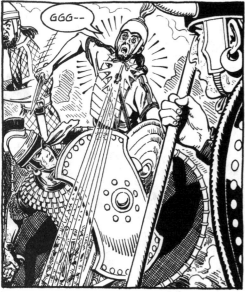

GGG--

100

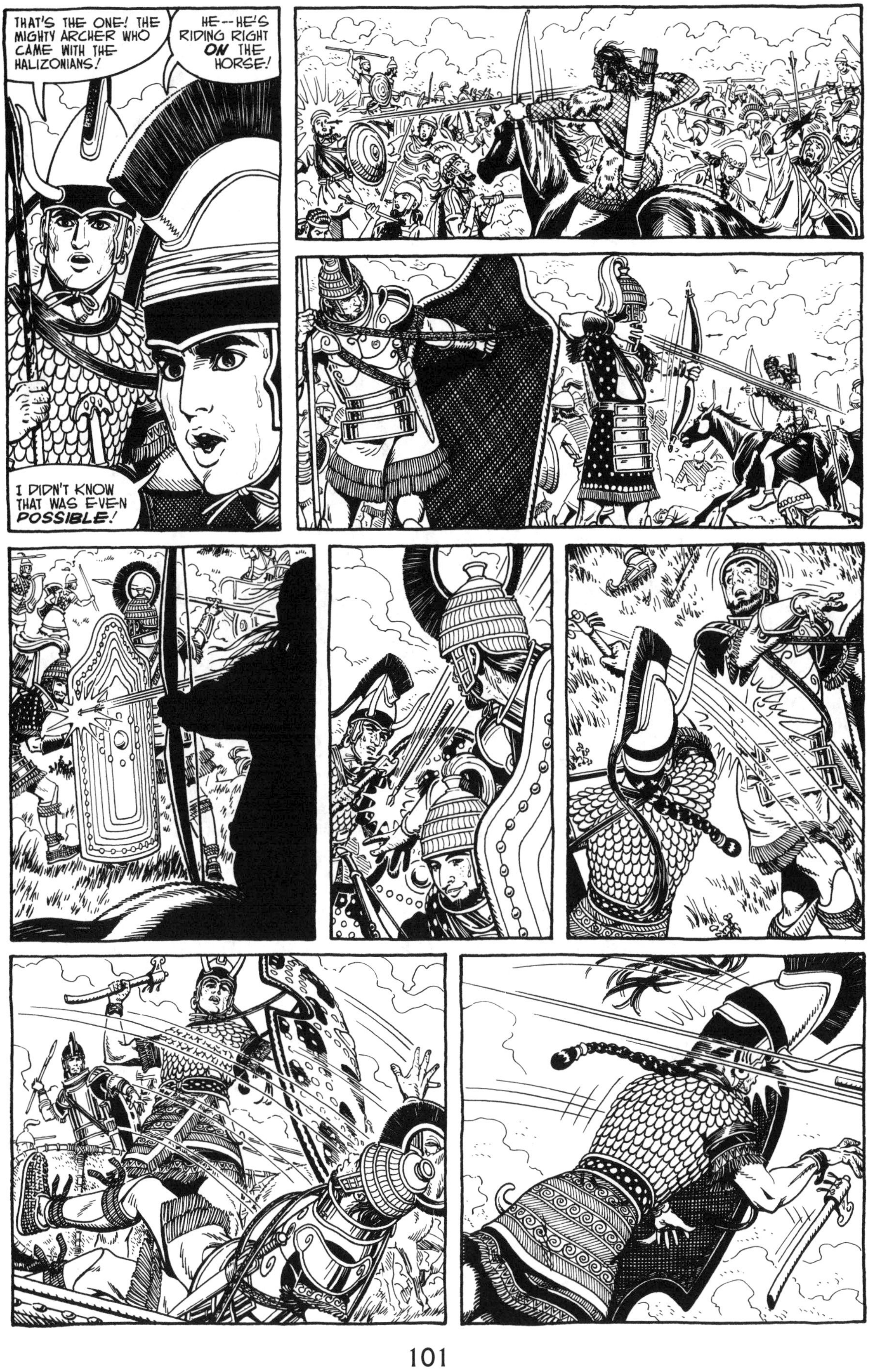
THAT'S THE ONE! THE MIGHTY ARCHER WHO CAME WITH THE HALIZONIANS!
HE--HE'S RIDING RIGHT ON THE HORSE!
I DIDN'T KNOW THAT WAS EVEN POSSIBLE!

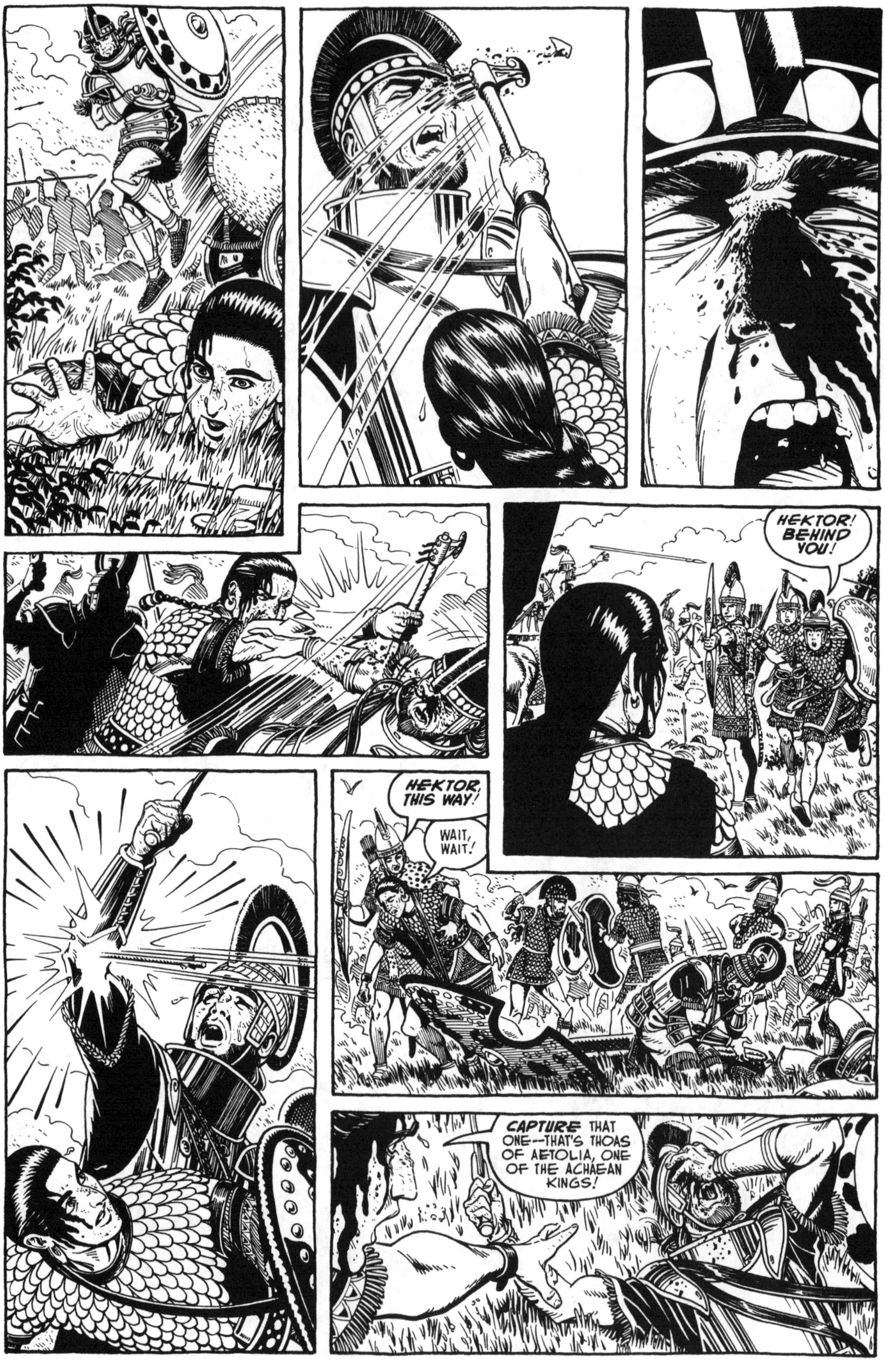
HEKTOR! BEHIND YOU!
HEKTOR, THIS WAY!
WAIT, WAIT!
CAPTURE THAT ONE--THAT'S THOAS OF AETOLIA, ONE OF THE ACHAEAN KINGS!

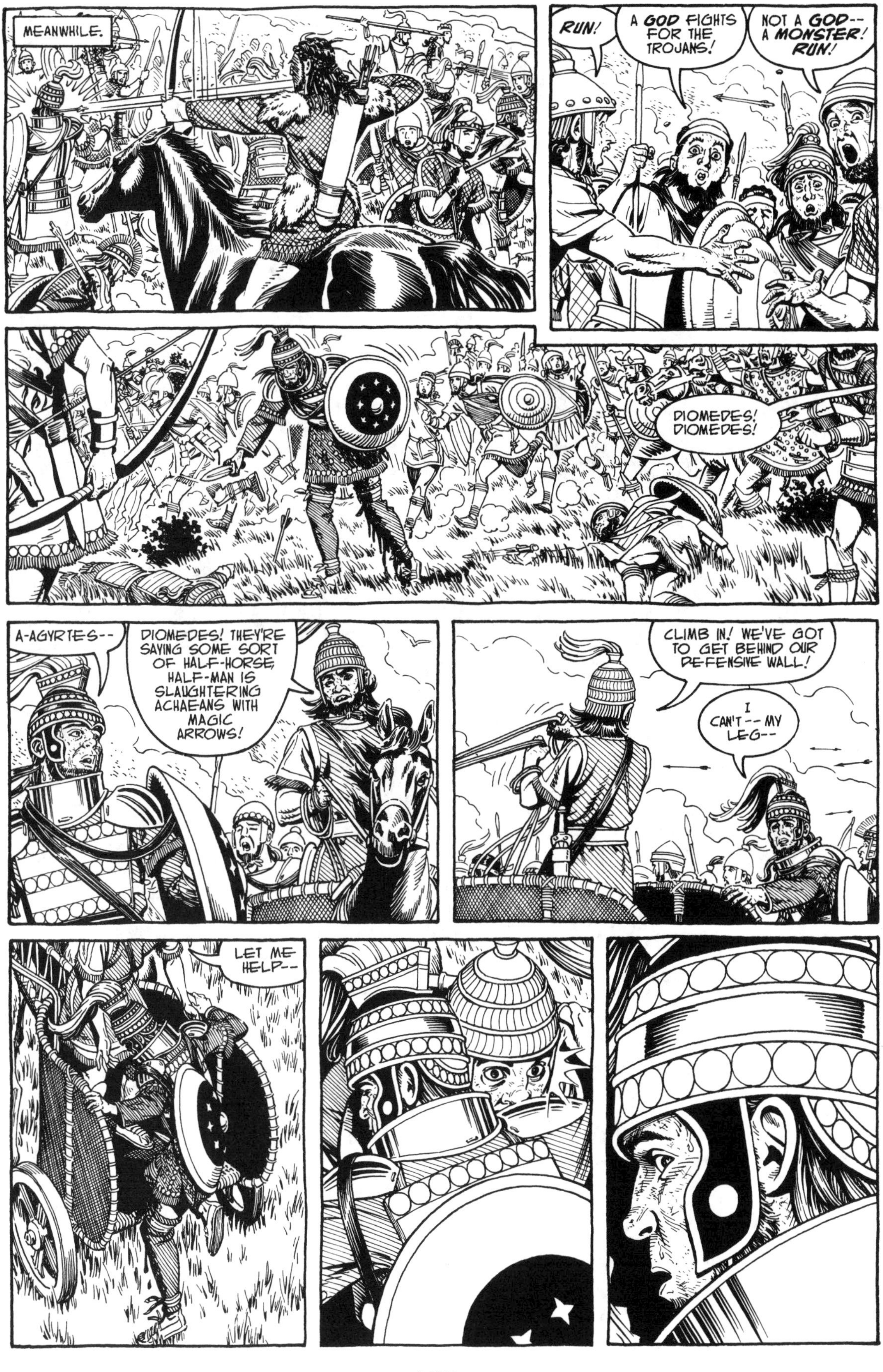
MEANWHILE.
RUN!
A GOD FIGHTS FOR THE TROJANS!
NOT A GOD-- A MONSTER! RUN!
DIOMEDES! DIOMEDES!
A-AGYRTES--
DIOMEDES! THEY'RE SAYING SOME SORT OF HALF-HORSE, HALF-MAN IS SLAUGHTERING ACHAEANS WITH MAGIC ARROWS!
CLIMB IN! WE'VE GOT TO GET BEHIND OUR DEFENSIVE WALL!
I CAN'T -- MY LEG--
LET ME HELP--

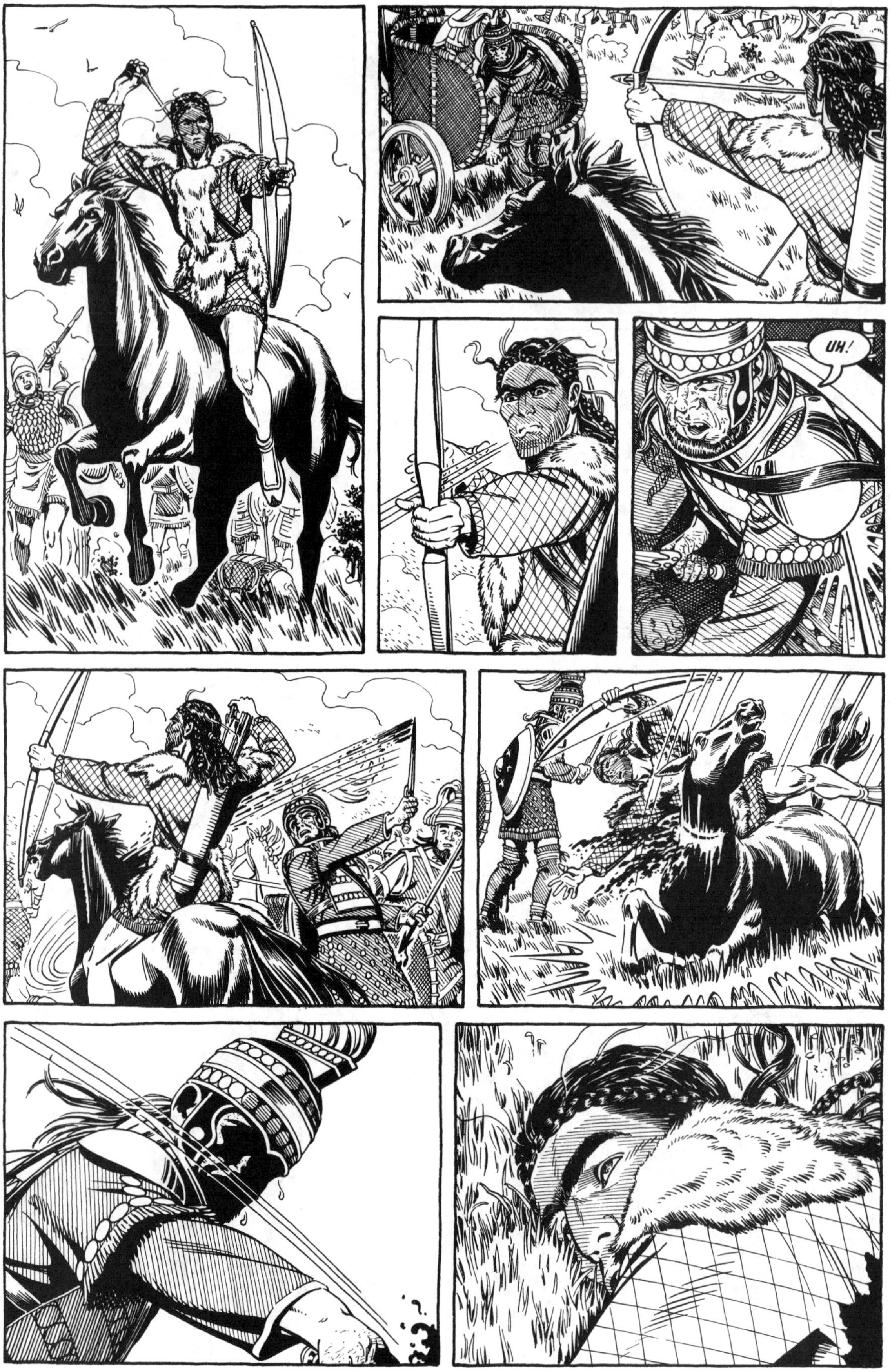
UH!

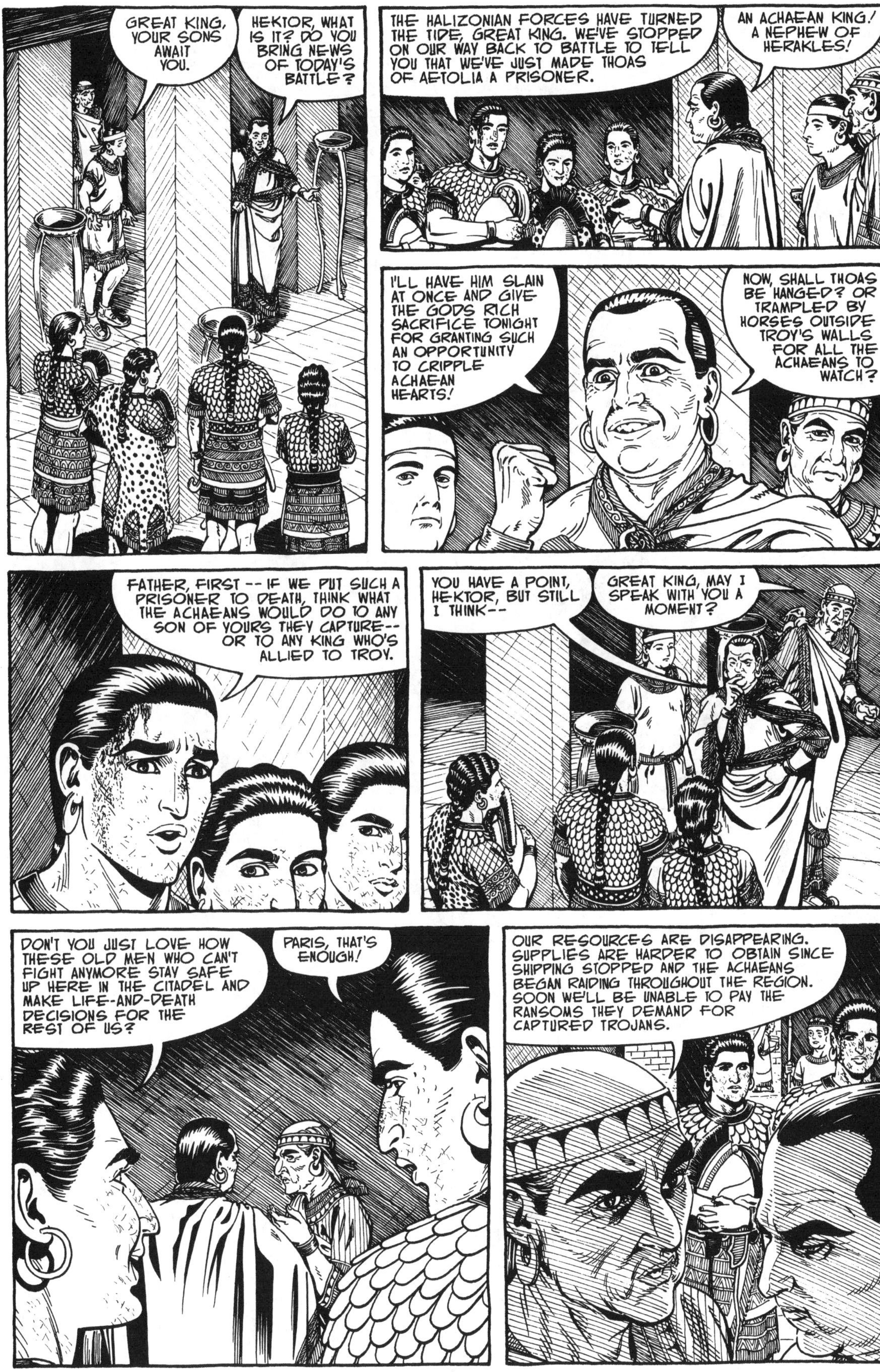
GREAT KING, YOUR SONS AWAIT YOU.
HEKTOR, WHAT IS IT? DO YOU BRING NEWS OF TODAY'S BATTLE?
THE HALIZONIAN FORCES HAVE TURNED THE TIDE, GREAT KING. WE'VE STOPPED ON OUR WAY BACK TO BATTLE TO TELL YOU THAT WE'VE JUST MADE THOAS OF AETOLIA A PRISONER.
AN ACHAEAN KING! A NEPHEW OF HERAKLES!
I'LL HAVE HIM SLAIN AT ONCE AND GIVE THE GODS RICH SACRIFICE TONIGHT FOR GRANTING SUCH AN OPPORTUNITY TO CRIPPLE ACHAEAN HEARTS!
NOW, SHALL THOAS BE HANGED? OR TRAMPLED BY HORSES OUTSIDE TROY'S WALLS FOR ALL THE ACHAEANS TO WATCH?
FATHER, FIRST -- IF WE PUT SUCH A PRISONER TO DEATH, THINK WHAT THE ACHAEANS WOULD DO TO ANY SON OF YOURS THEY CAPTURE-- OR TO ANY KING WHO'S ALLIED TO TROY.
YOU HAVE A POINT, HEKTOR, BUT STILL I THINK--
GREAT KING, MAY I SPEAK WITH YOU A MOMENT?
DON'T YOU JUST LOVE HOW THESE OLD MEN WHO CAN'T FIGHT ANYMORE STAY SAFE UP HERE IN THE CITADEL AND MAKE LIFE-AND-DEATH DECISIONS FOR THE REST OF US?
PARIS, THAT'S ENOUGH!
OUR RESOURCES ARE DISAPPEARING. SUPPLIES ARE HARDER TO OBTAIN SINCE SHIPPING STOPPED AND THE ACHAEANS BEGAN RAIDING THROUGHOUT THE REGION. SOON WE'LL BE UNABLE TO PAY THE RANSOMS THEY DEMAND FOR CAPTURED TROJANS.

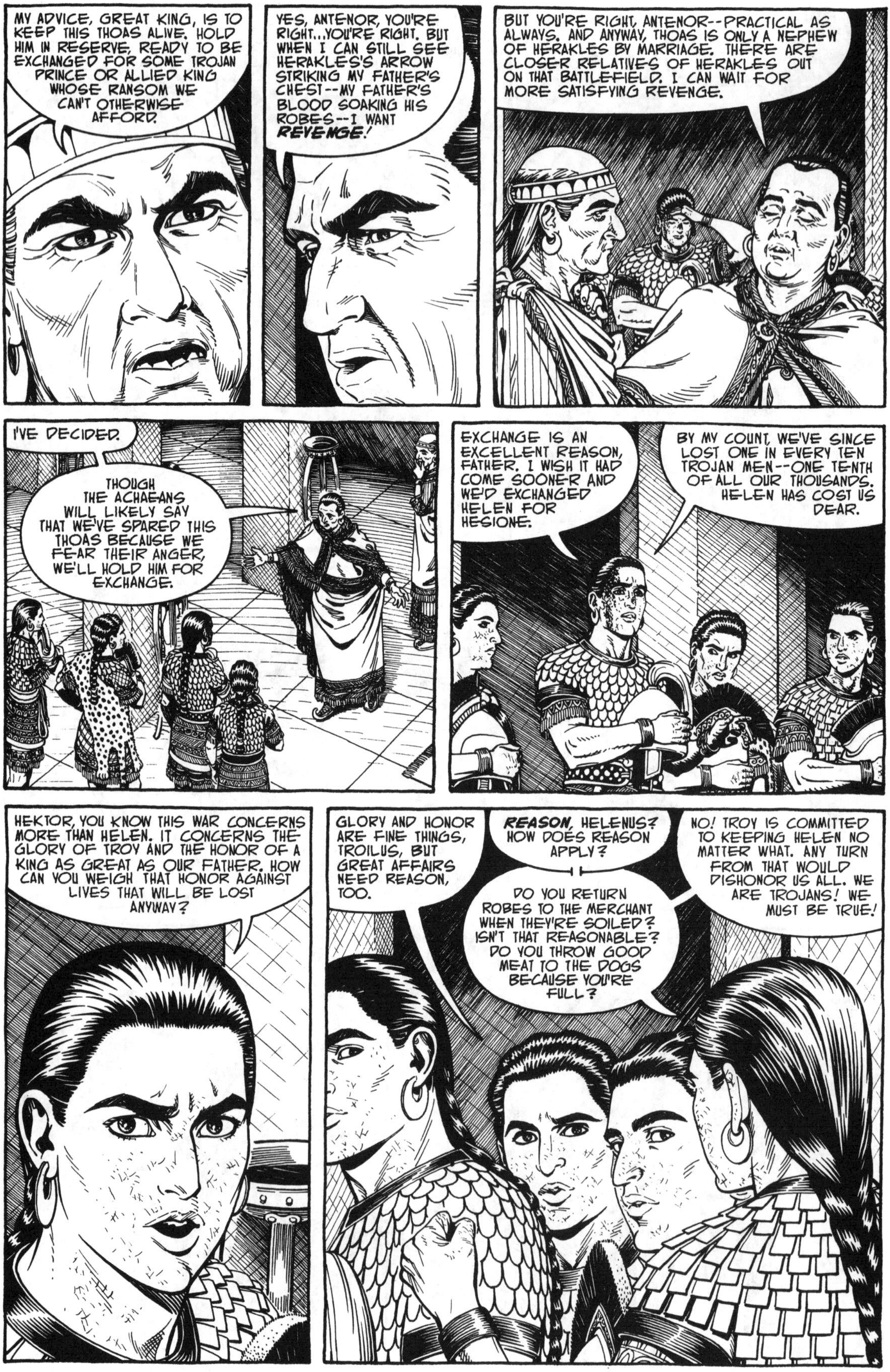
MY ADVICE, GREAT KING, IS TO KEEP THIS THOAS ALIVE. HOLD HIM IN RESERVE, READY TO BE EXCHANGED FOR SOME TROJAN PRINCE OR ALLIED KING WHOSE RANSOM WE CAN'T OTHERWISE AFFORD.
YES, ANTENOR, YOU'RE RIGHT... YOU'RE RIGHT. BUT WHEN I CAN STILL SEE HERAKLES'S ARROW STRIKING MY FATHER'S CHEST--MY FATHER'S BLOOD SOAKING HIS ROBES--I WANT REVENGE!
BUT YOU'RE RIGHT, ANTENOR--PRACTICAL AS ALWAYS. AND ANYWAY, THOAS IS ONLY A NEPHEW OF HERAKLES BY MARRIAGE. THERE ARE CLOSER RELATIVES OF HERAKLES OUT ON THAT BATTLEFIELD. I CAN WAIT FOR MORE SATISFYING REVENGE.
I'VE DECIDED.
THOUGH THE ACHAEANS WILL LIKELY SAY THAT WE'VE SPARED THIS THOAS BECAUSE WE FEAR THEIR ANGER, WE'LL HOLD HIM FOR EXCHANGE.
EXCHANGE IS AN EXCELLENT REASON, FATHER. I WISH IT HAD COME SOONER AND WE'D EXCHANGED HELEN FOR HESIONE.
BY MY COUNT, WE'VE SINCE LOST ONE IN EVERY TEN TROJAN MEN--ONE TENTH OF ALL OUR THOUSANDS. HELEN HAS COST US DEAR.
HEKTOR, YOU KNOW THIS WAR CONCERNS MORE THAN HELEN. IT CONCERNS THE GLORY OF TROY AND THE HONOR OF A KING AS GREAT AS OUR FATHER. HOW CAN YOU WEIGH THAT HONOR AGAINST LIVES THAT WILL BE LOST ANYWAY?
GLORY AND HONOR ARE FINE THINGS, TROILUS, BUT GREAT AFFAIRS NEED REASON, TOO.
REASON, HELENUS? HOW DOES REASON APPLY?
DO YOU RETURN ROBES TO THE MERCHANT WHEN THEY'RE SOILED? ISN'T THAT REASONABLE? DO YOU THROW GOOD MEAT TO THE DOGS BECAUSE YOU'RE FULL?
NO! TROY IS COMMITTED TO KEEPING HELEN NO MATTER WHAT. ANY TURN FROM THAT WOULD DISHONOR US ALL. WE ARE TROJANS! WE MUST BE TRUE!

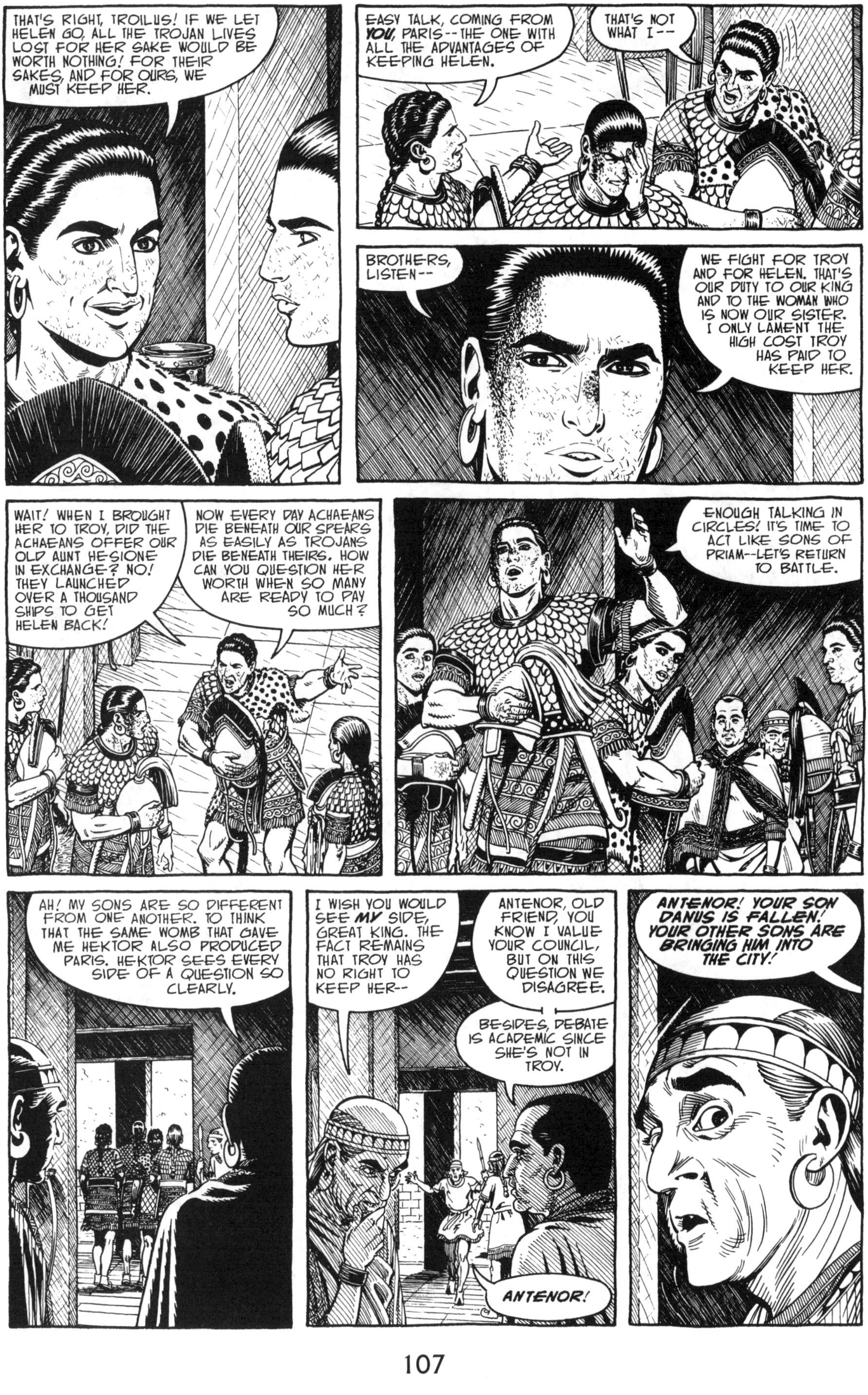
THAT'S RIGHT, TROILUS! IF WE LET HELEN GO, ALL THE TROJAN LIVES LOST FOR HER SAKE WOULD BE WORTH NOTHING! FOR THEIR SAKES, AND FOR OURS, WE MUST KEEP HER.
EASY TALK, COMING FROM *YOU*, PARIS--THE ONE WITH ALL THE ADVANTAGES OF KEEPING HELEN.
THAT'S NOT WHAT I--
BROTHERS, LISTEN--
WE FIGHT FOR TROY AND FOR HELEN. THAT'S OUR DUTY TO OUR KING AND TO THE WOMAN WHO IS NOW OUR SISTER. I ONLY LAMENT THE HIGH COST TROY HAS PAID TO KEEP HER.
WAIT! WHEN I BROUGHT HER TO TROY, DID THE ACHAEANS OFFER OUR OLD AUNT HESIONE IN EXCHANGE? NO! THEY LAUNCHED OVER A THOUSAND SHIPS TO GET HELEN BACK!
NOW EVERY DAY ACHAEANS DIE BENEATH OUR SPEARS AS EASILY AS TROJANS DIE BENEATH THEIRS. HOW CAN YOU QUESTION HER WORTH WHEN SO MANY ARE READY TO PAY SO MUCH?
ENOUGH TALKING IN CIRCLES! IT'S TIME TO ACT LIKE SONS OF PRIAM--LET'S RETURN TO BATTLE.
AH! MY SONS ARE SO DIFFERENT FROM ONE ANOTHER. TO THINK THAT THE SAME WOMB THAT GAVE ME HEKTOR ALSO PRODUCED PARIS. HEKTOR SEES EVERY SIDE OF A QUESTION SO CLEARLY.
I WISH YOU WOULD SEE *MY* SIDE, GREAT KING. THE FACT REMAINS THAT TROY HAS NO RIGHT TO KEEP HER--
ANTENOR, OLD FRIEND, YOU KNOW I VALUE YOUR COUNCIL, BUT ON THIS QUESTION WE DISAGREE.
BESIDES, DEBATE IS ACADEMIC SINCE SHE'S NOT IN TROY.
ANTENOR!
ANTENOR! YOUR SON DANUS IS FALLEN! YOUR OTHER SONS ARE BRINGING HIM INTO THE CITY!

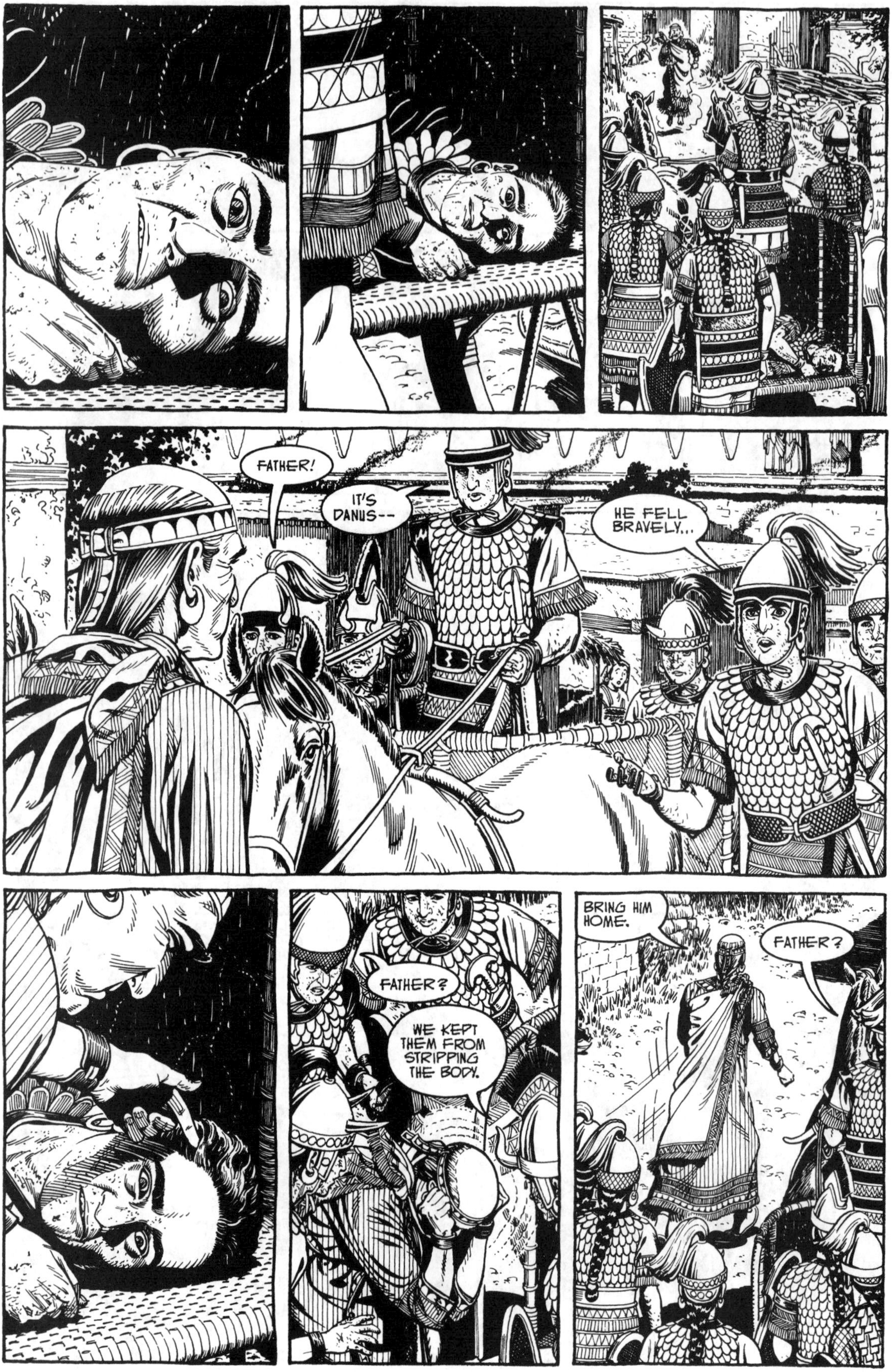
FATHER!
IT'S DANUS--
HE FELL BRAVELY...
FATHER?
WE KEPT THEM FROM STRIPPING THE BODY.
BRING HIM HOME.
FATHER?

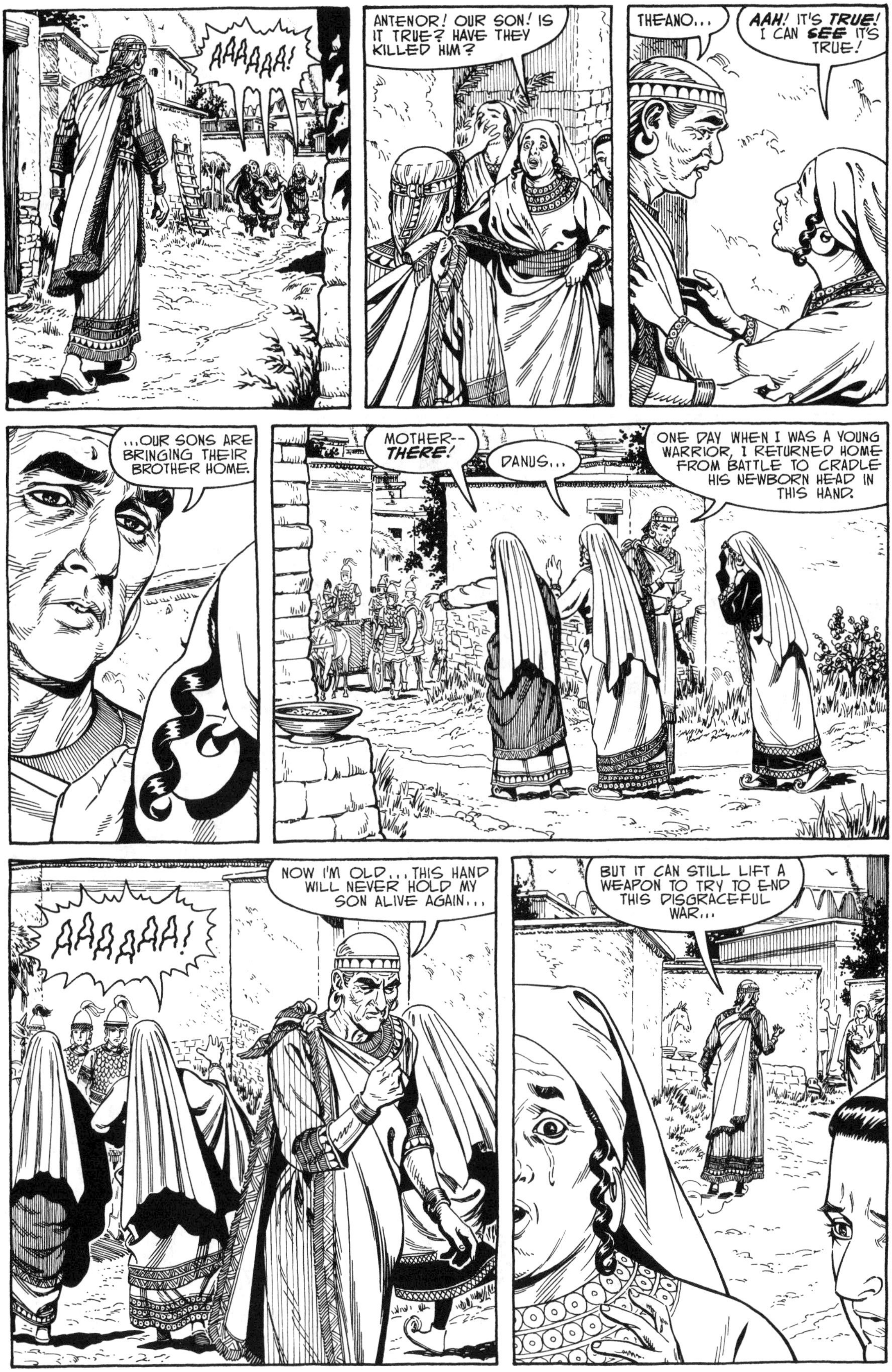
AAAAAA!
ANTENOR! OUR SON! IS IT TRUE? HAVE THEY KILLED HIM?
THEANO...
AAH! IT'S TRUE! I CAN SEE IT'S TRUE!
...OUR SONS ARE BRINGING THEIR BROTHER HOME.
MOTHER-- THERE!
DANUS...
ONE DAY WHEN I WAS A YOUNG WARRIOR, I RETURNED HOME FROM BATTLE TO CRADLE HIS NEWBORN HEAD IN THIS HAND.
AAAAAA!
NOW I'M OLD... THIS HAND WILL NEVER HOLD MY SON ALIVE AGAIN...
BUT IT CAN STILL LIFT A WEAPON TO TRY TO END THIS DISGRACEFUL WAR...

...AND THAT'S EXACTLY WHAT I MEAN TO DO.

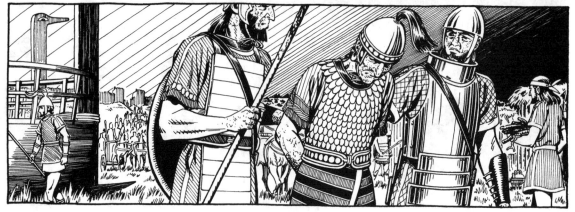

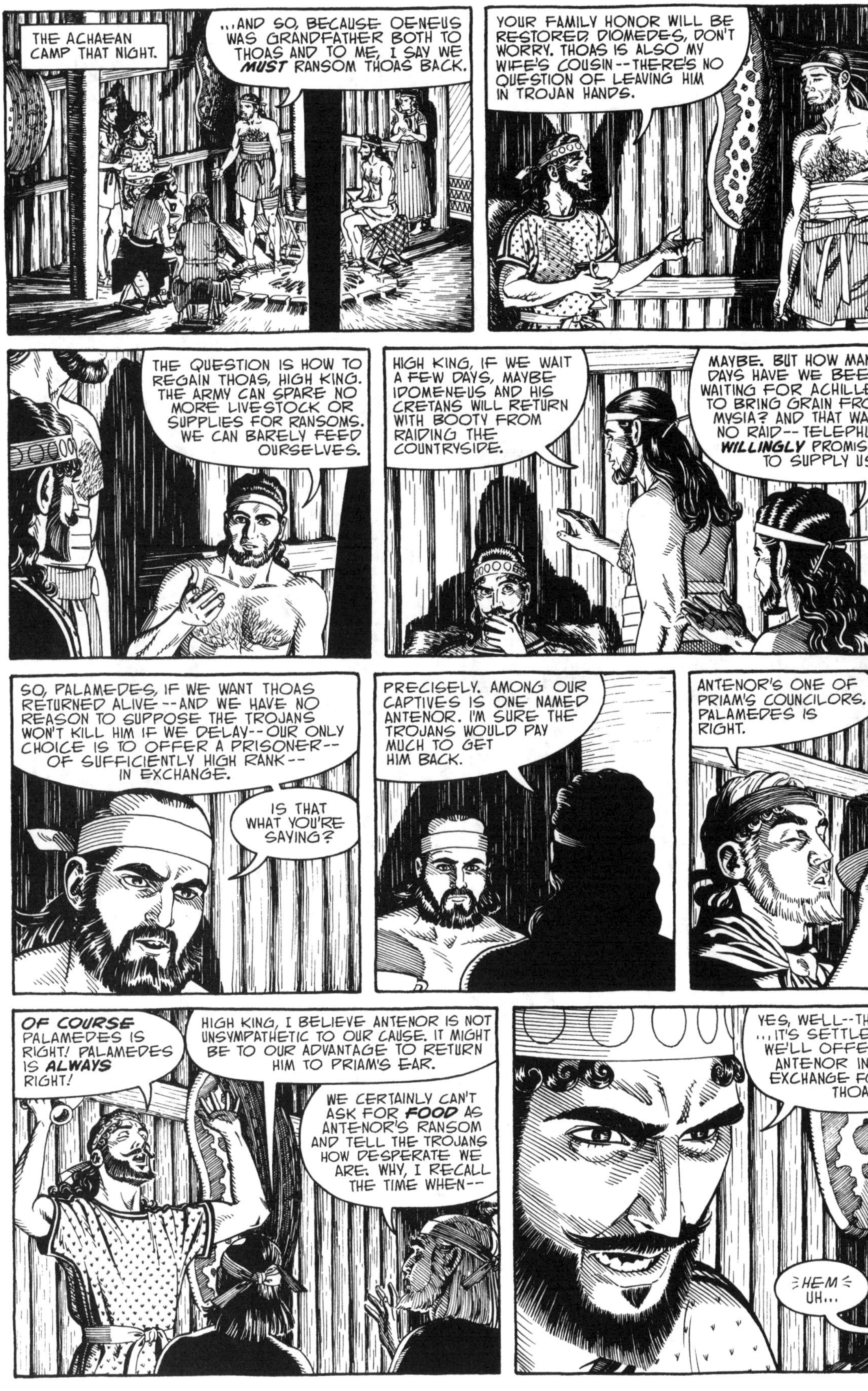
THE ACHAEAN CAMP THAT NIGHT.
...AND SO, BECAUSE OENEUS WAS GRANDFATHER BOTH TO THOAS AND TO ME, I SAY WE MUST RANSOM THOAS BACK.
YOUR FAMILY HONOR WILL BE RESTORED DIOMEDES, DON'T WORRY. THOAS IS ALSO MY WIFE'S COUSIN--THERE'S NO QUESTION OF LEAVING HIM IN TROJAN HANDS.
THE QUESTION IS HOW TO REGAIN THOAS, HIGH KING. THE ARMY CAN SPARE NO MORE LIVESTOCK OR SUPPLIES FOR RANSOMS. WE CAN BARELY FEED OURSELVES.
HIGH KING, IF WE WAIT A FEW DAYS, MAYBE IDOMENEUS AND HIS CRETANS WILL RETURN WITH BOOTY FROM RAIDING THE COUNTRYSIDE.
MAYBE. BUT HOW MANY DAYS HAVE WE BEEN WAITING FOR ACHILLES TO BRING GRAIN FROM MYSIA? AND THAT WAS NO RAID--TELEPHUS WILLINGLY PROMISED TO SUPPLY US.
SO, PALAMEDES, IF WE WANT THOAS RETURNED ALIVE--AND WE HAVE NO REASON TO SUPPOSE THE TROJANS WON'T KILL HIM IF WE DELAY--OUR ONLY CHOICE IS TO OFFER A PRISONER--OF SUFFICIENTLY HIGH RANK--IN EXCHANGE.
IS THAT WHAT YOU'RE SAYING?
PRECISELY. AMONG OUR CAPTIVES IS ONE NAMED ANTENOR. I'M SURE THE TROJANS WOULD PAY MUCH TO GET HIM BACK.
ANTENOR'S ONE OF PRIAM'S COUNCILORS. PALAMEDES IS RIGHT.
OF COURSE PALAMEDES IS RIGHT! PALAMEDES IS ALWAYS RIGHT!
HIGH KING, I BELIEVE ANTENOR IS NOT UNSYMPATHETIC TO OUR CAUSE. IT MIGHT BE TO OUR ADVANTAGE TO RETURN HIM TO PRIAM'S EAR.
WE CERTAINLY CAN'T ASK FOR FOOD AS ANTENOR'S RANSOM AND TELL THE TROJANS HOW DESPERATE WE ARE. WHY, I RECALL THE TIME WHEN--
YES, WELL--THEN ...IT'S SETTLED. WE'LL OFFER ANTENOR IN EXCHANGE FOR THOAS.
HEM
UH...

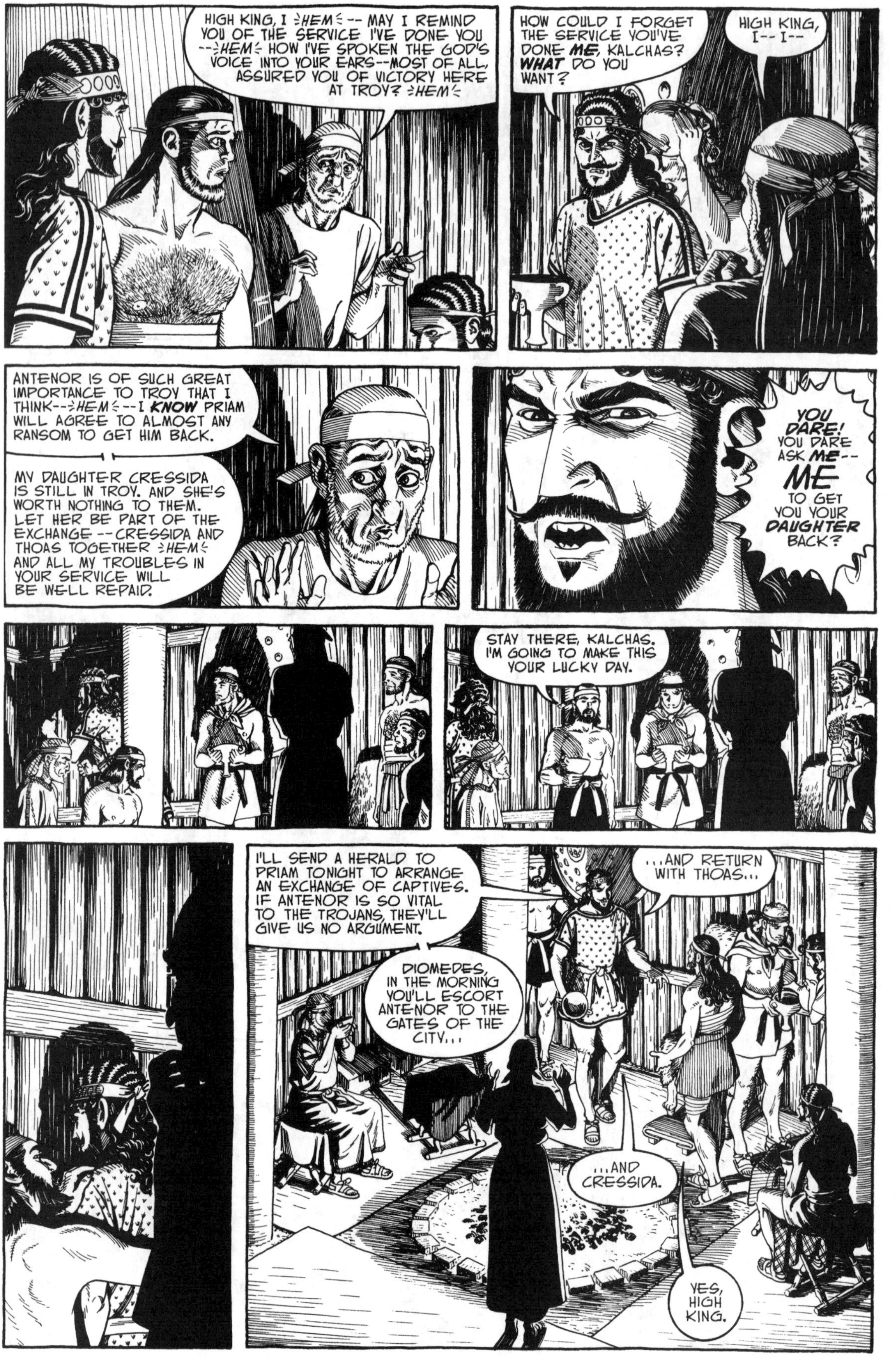
HIGH KING, I ⋛HEM⋚ -- MAY I REMIND YOU OF THE SERVICE I'VE DONE YOU --⋛HEM⋚ HOW I'VE SPOKEN THE GOD'S VOICE INTO YOUR EARS--MOST OF ALL, ASSURED YOU OF VICTORY HERE AT TROY? ⋛HEM⋚
HOW COULD I FORGET THE SERVICE YOU'VE DONE **ME**, KALCHAS? **WHAT** DO YOU WANT?
HIGH KING, I-- I--
ANTENOR IS OF SUCH GREAT IMPORTANCE TO TROY THAT I THINK--⋛HEM⋚--I **KNOW** PRIAM WILL AGREE TO ALMOST ANY RANSOM TO GET HIM BACK.
MY DAUGHTER CRESSIDA IS STILL IN TROY. AND SHE'S WORTH NOTHING TO THEM. LET HER BE PART OF THE EXCHANGE --CRESSIDA AND THOAS TOGETHER ⋛HEM⋚ AND ALL MY TROUBLES IN YOUR SERVICE WILL BE WELL REPAID.
YOU DARE! YOU DARE ASK **ME**-- **ME** TO GET YOU YOUR **DAUGHTER** BACK?
STAY THERE, KALCHAS. I'M GOING TO MAKE THIS YOUR LUCKY DAY.
I'LL SEND A HERALD TO PRIAM TONIGHT TO ARRANGE AN EXCHANGE OF CAPTIVES. IF ANTENOR IS SO VITAL TO THE TROJANS, THEY'LL GIVE US NO ARGUMENT.
DIOMEDES, IN THE MORNING YOU'LL ESCORT ANTENOR TO THE GATES OF THE CITY...
...AND RETURN WITH THOAS...
...AND CRESSIDA.
YES, HIGH KING.

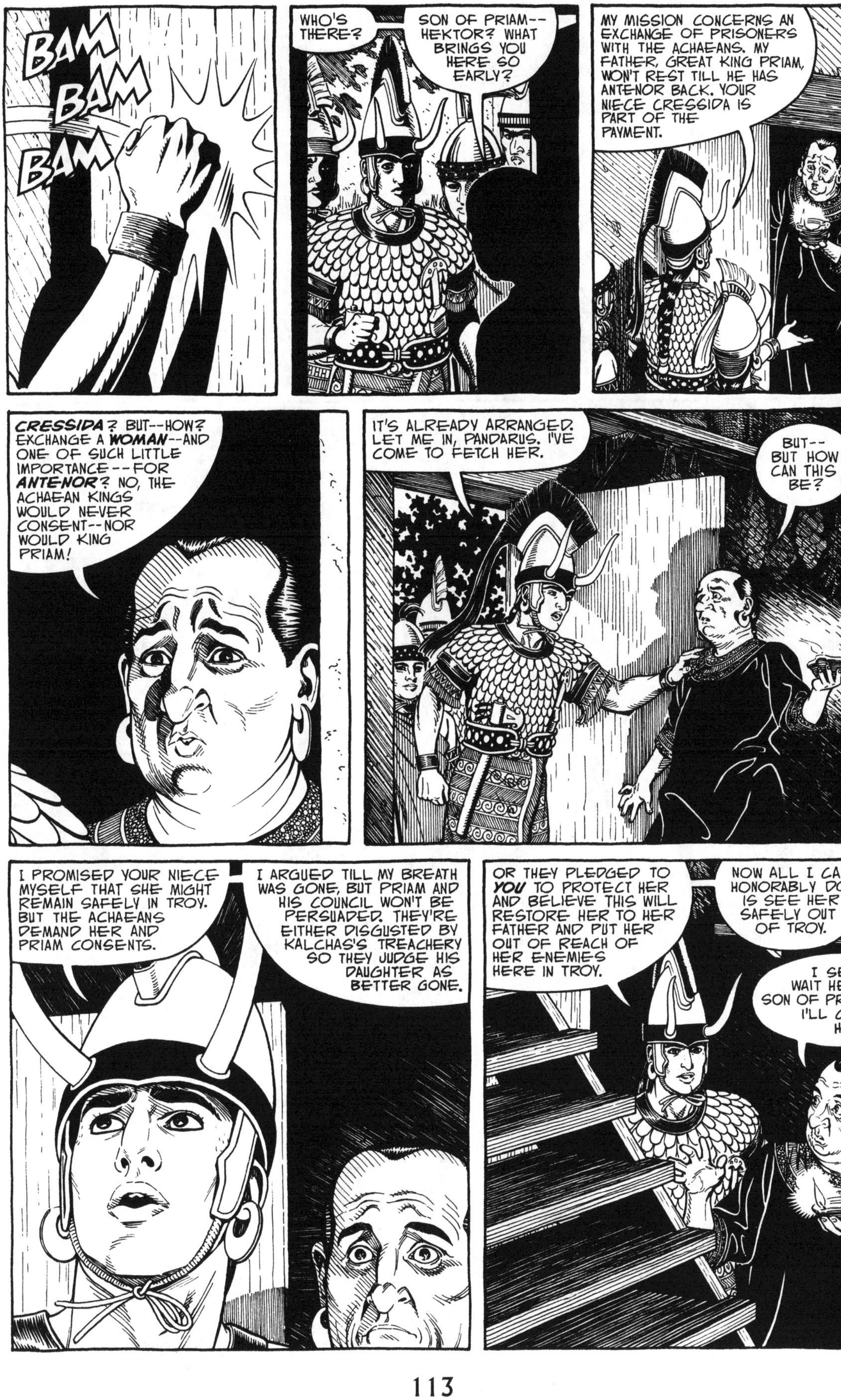
BAM BAM BAM
WHO'S THERE?
SON OF PRIAM--HEKTOR? WHAT BRINGS YOU HERE SO EARLY?
MY MISSION CONCERNS AN EXCHANGE OF PRISONERS WITH THE ACHAEANS. MY FATHER, GREAT KING PRIAM, WON'T REST TILL HE HAS ANTENOR BACK. YOUR NIECE CRESSIDA IS PART OF THE PAYMENT.
CRESSIDA? BUT--HOW? EXCHANGE A WOMAN--AND ONE OF SUCH LITTLE IMPORTANCE--FOR ANTENOR? NO, THE ACHAEAN KINGS WOULD NEVER CONSENT--NOR WOULD KING PRIAM!
IT'S ALREADY ARRANGED. LET ME IN, PANDARUS. I'VE COME TO FETCH HER.
BUT--BUT HOW CAN THIS BE?
I PROMISED YOUR NIECE MYSELF THAT SHE MIGHT REMAIN SAFELY IN TROY. BUT THE ACHAEANS DEMAND HER AND PRIAM CONSENTS.
I ARGUED TILL MY BREATH WAS GONE, BUT PRIAM AND HIS COUNCIL WON'T BE PERSUADED. THEY'RE EITHER DISGUSTED BY KALCHAS'S TREACHERY SO THEY JUDGE HIS DAUGHTER AS BETTER GONE.
OR THEY PLEDGED TO YOU TO PROTECT HER AND BELIEVE THIS WILL RESTORE HER TO HER FATHER AND PUT HER OUT OF REACH OF HER ENEMIES HERE IN TROY.
NOW ALL I CAN HONORABLY DO IS SEE HER SAFELY OUT OF TROY.
I SEE.. WAIT HERE, SON OF PRIAM. I'LL CALL HER.

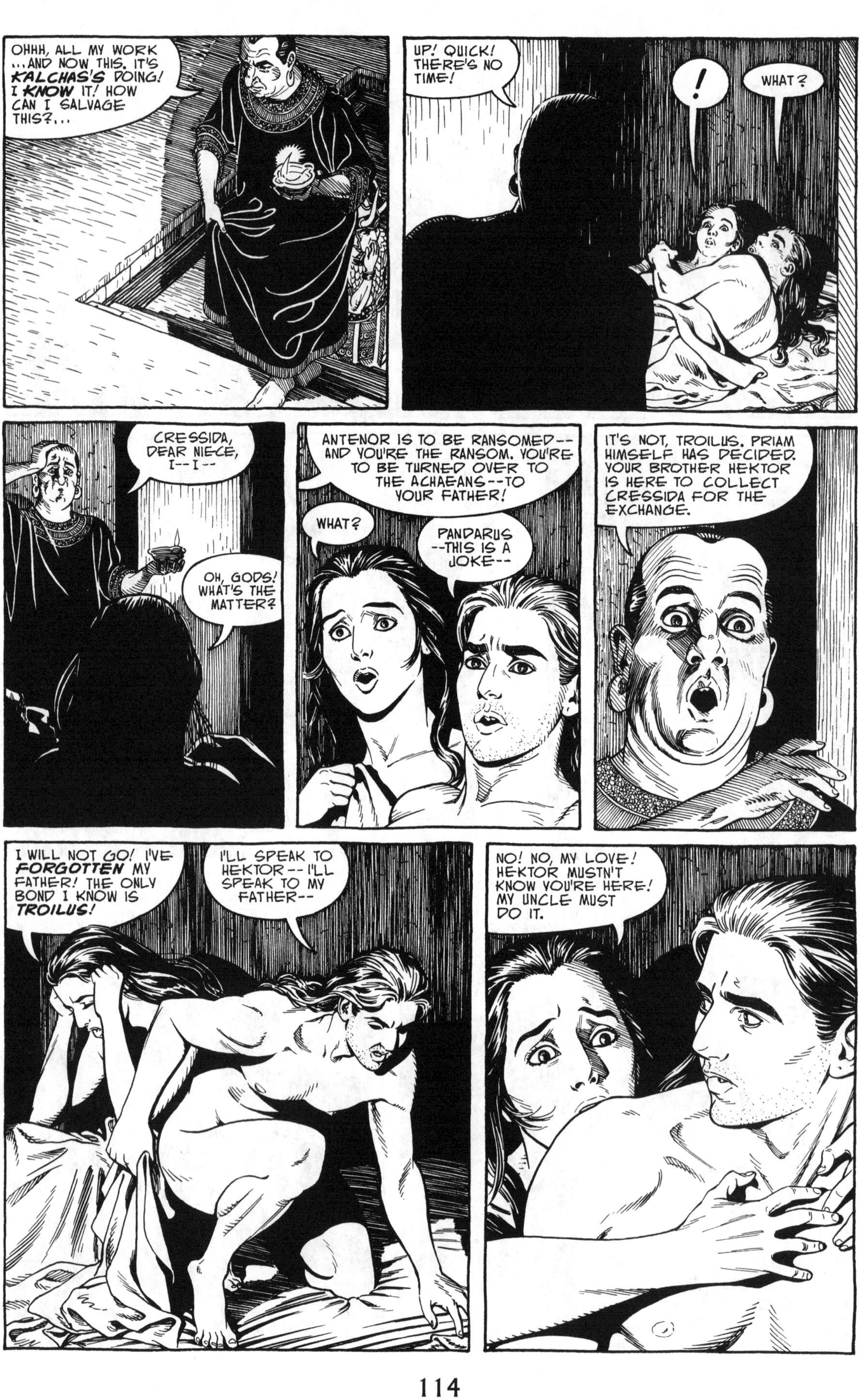
OHHH, ALL MY WORK ...AND NOW THIS. IT'S KALCHAS'S DOING! I KNOW IT! HOW CAN I SALVAGE THIS?...
UP! QUICK! THERE'S NO TIME!
!
WHAT?
CRESSIDA, DEAR NIECE, I-- I--
OH, GODS! WHAT'S THE MATTER?
ANTENOR IS TO BE RANSOMED-- AND YOU'RE THE RANSOM. YOU'RE TO BE TURNED OVER TO THE ACHAEANS--TO YOUR FATHER!
WHAT?
PANDARUS --THIS IS A JOKE--
IT'S NOT, TROILUS. PRIAM HIMSELF HAS DECIDED. YOUR BROTHER HEKTOR IS HERE TO COLLECT CRESSIDA FOR THE EXCHANGE.
I WILL NOT GO! I'VE FORGOTTEN MY FATHER! THE ONLY BOND I KNOW IS TROILUS!
I'LL SPEAK TO HEKTOR-- I'LL SPEAK TO MY FATHER--
NO! NO, MY LOVE! HEKTOR MUSTN'T KNOW YOU'RE HERE! MY UNCLE MUST DO IT.

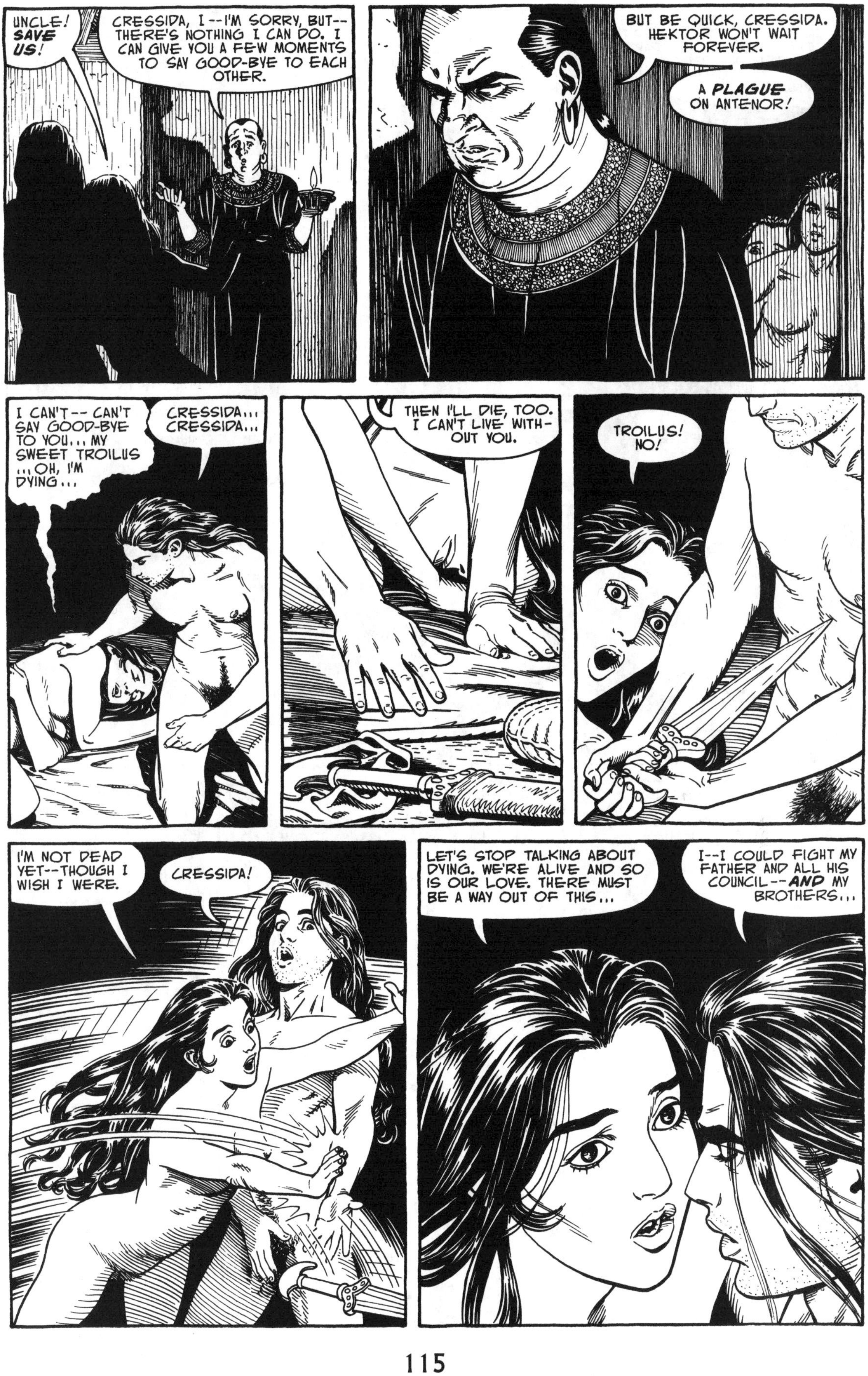
UNCLE! **SAVE US!**
CRESSIDA, I--I'M SORRY, BUT--THERE'S NOTHING I CAN DO. I CAN GIVE YOU A FEW MOMENTS TO SAY GOOD-BYE TO EACH OTHER.
BUT BE QUICK, CRESSIDA. HEKTOR WON'T WAIT FOREVER.
A **PLAGUE** ON ANTENOR!
I CAN'T-- CAN'T SAY GOOD-BYE TO YOU... MY SWEET TROILUS ...OH, I'M DYING...
CRESSIDA... CRESSIDA...
THEN I'LL DIE, TOO. I CAN'T LIVE WITHOUT YOU.
TROILUS! NO!
I'M NOT DEAD YET--THOUGH I WISH I WERE.
CRESSIDA!
LET'S STOP TALKING ABOUT DYING. WE'RE ALIVE AND SO IS OUR LOVE. THERE MUST BE A WAY OUT OF THIS...
I--I COULD FIGHT MY FATHER AND ALL HIS COUNCIL--**AND** MY BROTHERS...

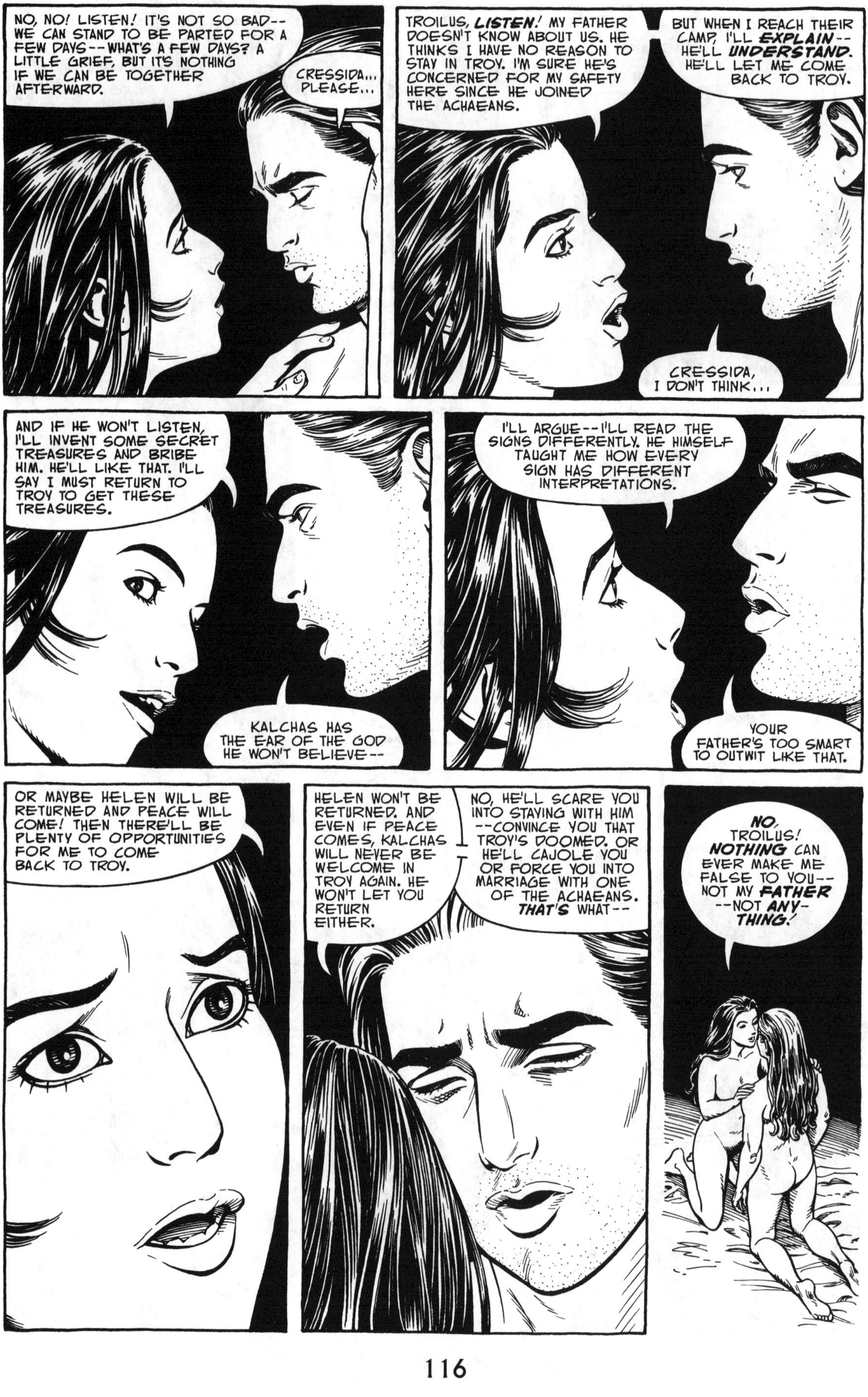
NO, NO! LISTEN! IT'S NOT SO BAD-- WE CAN STAND TO BE PARTED FOR A FEW DAYS--WHAT'S A FEW DAYS? A LITTLE GRIEF, BUT IT'S NOTHING IF WE CAN BE TOGETHER AFTERWARD.
CRESSIDA... PLEASE...
TROILUS, LISTEN! MY FATHER DOESN'T KNOW ABOUT US. HE THINKS I HAVE NO REASON TO STAY IN TROY. I'M SURE HE'S CONCERNED FOR MY SAFETY HERE SINCE HE JOINED THE ACHAEANS.
BUT WHEN I REACH THEIR CAMP, I'LL EXPLAIN-- HE'LL UNDERSTAND. HE'LL LET ME COME BACK TO TROY.
CRESSIDA, I DON'T THINK...
AND IF HE WON'T LISTEN, I'LL INVENT SOME SECRET TREASURES AND BRIBE HIM. HE'LL LIKE THAT. I'LL SAY I MUST RETURN TO TROY TO GET THESE TREASURES.
KALCHAS HAS THE EAR OF THE GOD HE WON'T BELIEVE--
I'LL ARGUE--I'LL READ THE SIGNS DIFFERENTLY. HE HIMSELF TAUGHT ME HOW EVERY SIGN HAS DIFFERENT INTERPRETATIONS.
YOUR FATHER'S TOO SMART TO OUTWIT LIKE THAT.
OR MAYBE HELEN WILL BE RETURNED AND PEACE WILL COME! THEN THERE'LL BE PLENTY OF OPPORTUNITIES FOR ME TO COME BACK TO TROY.
HELEN WON'T BE RETURNED. AND EVEN IF PEACE COMES, KALCHAS WILL NEVER BE WELCOME IN TROY AGAIN. HE WON'T LET YOU RETURN EITHER.
NO, HE'LL SCARE YOU INTO STAYING WITH HIM --CONVINCE YOU THAT TROY'S DOOMED. OR HE'LL CAJOLE YOU OR FORCE YOU INTO MARRIAGE WITH ONE OF THE ACHAEANS. THAT'S WHAT--
NO, TROILUS! NOTHING CAN EVER MAKE ME FALSE TO YOU-- NOT MY FATHER --NOT ANY-THING!

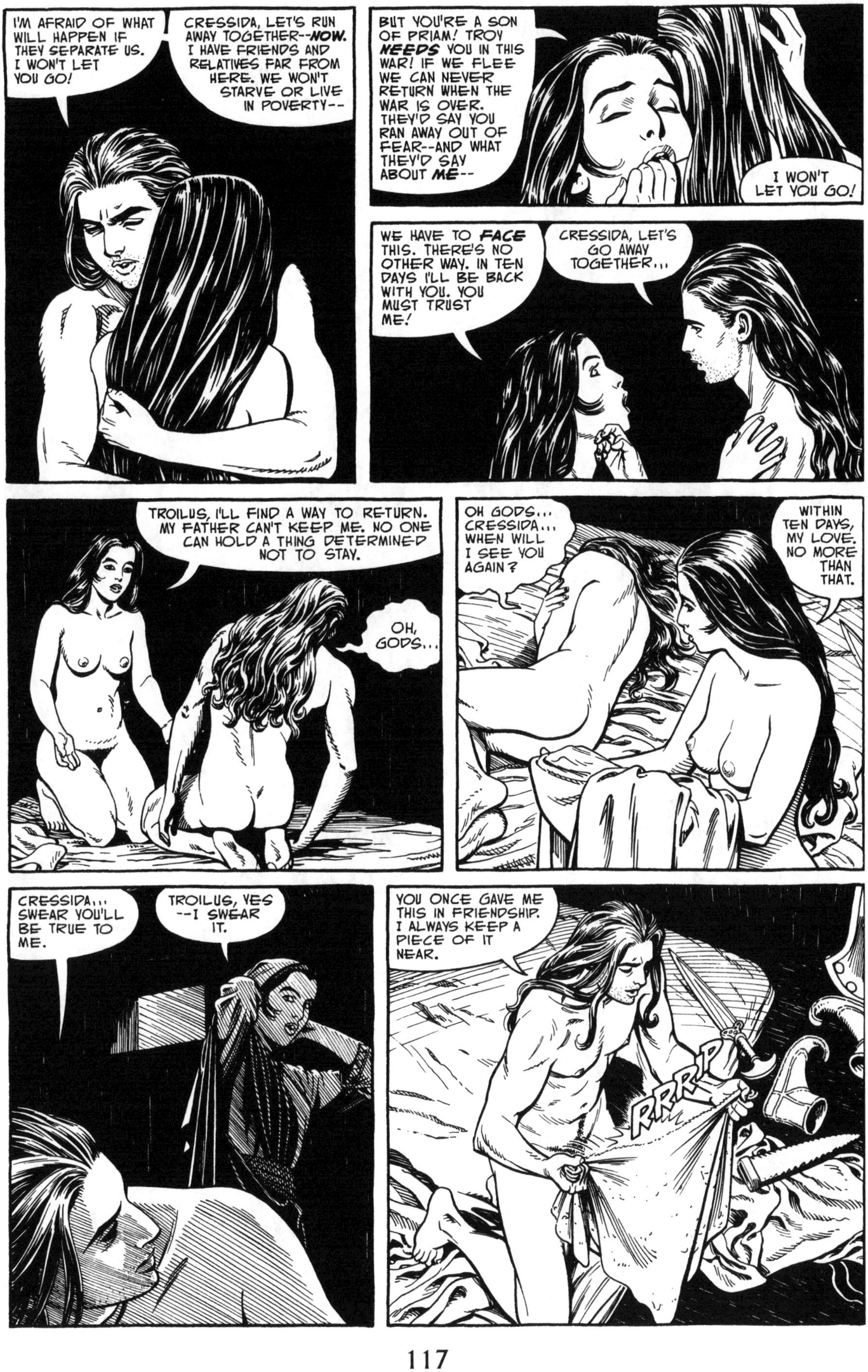
I'M AFRAID OF WHAT WILL HAPPEN IF THEY SEPARATE US. I WON'T LET YOU GO!
CRESSIDA, LET'S RUN AWAY TOGETHER--*NOW*. I HAVE FRIENDS AND RELATIVES FAR FROM HERE. WE WON'T STARVE OR LIVE IN POVERTY--
BUT YOU'RE A SON OF PRIAM! TROY *NEEDS* YOU IN THIS WAR! IF WE FLEE WE CAN NEVER RETURN WHEN THE WAR IS OVER. THEY'D SAY YOU RAN AWAY OUT OF FEAR--AND WHAT THEY'D SAY ABOUT *ME*--
I WON'T LET YOU GO!
WE HAVE TO *FACE* THIS. THERE'S NO OTHER WAY. IN TEN DAYS I'LL BE BACK WITH YOU. YOU MUST TRUST ME!
CRESSIDA, LET'S GO AWAY TOGETHER...
TROILUS, I'LL FIND A WAY TO RETURN. MY FATHER CAN'T KEEP ME. NO ONE CAN HOLD A THING DETERMINED NOT TO STAY.
OH, GODS...
OH GODS... CRESSIDA... WHEN WILL I SEE YOU AGAIN?
WITHIN TEN DAYS, MY LOVE. NO MORE THAN THAT.
CRESSIDA... SWEAR YOU'LL BE TRUE TO ME.
TROILUS, YES --I SWEAR IT.
YOU ONCE GAVE ME THIS IN FRIENDSHIP. I ALWAYS KEEP A PIECE OF IT NEAR.
RRRIP

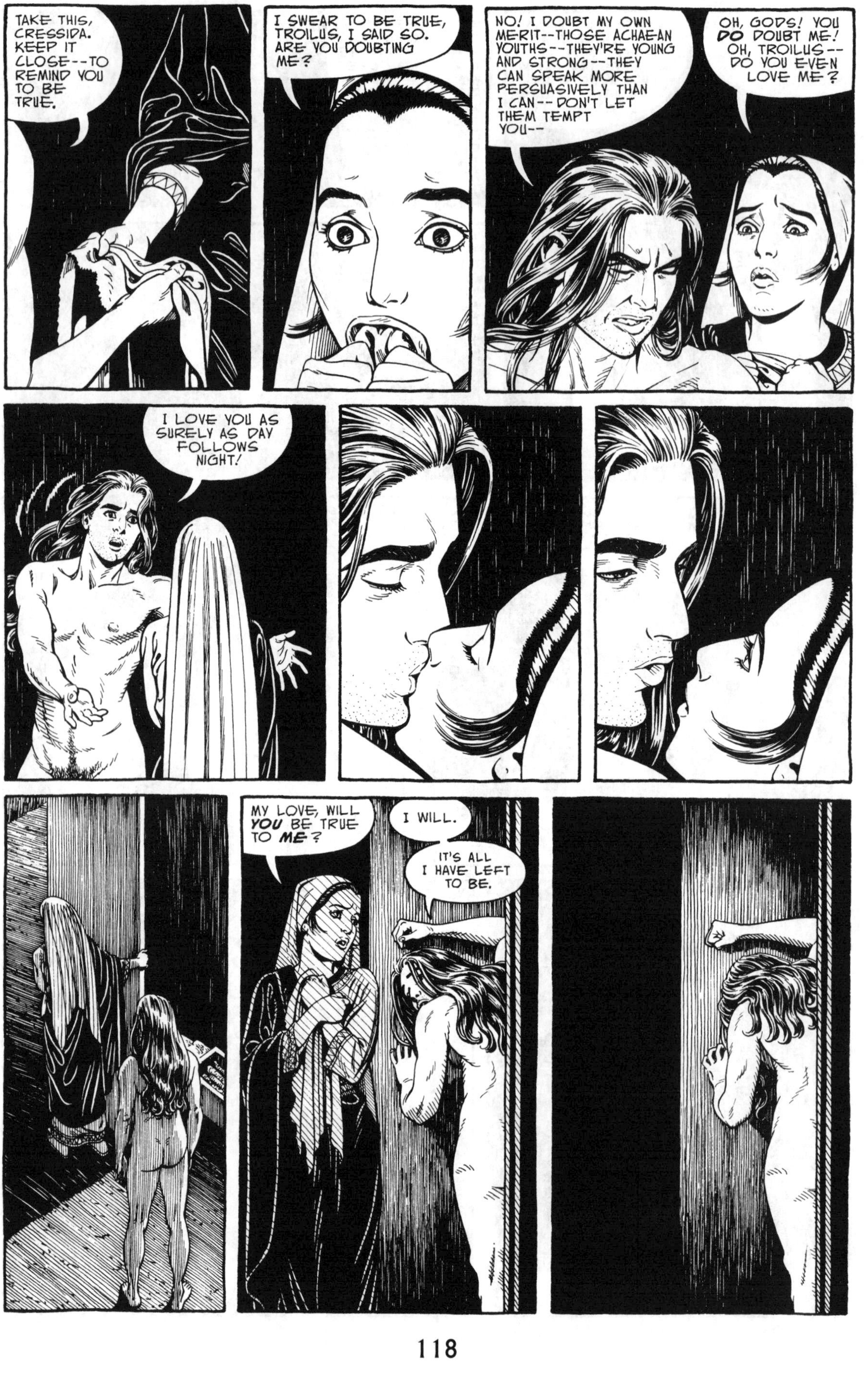
TAKE THIS, CRESSIDA. KEEP IT CLOSE--TO REMIND YOU TO BE TRUE.
I SWEAR TO BE TRUE, TROILUS, I SAID SO. ARE YOU DOUBTING ME?
NO! I DOUBT MY OWN MERIT--THOSE ACHAEAN YOUTHS--THEY'RE YOUNG AND STRONG--THEY CAN SPEAK MORE PERSUASIVELY THAN I CAN--DON'T LET THEM TEMPT YOU--
OH, GODS! YOU DO DOUBT ME! OH, TROILUS--DO YOU EVEN LOVE ME?
I LOVE YOU AS SURELY AS DAY FOLLOWS NIGHT!
MY LOVE, WILL YOU BE TRUE TO ME?
I WILL.
IT'S ALL I HAVE LEFT TO BE.

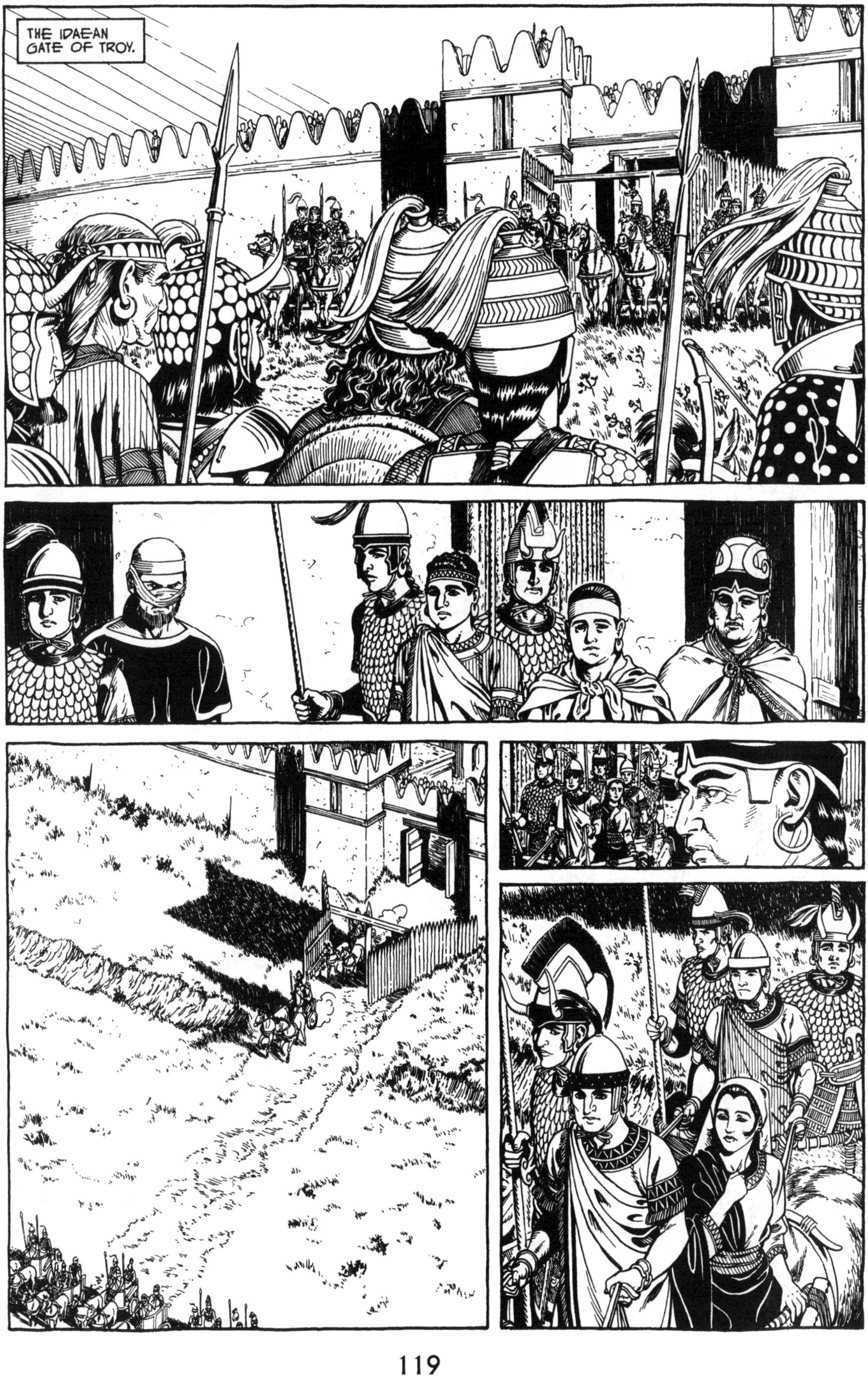
THE IDAEAN
GATE OF TROY.

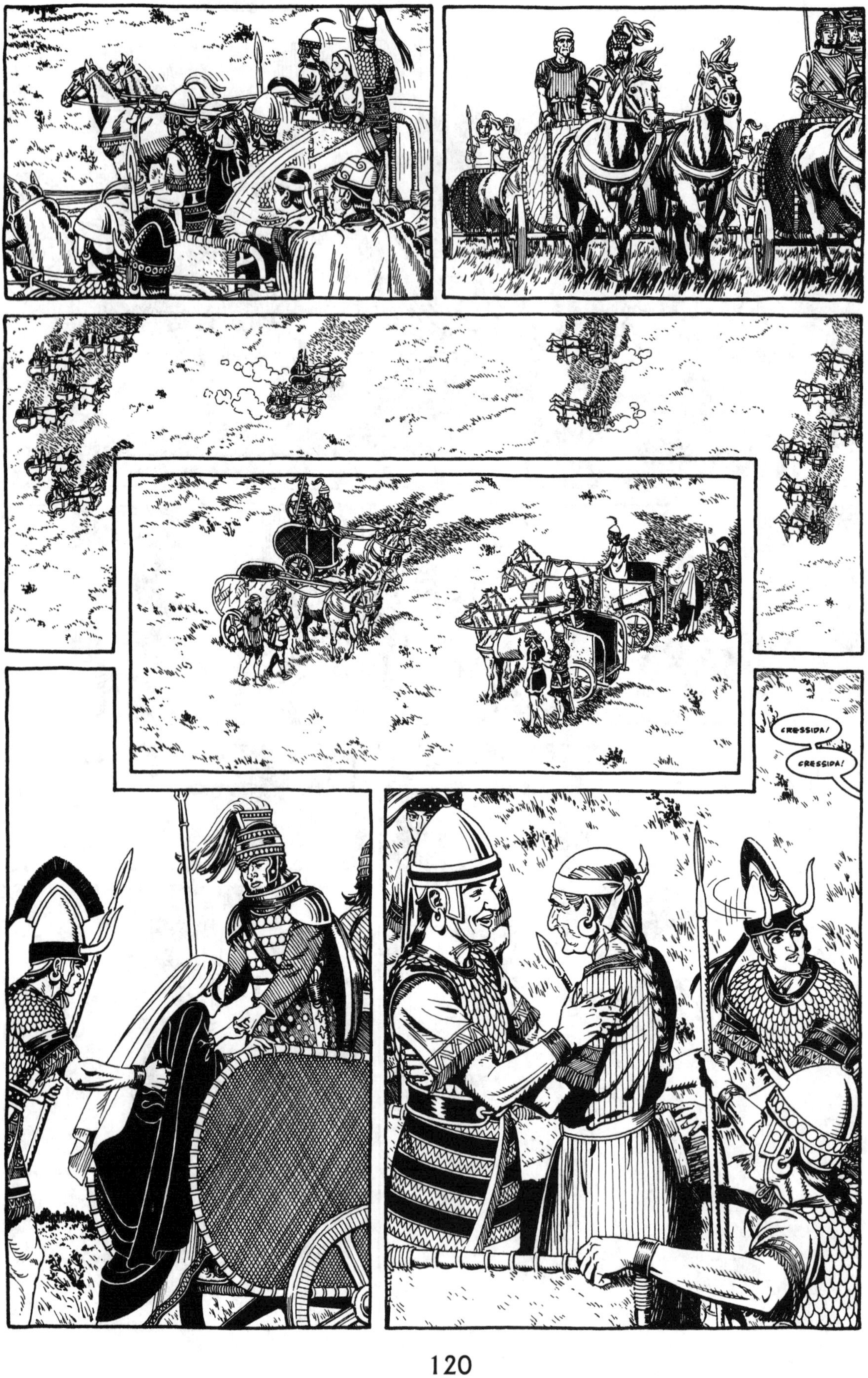
CRESSIDA!
CRESSIDA!

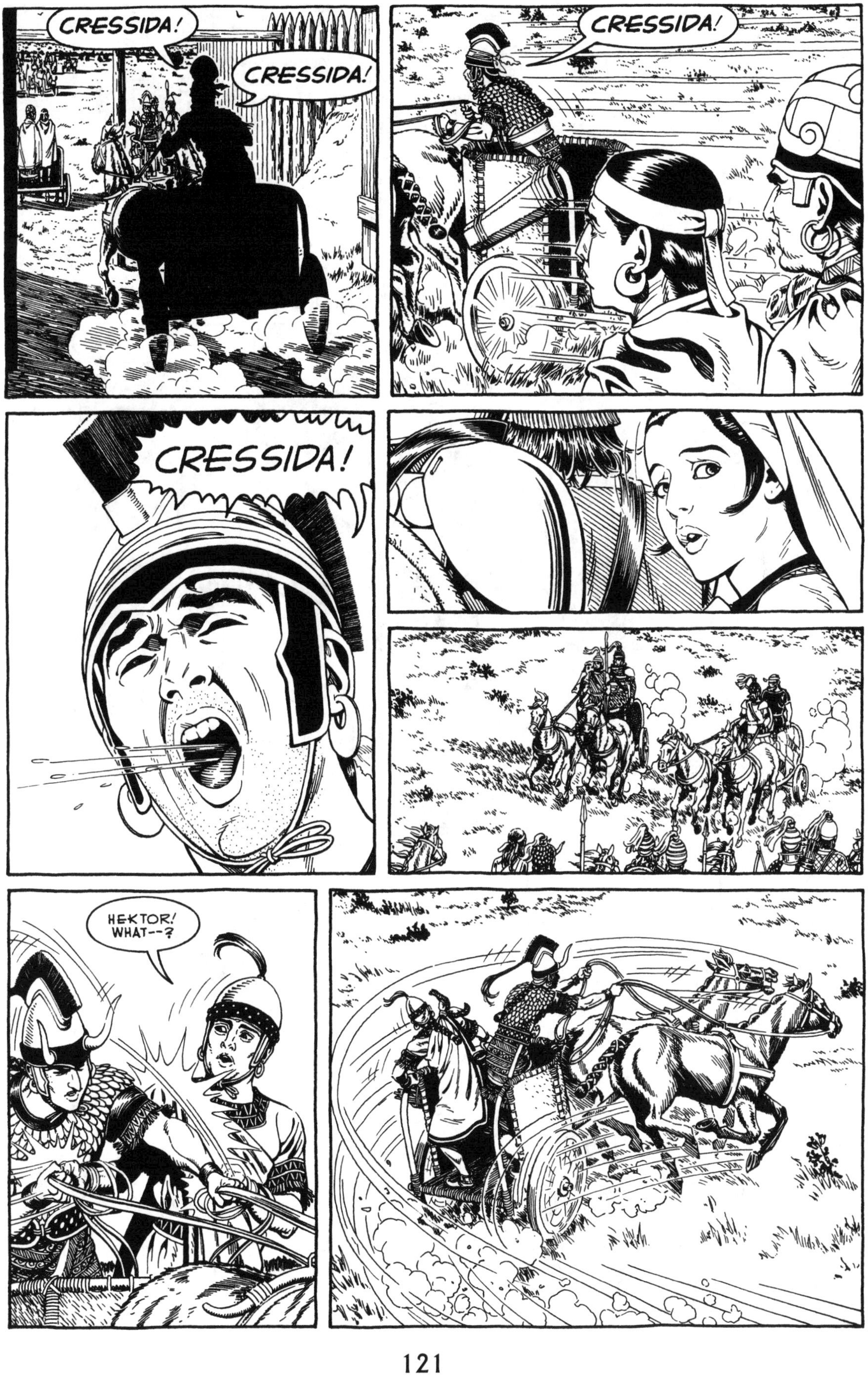
CRESSIDA!
CRESSIDA!
CRESSIDA!
CRESSIDA!
HEKTOR! WHAT--?

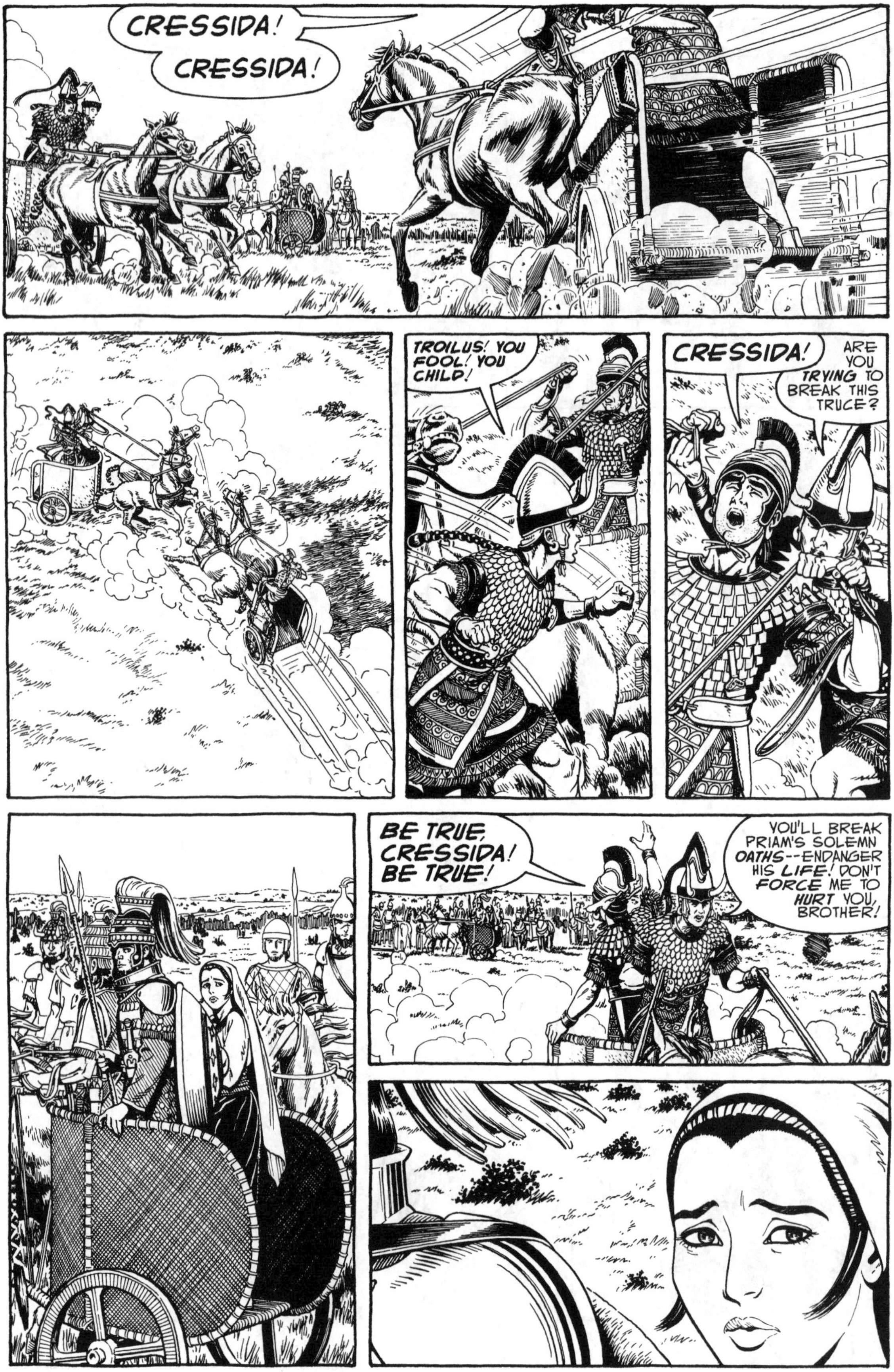

CRESSIDA! CRESSIDA!
TROILUS! YOU FOOL! YOU CHILD!
CRESSIDA!
ARE YOU TRYING TO BREAK THIS TRUCE?
BE TRUE, CRESSIDA! BE TRUE!
YOU'LL BREAK PRIAM'S SOLEMN OATHS--ENDANGER HIS LIFE! DON'T FORCE ME TO HURT YOU, BROTHER!

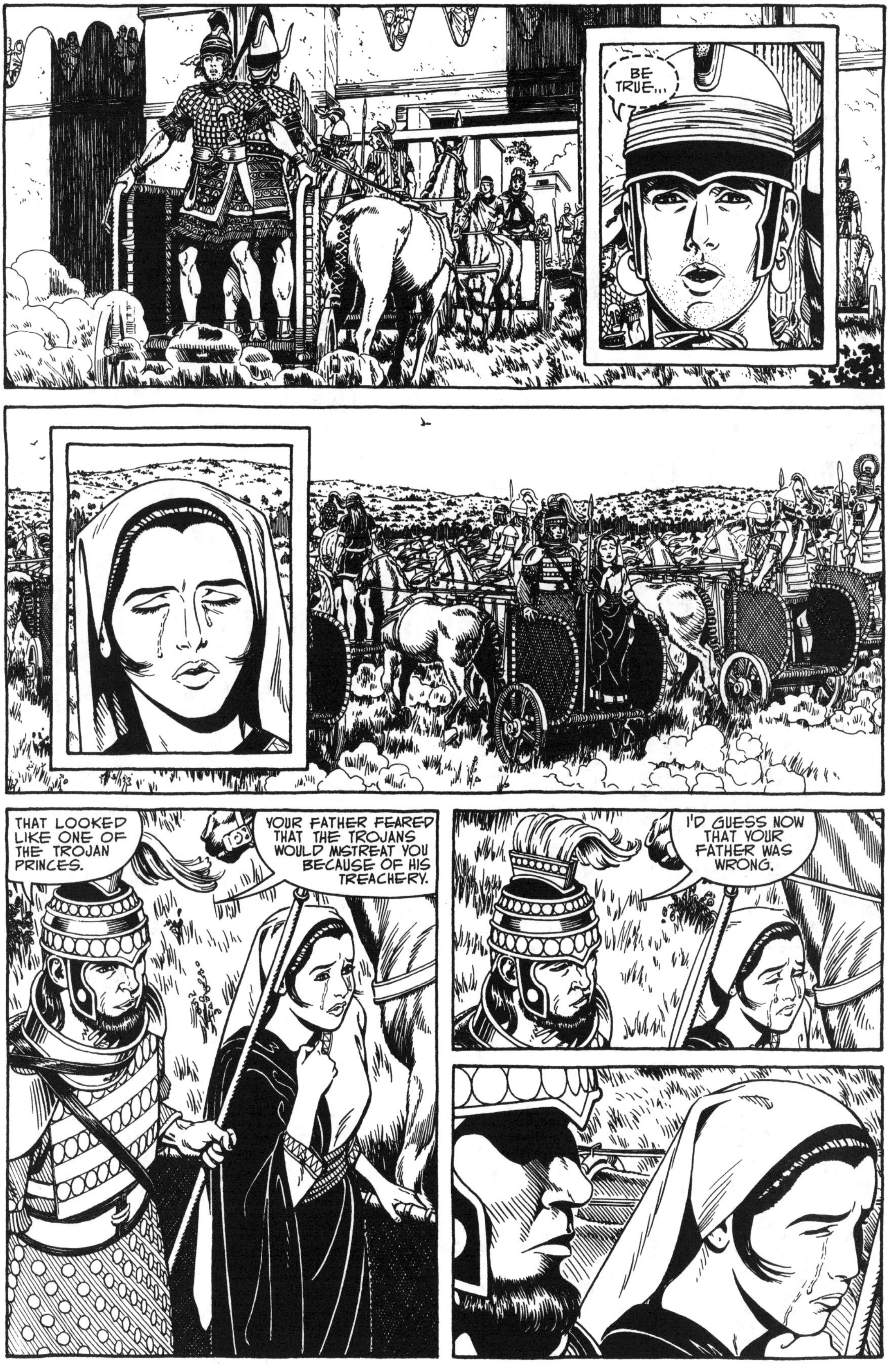
BE TRUE...
THAT LOOKED LIKE ONE OF THE TROJAN PRINCES.
YOUR FATHER FEARED THAT THE TROJANS WOULD MISTREAT YOU BECAUSE OF HIS TREACHERY.
I'D GUESS NOW THAT YOUR FATHER WAS WRONG.

WELL...

FORGET TROY AND DRY YOUR TEARS.

YOU WON'T FIND THE CAMP SO BAD. I GUESS IT WON'T BE WHAT YOU'RE USED TO.

BUT YOU'LL BE WITH YOUR FATHER.

AND I THINK A FEW OF THE ACHAEANS MIGHT SEEK YOUR FAVOR.

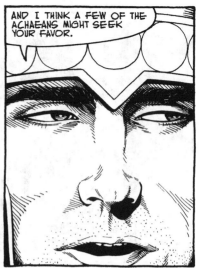

SOON.

HIGH KING, THOAS OF AETOLIA IS BACK -- WITH HIS BEAUTY ONLY SLIGHTLY MARRED.

WELCOME BACK, COUSIN!

I'VE NEVER BOASTED OF BEAUTY --BUT MY *ARMS* ARE AS STRONG AS EVER AND READY TO SLAY *TROJANS!*

AND HERE'S KALCHAS'S DAUGHTER...BRINGING A DIFFERENT KIND OF BEAUTY.

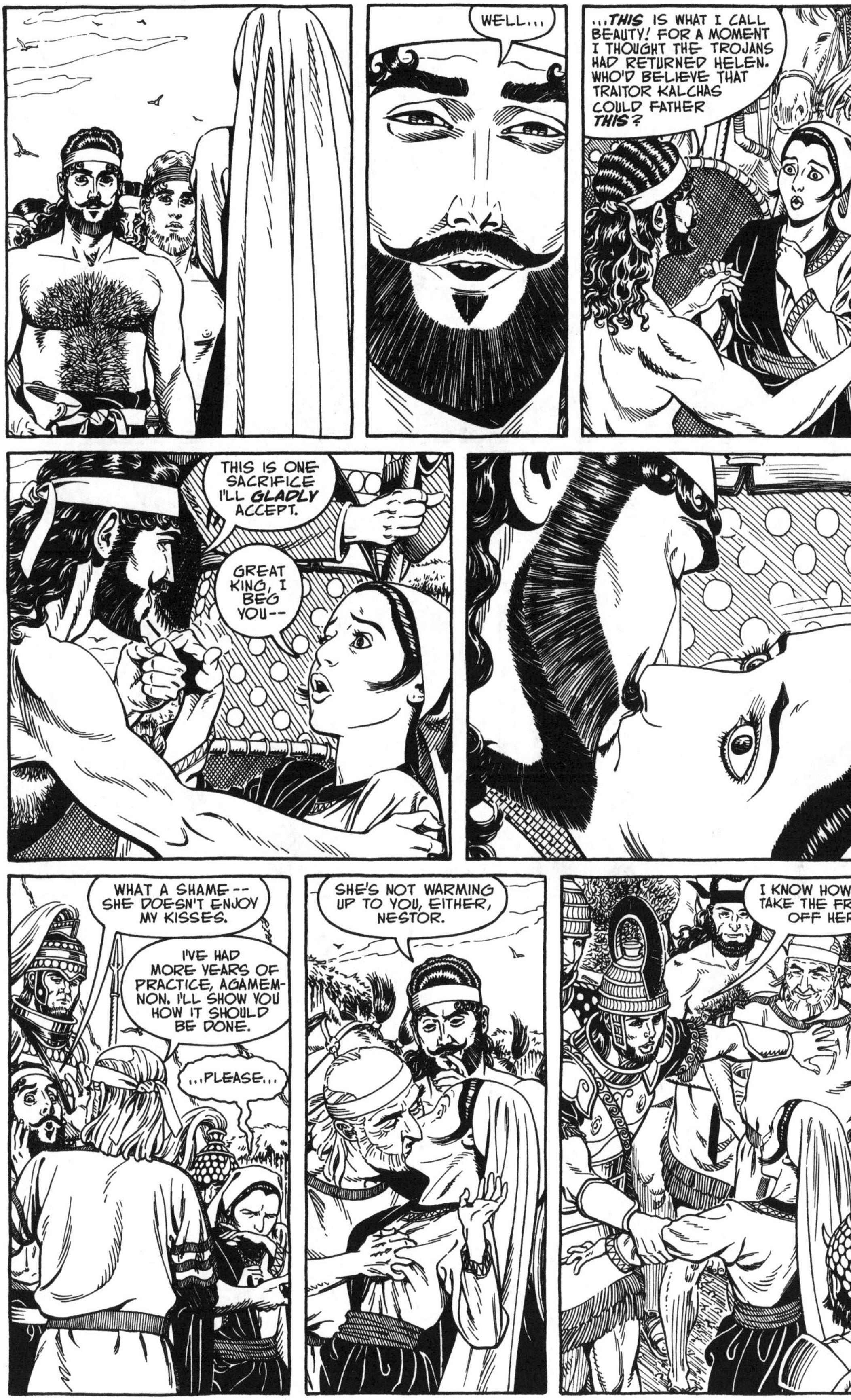
WELL...
...THIS IS WHAT I CALL BEAUTY! FOR A MOMENT I THOUGHT THE TROJANS HAD RETURNED HELEN. WHO'D BELIEVE THAT TRAITOR KALCHAS COULD FATHER THIS?
THIS IS ONE SACRIFICE I'LL GLADLY ACCEPT.
GREAT KING, I BEG YOU--
WHAT A SHAME--SHE DOESN'T ENJOY MY KISSES.
I'VE HAD MORE YEARS OF PRACTICE, AGAMEMNON. I'LL SHOW YOU HOW IT SHOULD BE DONE.
...PLEASE...
SHE'S NOT WARMING UP TO YOU, EITHER, NESTOR.
I KNOW HOW TO TAKE THE FROST OFF HER.

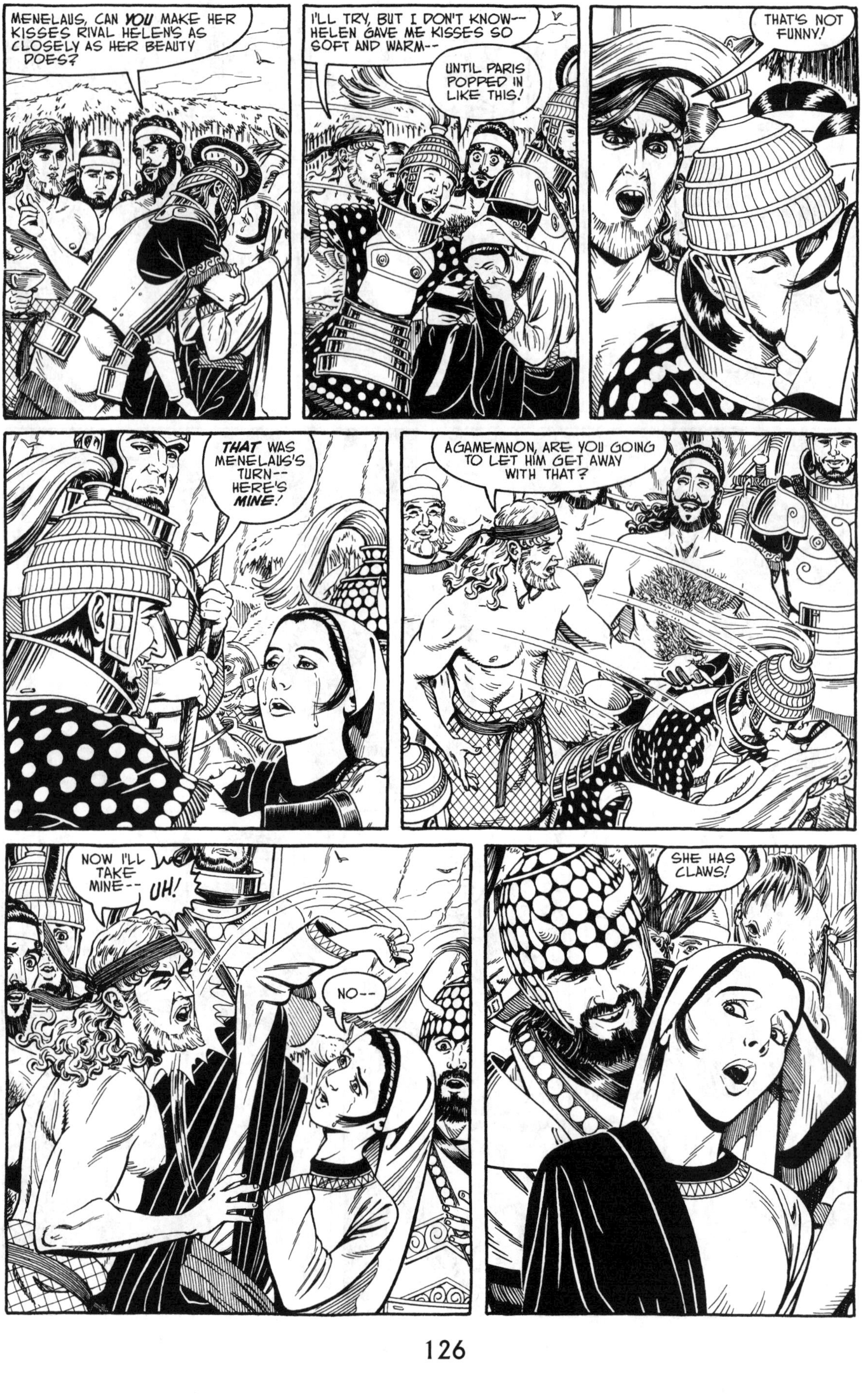
MENELAUS, CAN **YOU** MAKE HER KISSES RIVAL HELEN'S AS CLOSELY AS HER BEAUTY DOES?
I'LL TRY, BUT I DON'T KNOW-- HELEN GAVE ME KISSES SO SOFT AND WARM--
UNTIL PARIS POPPED IN LIKE THIS!
THAT'S NOT FUNNY!
THAT WAS MENELAUS'S TURN-- HERE'S **MINE**!
AGAMEMNON, ARE YOU GOING TO LET HIM GET AWAY WITH THAT?
NOW I'LL TAKE MINE--
UH!
NO--
SHE HAS CLAWS!

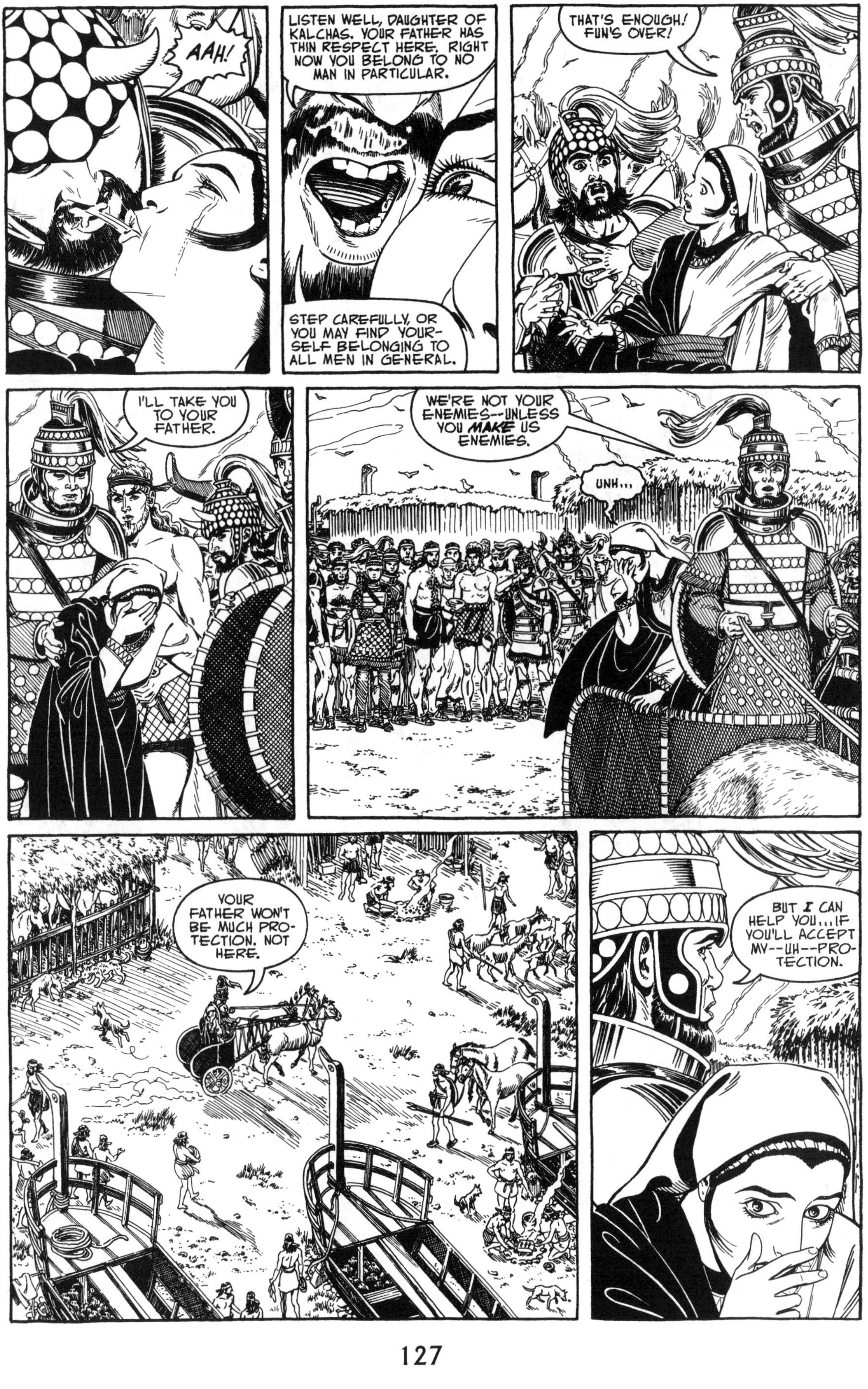
AAH!
LISTEN WELL, DAUGHTER OF KALCHAS. YOUR FATHER HAS THIN RESPECT HERE. RIGHT NOW YOU BELONG TO NO MAN IN PARTICULAR.
STEP CAREFULLY, OR YOU MAY FIND YOURSELF BELONGING TO ALL MEN IN GENERAL.
THAT'S ENOUGH! FUN'S OVER!
I'LL TAKE YOU TO YOUR FATHER.
WE'RE NOT YOUR ENEMIES--UNLESS YOU MAKE US ENEMIES.
UNH...
YOUR FATHER WON'T BE MUCH PROTECTION. NOT HERE.
BUT I CAN HELP YOU...IF YOU'LL ACCEPT MY--UH--PROTECTION.

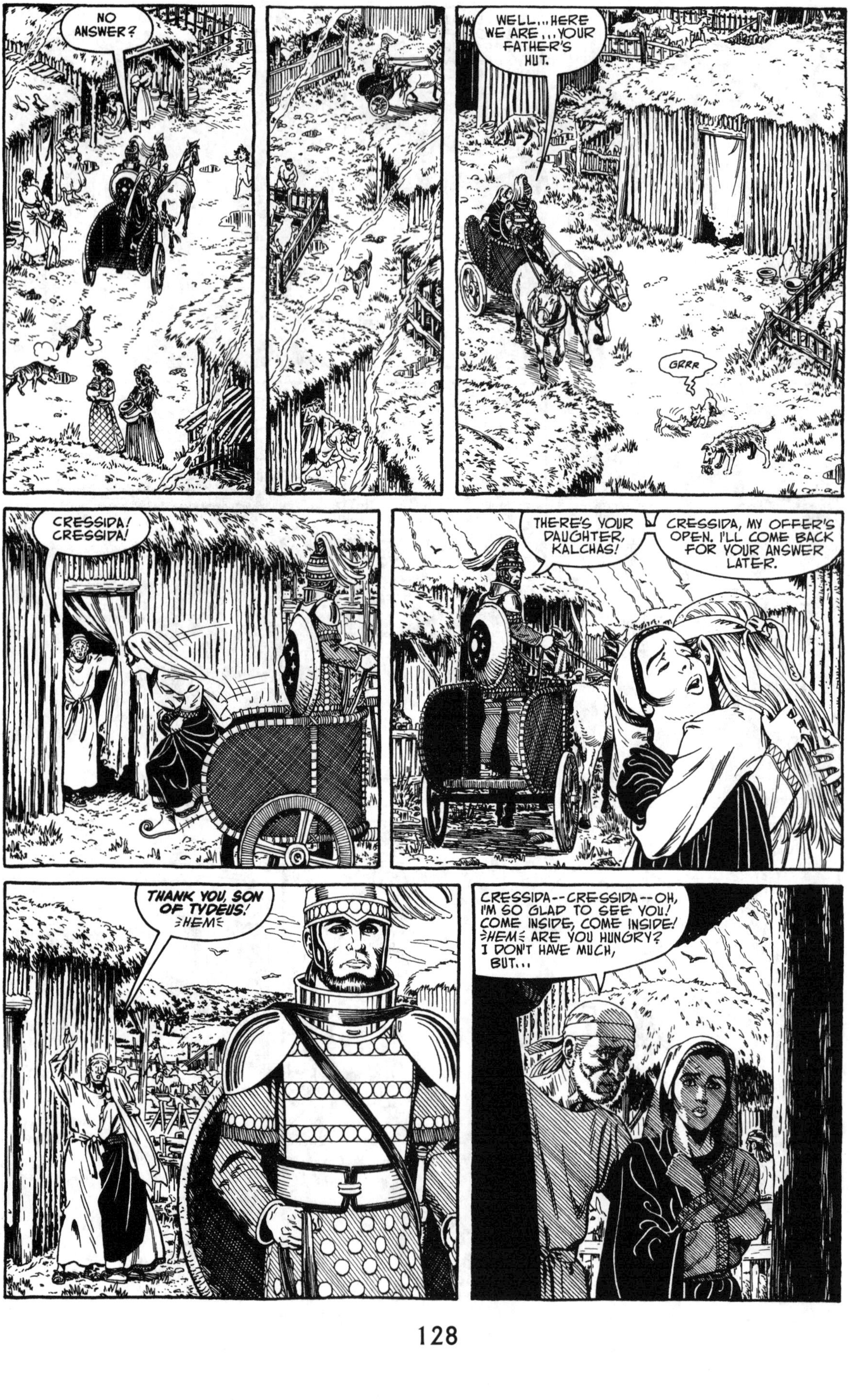
NO ANSWER?
WELL... HERE WE ARE... YOUR FATHER'S HUT.
GRRR
CRESSIDA! CRESSIDA!
THERE'S YOUR DAUGHTER, KALCHAS!
CRESSIDA, MY OFFER'S OPEN. I'LL COME BACK FOR YOUR ANSWER LATER.
THANK YOU, SON OF TYDEUS! HEM
CRESSIDA--CRESSIDA--OH, I'M SO GLAD TO SEE YOU! COME INSIDE, COME INSIDE! HEM ARE YOU HUNGRY? I DON'T HAVE MUCH, BUT...

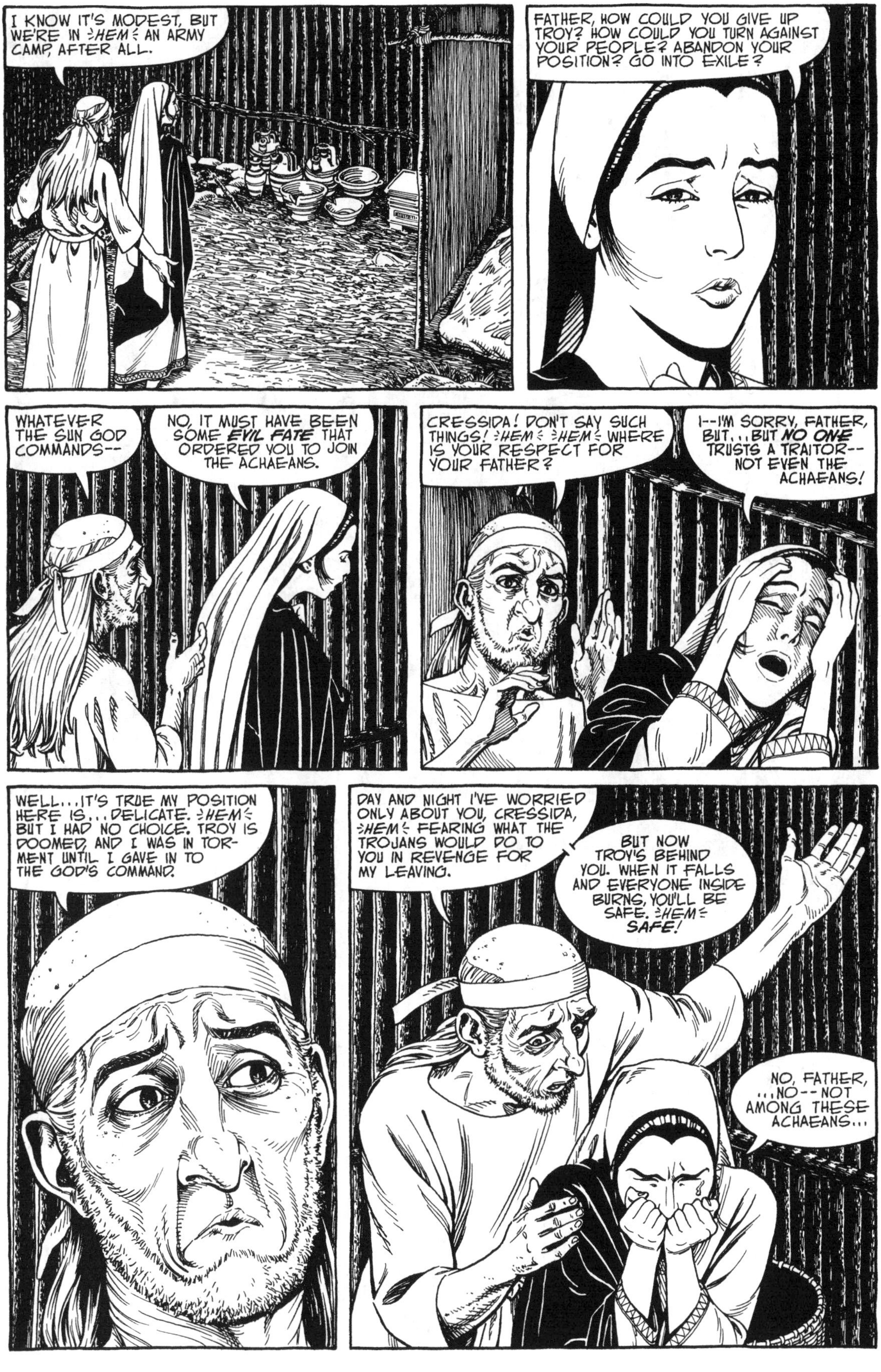
I KNOW IT'S MODEST, BUT WE'RE IN *HEM* AN ARMY CAMP, AFTER ALL.
FATHER, HOW COULD YOU GIVE UP TROY? HOW COULD YOU TURN AGAINST YOUR PEOPLE? ABANDON YOUR POSITION? GO INTO EXILE?
WHATEVER THE SUN GOD COMMANDS--
NO, IT MUST HAVE BEEN SOME EVIL FATE THAT ORDERED YOU TO JOIN THE ACHAEANS.
CRESSIDA! DON'T SAY SUCH THINGS! *HEM* *HEM* WHERE IS YOUR RESPECT FOR YOUR FATHER?
I--I'M SORRY, FATHER, BUT...BUT NO ONE TRUSTS A TRAITOR--NOT EVEN THE ACHAEANS!
WELL...IT'S TRUE MY POSITION HERE IS...DELICATE. *HEM* BUT I HAD NO CHOICE. TROY IS DOOMED, AND I WAS IN TORMENT UNTIL I GAVE IN TO THE GOD'S COMMAND.
DAY AND NIGHT I'VE WORRIED ONLY ABOUT YOU, CRESSIDA, *HEM* FEARING WHAT THE TROJANS WOULD DO TO YOU IN REVENGE FOR MY LEAVING.
BUT NOW TROY'S BEHIND YOU. WHEN IT FALLS AND EVERYONE INSIDE BURNS, YOU'LL BE SAFE. *HEM* SAFE!
NO, FATHER, ...NO--NOT AMONG THESE ACHAEANS...

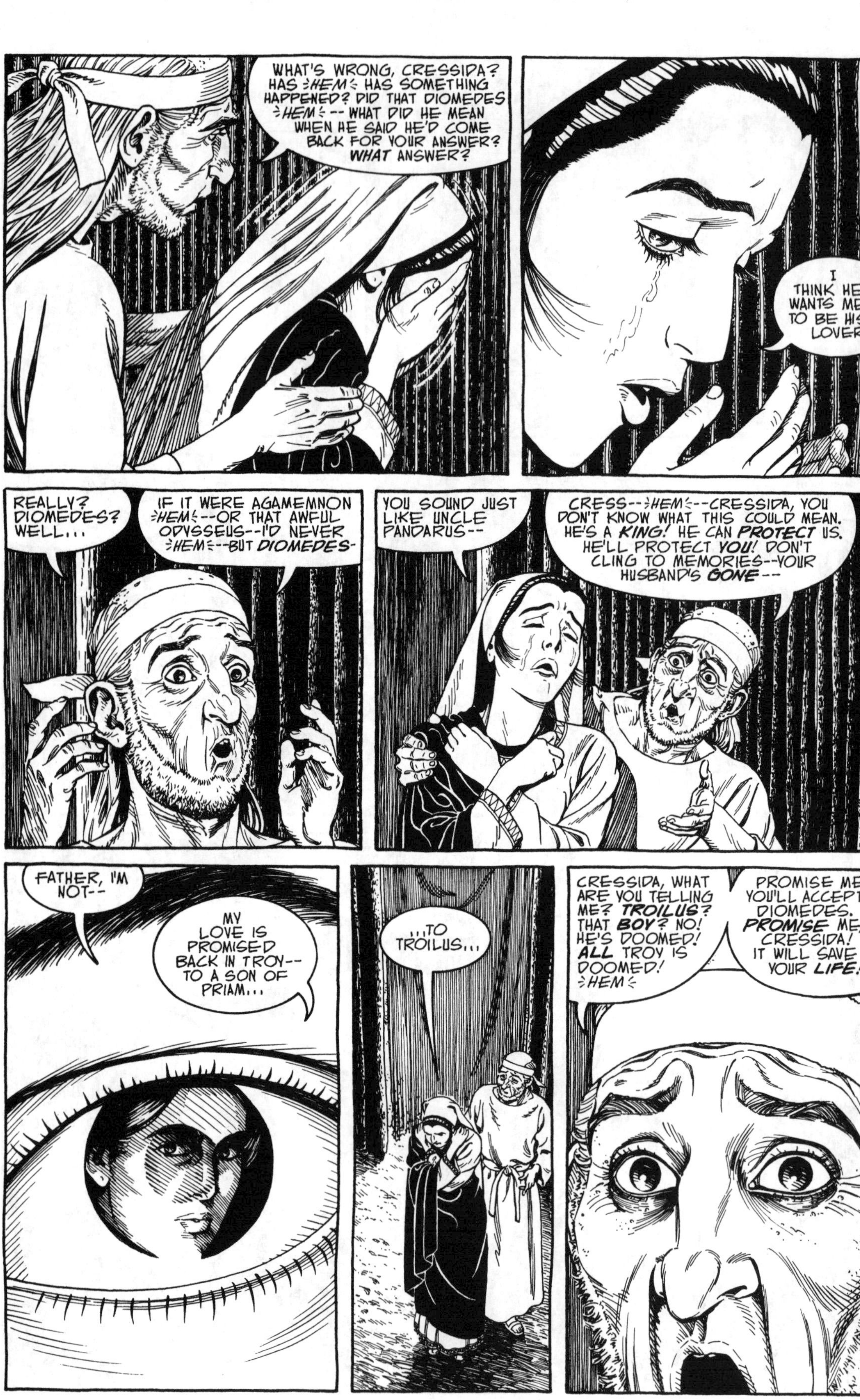
WHAT'S WRONG, CRESSIDA? HAS ⋟HEM⋞ HAS SOMETHING HAPPENED? DID THAT DIOMEDES ⋟HEM⋞ -- WHAT DID HE MEAN WHEN HE SAID HE'D COME BACK FOR YOUR ANSWER? WHAT ANSWER?
I THINK HE WANTS ME TO BE HIS LOVER.
REALLY? DIOMEDES? WELL...
IF IT WERE AGAMEMNON ⋟HEM⋞ --OR THAT AWFUL ODYSSEUS--I'D NEVER ⋟HEM⋞ --BUT DIOMEDES-
YOU SOUND JUST LIKE UNCLE PANDARUS--
CRESS--⋟HEM⋞--CRESSIDA, YOU DON'T KNOW WHAT THIS COULD MEAN. HE'S A KING! HE CAN PROTECT US. HE'LL PROTECT YOU! DON'T CLING TO MEMORIES--YOUR HUSBAND'S GONE--
FATHER, I'M NOT--
MY LOVE IS PROMISED BACK IN TROY-- TO A SON OF PRIAM...
...TO TROILUS...
CRESSIDA, WHAT ARE YOU TELLING ME? TROILUS? THAT BOY? NO! HE'S DOOMED! ALL TROY IS DOOMED! ⋟HEM⋞
PROMISE ME YOU'LL ACCEPT DIOMEDES. PROMISE ME, CRESSIDA! IT WILL SAVE YOUR LIFE!

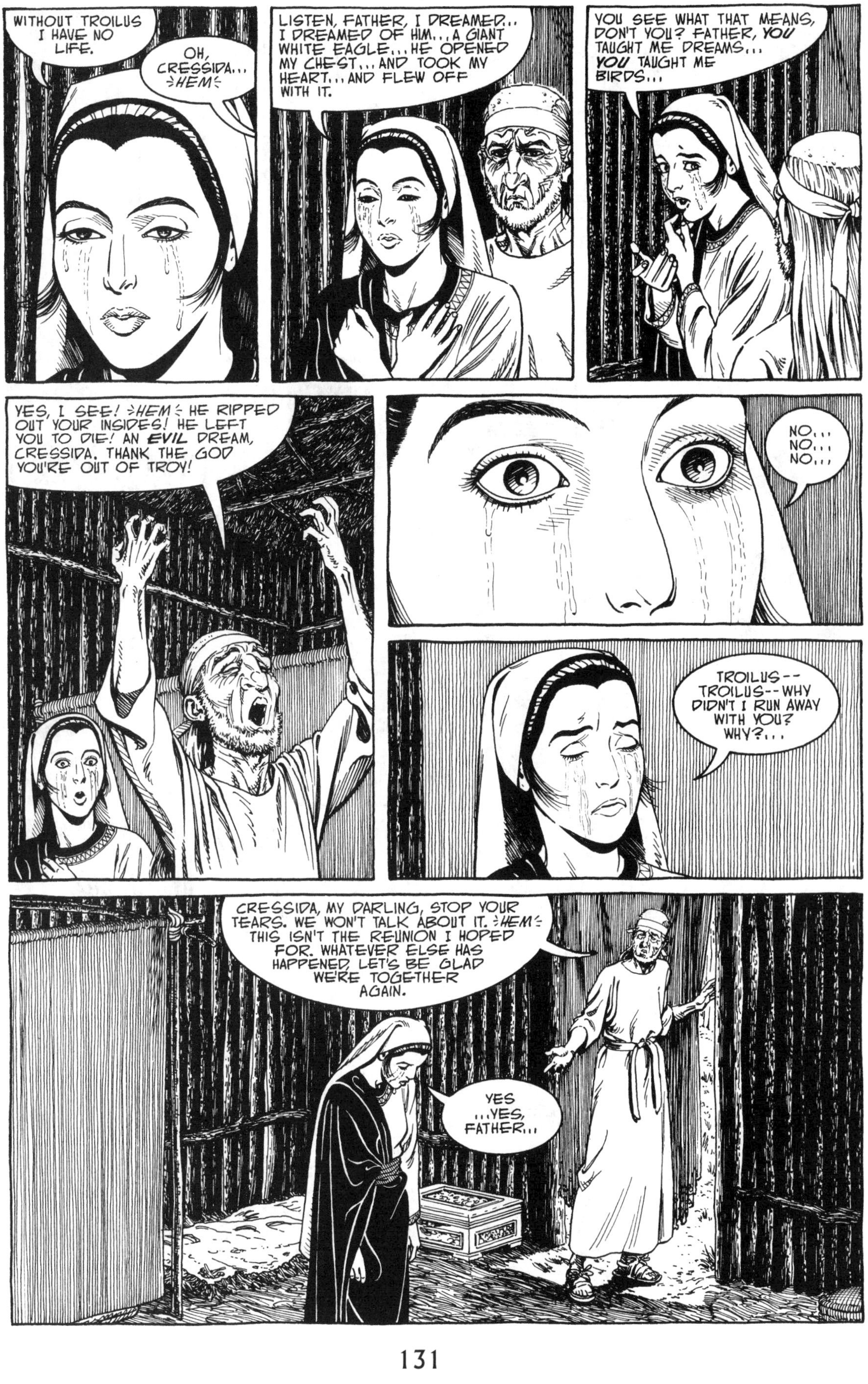
WITHOUT TROILUS I HAVE NO LIFE.
OH, CRESSIDA... ⋺HEM⋲
LISTEN, FATHER, I DREAMED... I DREAMED OF HIM... A GIANT WHITE EAGLE... HE OPENED MY CHEST... AND TOOK MY HEART... AND FLEW OFF WITH IT.
YOU SEE WHAT THAT MEANS, DON'T YOU? FATHER, **YOU** TAUGHT ME DREAMS... **YOU** TAUGHT ME BIRDS...
YES, I SEE! ⋺HEM⋲ HE RIPPED OUT YOUR INSIDES! HE LEFT YOU TO DIE! AN **EVIL** DREAM, CRESSIDA. THANK THE GOD YOU'RE OUT OF TROY!
NO... NO... NO...
TROILUS-- TROILUS--WHY DIDN'T I RUN AWAY WITH YOU? WHY?...
CRESSIDA, MY DARLING, STOP YOUR TEARS. WE WON'T TALK ABOUT IT. ⋺HEM⋲ THIS ISN'T THE REUNION I HOPED FOR. WHATEVER ELSE HAS HAPPENED, LET'S BE GLAD WE'RE TOGETHER AGAIN.
YES ...YES, FATHER...

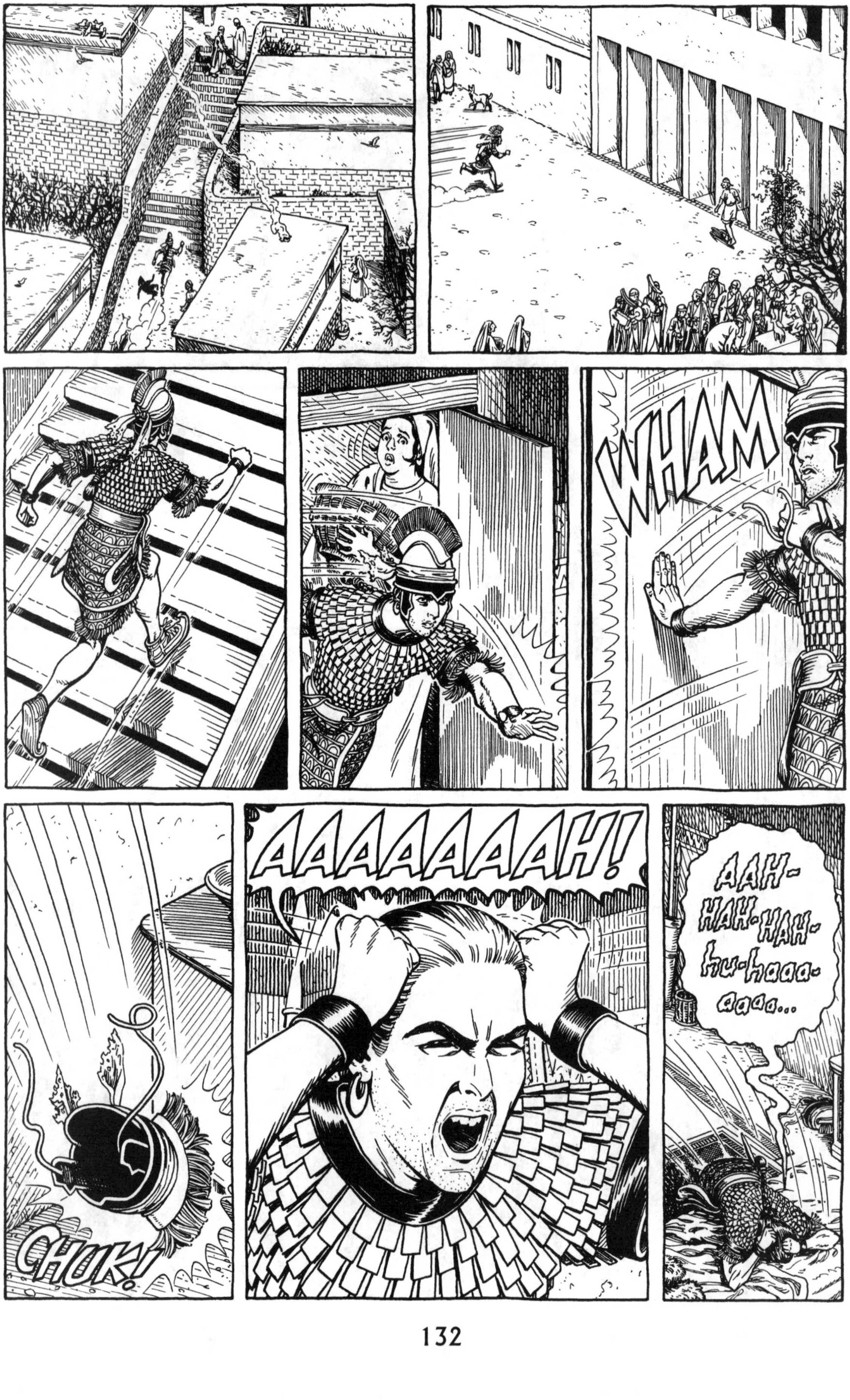
WHAM
CHUK!
AAAAAAAAH!
AAH-HAH-HAH-hu-haaa-aaaa...

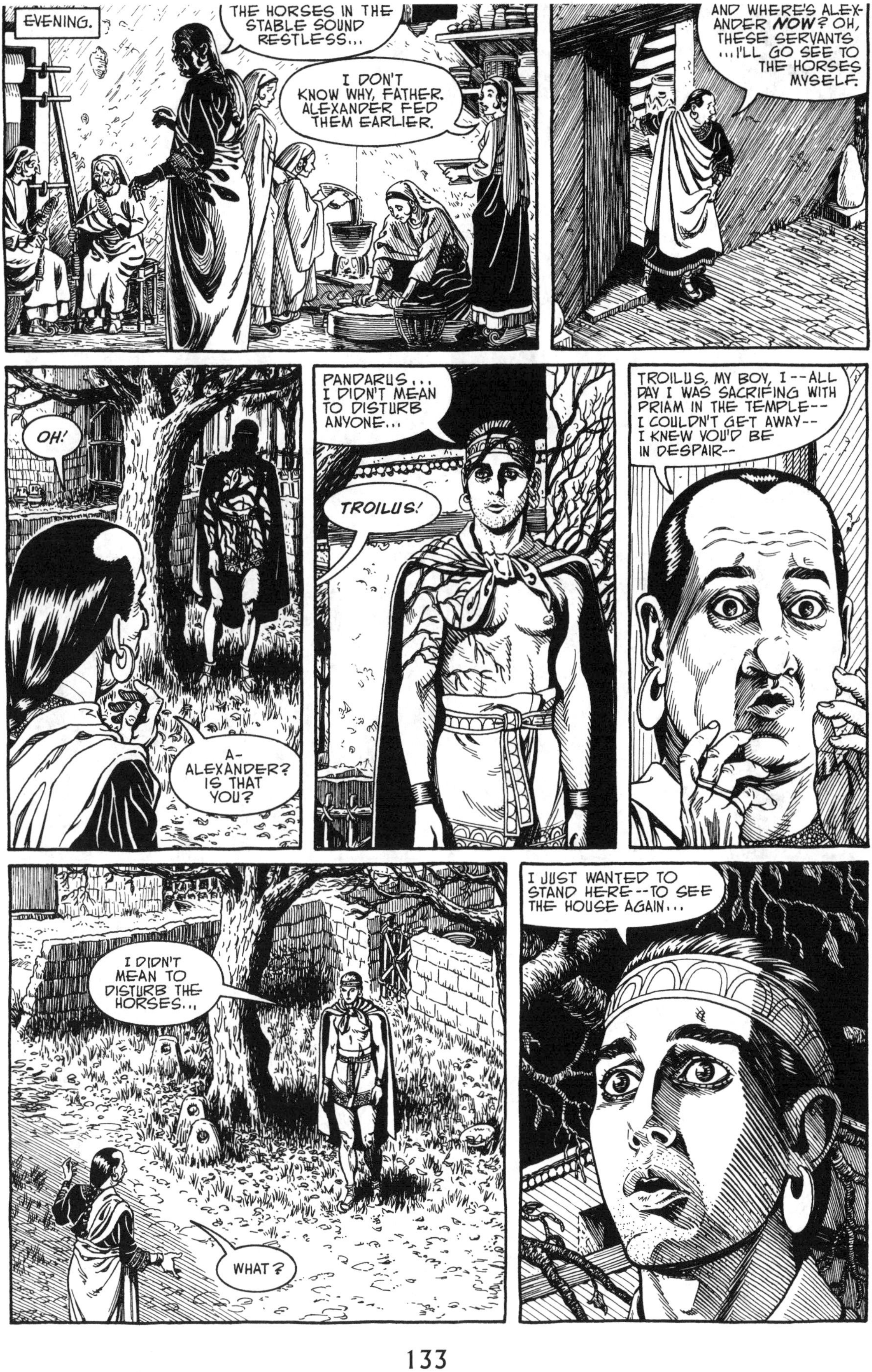
EVENING.
THE HORSES IN THE STABLE SOUND RESTLESS...
I DON'T KNOW WHY, FATHER. ALEXANDER FED THEM EARLIER.
AND WHERE'S ALEXANDER *NOW*? OH, THESE SERVANTS ...I'LL GO SEE TO THE HORSES MYSELF.
OH!
A- ALEXANDER? IS THAT YOU?
PANDARUS... I DIDN'T MEAN TO DISTURB ANYONE...
TROILUS!
TROILUS, MY BOY, I--ALL DAY I WAS SACRIFING WITH PRIAM IN THE TEMPLE-- I COULDN'T GET AWAY-- I KNEW YOU'D BE IN DESPAIR--
I DIDN'T MEAN TO DISTURB THE HORSES...
WHAT?
I JUST WANTED TO STAND HERE--TO SEE THE HOUSE AGAIN...

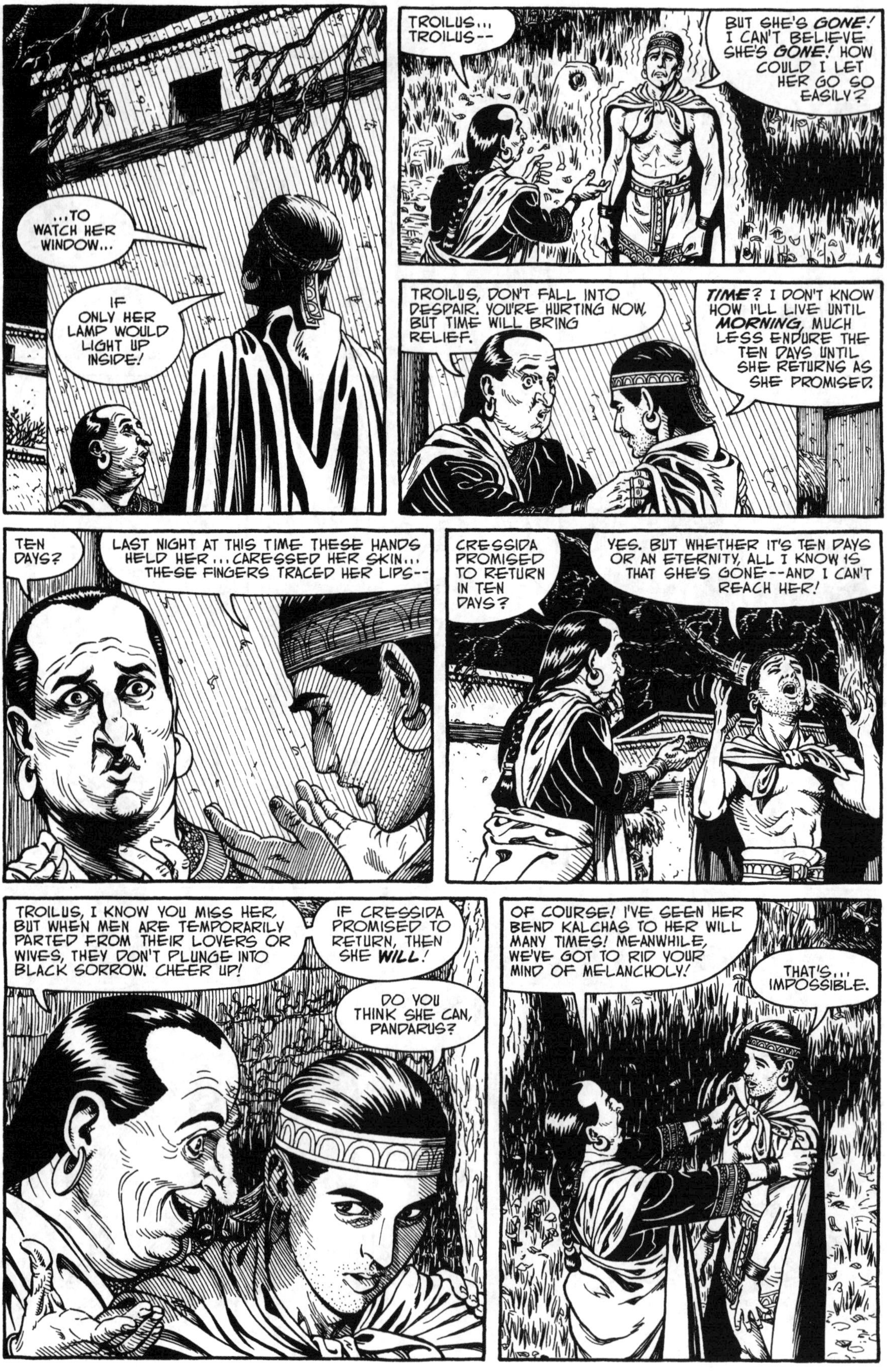
...TO WATCH HER WINDOW...
IF ONLY HER LAMP WOULD LIGHT UP INSIDE!
TROILUS... TROILUS--
BUT SHE'S *GONE!* I CAN'T BELIEVE SHE'S *GONE!* HOW COULD I LET HER GO SO EASILY?
TROILUS, DON'T FALL INTO DESPAIR. YOU'RE HURTING NOW, BUT TIME WILL BRING RELIEF.
TIME? I DON'T KNOW HOW I'LL LIVE UNTIL *MORNING*, MUCH LESS ENDURE THE TEN DAYS UNTIL SHE RETURNS AS SHE PROMISED.
TEN DAYS?
LAST NIGHT AT THIS TIME THESE HANDS HELD HER... CARESSED HER SKIN... THESE FINGERS TRACED HER LIPS--
CRESSIDA PROMISED TO RETURN IN TEN DAYS?
YES. BUT WHETHER IT'S TEN DAYS OR AN ETERNITY, ALL I KNOW IS THAT SHE'S GONE--AND I CAN'T REACH HER!
TROILUS, I KNOW YOU MISS HER, BUT WHEN MEN ARE TEMPORARILY PARTED FROM THEIR LOVERS OR WIVES, THEY DON'T PLUNGE INTO BLACK SORROW. CHEER UP!
IF CRESSIDA PROMISED TO RETURN, THEN SHE *WILL*!
DO YOU THINK SHE CAN, PANDARUS?
OF COURSE! I'VE SEEN HER BEND KALCHAS TO HER WILL MANY TIMES! MEANWHILE, WE'VE GOT TO RID YOUR MIND OF MELANCHOLY!
THAT'S... IMPOSSIBLE.

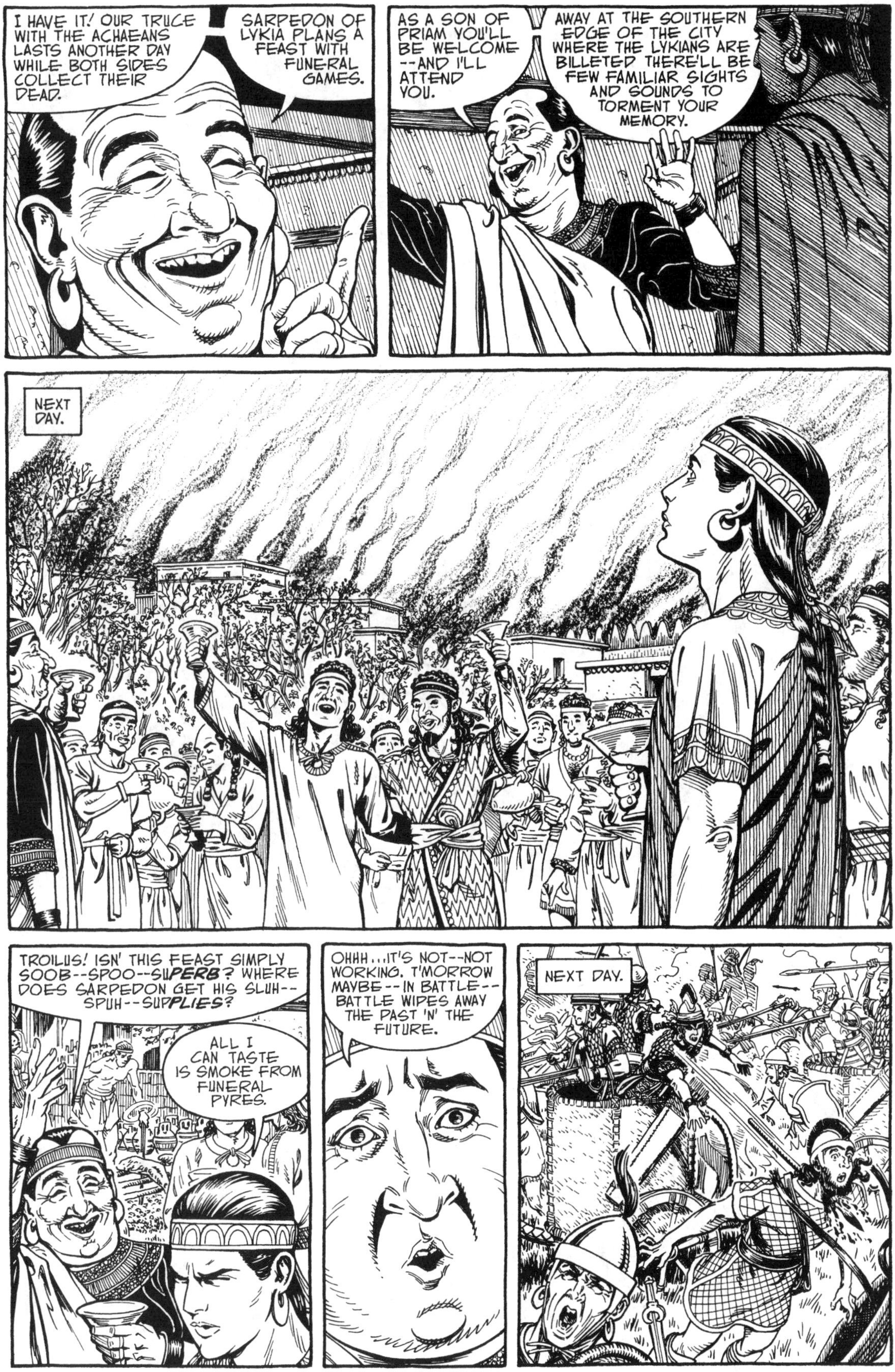
I HAVE IT! OUR TRUCE WITH THE ACHAEANS LASTS ANOTHER DAY WHILE BOTH SIDES COLLECT THEIR DEAD.
SARPEDON OF LYKIA PLANS A FEAST WITH FUNERAL GAMES.
AS A SON OF PRIAM YOU'LL BE WELCOME --AND I'LL ATTEND YOU.
AWAY AT THE SOUTHERN EDGE OF THE CITY WHERE THE LYKIANS ARE BILLETED THERE'LL BE FEW FAMILIAR SIGHTS AND SOUNDS TO TORMENT YOUR MEMORY.
NEXT DAY.
TROILUS! ISN' THIS FEAST SIMPLY SOOB--SPOO--SU***PERB***? WHERE DOES SARPEDON GET HIS SLUH--SPUH--SUP***PLIES***?
ALL I CAN TASTE IS SMOKE FROM FUNERAL PYRES.
OHHH...IT'S NOT--NOT WORKING. T'MORROW MAYBE--IN BATTLE--BATTLE WIPES AWAY THE PAST 'N' THE FUTURE.
NEXT DAY.

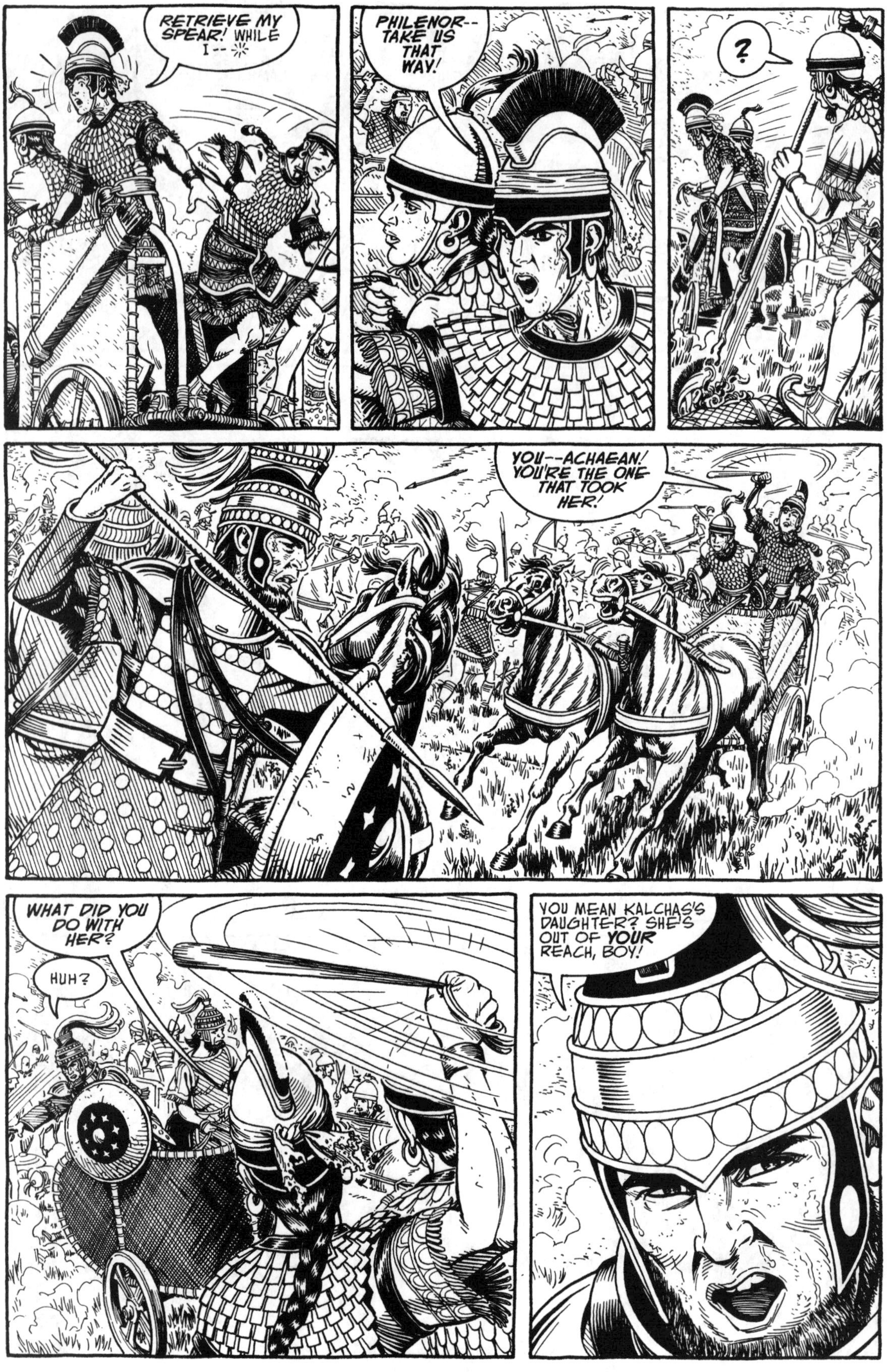
RETRIEVE MY SPEAR! WHILE I--
PHILENOR-- TAKE US THAT WAY!
?
YOU--ACHAEAN! YOU'RE THE ONE THAT TOOK HER!
WHAT DID YOU DO WITH HER?
HUH?
YOU MEAN KALCHAS'S DAUGHTER? SHE'S OUT OF **YOUR** REACH, BOY!

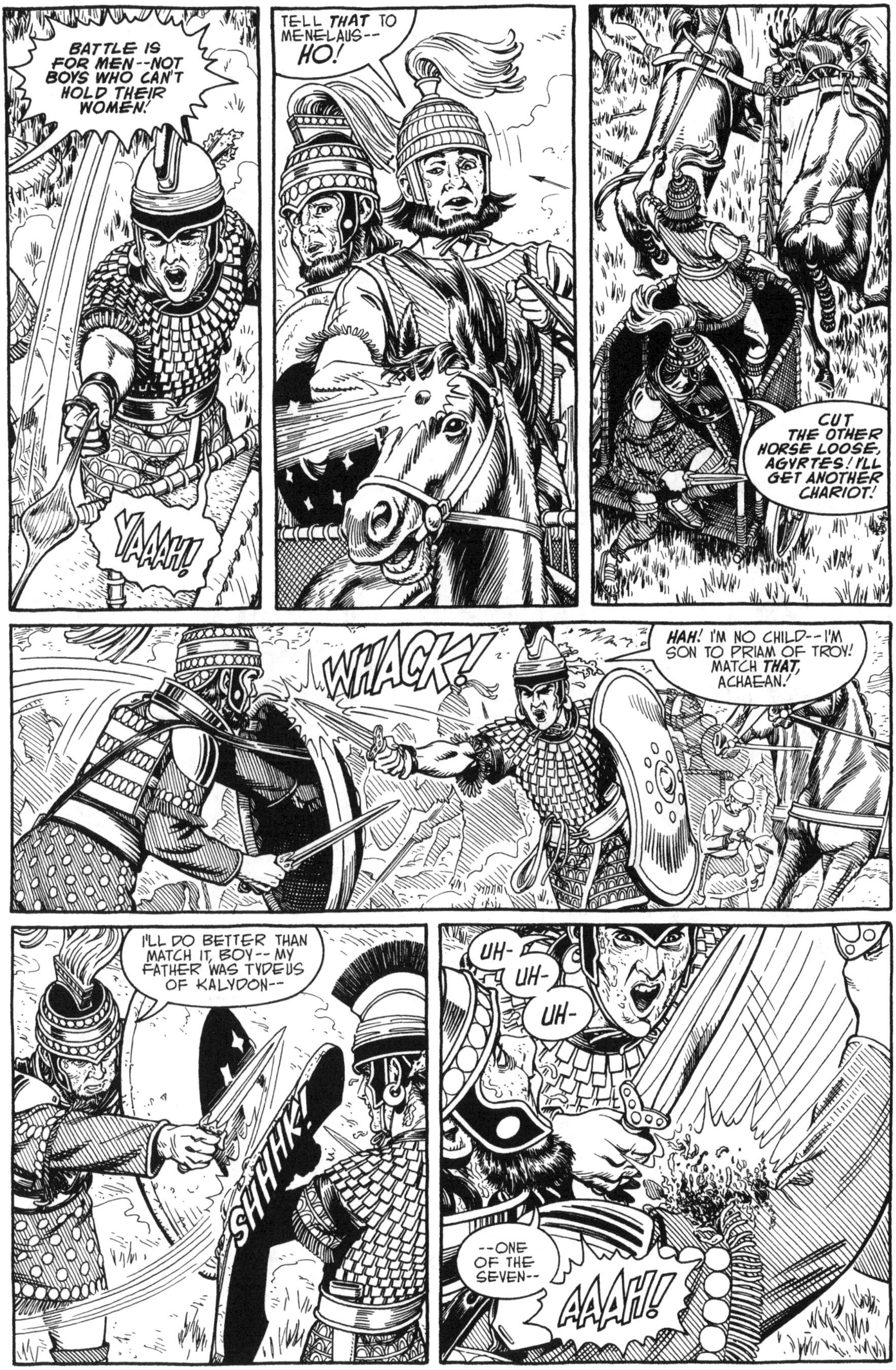
BATTLE IS FOR MEN--NOT BOYS WHO CAN'T HOLD THEIR WOMEN!
YAAAH!
TELL THAT TO MENELAUS--HO!
CUT THE OTHER HORSE LOOSE, AGYRTES! I'LL GET ANOTHER CHARIOT!
WHACK!
HAH! I'M NO CHILD--I'M SON TO PRIAM OF TROY! MATCH THAT, ACHAEAN!
I'LL DO BETTER THAN MATCH IT, BOY--MY FATHER WAS TYDEUS OF KALYDON--
SHHHK!
UH-
UH-
UH-
--ONE OF THE SEVEN--
AAAH!

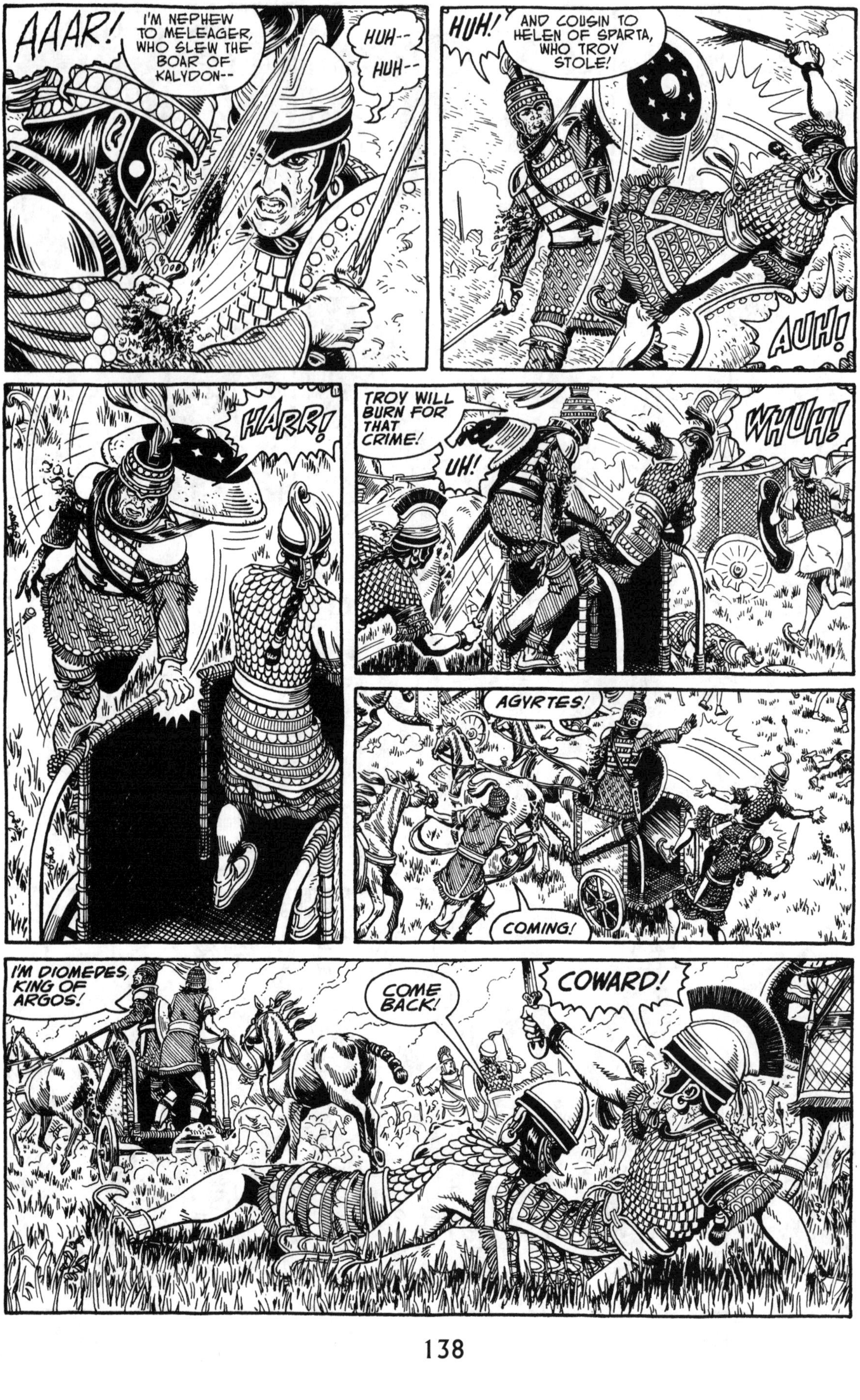
AAAR!
I'M NEPHEW TO MELEAGER, WHO SLEW THE BOAR OF KALYDON--
HUH-- HUH--
HUH!
AND COUSIN TO HELEN OF SPARTA, WHO TROY STOLE!
AUH!
HARR!
TROY WILL BURN FOR THAT CRIME!
UH!
WHUH!
AGYRTES!
COMING!
I'M DIOMEDES, KING OF ARGOS!
COME BACK!
COWARD!

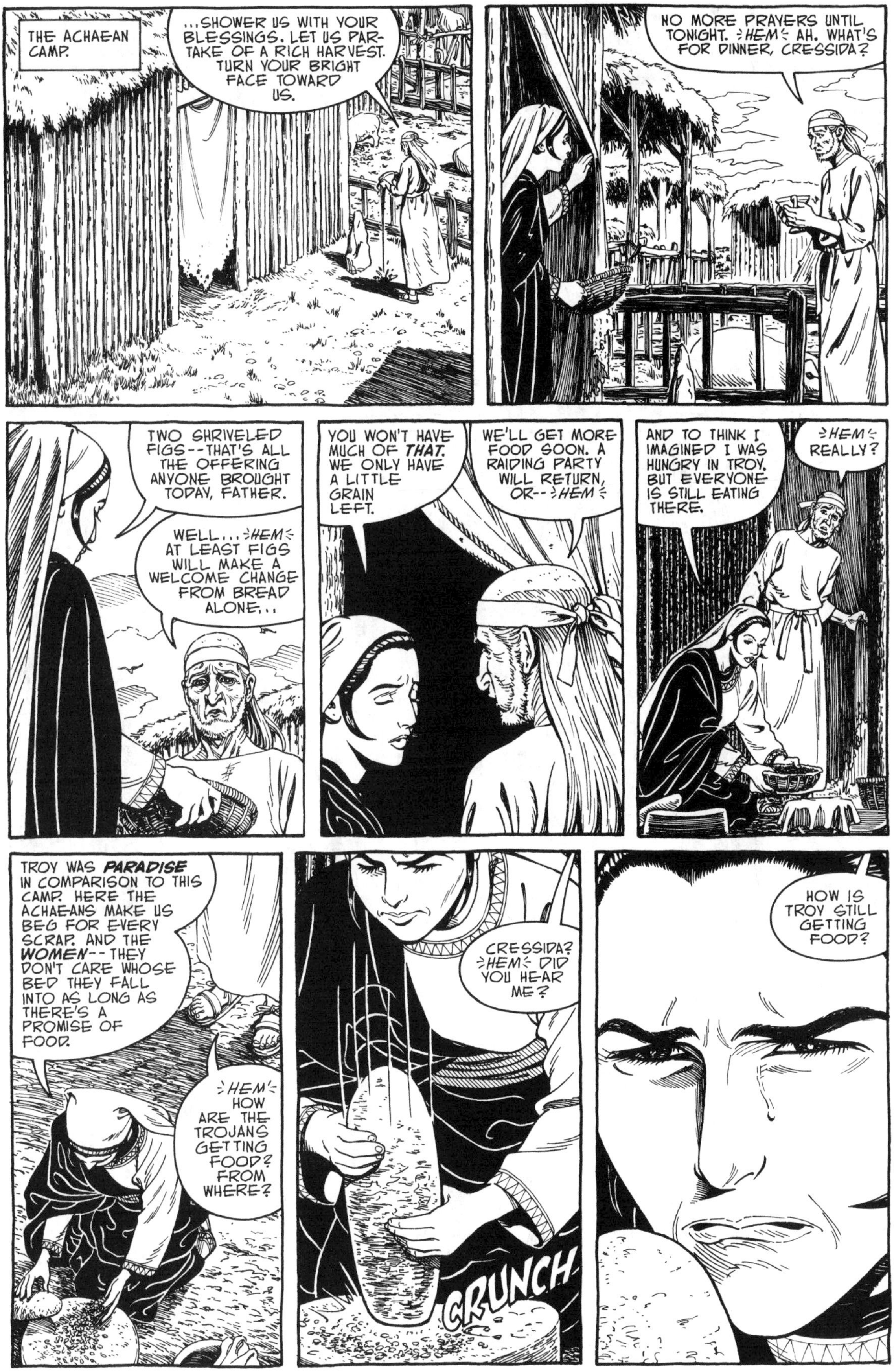
THE ACHAEAN CAMP.
...SHOWER US WITH YOUR BLESSINGS. LET US PARTAKE OF A RICH HARVEST. TURN YOUR BRIGHT FACE TOWARD US.
NO MORE PRAYERS UNTIL TONIGHT. *HEM* AH. WHAT'S FOR DINNER, CRESSIDA?
TWO SHRIVELED FIGS--THAT'S ALL THE OFFERING ANYONE BROUGHT TODAY, FATHER.
WELL... *HEM* AT LEAST FIGS WILL MAKE A WELCOME CHANGE FROM BREAD ALONE...
YOU WON'T HAVE MUCH OF **THAT.** WE ONLY HAVE A LITTLE GRAIN LEFT.
WE'LL GET MORE FOOD SOON. A RAIDING PARTY WILL RETURN, OR-- *HEM*
AND TO THINK I IMAGINED I WAS HUNGRY IN TROY. BUT EVERYONE IS STILL EATING THERE.
HEM REALLY?
TROY WAS **PARADISE** IN COMPARISON TO THIS CAMP. HERE THE ACHAEANS MAKE US BEG FOR EVERY SCRAP. AND THE **WOMEN**-- THEY DON'T CARE WHOSE BED THEY FALL INTO AS LONG AS THERE'S A PROMISE OF FOOD.
HEM HOW ARE THE TROJANS GETTING FOOD? FROM WHERE?
CRESSIDA? *HEM* DID YOU HEAR ME?
CRUNCH
HOW IS TROY STILL GETTING FOOD?

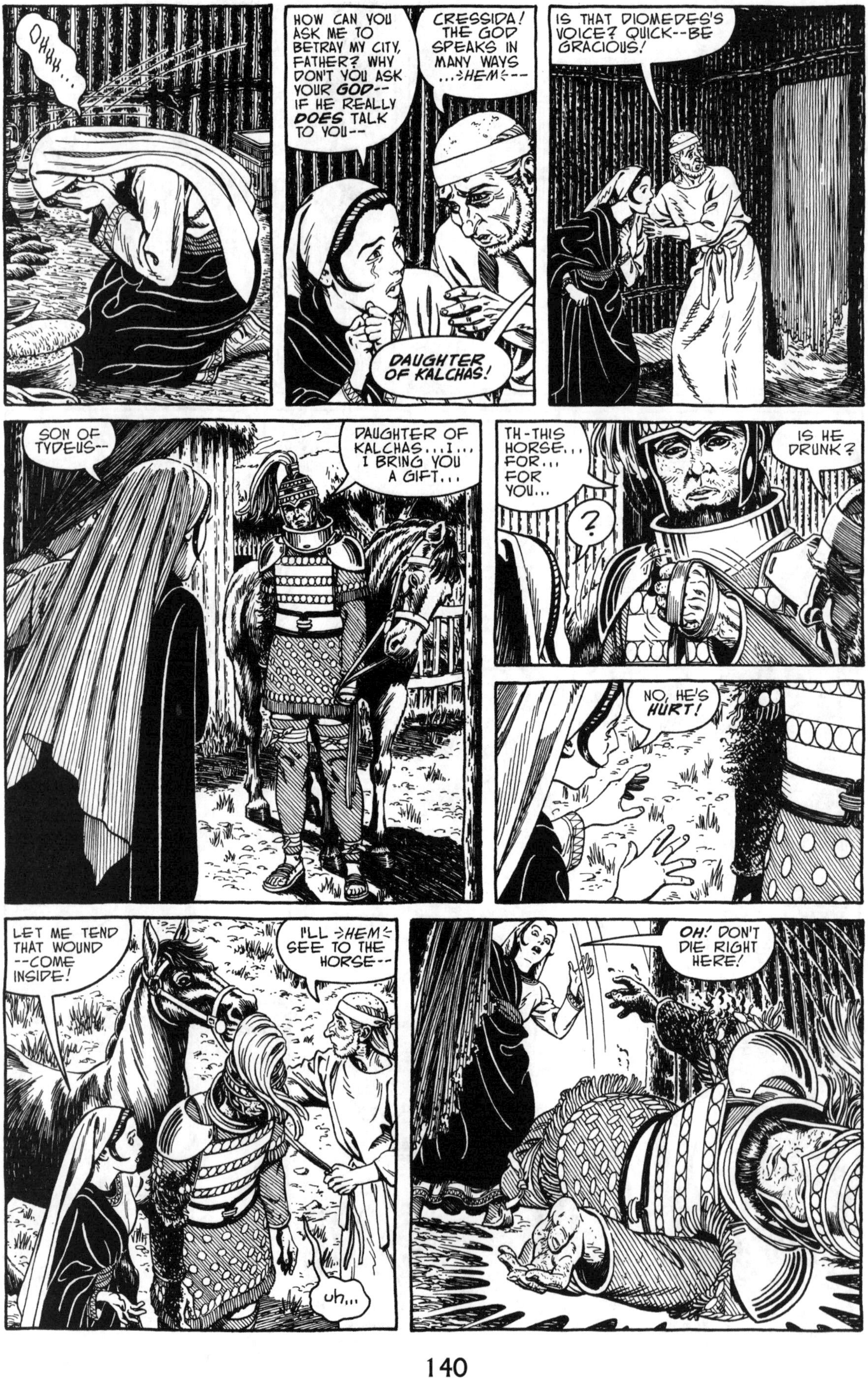
OHHH...
HOW CAN YOU ASK ME TO BETRAY MY CITY, FATHER? WHY DON'T YOU ASK YOUR GOD-- IF HE REALLY DOES TALK TO YOU--
CRESSIDA! THE GOD SPEAKS IN MANY WAYS ...HEM--
DAUGHTER OF KALCHAS!
IS THAT DIOMEDES'S VOICE? QUICK--BE GRACIOUS!
SON OF TYDEUS--
DAUGHTER OF KALCHAS...I... I BRING YOU A GIFT...
TH-THIS HORSE... FOR... FOR YOU...
?
IS HE DRUNK?
NO, HE'S HURT!
LET ME TEND THAT WOUND --COME INSIDE!
I'LL HEM SEE TO THE HORSE--
uh...
OH! DON'T DIE RIGHT HERE!

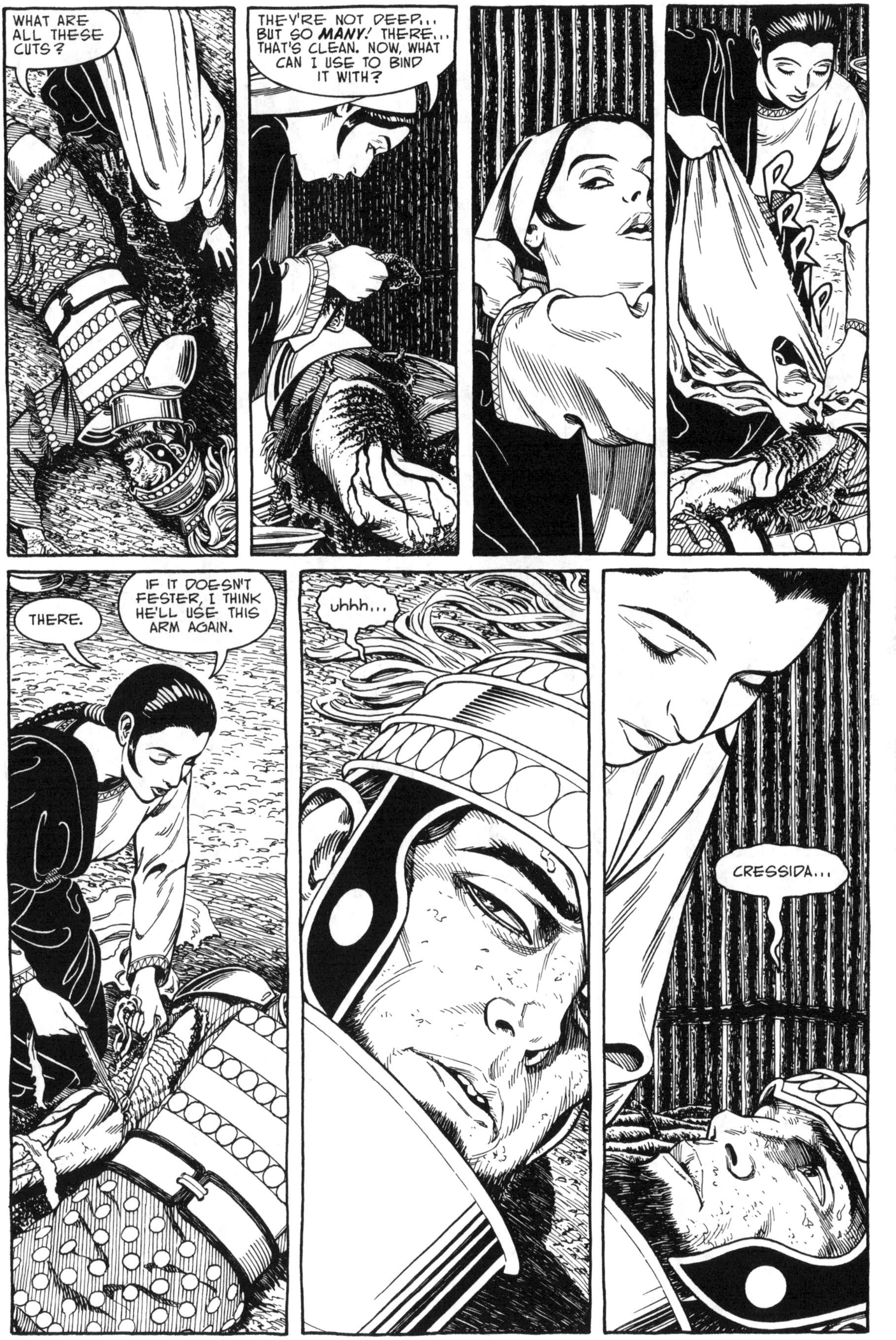
WHAT ARE ALL THESE CUTS?
THEY'RE NOT DEEP... BUT SO *MANY!* THERE... THAT'S CLEAN. NOW, WHAT CAN I USE TO BIND IT WITH?
RRRRRP
THERE.
IF IT DOESN'T FESTER, I THINK HE'LL USE THIS ARM AGAIN.
uhhh...
CRESSIDA...

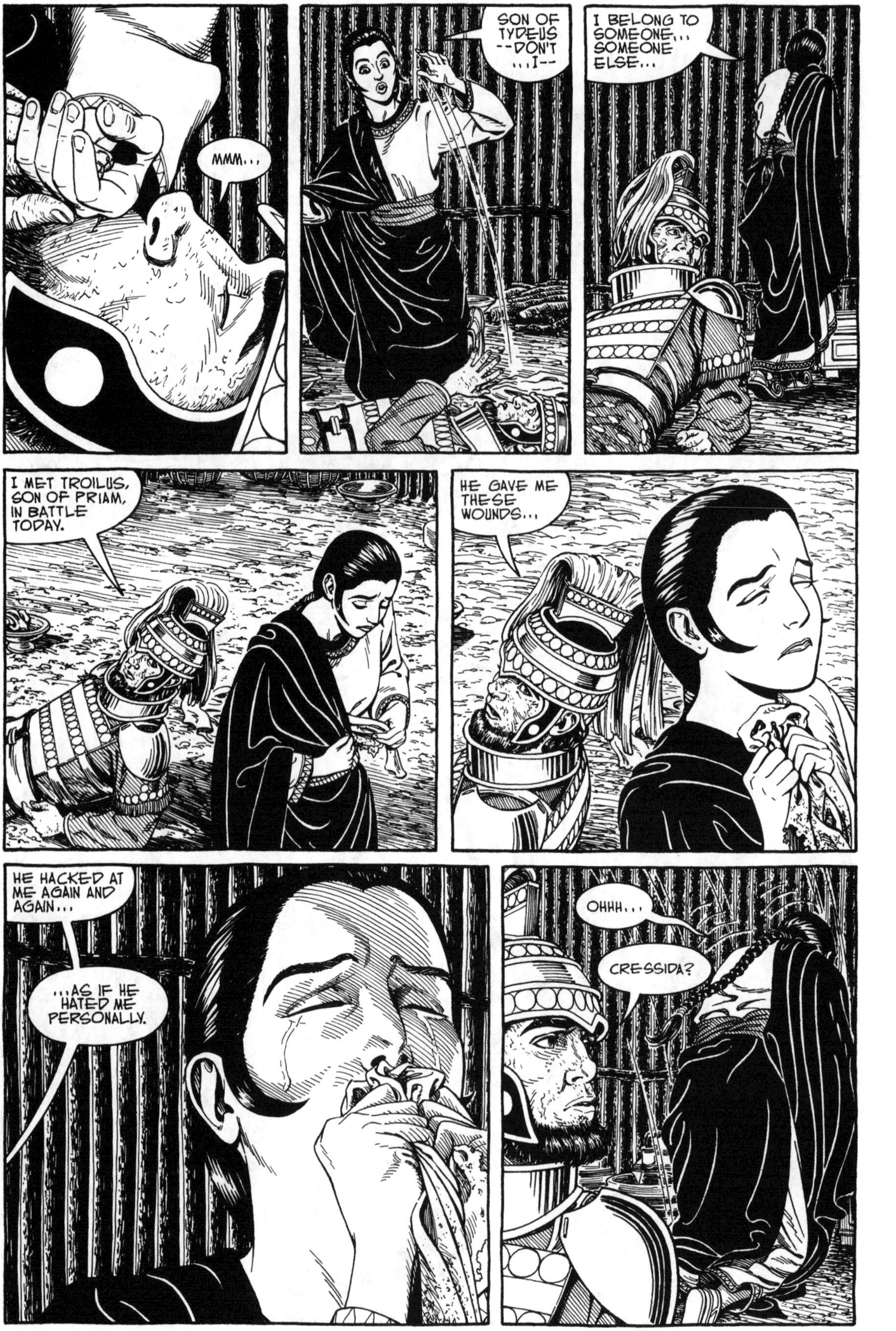
MMM...
SON OF TYDEUS --DON'T ...I--
I BELONG TO SOMEONE... SOMEONE ELSE...
I MET TROILUS, SON OF PRIAM, IN BATTLE TODAY.
HE GAVE ME THESE WOUNDS...
HE HACKED AT ME AGAIN AND AGAIN...
...AS IF HE HATED ME PERSONALLY.
OHHH...
CRESSIDA?

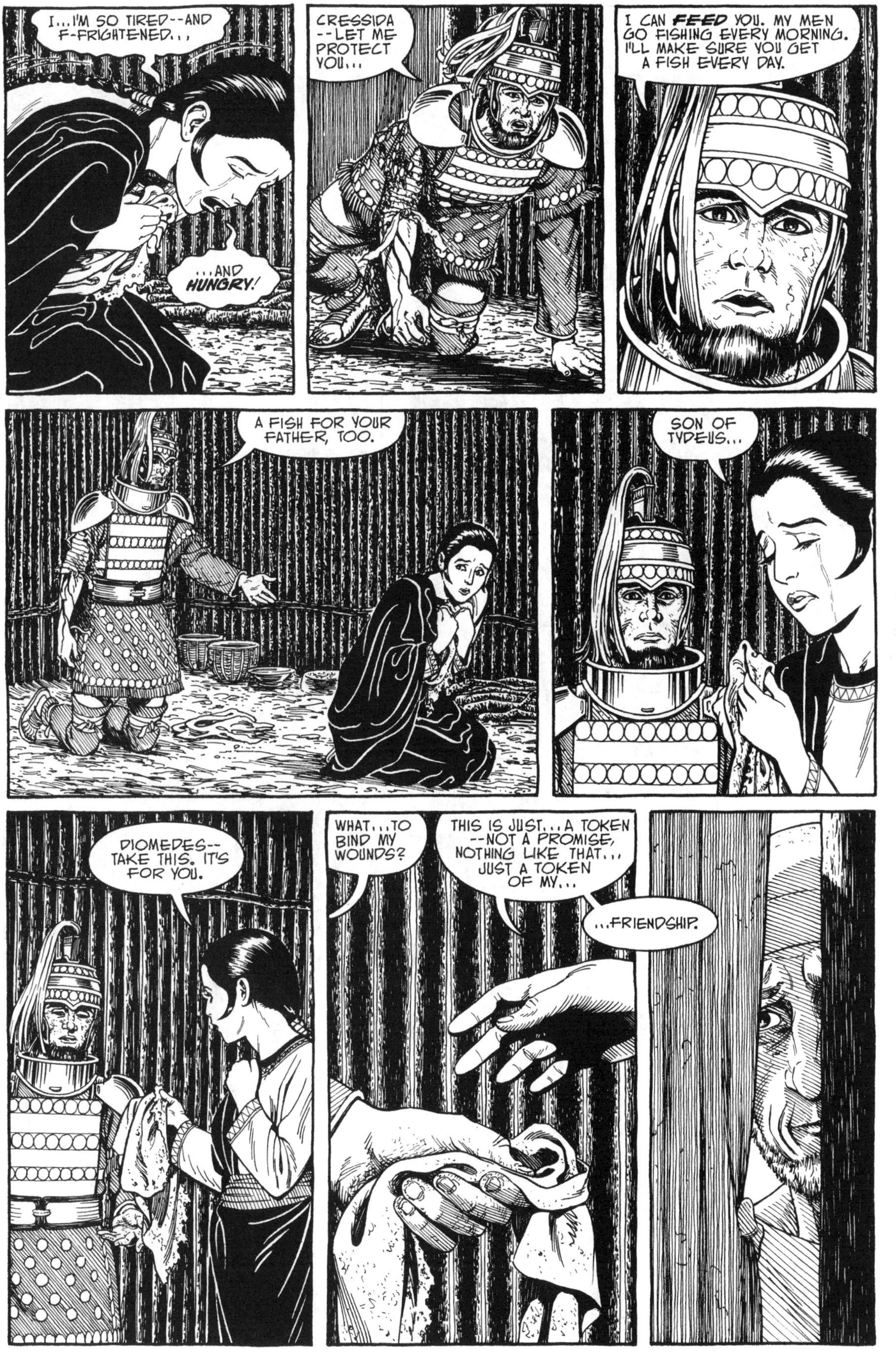
I...I'M SO TIRED--AND F-FRIGHTENED...
...AND HUNGRY!
CRESSIDA --LET ME PROTECT YOU...
I CAN FEED YOU. MY MEN GO FISHING EVERY MORNING. I'LL MAKE SURE YOU GET A FISH EVERY DAY.
A FISH FOR YOUR FATHER, TOO.
SON OF TYDEUS...
DIOMEDES-- TAKE THIS. IT'S FOR YOU.
WHAT...TO BIND MY WOUNDS?
THIS IS JUST...A TOKEN --NOT A PROMISE, NOTHING LIKE THAT... JUST A TOKEN OF MY...
...FRIENDSHIP.

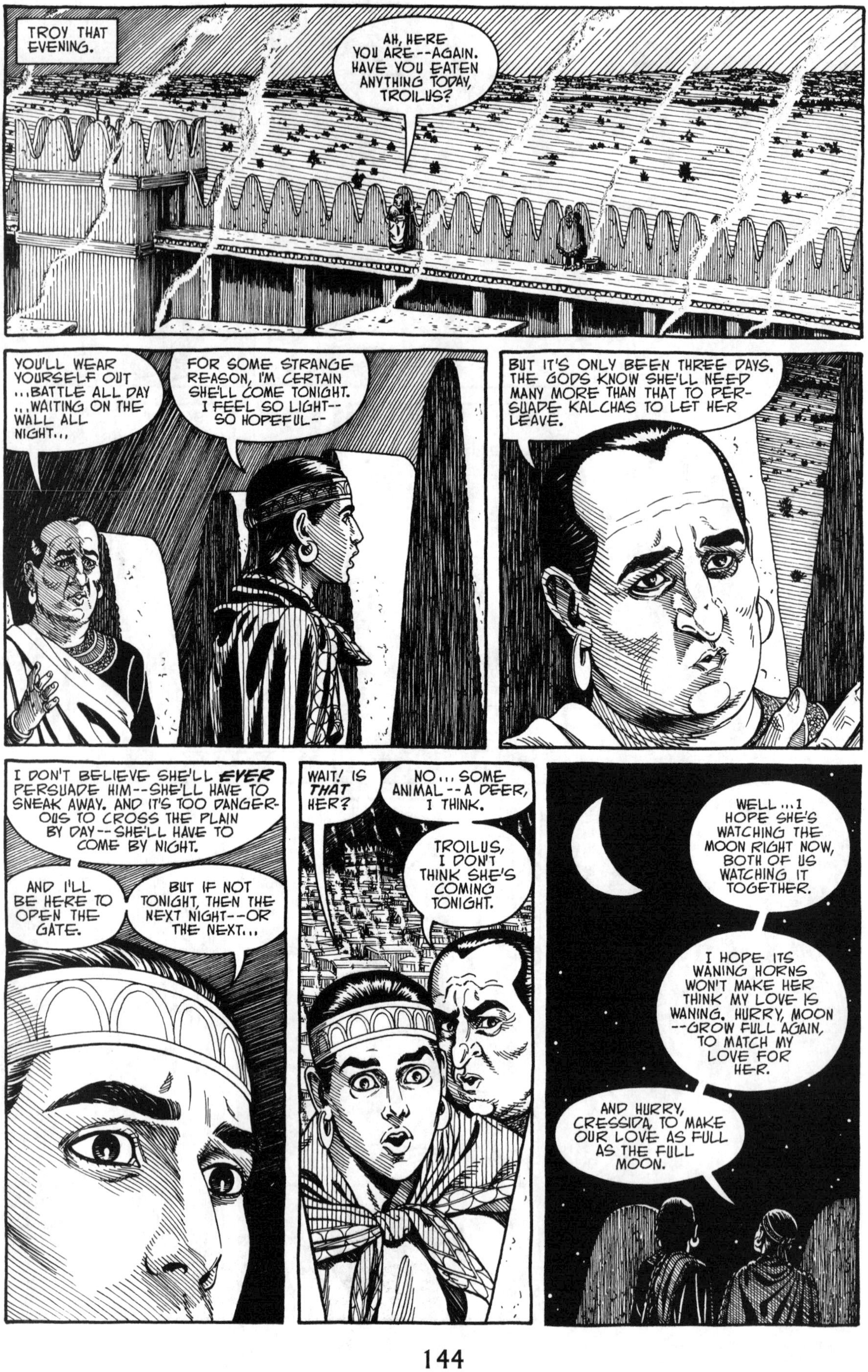

TROY THAT EVENING.
AH, HERE YOU ARE--AGAIN. HAVE YOU EATEN ANYTHING TODAY, TROILUS?
YOU'LL WEAR YOURSELF OUT ...BATTLE ALL DAY ...WAITING ON THE WALL ALL NIGHT...
FOR SOME STRANGE REASON, I'M CERTAIN SHE'LL COME TONIGHT. I FEEL SO LIGHT-- SO HOPEFUL--
BUT IT'S ONLY BEEN THREE DAYS. THE GODS KNOW SHE'LL NEED MANY MORE THAN THAT TO PERSUADE KALCHAS TO LET HER LEAVE.
I DON'T BELIEVE SHE'LL **EVER** PERSUADE HIM--SHE'LL HAVE TO SNEAK AWAY. AND IT'S TOO DANGEROUS TO CROSS THE PLAIN BY DAY--SHE'LL HAVE TO COME BY NIGHT.
AND I'LL BE HERE TO OPEN THE GATE.
BUT IF NOT TONIGHT, THEN THE NEXT NIGHT--OR THE NEXT...
WAIT! IS **THAT** HER?
NO... SOME ANIMAL--A DEER, I THINK.
TROILUS, I DON'T THINK SHE'S COMING TONIGHT.
WELL...I HOPE SHE'S WATCHING THE MOON RIGHT NOW, BOTH OF US WATCHING IT TOGETHER.
I HOPE ITS WANING HORNS WON'T MAKE HER THINK MY LOVE IS WANING. HURRY, MOON --GROW FULL AGAIN, TO MATCH MY LOVE FOR HER.
AND HURRY, CRESSIDA, TO MAKE OUR LOVE AS FULL AS THE FULL MOON.

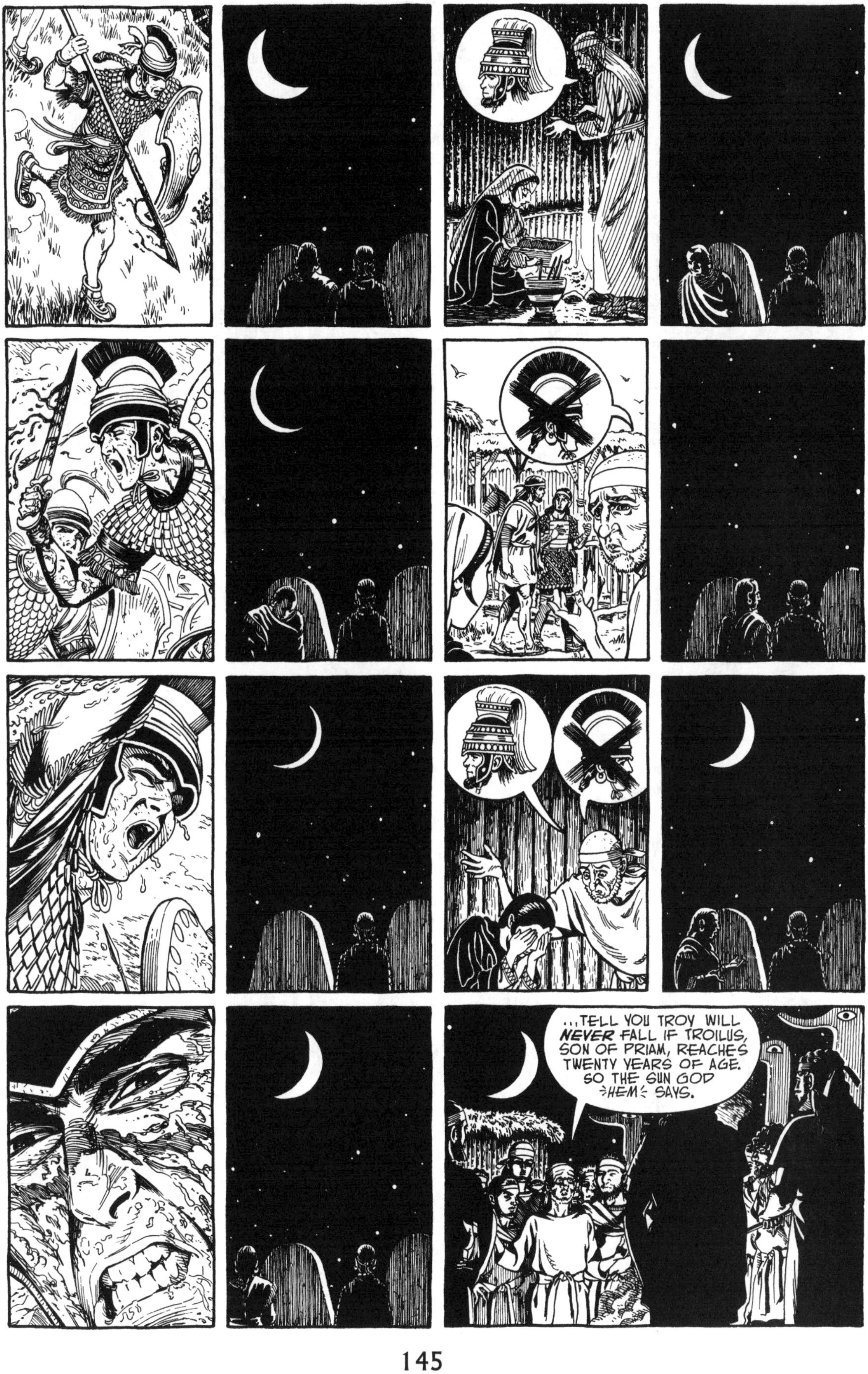

...TELL YOU TROY WILL **NEVER** FALL IF TROILUS, SON OF PRIAM, REACHES TWENTY YEARS OF AGE. SO THE SUN GOD HEM SAYS.

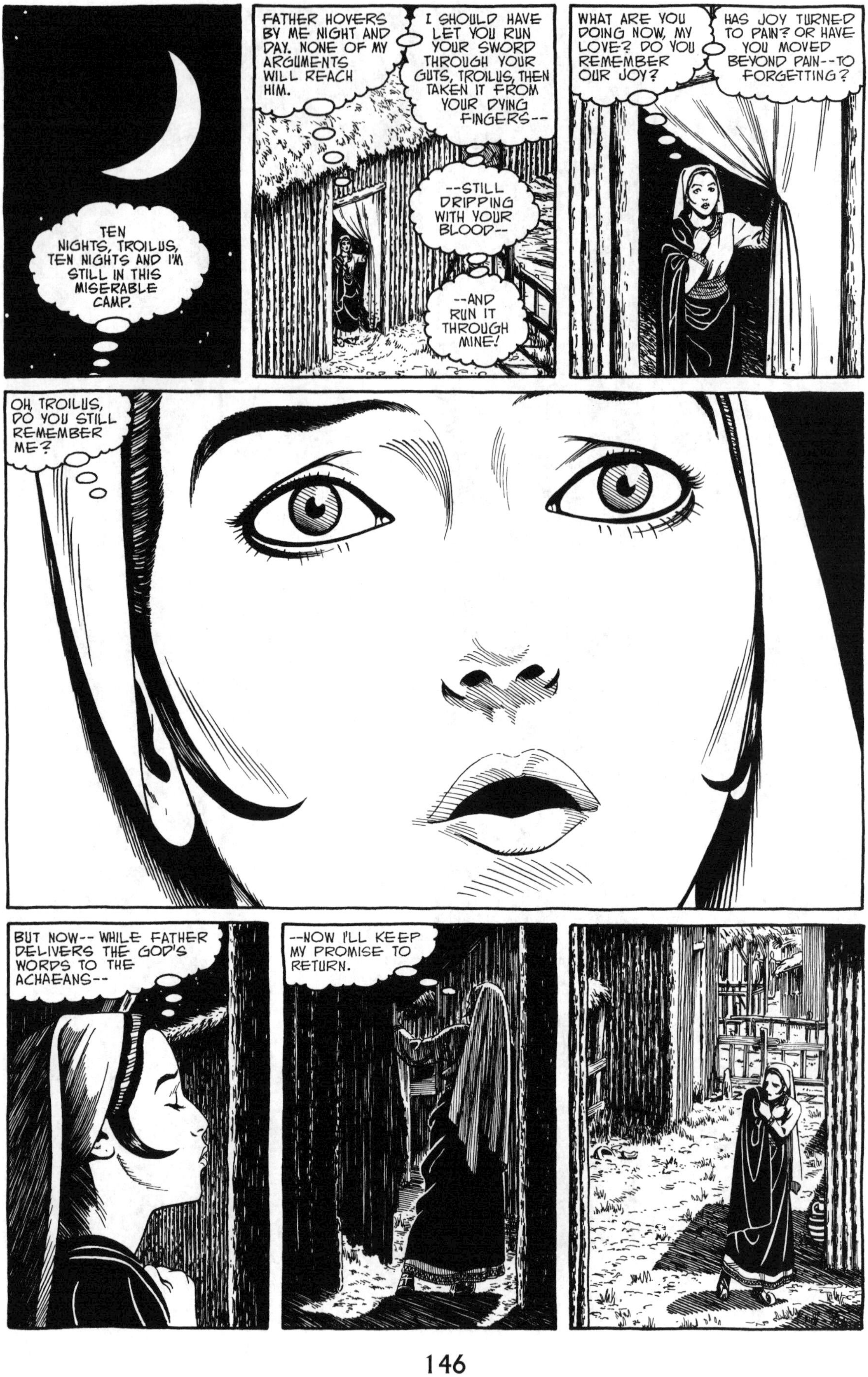
TEN NIGHTS, TROILUS, TEN NIGHTS AND I'M STILL IN THIS MISERABLE CAMP.
FATHER HOVERS BY ME NIGHT AND DAY. NONE OF MY ARGUMENTS WILL REACH HIM.
I SHOULD HAVE LET YOU RUN YOUR SWORD THROUGH YOUR GUTS, TROILUS, THEN TAKEN IT FROM YOUR DYING FINGERS--
--STILL DRIPPING WITH YOUR BLOOD--
--AND RUN IT THROUGH MINE!
WHAT ARE YOU DOING NOW, MY LOVE? DO YOU REMEMBER OUR JOY?
HAS JOY TURNED TO PAIN? OR HAVE YOU MOVED BEYOND PAIN--TO FORGETTING?
OH, TROILUS, DO YOU STILL REMEMBER ME?
BUT NOW-- WHILE FATHER DELIVERS THE GOD'S WORDS TO THE ACHAEANS--
--NOW I'LL KEEP MY PROMISE TO RETURN.

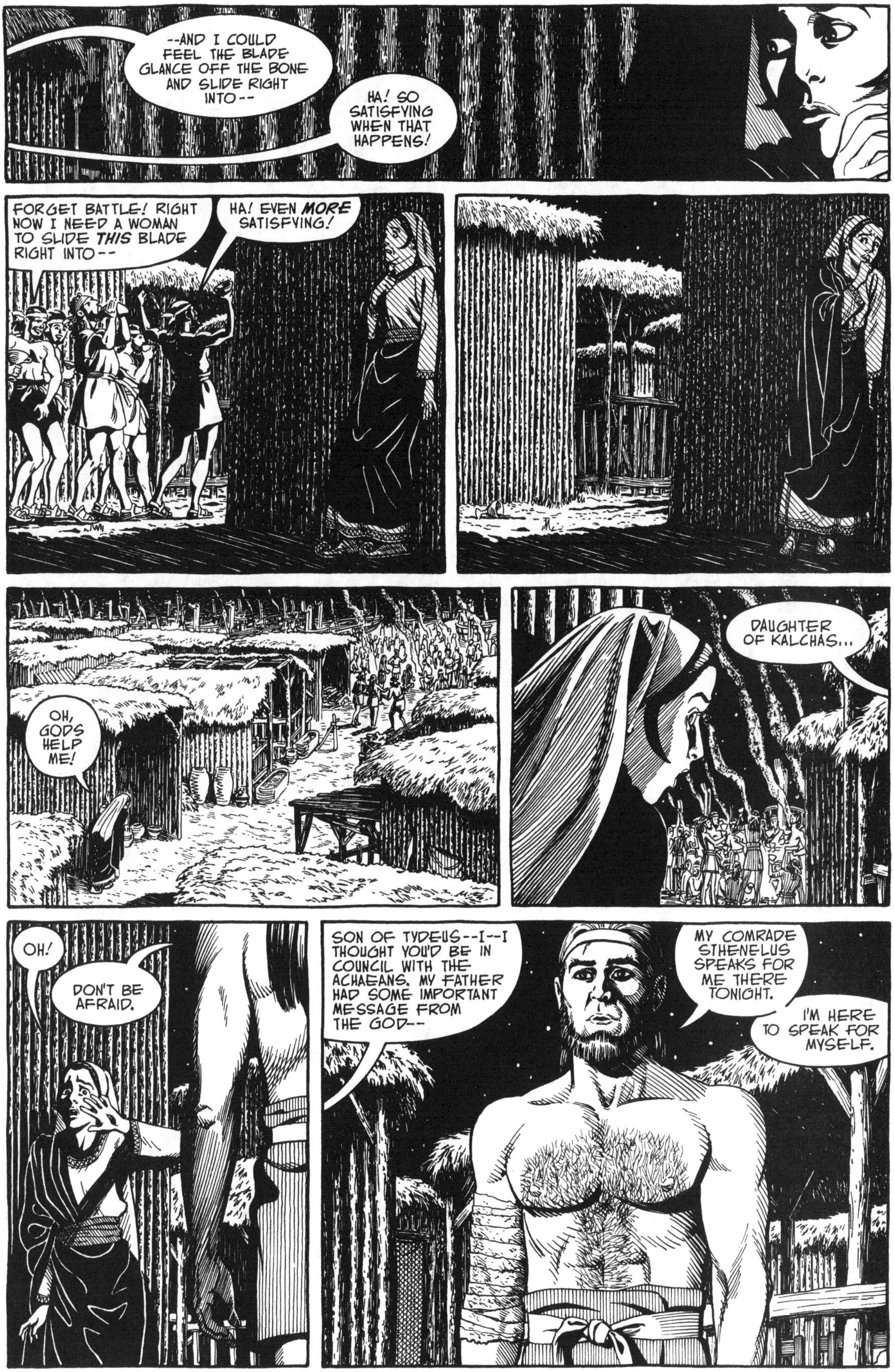
--AND I COULD FEEL THE BLADE GLANCE OFF THE BONE AND SLIDE RIGHT INTO--
HA! SO SATISFYING WHEN THAT HAPPENS!
FORGET BATTLE! RIGHT NOW I NEED A WOMAN TO SLIDE THIS BLADE RIGHT INTO--
HA! EVEN MORE SATISFYING!
OH, GODS HELP ME!
DAUGHTER OF KALCHAS...
OH!
DON'T BE AFRAID.
SON OF TYDEUS--I--I THOUGHT YOU'D BE IN COUNCIL WITH THE ACHAEANS. MY FATHER HAD SOME IMPORTANT MESSAGE FROM THE GOD--
MY COMRADE STHENELUS SPEAKS FOR ME THERE TONIGHT.
I'M HERE TO SPEAK FOR MYSELF.

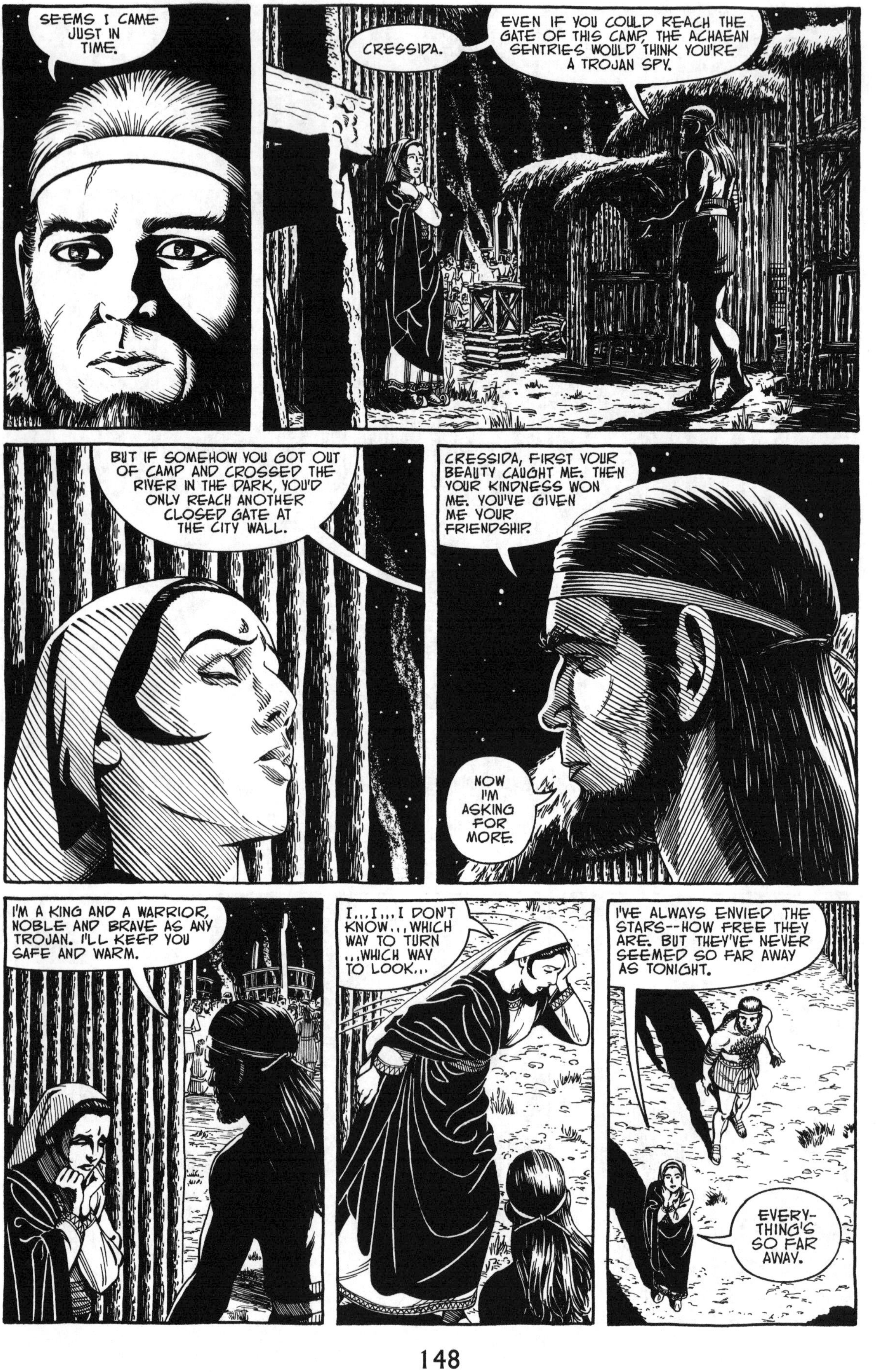
SEEMS I CAME JUST IN TIME.
CRESSIDA.
EVEN IF YOU COULD REACH THE GATE OF THIS CAMP, THE ACHAEAN SENTRIES WOULD THINK YOU'RE A TROJAN SPY.
BUT IF SOMEHOW YOU GOT OUT OF CAMP AND CROSSED THE RIVER IN THE DARK, YOU'D ONLY REACH ANOTHER CLOSED GATE AT THE CITY WALL.
CRESSIDA, FIRST YOUR BEAUTY CAUGHT ME. THEN YOUR KINDNESS WON ME. YOU'VE GIVEN ME YOUR FRIENDSHIP.
NOW I'M ASKING FOR MORE.
I'M A KING AND A WARRIOR, NOBLE AND BRAVE AS ANY TROJAN. I'LL KEEP YOU SAFE AND WARM.
I...I...I DON'T KNOW...WHICH WAY TO TURN ...WHICH WAY TO LOOK...
I'VE ALWAYS ENVIED THE STARS--HOW FREE THEY ARE. BUT THEY'VE NEVER SEEMED SO FAR AWAY AS TONIGHT.
EVERYTHING'S SO FAR AWAY.

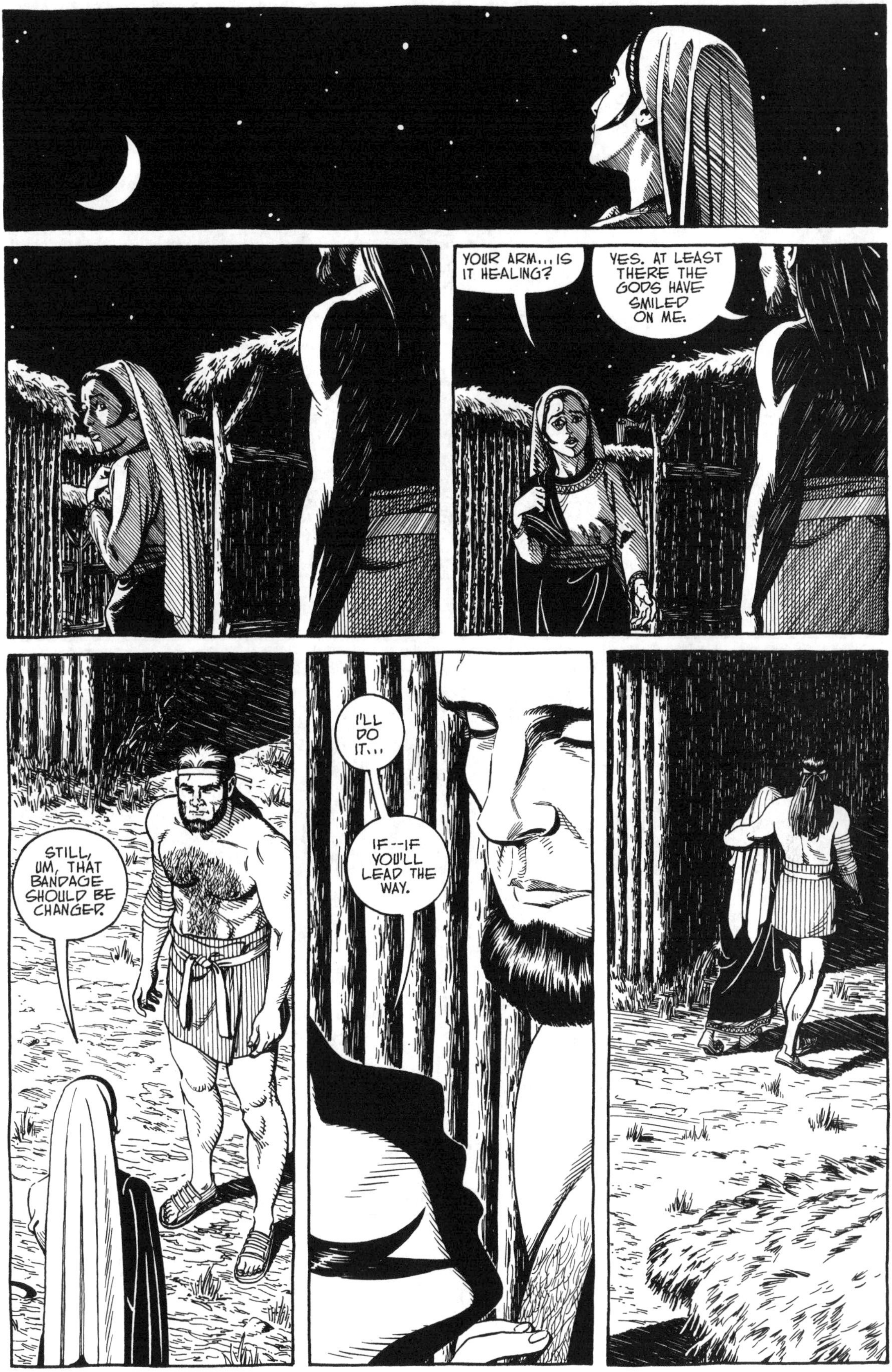
YOUR ARM... IS IT HEALING?
YES. AT LEAST THERE THE GODS HAVE SMILED ON ME.
STILL, UM, THAT BANDAGE SHOULD BE CHANGED.
I'LL DO IT...
IF--IF YOU'LL LEAD THE WAY.

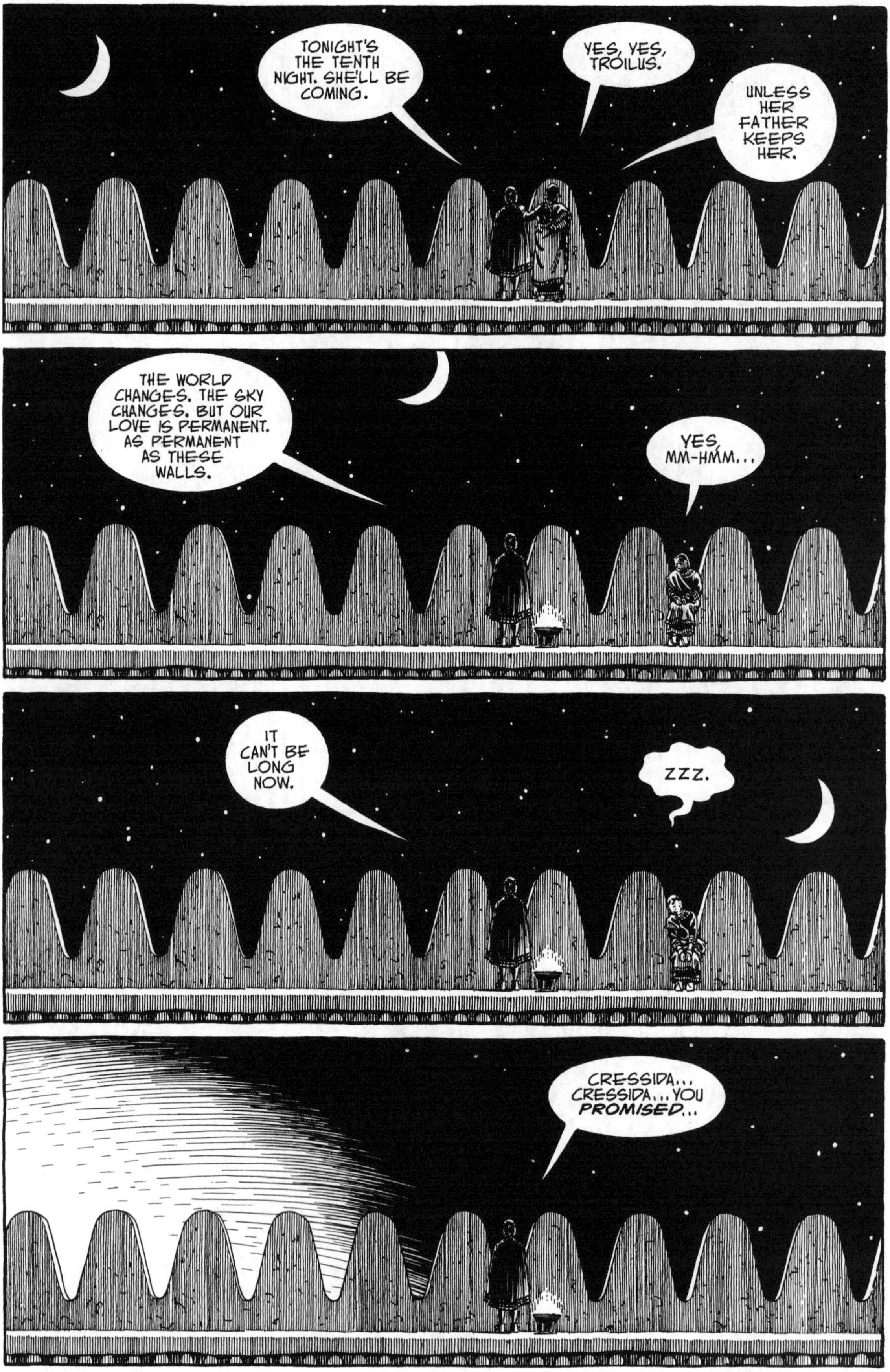
TONIGHT'S THE TENTH NIGHT. SHE'LL BE COMING.
YES, YES, TROILUS.
UNLESS HER FATHER KEEPS HER.
THE WORLD CHANGES. THE SKY CHANGES. BUT OUR LOVE IS PERMANENT. AS PERMANENT AS THESE WALLS.
YES, MM-HMM...
IT CAN'T BE LONG NOW.
ZZZ.
CRESSIDA... CRESSIDA... YOU *PROMISED*...

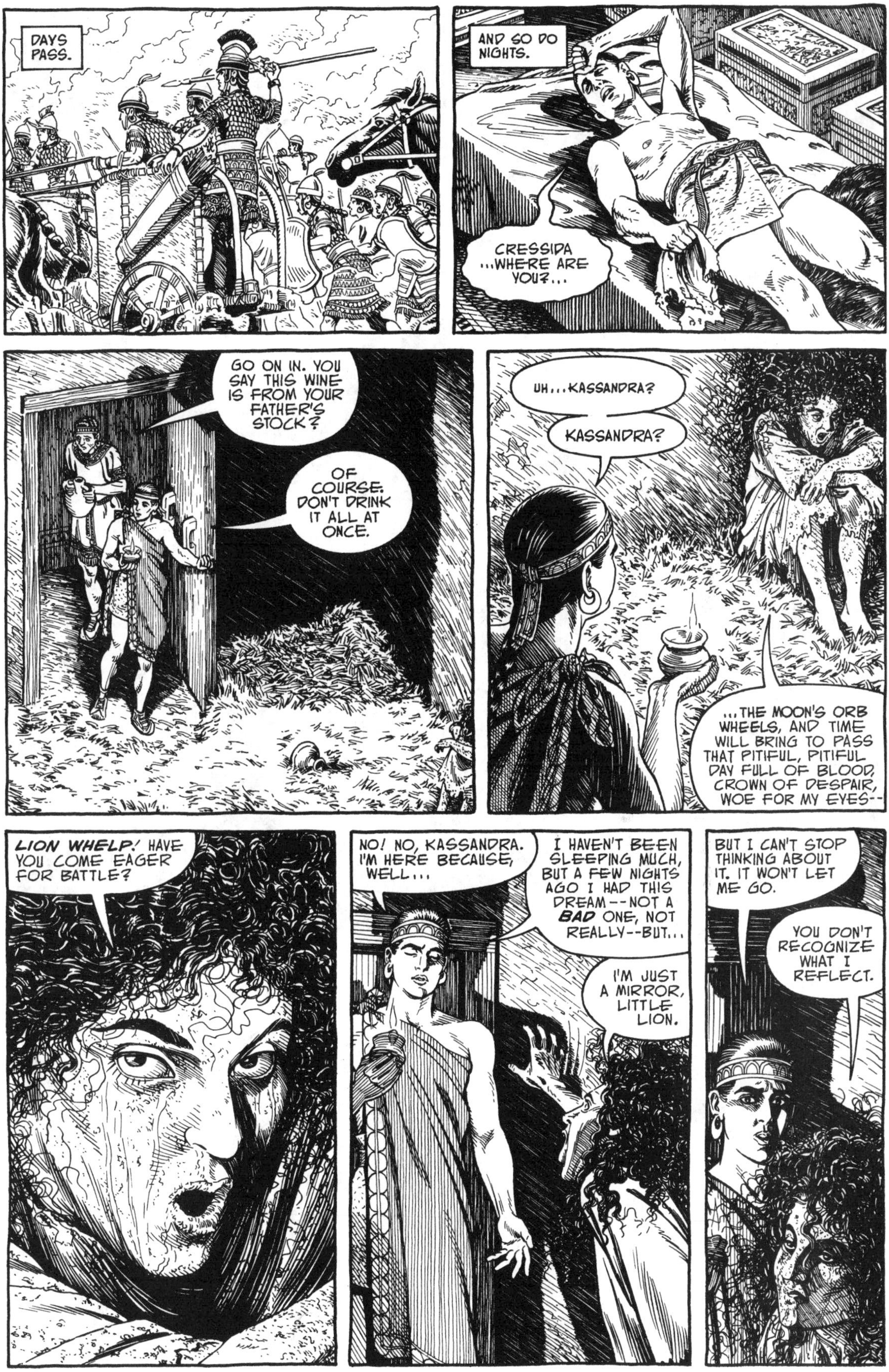
DAYS PASS.
AND SO DO NIGHTS.
CRESSIDA ...WHERE ARE YOU?...
GO ON IN. YOU SAY THIS WINE IS FROM YOUR FATHER'S STOCK?
OF COURSE. DON'T DRINK IT ALL AT ONCE.
UH... KASSANDRA?
KASSANDRA?
...THE MOON'S ORB WHEELS, AND TIME WILL BRING TO PASS THAT PITIFUL, PITIFUL DAY FULL OF BLOOD, CROWN OF DESPAIR, WOE FOR MY EYES--
LION WHELP! HAVE YOU COME EAGER FOR BATTLE?
NO! NO, KASSANDRA. I'M HERE BECAUSE, WELL...
I HAVEN'T BEEN SLEEPING MUCH, BUT A FEW NIGHTS AGO I HAD THIS DREAM--NOT A ***BAD*** ONE, NOT REALLY--BUT...
I'M JUST A MIRROR, LITTLE LION.
BUT I CAN'T STOP THINKING ABOUT IT. IT WON'T LET ME GO.
YOU DON'T RECOGNIZE WHAT I REFLECT.

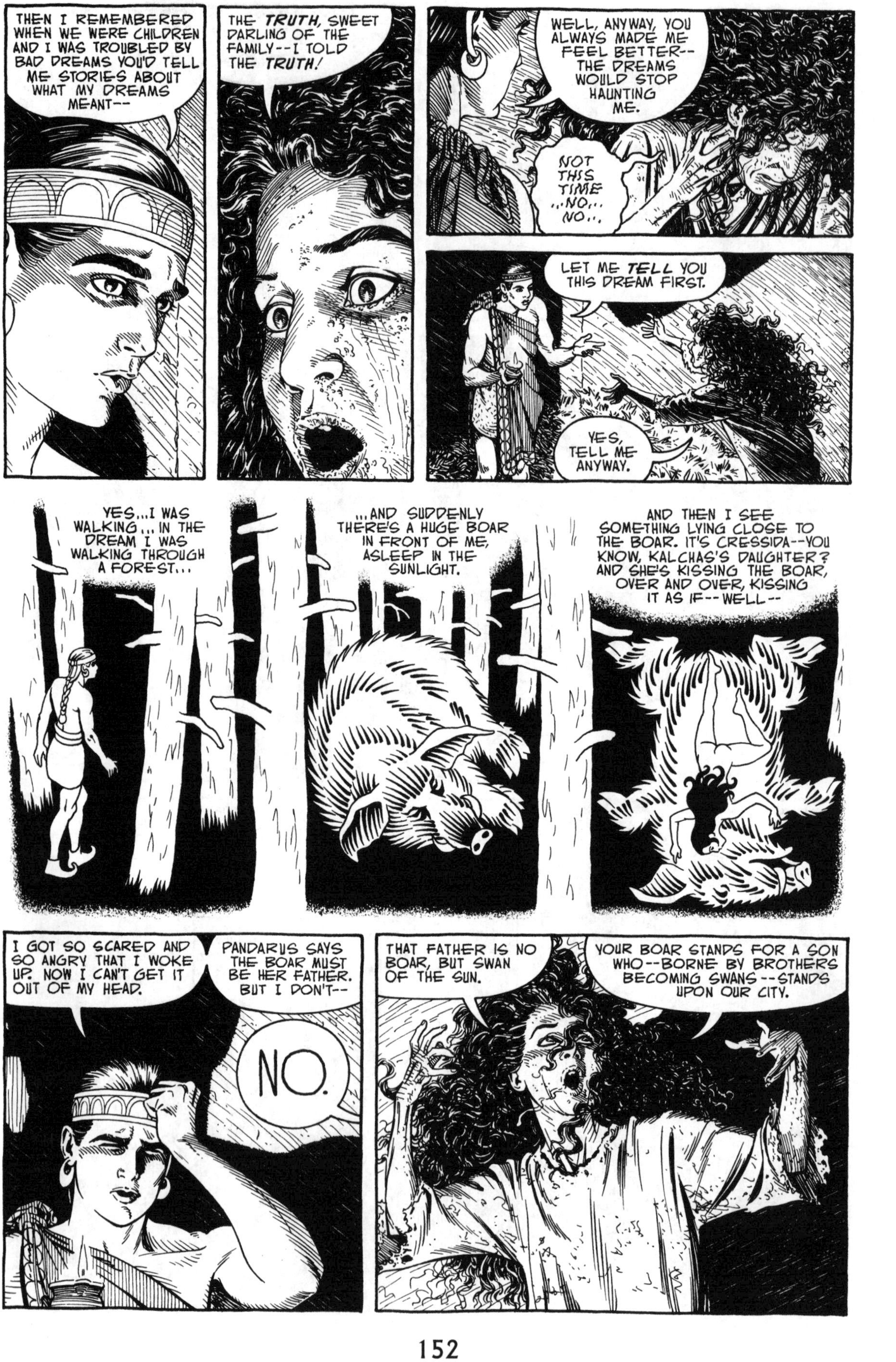
THEN I REMEMBERED WHEN WE WERE CHILDREN AND I WAS TROUBLED BY BAD DREAMS YOU'D TELL ME STORIES ABOUT WHAT MY DREAMS MEANT--
THE TRUTH, SWEET DARLING OF THE FAMILY--I TOLD THE TRUTH!
WELL, ANYWAY, YOU ALWAYS MADE ME FEEL BETTER-- THE DREAMS WOULD STOP HAUNTING ME.
NOT THIS TIME ...NO... NO...
LET ME TELL YOU THIS DREAM FIRST.
YES, TELL ME ANYWAY.
YES...I WAS WALKING... IN THE DREAM I WAS WALKING THROUGH A FOREST...
...AND SUDDENLY THERE'S A HUGE BOAR IN FRONT OF ME, ASLEEP IN THE SUNLIGHT.
AND THEN I SEE SOMETHING LYING CLOSE TO THE BOAR. IT'S CRESSIDA--YOU KNOW, KALCHAS'S DAUGHTER? AND SHE'S KISSING THE BOAR, OVER AND OVER, KISSING IT AS IF--WELL--
I GOT SO SCARED AND SO ANGRY THAT I WOKE UP. NOW I CAN'T GET IT OUT OF MY HEAD.
PANDARUS SAYS THE BOAR MUST BE HER FATHER. BUT I DON'T--
NO.
THAT FATHER IS NO BOAR, BUT SWAN OF THE SUN.
YOUR BOAR STANDS FOR A SON WHO--BORNE BY BROTHERS BECOMING SWANS--STANDS UPON OUR CITY.

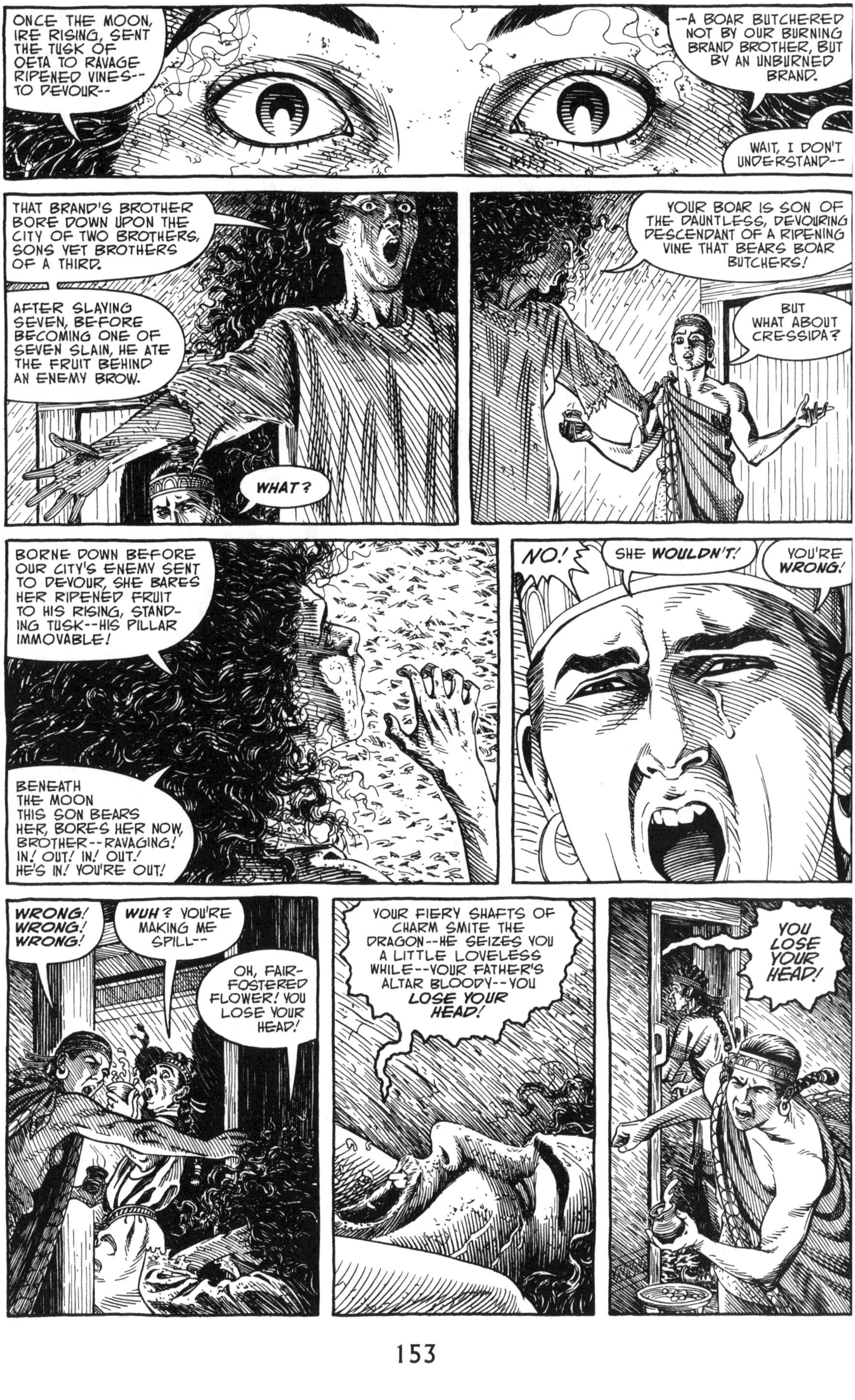
ONCE THE MOON, IRE RISING, SENT THE TUSK OF OETA TO RAVAGE RIPENED VINES-- TO DEVOUR--
--A BOAR BUTCHERED NOT BY OUR BURNING BRAND BROTHER, BUT BY AN UNBURNED BRAND.
WAIT, I DON'T UNDERSTAND--
THAT BRAND'S BROTHER BORE DOWN UPON THE CITY OF TWO BROTHERS, SONS YET BROTHERS OF A THIRD.
AFTER SLAYING SEVEN, BEFORE BECOMING ONE OF SEVEN SLAIN, HE ATE THE FRUIT BEHIND AN ENEMY BROW.
WHAT?
YOUR BOAR IS SON OF THE DAUNTLESS, DEVOURING DESCENDANT OF A RIPENING VINE THAT BEARS BOAR BUTCHERS!
BUT WHAT ABOUT CRESSIDA?
BORNE DOWN BEFORE OUR CITY'S ENEMY SENT TO DEVOUR, SHE BARES HER RIPENED FRUIT TO HIS RISING, STANDING TUSK--HIS PILLAR IMMOVABLE!
BENEATH THE MOON THIS SON BEARS HER, BORES HER NOW, BROTHER--RAVAGING! IN! OUT! IN! OUT! HE'S IN! YOU'RE OUT!
NO!
SHE WOULDN'T!
YOU'RE WRONG!
WRONG! WRONG! WRONG!
WUH? YOU'RE MAKING ME SPILL--
OH, FAIR-FOSTERED FLOWER! YOU LOSE YOUR HEAD!
YOUR FIERY SHAFTS OF CHARM SMITE THE DRAGON--HE SEIZES YOU A LITTLE LOVELESS WHILE--YOUR FATHER'S ALTAR BLOODY--YOU LOSE YOUR HEAD!
YOU LOSE YOUR HEAD!

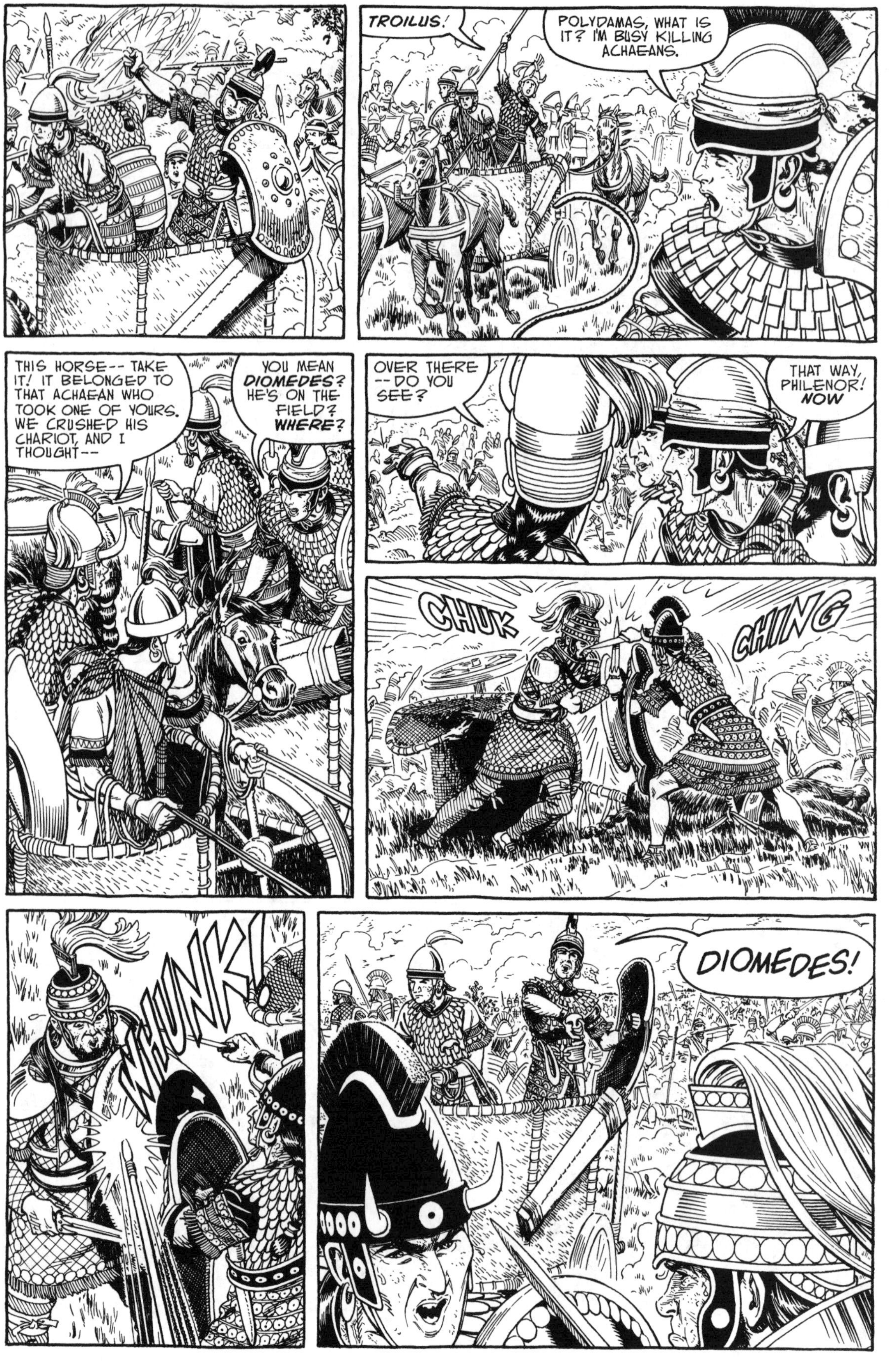
TROILUS!
POLYDAMAS, WHAT IS IT? I'M BUSY KILLING ACHAEANS.
THIS HORSE-- TAKE IT! IT BELONGED TO THAT ACHAEAN WHO TOOK ONE OF YOURS. WE CRUSHED HIS CHARIOT, AND I THOUGHT--
YOU MEAN DIOMEDES? HE'S ON THE FIELD? WHERE?
OVER THERE --DO YOU SEE?
THAT WAY, PHILENOR! NOW
CHUK
CHING
WHUNK!
DIOMEDES!

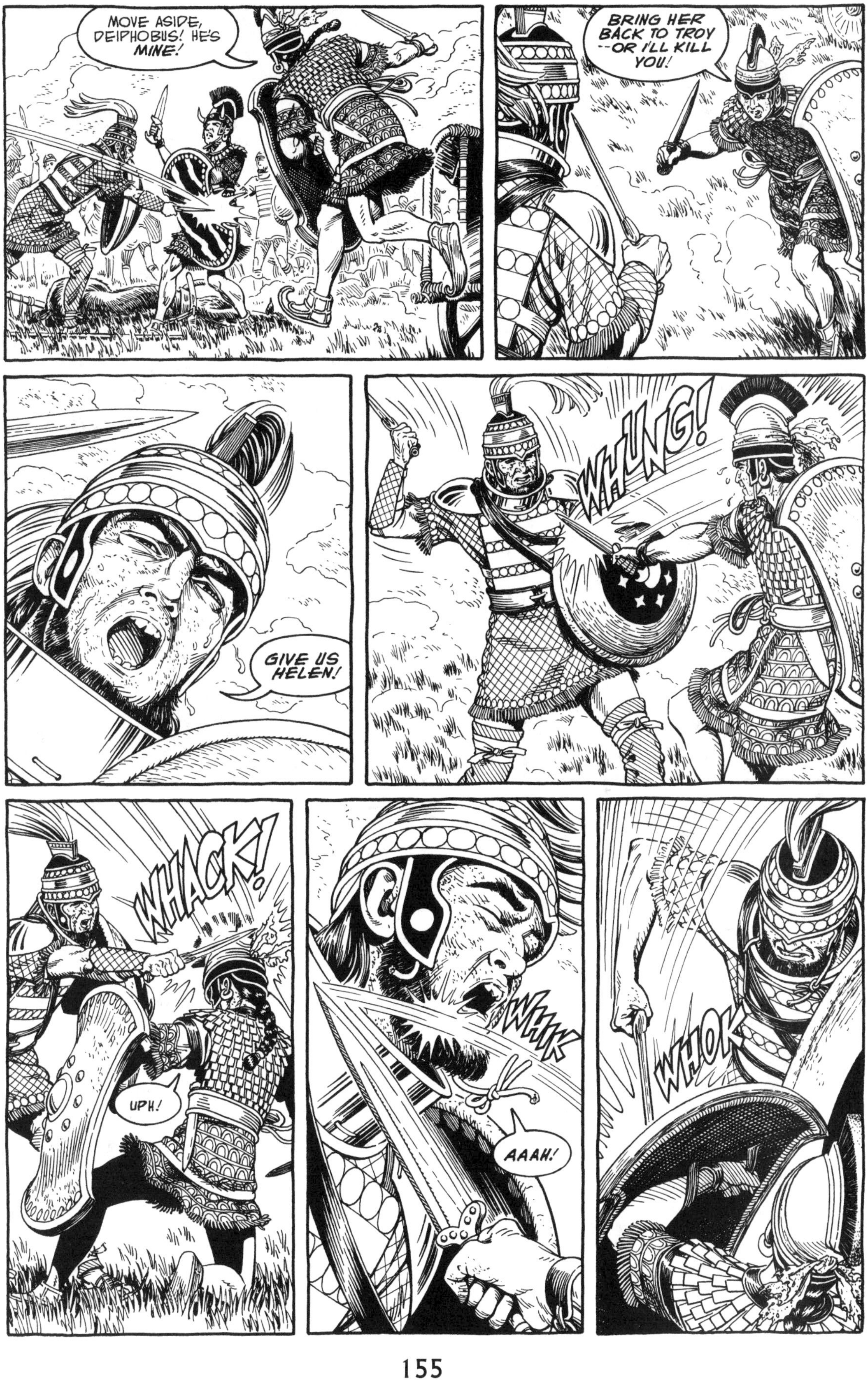

MOVE ASIDE, DEIPHOBUS! HE'S MINE!
BRING HER BACK TO TROY --OR I'LL KILL YOU!
GIVE US HELEN!
WHUNG!
WHACK!
UPH!
WHUK
AAAH!
WHOK

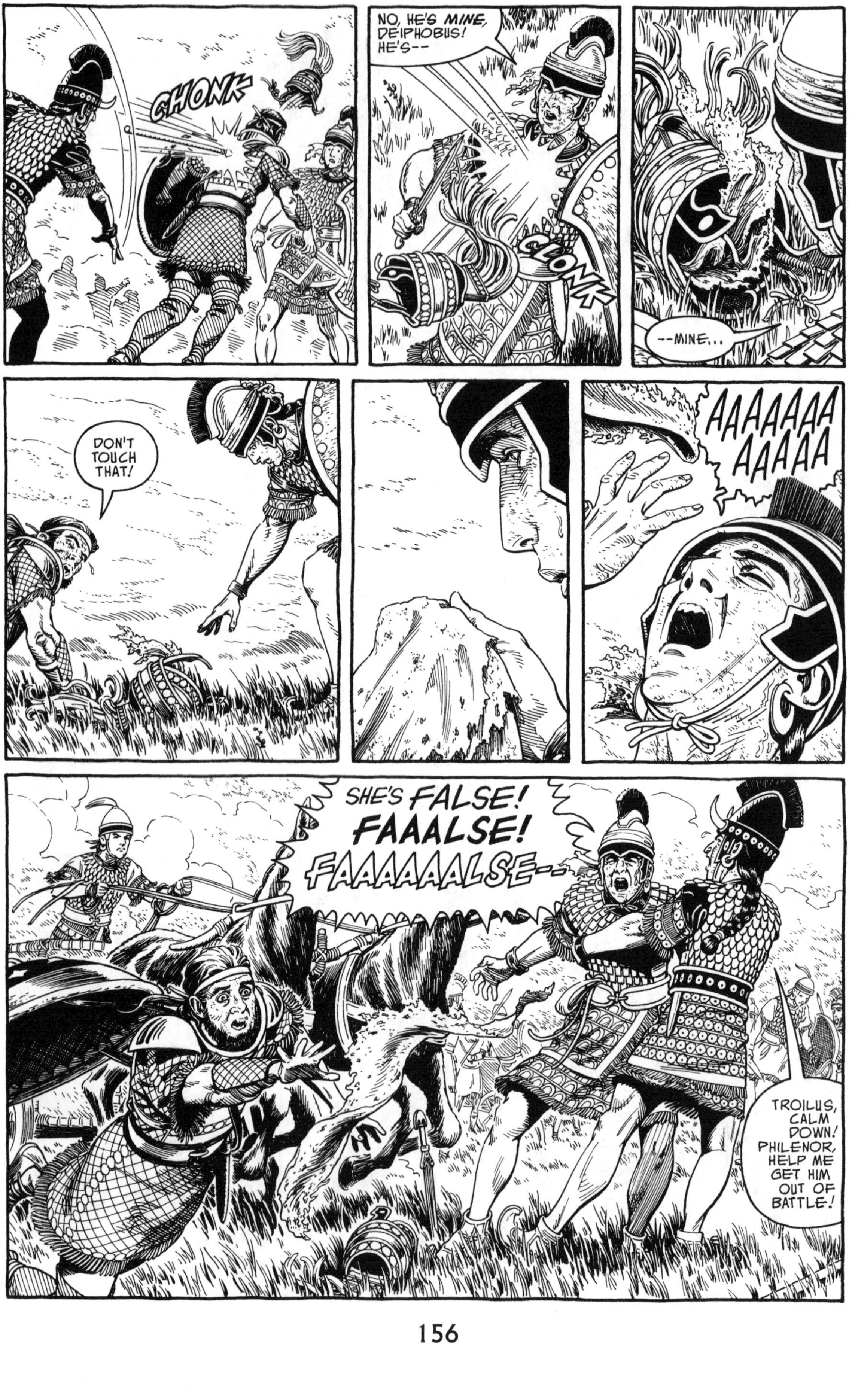
CHONK
NO, HE'S MINE, DEIPHOBUS! HE'S--
CLONK
--MINE...
DON'T TOUCH THAT!
AAAAAAA AAAAA
SHE'S FALSE! FAAALSE! FAAAAAALSE--
TROILUS, CALM DOWN! PHILENOR, HELP ME GET HIM OUT OF BATTLE!

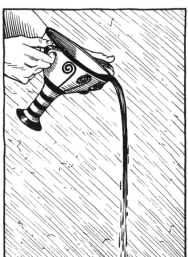

IF ALL THAT HAPPENS IS DIRECTED BY THE GODS, AS THE PRIESTS TELL US...

...DO I HAVE A CHOICE IN MY OWN DESTINY?

CAN I TAKE AN ACTION THAT ONE OF THE THOUSAND GODS HASN'T DECREED?

CAN I EVEN CONCEIVE A THOUGHT THAT A GOD HASN'T PUT INTO MY HEAD?

IF EACH OF US LIVES A LIFE THAT'S ALREADY DECIDED, THEN WHAT'S THE USE OF MAKING ANY EFFORT AT ALL?

IF THE GODS MEANT HER TO BE WITH ME, SHE WOULD BE.

AND IF THEY MEANT ME TO LOSE HER, THEN NOTHING I DO CAN CHANGE THAT.

157

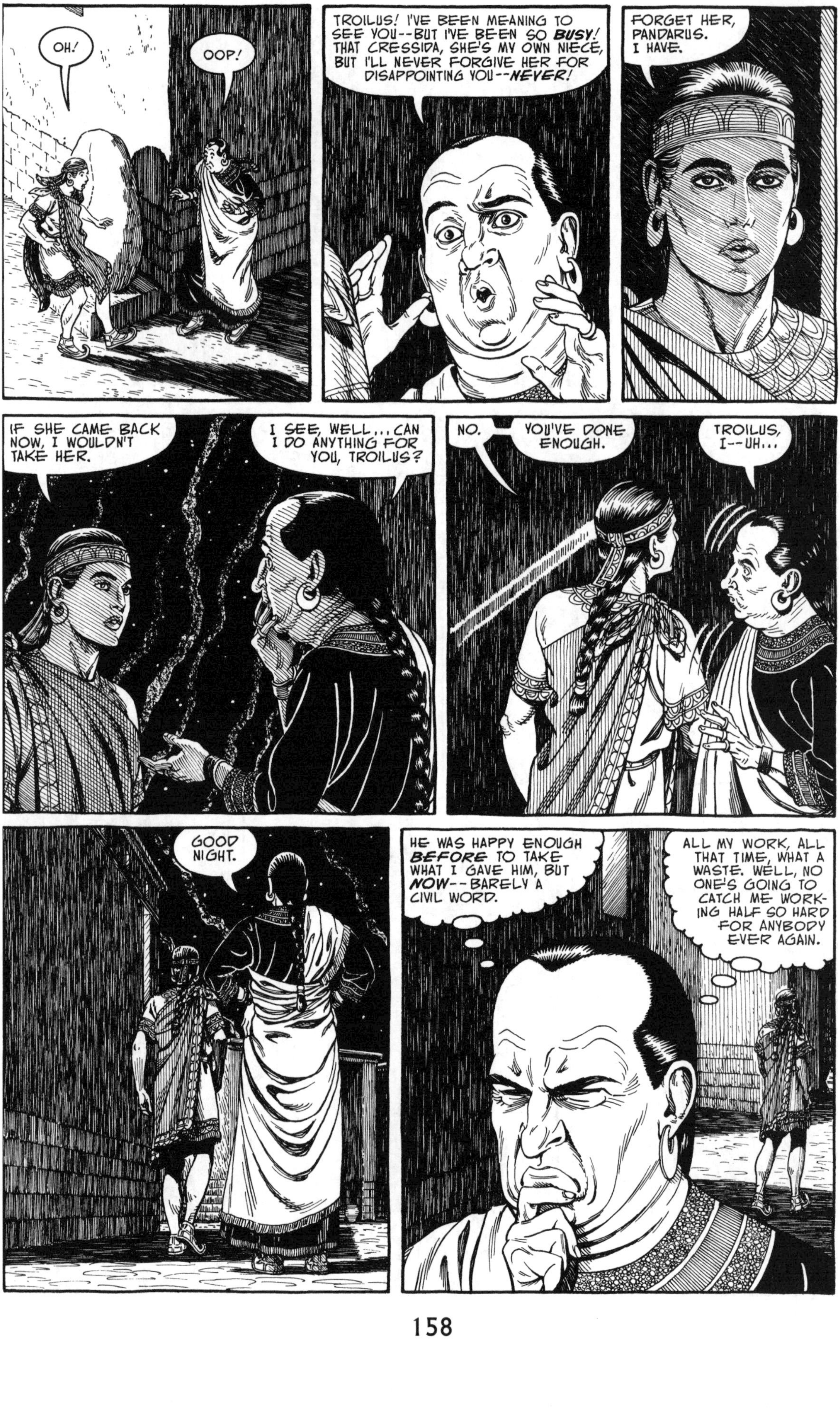
OH!
OOP!
TROILUS! I'VE BEEN MEANING TO SEE YOU--BUT I'VE BEEN SO **BUSY**! THAT CRESSIDA, SHE'S MY OWN NIECE, BUT I'LL NEVER FORGIVE HER FOR DISAPPOINTING YOU--**NEVER**!
FORGET HER, PANDARUS. I HAVE.
IF SHE CAME BACK NOW, I WOULDN'T TAKE HER.
I SEE, WELL... CAN I DO ANYTHING FOR YOU, TROILUS?
NO.
YOU'VE DONE ENOUGH.
TROILUS, I--UH...
GOOD NIGHT.
HE WAS HAPPY ENOUGH **BEFORE** TO TAKE WHAT I GAVE HIM, BUT **NOW**--BARELY A CIVIL WORD.
ALL MY WORK, ALL THAT TIME, WHAT A WASTE. WELL, NO ONE'S GOING TO CATCH ME WORKING HALF SO HARD FOR ANYBODY EVER AGAIN.

AGE OF

BRONZE™

THE STORY OF THE TROJAN WAR

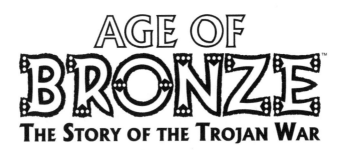

continues in

BETRAYAL PART THREE

GLOSSARY OF NAMES

Pronunciation of names can vary widely. What I present here is merely a guide and needn't be considered definitive.

Anyone seeking consistency among the forms of character and place names should look elsewhere. In general, I've used the more familiar Roman forms for the better-known characters—for instance, Achilles instead of Akhilleos, Helen instead of Helena. Lesser-known and minor characters use a more Greek form—for instance, Teukros instead of Teucer, Polydeukes instead of Pollux.

a as in lap	ee as in see	i as in sit	oo as in wool	u as in us
ay as in say	eye as in hike	o as in not	s as in less	uh as in duh
e as in bed	g as in get	oh as in note	th as in thick	

Listed alphabetically   Stress italicized syllable

Achaean(s) a-*kee*-an(z), the people of roughly the area of modern Greece, the army warring against Troy

Achilles a-*kil*-eez, son of Peleus and Thetis, Achaean prince of Phthia

Aeneas ee-*nee*-as, prince of Dardania, cousin of the Trojan royal family

Aetolia ee-*toh*-lee-a, Achaean land ruled by Thoas

Agamemnon a-ga-*mem*-non, High King of Mycenae, leader of the Achaean forces, brother of Menelaus

Agyrtes a-*jir*-teez, steward of Diomedes

Aithra *ay*-thra, servant of Helen, mother of Theseus, grandmother of Akamas

Ajax (great) *ay*-jax, son of Telamon, Achaean prince of Salamis

Akamas *a*-ka-mas, son of Theseus, grandson of Aithra

Alexander a-lek-*zan*-der, servant of Pandarus

Alkimus *al*-ki-mus, companion of Achilles

Amar-Addu a-*mar*-a-doo, a Levantine merchant

Andromache an-*dro*-ma-kee, daughter of Eetion of Thebes, wife of Hektor

Antenor an-*tee*-nor, Trojan elder, husband of Theano

Antigone an-*ti*-goh-nee, cousin of Cressida, daughter of Pandarus

Arachnus a-*rak*-nus, mountain overlooking Mycenae

Argolid *ar*-go-lid, the area containing the cities of Mycenae, Tiryns, and Argos

Argos *ar*-gos, city in the Argolid ruled by Diomedes

Argyve ar-*geye*-vee, mother of Cressida

Astyoche as-*teye*-o-kee, sister of Priam, wife of Telephus

Chersidamas kur-*si*-da-mas, son of Priam and a secondary wife, charioteer of Paris

Cressida *kres*-i-duh, widowed daughter of Kalchas, niece of Pandarus, lover of Troilus

Cretans *kree*-tanz, people of the island of Crete ruled by Idomeneus

Danus *day*-nus, son of Antenor and Theano

Dardanian Gate dar-*day*-nee-an, gate in Troy's southeastern lower city wall

Dardanus *dar*-da-nus, an area southeast of Troy

Deiphobus de-*if*-oh-bus, prince of Troy, son of Priam and Hekuba

Diomedes deye-o-*mee*-deez, Achaean king of Argos and Tiryns

Dymas *deye*-mas, father of Hekuba and Asius

Epistrophus e-*pis*-tro-fus, leader of the Halizonians, a Trojan ally

Euandrus yoo-*an*-drus, father of Sarpedon

Eurytus *yoo*-ri-tus, a Kentaur guest at the wedding of Peirithous

Evadne e-*vad*-nee, servant of Cressida

Glaukus *glaw*-kus, companion of Sarpedon, co-commander of Lykians

Hektor *hek*-tor, eldest son of Priam and Hekuba, prince of Troy

Halizonians ha-li-*zoh*-nee-anz, a people northeast of Troy, Trojan allies

Hekuba *hek*-yoo-buh, chief wife of Priam

Helen *he*-len, wife first of Menelaus and then of Paris

Helenus *he*-le-nus, prince of Troy, son of Priam and Hekuba, twin brother of Kassandra

Helikaon he-li-*kay*-on, son of Antenor, husband of Laodike

Hellespont *he*-le-spont, strait of water just north of Troy

Herakles *her*-a-kleez, greatest Achaean hero

Hesione he-*seye*-uh-nee, sister of Priam, wife of Telamon, mother of Teukros

Horaste hor-*ast,* fictional lover of Cressida, made up by Pandarus

Idaean Gate eye-*dee*-an, one of the southern gates in the lower city wall of Troy

Idomeneus eye-*do*-men-yoos, king of the island of Crete

Ikarus *i*-ka-rus, ruler of Karia who bought Theonoe from pirates

Iolaus eye-oh-*lay*-us, king of Phylake, first Achaean to land at Troy during war, brother of Podarkes

Iphiklus *eye*-fi-klus, former king of Phylake, father of Iolaus

Irt *irt,* a Levantine merchant

Ithaka *i*-tha-ka, island ruled by Odysseus

Kaeneus *kee*-nyoos, androgynous hero buried alive in battle at Peirithous's wedding

Kalchas *kal*-kas, former Trojan priest, now ally of the Achaeans, father of Cressida, brother of Pandarus

Kalydon *ka*-li-don, city in Aetolia ruled by Oeneus

Karia *kayr*-ee-a, an area south of Troy

Kassandra ka-*san*-dra, daughter of Priam and Hekuba, a seer

Kebriones ke-*breye*-o-neez, son of Priam by a secondary wife, charioteer of Hektor

Kentaurs *ken*-taurz, tribe of men that holds horses as holy

Kolonae ko-*loh*-nee, city ruled by Kyknos

Kolophon *ko*-lo-fon, city in Pamphylia south of Troy

Kreusa kree-*oo*-sa, eldest daughter of Priam and Hekuba, wife of Aeneas

Kyklopes *kik*-loh-peez, giant children of Earth and Sky

Kyknos *kik*-nos, albino king of Kolonae

Laodameia lay-o-da-*meye*-a, wife of Iolaus

Laodike lay-*o*-di-kee, daughter of Priam and Hekuba, wife of Helikaon

Leukippe lyoo-*kip*-ee, sister of Kalchas and Pandarus, aunt of Cressida

Lykia *li*-kee-a, area south of Troy ruled by Sarpedon

Lykians *li*-kee-anz, people of Lykia

Medesikaste mee-des-i-*kas*-tee, daughter of Priam and a secondary wife, wife of Imbrius

Medon *mee*-don, Achaean son of Oileus, half brother of Little Ajax

Meleager me-lee-*ay*-ger, son of Oeneus, slayer of the Kalydonian boar

Menelaus me-ne-*lay*-us, Achaean king of Lakedaemon, first husband of Helen, brother of Agamemnon

Menoetes me-*nee*-teez, a Lykian

Mestor *mes*-tor, prince of Troy, son of Priam and Hekuba

Minuus *min*-yoo-us, father of Epistrophus and Odius

Myrmidons *mur*-mi-donz, Achilles's soldiers from Phthia

Mysia *mi*-sha, area south of Troy where Telephus rules

Nauplius *naw*-plee-us, Achaean king of Nauplia, father of Palamedes and Oeax

Nestor *nes*-tor, elderly Achaean king of Pylos, father of Thrasymedes and Antilochus

Odius *od*-i-us, co-leader of the Halizonians, allied to Troy

Odysseus o-*dis*-yoos, Achaean king of Ithaka

Oeax *ee*-aks, younger brother of Palamedes, son of Nauplius

Oeneus *een*-yoos, grandfather of both Diomedes and Thoas, uncle of Thersites

Oeta *ee*-ta, the mountain where Herakles died, home of the Kalydonian boar

Olympus oh-*lim*-pus, mountain home of the highest Achaean gods

Orthrian *orth*-ree-an, of the dawn or morning, i. e. early

Palamedes pa-la-*mee*-deez, Achaean prince of Nauplia, cousin of Agamemnon, brother of Oeax, son of Nauplius

Pamphylia pam-*fi*-lee-a, coastal area south of Troy

Pandarus *pan*-da-rus, brother of Kalchas, uncle and guardian of Cressida

Paris *pa*-ris, Trojan prince, husband and lover of Helen

Patroklus pa-*trok*-lus, closest companion of Achilles

Pedaeon pe-*dee*-on, area ruled by Imbrius

Polymestor po-li-*mes*-tor, ruler in Thrace

Peleus *peel*-yoos, Achaean king of Phthia, father of Achilles

Philaemon fi-*lee*-mon, son of Priam and a secondary wife

Philenor feye-*lee*-nor, prince of Troy, son of Priam and a secondary wife, charioteer of Troilus

Philobia fi-*loh*-bee-a, wife of the Trojan ally Perseus of Dardanus

Phrontis *fron*-tis, steersman of Agamemnon

Phylake *fi*-la-kee, city ruled by Iolaus

Podarkes po-*dar*-keez, brother of Iolaus

Polydamas po-*li*-da-mas, son of Panthous, companion of Hektor

Polyxena poh-*liks*-ee-nuh, daughter of Priam and Hekuba

Priam *preye*-am, king of Troy

Protesilaus proh-tes-i-*lay*-us, posthumous name of Iolaus

Sarpedon sar-*pee*-don, king of Lykia, a Trojan ally

Skaean Gate *skee*-an, gate in western lower city wall of Troy

Sparta *spar*-ta, Achaean city in Lakedaemon ruled by Menelaus

Sthenelus *sthen*-e-lus, Achaean companion of Diomedes, co-commander of the forces from Argos and Tiryns

Tarba *tar*-ba, middle daughter of Pandarus

Tartarus *tar*-tar-us, the lowest underworld

Telamon *tel*-a-mon, Achaean king of the island of Salamis, father of Great Ajax and Teukros

Telephus *te*-le-fus, king of Mysia, son of Herakles and Auge

Telestes te-*les*-teez, son of Priam and a secondary wife

Tenedos *ten*-e-dos, island just off the coast southwest of Troy

Theano thee-*ay*-noh, Trojan priestess of the wisdom goddess, wife of Antenor

Theonoe thee-*on*-oh-ee, sister of Kalchas and Pandarus, aunt of Cressida

Theseus *thees*-yoos, great Achaean hero, son of Aithra, father of Akamas and Demophoon

Thetis *thee*-tis, influential Achaean priestess, mother of Achilles, former wife of Peleus

Thoas *thoh*-as, Achaean king of Aetolia

Thrace *thrays,* area northwest of Troy, north of the Aegean Sea

Tiryns *tir*-inz, city ruled by Diomedes

Titans *teye*-tanz, elder gods, first children of Earth and Sky

Troilus *troy*-lus, prince of Troy, son of Priam and Hekuba, lover of Cressida

Tydeus *teye*-dyoos, father of Diomedes, one of the seven attackers in the war against Thebes

Zeus *zyoos,* Achaean god of thunder and sky

Genealogical Chart: The Achaeans

Characters in bold appear and are named in *Betrayal Part Two.*

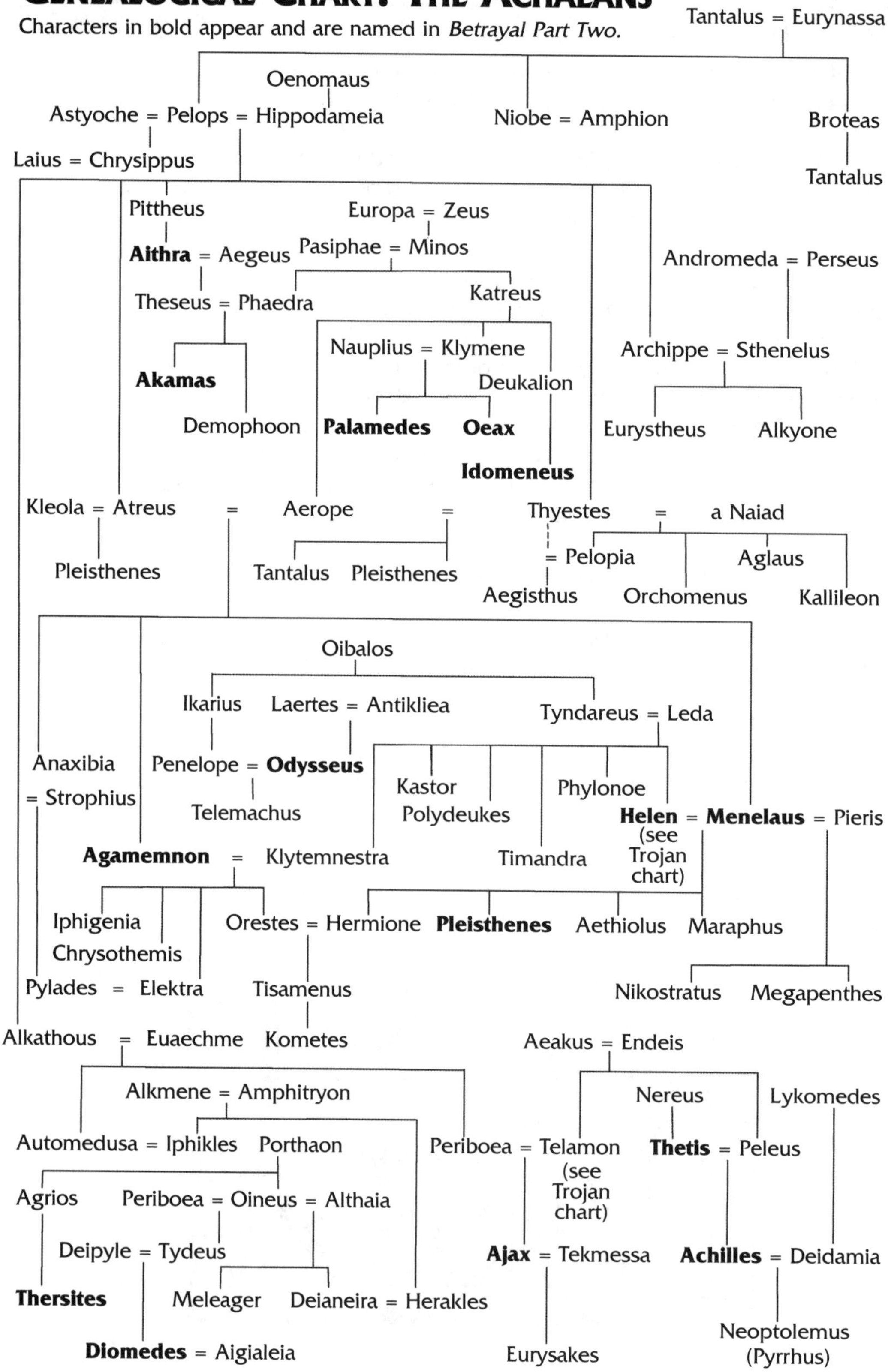
Tantalus = Eurynassa
Oenomaus
Astyoche = Pelops = Hippodameia
Niobe = Amphion
Broteas
Laius = Chrysippus
Tantalus
Pittheus
Europa = Zeus
Aithra = Aegeus
Pasiphae = Minos
Andromeda = Perseus
Theseus = Phaedra
Katreus
Nauplius = Klymene
Archippe = Sthenelus
Akamas
Deukalion
Demophoon
Palamedes
Oeax
Eurystheus
Alkyone
Idomeneus
Kleola = Atreus = Aerope = Thyestes = a Naiad
Pleisthenes
Tantalus
Pleisthenes
= Pelopia
Aglaus
Aegisthus
Orchomenus
Kallileon
Oibalos
Ikarius
Laertes = Antikliea
Tyndareus = Leda
Anaxibia
= Strophius
Penelope = **Odysseus**
Kastor
Polydeukes
Phylonoe
Telemachus
Helen = **Menelaus** = Pieris
(see Trojan chart)
Agamemnon = Klytemnestra
Timandra
Iphigenia
Chrysothemis
Orestes = Hermione
Pleisthenes
Aethiolus
Maraphus
Pylades = Elektra
Tisamenus
Nikostratus
Megapenthes
Alkathous = Euaechme
Kometes
Aeakus = Endeis
Alkmene = Amphitryon
Nereus
Lykomedes
Automedusa = Iphikles
Porthaon
Periboea = Telamon
(see Trojan chart)
Thetis = Peleus
Agrios
Periboea = Oineus = Althaia
Deipyle = Tydeus
Ajax = Tekmessa
Achilles = Deidamia
Thersites
Meleager
Deianeira = Herakles
Diomedes = Aigialeia
Eurysakes
Neoptolemus
(Pyrrhus)

Genealogical Chart: The Trojan Royal Family

Characters in bold appear and are named in *Betrayal Part Two.*

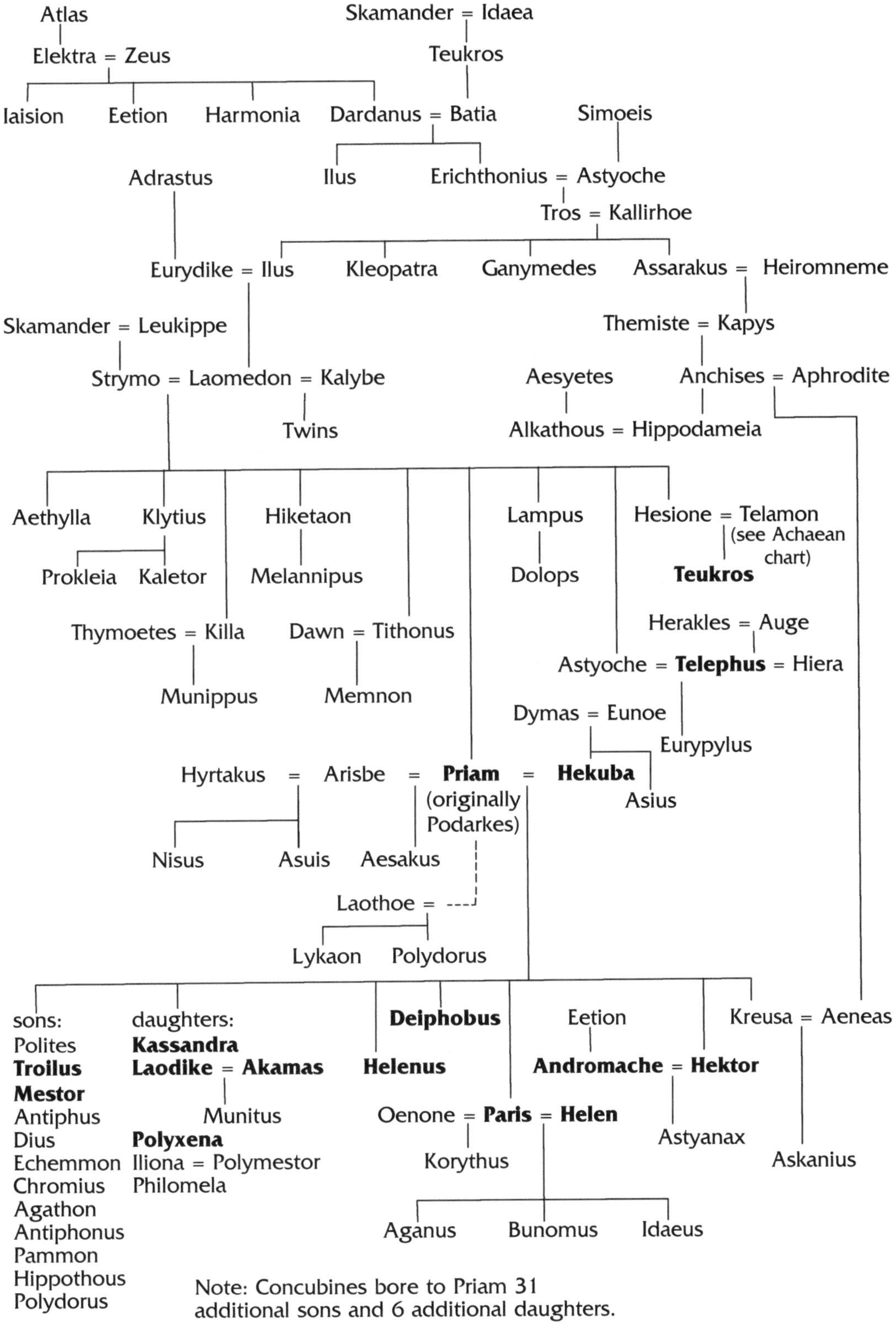

Atlas
Skamander = Idaea
Elektra = Zeus
Teukros
Iaision
Eetion
Harmonia
Dardanus = Batia
Simoeis
Adrastus
Ilus
Erichthonius = Astyoche
Tros = Kallirhoe
Eurydike = Ilus
Kleopatra
Ganymedes
Assarakus = Heiromneme
Skamander = Leukippe
Themiste = Kapys
Strymo = Laomedon = Kalybe
Aesyetes
Anchises = Aphrodite
Twins
Alkathous = Hippodameia
Aethylla
Klytius
Hiketaon
Lampus
Hesione = Telamon
(see Achaean chart)
Prokleia
Kaletor
Melannipus
Dolops
Teukros
Thymoetes = Killa
Dawn = Tithonus
Herakles = Auge
Astyoche = **Telephus** = Hiera
Munippus
Memnon
Dymas = Eunoe
Eurypylus
Hyrtakus = Arisbe = **Priam** = **Hekuba**
(originally Podarkes)
Asius
Nisus
Asuis
Aesakus
Laothoe = ----
Lykaon
Polydorus
sons:
Polites
Troilus
Mestor
Antiphus
Dius
Echemmon
Chromius
Agathon
Antiphonus
Pammon
Hippothous
Polydorus
daughters:
Kassandra
Laodike = **Akamas**
Munitus
Polyxena
Iliona = Polymestor
Philomela
Deiphobus
Helenus
Eetion
Andromache = **Hektor**
Kreusa = Aeneas
Oenone = **Paris** = **Helen**
Korythus
Astyanax
Askanius
Aganus
Bunomus
Idaeus
Note: Concubines bore to Priam 31 additional sons and 6 additional daughters.

COME TO THE DEFENSE OF TROY!

Every summer from 1988 through 2012 the International Troy Excavation Project, a team of archaeologists and other scientists, undertook the most extensive excavation yet conducted of the hill of Hisarlik in northwestern Turkey, the site identified as the ancient city of Troy. Study and publication of the finds will follow for years as the evidence is sifted and understood. And what finds they are! A previously unsuspected Bronze Age defensive ditch surrounding the city—a magnificent statue of the Roman Emperor Hadrian—as well as finds less spectacular but no less valuable to our understanding of the architecture, culture, and religion of the Trojan people for a period spanning more than 2000 years.

Help support the International Troy Excavation Project by joining the Friends of Troy, a group of people from all over the world with one thing in common—an interest in this most legendary of archaeological sites. As a Friend of Troy, you will receive periodic updates as well as notices of events of interest to Troy enthusiasts. All it takes to join each year is a donation—any amount is welcome. Your donation is tax deductible since Friends of Troy is a 501 (c) 3 non-profit organization.

www.uni-tuebingen.de/troia/eng/freunde.html

Send donations to Friends of Troy to:
Institute for Mediterranean Studies
7086 Aracoma Drive
Cincinnati, OH 45237, USA
Phone: 513/631-8049
Fax: 513/631-1715
E-mail: studies@usa.net

The Troia Foundation supports the International Troy Excavation Project, study and publication of finds, and the ongoing conservation and restoration of Troy and the surrounding area as a UNESCO monument. The Troia Foundation has two branches, one at Tubingen University, German partner of the 1988-2012 Troy excavation, and the other is Canakkale-Tubingen Troia Vakfi in Canakkale, Turkey, near Troy.

www.uni-tuebingen.de/troia/eng/troiastiftung.html (Germany)
www.troiavakfi.com/ing_default.asp (Turkey)

A new archaeological expedition to Troy will begin in the summer of 2013, led by Professor William Aylward of the University of Wisconsin-Madison in partnershop with Canakkale Onsekiz Mart University in Turkey. Opportunities for the public to support the new excavations haven't been annnounced yet, but keep your eyes open.

BE A WATCHER ON THE COAST AT PYLOS

At the end of the Bronze Age in Greece the great Mycenaean civilization was disintegrating. At Pylos, where in legend King Nestor ruled, watchmen were posted along the coast. It's not clear who the Pylians specifically feared, but the palace at Pylos was eventually burned and abandoned.

Centuries later in 1939 Carl W. Blegen uncovered the remains of the Mycenaean palace of King Nestor at Pylos. Even Heinrich Schliemann, excavator of Troy and Mycenae, had failed in his attempts to find it. Excavations at Pylos until 1970 revealed the remains of the best preserved seat of any of the chieftains who followed Agamemnon to Troy. The remains included colorful wall frescoes, painted floors, and even parts of a chimney over the central hearth.

A team from the University of Cincinnati under the direction of Sharon Stocker and Jack Davis is now working hard to preserve these important discoveries and to bring their significance to the attention of a wider public.

You can help in this effort while becoming part of the legacy of ancient Pylos. For more information and details on how you can help preserve the palace at Pylos and finds from the surrounding area, contact Professor Sharon Stocker at:

Sharon.Stocker@UC.edu

Friends of Pylos
Department of Classics
University of Cincinnati
Cincinnati, Ohio 45221-0226

BIBLIOGRAPHY

The following list of sources is an addendum to the lists in previous volumes.

THE STORY

"Whan Cresseyde came from Troye." In *Tottel's Miscellany II*. Ed. Hyder Edward Rollins. Cambridge: Harvard University Press, 1966, 294-5.

Akhurst, W. M. *Paris the Prince, and Helen the Fair; or, the Giant Horse, and the Siege of Troy*. Melbourne: R. Bell, 1869.

Alexander, Caroline. *The War That Killed Achilles*. New York: Viking, 2009.

Ausonius. *The Works of Ausonius*. Ed. R. P. H. Green. Oxford: Clarendon Press, 1991.

Austin, Norman. *Helen of Troy and Her Shameless Phantom*. Ithaca, NY, and London: Cornell University Press, 1994.

Baily, William Entriken. "Priam, King of Troy." In *Dramatic Poems*. Philadelphia: Printed for the Author, 1894, 38-68.

Bankes, John. *The Destruction of Troy, a Tragedy, Acted at His Royal Highness the Duke's Theatre*. London: Printed by A. G. and J. P., 1679.

Benson, C. David. *The History of Troy in Middle English Literature: Guido delle Colonne's Historia Destructionis Troiae in Medieval England*. Woodbridge, UK: D. S. Brewer; Totowa, NJ: Rowman & Littlefield, 1980.

Binyon, Laurence. "Memnon." In *Three Short Plays*. London: Sidgwick & Jackson, Ltd., 1930, 37-47.

—. *Paris and Oenone*. London: Archibald Constable and Co., Ltd., 1906.

—. *Penthesilea*. London: Archibald Constable and Company, Ltd., 1905.

Bird, Graeme D. *Multitextuality in the Homeric Iliad: The Witness of the Ptolemaic Papyri*. Center For Hellenic Studies. Cambridge and London: Harvard University Press, 2010.

Brilliant, Richard. *Visual Narratives: Storytelling in Etruscan and Roman Art*. Ithaca, NY, and London: Cornell University Press, 1984.

Burgess, Jonathan S. *The Death and Afterlife of Achilles*. Baltimore: The Johns Hopkins University Press, 2009.

Campbell, Malcolm. *A Commentary on Quintus Smyrnaeus Posthomerica XII*. Mnemosyne. Leiden: E. J. Brill, 1981.

Chapman, John Jay. *Homeric Scenes: Hector's Farewell and The Wrath of Achilles*. New York: Laurence J. Gomme, 1914.

Collins, Leslie. *Studies in Characterization in the Iliad*. Frankfurt am Main: Athenaeum, 1988.

De Selincourt, E. "Troilus and Cressida" and "Troilus and Criseyde." In *Oxford Lectures on Poetry*. Oxford: Clarendon Press, 1934.

Demangeot, Cedric. *Philoctete*. Barre, France: barre parallele, 2008.

Due, Casey, and Mary Ebbott. *Iliad 10 and the Poetics of Ambush*. Center for Hellenic Studies. Cambridge and London: Harvard University Press, 2010.

Forsyth, William H. "The Trojan War in Medieval Tapestries." In *Metropolitan Museum of Art Bulletin,* New ser., v. 14, no. 3 (November, 1955). New York: Metropolitan Museum of Art, 1955, 76-84.

Frame, Douglas. *Hippota Nestor*. Washington, DC: Center for Hellenic Studies, Trustees for Harvard University, 2009.

Fury of Achilles. Dir. Marino Girolami. Perf. Gordon Mitchell, Jacques Bergerac, Cristina Gaioni. Uneurop Film, 1962.

Gottschall, Jonathan. *The Rape of Troy*. Cambridge: Cambridge University Press, 2008.

Griffin, Nathaniel E. "Un-Homeric Elements in the Medieval Story of Troy." In *The Journal of English and Germanic Philology,* Vol. VII, no. 1. 1907-1908. Urbana, IL: The University of Illinois, 32-52.

Hamilton, George A. *The Indebtedness of Chaucer's Troilus and Criseyde to Guido delle Colonne's Historia Trojana.* New York: AMS Press, Inc., 1966. (Reprint of 1903 edition.)

Hatchett, William. *The Rival Father: or, the Death of Achilles. A Tragedy: As it is Acted at the New Theatre in the Hay-Market.* London: Printed for William Mears, at the Lamb; and Thomas Corbett, at Addison's Head, 1730.

Heywood, Thomas. *Troia Britanica: or, Great Britaines Troy.* Amsterdam: Theatrum Orbis Terrarum; Norwood, NJ: W. J. Johnson, 1974.

Hillman, Richard. "Chapter Two: Troilus and Cressida." In *William Shakespeare: the Problem Plays.* New York: Twayne Publishers; Toronto: Maxwell Macmillan Canada; et. al., 1993, 17-53.

Horstall, Nicholas. *Virgil, Aeneid 2: A Commentary.* Leiden: Brill, 2008.

Ibycus. "Fragments." In *Greek Lyric III.* Ed. and trans. David A. Campbell. Loeb Classical Library 476. Cambridge and London: Harvard University Press, 1991, 221-63.

An Iliad. By Lisa Peterson and Denis O'Hare. Dir. Penny Metropulos. Syracuse Stage, Syracuse, NY. 30 May 2013.

Kelly, Douglas. "Guerre et Parente dans le Roman de Troie." In *Entre Fiction et Histoire: Troie et Rome au Moyen Age.* Ed. Emmanuele Baumgartner and Laurence Harf-Lancner. Paris: Presses de la Sorbonne Nouvelle, 1997, 53-71.

Kem, Judy. *Jean Lemaire de Belges's Les Illustrations de Gaule et singularitez de Troye: The Trojan Legend in the Late Middle Ages and Early Renaissance.* Currents in Comparative Romance Languages and Literatures, vol. 15. New York: Peter Lang, 1994.

Konstan, David. "Afterword." In *Broken Columns: Two Roman Epic Fragments.* Trans. David R. Slavitt. Philadelphia: University of Pennsylvania Press, 1997, 79-98.

Lanii Triumphantes, or, The Butcher's Prize: Being a Description of the Famous Battel Between Achilles a Butcher of Greece and Hector a Weaver of Troy, Occasion'd by the Rape of a Daughty Damosill y-clep'd Hellen the Bright. London: printed by J. B. for William Crook, 1665.

Lexicon Iconographicum Mythologiae Classicae. Zurich, Munchen, Dusseldorf: Artemis & Winkler Verlag, 1981-1999.

Loschi of Vicenza, Antonio. "Achilles." In *Humanist Tragedies.* Trans. Gary R. Grund. I Tatti Renaissance Library. Cambridge and London: Harvard University Press, 2011, 48-109.

Lowenstam, Steven. *As Witnessed by Images: The Trojan War Tradition in Greek and Etruscan Art.* Baltimore: The Johns Hopkins University Press, 2008.

Lyons, Clifford P. "The Hector-Achilles Encounters in Shakespeare's *Troilus & Cressida.*" In *. . . All These to Teach.* Ed. Robert A. Bryan, Alton C. Morris, A. A. Murphree, and Aubrey L. Williams. Gainesville, FL: University of Florida Press, 1965, 67-79.

Masefield, John. *A King's Daughter.* New York: The Macmillan Company, 1923.

Mee, Charles L. "The Trojan Women, a Love Story." In *History Plays.* Baltimore and London: The Johns Hopkins University Press, 1998, 159-250.

Moret, Jean-Marc. *Les pierres gravees antiques representant le rapt du Palladion.* Mainz: Philipp von Zabern, 1997.

Morris, Sir Lewis. *The Epic of Hades.* Boston: Roberts Brothers, 1891.

Morris, William. "Scenes from the Fall of Troy." In *The Collected Works of William Morris.* London: Longmans Green and Company, 1915, 3-51.

—. "The Death of Paris." In *The Earthly Paradise,* vol. 2. Ed. Florence S. Boos. New York and London: Routledge, 2002, 7-29.

—. "The Death of Paris." In *The Earthly Paradise: a Poem.* New York, et al: Longmans, Green, and Co., 1923, 189-96.

O., I. *The Lamentation of Troy for the Death of Hector whereunto is annexed an Olde Womans Tale in hir Solitarie Cell.* Ed. Elkin Calhoun Wilson. Chicago: Institute of Elizabethan Studies, 1959. (Original publication 1594.)

O'Keeffe, John. *The Siege of Troy; or, Famous Trojan Horse, a Grand Heroic, Serio-Comic, Tragic Spectacle.* London: printed by H. Pace, 1795.

Papaioannou, Sophia. *Redesigning Achilles: 'Recycling' the Epic Cycle in the 'Little Iliad' (Ovid, Metamorphoses 12.1-13.622).* Untersuchungen zur antiken Literatur und Geschichte, band 89. Berlin and New York: Walter de Gruyter, 2007.

Partridge, John. *The notable hystorie of two famous Princes of the worlde, Astianax and Polixena: wherin is set forth the cursed treason of Caulcas.* London: Henry Denham, for Thomas Hacket, 1566.

Pepin, Ronald E. *The Vatican Mythographers.* New York: Fordham University Press, 2008.

Perkell, Christine. "Reading the Laments of *Iliad* 24." In *Lament.* Ed. Ann Suter. Oxford: Oxford University Press, 2008, 93-117.

Pfister, Friedrich. *Greek Gods and Heroes.* London: MacGibbon & Kee, 1961.

Rabel, Robert J. *Plot and Point of View in the* Iliad. Ann Arbor, MI: The University of Michigan Press, 1997.

Rennell, James. *Observations of the Topography of the Plain of Troy; and on the Principal Objects within, and around it Described, or Alluded to, in the* Iliad. London: Printed by W. Bulmer and Co. Cleveland-Row, St. James, 1814.

Rossetti, Dante Gabriel. "Cassandra." In *Dante Gabriel Rossetti: Collected Writings.* Ed. Jan Marsh. London: J. M. Dent, 1999, 251.

Salimbeti, Andrea, and Raffaele D'Amato. "Clash Amongst the Kings—the Seven Against Thebes." *Ancient Warfare.* June/July 2009: 24-31.

Schefold, Karl. *Gods and Heroes in Late Archaic Greek Art.* Trans. Alan Griffiths. Cambridge: Cambridge University Press, 1992.

Schefold, Karl. *Myth and Legend in Early Greek Art.* New York: Harry N. Abrams, Inc., n. d.

Shakespeare, William. *The Rape of Lucrece.* 1594. <http://www.william-shakespeare.info/william-shakespeare-poem-the-rape-of-lucrece.htm> 19 April 2008. 26 October 2008.

Sophocles. *Sophocles: Selected Fragmentary Plays, Volume I.* Trans. A. H. Sommerstein, D. Fitzpatrick, and T. Talboy. Oxford: Aris & Phillips, 2006.

—. *Sophocles: Selected Fragmentary Plays, Volume II.* Trans. A. H. Sommerstein and T. H. Talboy. Oxford: Aris & Phillips, 2012.

Statius, Publius Papinius. *The Thebaid: Seven Against Thebes.* Trans. and introduction by Charles Stanley Ross. Baltimore and London: The Johns Hopkins University Press, 2004.

The famous history of Hector, Prince of Troy; or, the three destructions of Troy. . . . Together with the noble actions of Hector, Achilles, the Amazon queen, and divers other princes. [London]: printed and sold in London, [1780?].

The Greeks and Trojans Wars. [London]: Printed for F. Coles, T. VeWright [sic], and L. Clark, n. d. [1675?].

Trevelyan, Humphry. *Goethe and the Greeks.* London: Cambridge University Press, 1942.

Trojan Tales, Related by Ulysses, Helenus, Hector, Achilles, and Priam. London: printed for F. Burleigh; J. Graves; J. Richardson; J. Browne; and A. Dodd, 1714.

Troyer, Pamela Luff. "Smiting High Culture in the 'Fondemont': The Seege of Troye as Medieval Burlesque." In *Fantasies of Troy.* Ed. Alan Shepard and Stephen D. Powell. Toronto: Centre for Reformation and Renaissance Studies, 2004.

Vandiver, Elizabeth. *The* Iliad *of Homer.* The Great Courses. Chantilly, VA: The Teaching Company, 1999. Audio tapes.

Vellay, Charles. *Les Legendes du Cycle Troyen.* Vols. 1 and 2. Monaco: Imprimerie Nationale de Monaco, n. d.

War Music. Writer and Dir. Lillian Groag. American Conservatory Theater, San Francisco. 4 April 2009.

White, Edward Lucas. *Helen.* New York: George H. Doran Company, 1925.

Settings in General

Bachhuber, Christoph, and R. Gareth Roberts, eds. *Forces of Transformation: The End of the Bronze Age in the Mediterranean.* Themes from the Ancient Near East BANEA Publication Series, Vol. 1. Oxford: Oxbow Books, 2009.

Beckman, Gary M., Trevor Bryce, and Eric Cline. *The Ahhiyawa Texts.* Writings from the Ancient World no. 28. Atlanta: Society of Biblical Literature, 2011.

Bryce, Trevor. "Relations between Hatti and Ahhiyawa in the Last Decades of the Bronze Age." In *Hittite Studies in Honor of Harry A. Hoffner Jr.* Ed. Gary Beckman, Richard Beal, and Gregory McMahon. Winona Lake, IN: Eisenbrauns, 2003, 59-72.

Burke, Brendan. "Mycenaean Memory and Bronze Age Lament." In *Lament.* Ed. Ann Suter. Oxford: Oxford University Press, 2008, 70-92.

From Minos to Midas: Ancient Cloth Production in the Aegean and in Anatolia. Ancient Textiles Series vol. 7. Oxford and Oakville: Oxbow Books, 2010.

Collins, Billie Jean, Mary R. Bachvarova, and Ian C. Rutherford, eds. *Anatolian Interfaces: Hittites, Greeks and Their Neighbors.* Oxford: Oxbow Books, 2008.

Crouwel, Joost. "Ahhiyawa, Argos and the Argive Plain." In *Dioskouroi: Studies presented to W. G. Cavanagh and C. B. Mee on the anniversary of their 30-year joint contribution to Aegean Archaeology.* Ed. C. Gallou, M. Georgiadis, and G. M. Muskett. BAR International Series 1889. Oxford: Archaeopress, 2008, 265-73.

Dickinson, Oliver. "Was There Really a Trojan War?" In *Dioskouroi: Studies presented to W. G. Cavanagh and C. B. Mee on the anniversary of their 30-year joint contribution to Aegean Archaeology.* Ed. C. Gallou, M. Georgiadis, and G. M. Muskett. BAR International Series 1889. Oxford: Archaeopress, 2008, 189-97.

Furumark, Anne. *Mycenaean Pottery,* vol. 1, Analysis and Classification. Stockholm: Svenska Institutet I Athen, 1972.

Graziodio, Giampaolo. "Cretan Perfumed Oils at Enkomi (Cyprus) in the 13th Century B.C.?" In *Our Cups Are Full: Pottery and Society in the Aegean Bronze Age.* Ed. Walter Gauss, Michael Lindblom, R. Angus K. Smith, et al. Oxford: Archaeopress, 2011, 88-96.

Huxley, George L. "A Heifer to Ithaca." In *Dioskouroi: Studies presented to W. G. Cavanagh and C. B. Mee on the anniversary of their 30-year joint contribution to Aegean Archaeology.* Ed. C. Gallou, M. Georgiadis, and G. M. Muskett. BAR International Series 1889. Oxford: Archaeopress, 2008, 198-9.

Martin, Richard P. "Keens from the Absent Chorus." In *Lament.* Ed. Ann Suter. Oxford: Oxford University Press, 2008, 118-138.

Mayor, Adrienne. *The First Fossil Hunters: Paleontology in Greek and Roman Times.* Princeton: Princeton University Press, 2000.

Steel, Louise. "Creation and Expression of Identity in Cyprus at the End of the Late Bronze Age." In *Dioskouroi: Studies presented to W. G. Cavanagh and C. B. Mee on the anniversary of their 30-year joint contribution to Aegean Archaeology.* Ed. C. Gallou, M. Georgiadis, and G. M. Muskett. BAR International Series 1889. Oxford: Archaeopress, 2008, 54-175.

Wachsmann, Shelley. "On Drawing the Bow." In *Eretz-Israel* 29 (In Honor of Ephraim Stern). Ed. J. Aviram, A. Ben-Tor, I. Eph'al, S. Gitin, and R. Reich. Jerusalem: Israel Exploration Society, 238-257.

Watkins, Calvert. "Homer and Hittite Revisited II." In *Recent Developments in Hittite Archaeology and History.* Ed. K. Aslihan Yener and Harry A. Hoffner Jr. Winona Lake, IN: Eisenbrauns, 2002, 167-76.

Yassur-Landau, Assaf. *The Philistines and Aegean Migration at the End of the Late Bronze Age.* New York: Cambridge University Press, 2010.

Younger, John. *Music in the Aegean Bronze Age.* Jonsered, Sweden: Paul Astroms Forlag, 1988.

Troy and the Trojans

Guterbock, Hans Gustav. "The Hittite Palace," "An Outline of the Hittite AN.TAH.SUM Festival," "An Initiation Rite for a Hittite Prince," and "Authority and Law in the Hittite Kingdom." In *Perspectives on Hittite Civilization: Selected Writings of Hans Gustav Guterbock.* Ed. Harry A. Hoffner, Jr. Chicago: The Oriental Institute of the University of Chicago, 1997, 75-9, 95-7, 111-12, 229-32.

Haroutunian, Hripsime. "Bearded or Beardless? Some Speculations on the Function of the Beard among the Hittites." In *Recent Developments in Hittite Archaeology and History.* Ed. K. Aslihan Yener and Harry A. Hoffner Jr. Winona Lake, IN: Eisenbrauns, 2002, 43-52.

—. "The Hittite Ritual against a Curse (CTH 429)." In *Hittite Studies in Honor of Harry A. Hoffner Jr.* Ed. Gary Beckman, Richard Beal, and Gregory McMahon. Winona Lake, IN: Eisenbrauns, 2003, 149-68.

Hiller, Stefan. "Palm and Altar." In *Our Cups Are Full: Pottery and Society in the Aegean Bronze Age.* Ed. Walter Gauss, Michael Lindblom, R. Angus K. Smith, et al. Oxford: Archaeopress, 2011, 104-14.

Hoffner, Harry A., Jr. "The Treatment and Long-Term Use of Persons Captured in Battle according to the Masat Texts." In *Recent Developments in Hittite Archaeology and History.* Ed. K. Aslihan Yener and Harry A. Hoffner Jr. Winona Lake, IN: Eisenbrauns, 2002, 61-70.

Karasu, Cem. "Why Did the Hittites Have a Thousand Deities?" In *Hittite Studies in Honor of Harry A. Hoffner Jr.* Ed. Gary Beckman, Richard Beal, and Gregory McMahon. Winona Lake, IN: Eisenbrauns, 2003, 221-35.

Kassian, Alexei, Andrej Korolev, and Andrej Sidel'tsev. *Hittite Funerary Ritual.* Alter Orient und Altes Testament, band 288. Munster: Ugarit-Verlag, 2002.

Rutherford, Ian. " 'When You Go to the Meadow . . .' ": The Lament of the *Taptara*-Women in the Hittite *Sallis Wastais* Ritual." In *Lament.* Ed. Ann Suter. Oxford: Oxford University Press, 2008, 53-69.

Studia Troica. Band 16. Mainz am Rhein: Verlag Philipp von Zabern, 2006.

Studia Troica. Band 17. Mainz am Rhein: Verlag Philipp von Zabern, 2007.

Studia Troica. Band 18. Mainz am Rhein: Verlag Philipp von Zabern, 2008.

Taggar-Cohen, Ada. *Hittite Priesthood.* Heidelberg: Universitatsverlag Winter, 2006.

Taracha, Piotr. "Is Tuthaliya's Sword Really Aegean?" In *Hittite Studies in Honor of Harry A. Hoffner Jr.* Ed. Gary Beckman, Richard Beal, and Gregory McMahon. Winona Lake, IN: Eisenbrauns, 2003, 367-376.

The Mycenaeans

Aamont, Christina. "Mycenaean Cult Practice: 'Private' and 'Public' Ritual Acts." In *Dioskouroi: Studies presented to W. G. Cavanagh and C. B. Mee on the anniversary of their 30-year joint contribution to Aegean Archaeology.* Ed. C. Gallou, M. Georgiadis, and G. M. Muskett. BAR International Series 1889. Oxford: Archaeopress, 2008, 30-41.

D'Amato, Raffaele, and Andrea Salimbeti. *Bronze Age Greek Warrior 1600-1100 BC.* Warrior series vol. 153. Oxford: Osprey Publishing, 2011.

Desborough, V. R. d'A. *The Last Mycenaeans and Their Successors.* Oxford: Clarendon Press, 1964.

Faure, Paul. *La Grece au temps de la guerre de Troie.* Mesnil-sur-l'Estree: Hachette, 1994.

French, Elizabeth. "The Stirrup Jar: Does the West House Evidence Help or Complicate the Problems?" In *Our Cups Are Full: Pottery and Society in the Aegean Bronze Age.* Ed.

Walter Gauss, Michael Lindblom, R. Angus K. Smith, et al. Oxford: Archaeopress, 2011, 68-75.

Immerwahr, Sara Anderson. *Aegean Painting in the Bronze Age.* University Park, PA: Pennsylvania State University Press, 1990.

Kontroli-Papadopoulou, Litsa. *Aegean Frescoes of Religious Character.* Studies in Mediterranean Archaeology Vol. CXVII. Goteborg, Sweden: Paul Astroms Forlag, 1996.

Lobell, Jarrett A. "Search for the Mycenaeans." *Archaeology Magazine.* January/February 2008: 29.

Maran, Joseph. "Contested Pasts—The Society of the 12th c. B.C.E. Argolid and the Memory of the Mycenaean Palatial Period." In *Our Cups Are Full: Pottery and Society in the Aegean Bronze Age.* Ed. Walter Gauss, Michael Lindblom, R. Angus K. Smith, et al. Oxford: Archaeopress, 2011, 169-78.

Muskett, Georgina. "Gender Boundaries in Late Bronze Age Greece: The Contribution of Dress." In *Dioskouroi: Studies presented to W. G. Cavanagh and C. B. Mee on the anniversary of their 30-year joint contribution to Aegean Archaeology.* Ed. C. Gallou, M. Georgiadis, and G. M. Muskett. BAR International Series 1889. Oxford: Archaeopress, 2008, 90-96.

Mylonas, George E. *Mycenae: A Guide to its Ruins and its History.* Athens: N.P., 1967.

Peterson, Suzanne Elaine. *Wall Painting in the Aegean Bronze Age: The Procession Frescoes.* Ph.D. Thesis. N. P.: University Microfilms International, 1982.

Vetters, Melissa. "Seats of Power? Making the Most of Miniatures—The Role of Terracotta Throne Models in Disseminating Mycenaean Religious Ideology." In *Our Cups Are Full: Pottery and Society in the Aegean Bronze Age.* Ed. Walter Gauss, Michael Lindblom, R. Angus K. Smith, et al. Oxford: Archaeopress, 2011. 319-330.

Whittaker, Helene. *Mycenaean Cult Buildings.* Monographs from the Norwegian Institute at Athens. Vol. 1. Bergen, Norway: The Norwegian Institute at Athens, 1997.

Younger, John. "The Knossos 'Jewel Fresco' Reconsidered." In *Dioskouroi: Studies presented to W. G. Cavanagh and C. B. Mee on the anniversary of their 30-year joint contribution to Aegean Archaeology.* Ed. C. Gallou, M. Georgiadis, and G. M. Muskett. BAR International Series 1889. Oxford: Archaeopress, 2008, 76-89.

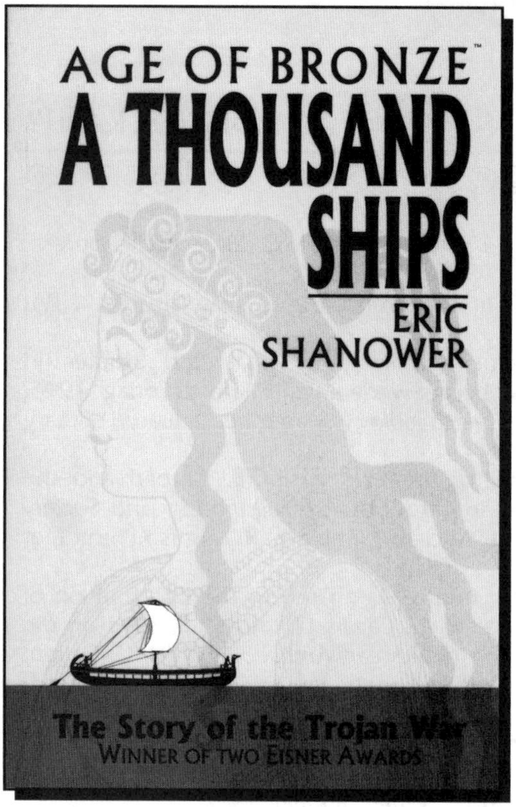
AGE OF BRONZE™
A THOUSAND SHIPS
ERIC SHANOWER
The Story of the Trojan War
WINNER OF TWO EISNER AWARDS

ISBN: 978-1582402000

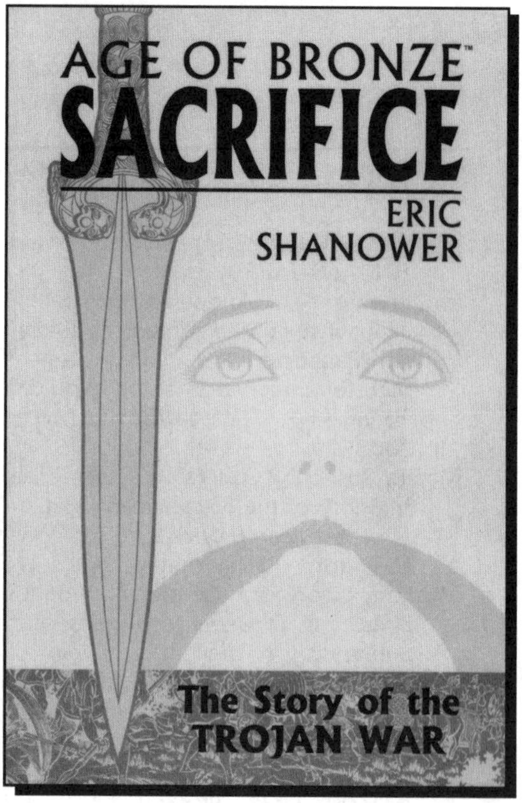
AGE OF BRONZE™
SACRIFICE
ERIC SHANOWER
The Story of the TROJAN WAR

ISBN: 978-1582403991

ALSO AVAILABLE FROM ERIC SHANOWER AND IMAGE COMICS

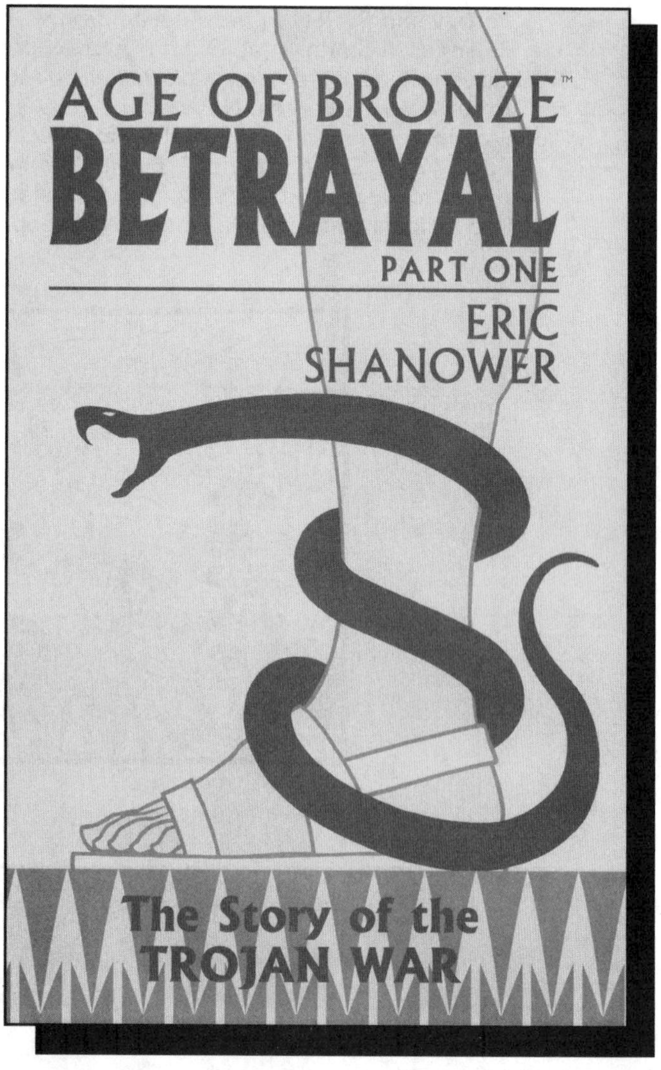
AGE OF BRONZE™
BETRAYAL
PART ONE
ERIC SHANOWER
The Story of the TROJAN WAR

ISBN: 978-1582407555